·新体验商务英语系列教材·

商务报刊选读（修订本）

Reading Course of Business English News Publications

主　编　束光辉
副主编　东　刚

刮开涂层，扫描二维码，可获取配套电子资源

清华大学出版社
北京交通大学出版社
·北京·

内容简介

本书所选材料均来自英、美等国家或地区近年来主要的商业杂志和报纸,并按主题分为9个单元,包括中国对外贸易与经济、地区经济与行业、金融与投资、企业发展与战略、营销与管理、人力资源、企业文化、企业家、贸易机构与合作会议等。本书旨在帮助学生掌握阅读和理解西方经贸报刊文章的方法和技巧,使他们熟悉当今经济贸易领域的专业知识、语言特色、惯用表达和句式,以提高其业务写作和商务交际能力。

本书可供英语专业学生、商务英语专业学生及具有较好英语基础的其他经贸专业学生作为教材使用,同时也可用作外企白领阶层和其他商务英语爱好者的自学用书。

本书封面贴有清华大学出版社防伪标签,无标签者不得销售。
版权所有,侵权必究。侵权举报电话:010 - 62782989　13501256678　13801310933

图书在版编目(CIP)数据

商务报刊选读:英文/束光辉主编. —修订本. — 北京:北京交通大学出版社:清华大学出版社,2016.4(2022.1重印)
ISBN 978 - 7 - 5121 - 1820 - 1

Ⅰ. ①商… Ⅱ. ①束… Ⅲ. ①商务 - 英语 - 阅读教学 - 教材 Ⅳ. ①H319.4

中国版本图书馆 CIP 数据核字(2014)第 020399 号

商务报刊选读
SHANGWU BAOKAN XUANDU

责任编辑:	张利军
出版发行:	清 华 大 学 出 版 社　邮编:100084　电话:010 - 62776969
	北京交通大学出版社　邮编:100044　电话:010 - 51686414
印　刷　者:	北京鑫海金澳胶印有限公司
经　　销:	全国新华书店
开　　本:	185 mm×260 mm　　印张:19.25　　字数:480 千字
版 印 次:	2020 年 1 月第 1 次修订　2022 年 1 月第 3 次印刷
印　　数:	3 001 ~ 4 000 册　　定价:48.00 元

本书如有质量问题,请向北京交通大学出版社质监组反映。对您的意见和批评,我们表示欢迎和感谢。
投诉电话:010 - 51686043,51686008;传真:010 - 62225406;E-mail:press@ bjtu. edu. cn。

进入 21 世纪，随着全球经济一体化进程的加快，我国与世界的经贸联系更加紧密，贸易形式更趋多元化。与此相伴的是，中国的商务英语教学与研究也发生了巨大的变化。这至少表现在以下几个方面：第一，如今，商务英语已是一个相当大的概念，它已从最早的一门单一的"外贸英语函电"课程发展到了涉及金融、保险、国际企业管理、国际经济法、海外投资与企业合作等多领域的学科；第二，人们对商务英语学习的需求持续旺盛，不仅几乎全国所有的高校都开设了商务英语专业或课程，而且越来越多的企业在职人员也迫切需要学习商务英语；第三，外语界对商务英语的研究也提高到了一个新的层次。

为了适应新的形势，许多高校都正在对一些传统的经贸英语类课程进行调整、改革和扩充，以培养新型的国际商务专业人才。这就向教材建设提出了更高的要求。教材不仅是教学内容的表现，更体现了人才培养的规格。纵观过去的一些教材，我们便不难发现，无论从内容上还是体例上，它们都已远远落后于当今国际经贸发展的形势，例如大多围绕语法、词汇和翻译等来展开，缺乏商务英语专业的实践性和语言的真实性，难以满足工作的需要。而另一些教材则又过于突出"专业"的内容，把商务英语教材混同于国际商务专业教材。因此，编写能够适应时代要求的国际商务英语教材显得尤为重要。正是在这样的背景下，由束光辉老师主编的"新体验商务英语系列教材"面世了，它体现了"贴近时代，融合语言与专业"的编写理念，是一次积极而大胆的尝试。

该系列包括《进出口贸易实务》《现代商务英语写作》《商务英语函电与合同》《商务报刊选读》《商务汉英翻译教程》《跨文化商务沟通》等教材。它们在内容设计和编写形式上具有以下特点。

1. 融专业性与语言技能于一体

该系列教材在编写上突出了以培养学生的实际工作能力为目标的思路，所选材料涉及了商务环境的各个方面，均能反映出商务工作实践性的特点，同时也体现了语言技能系统化培养的理念。该系列教材通过拟定各种商务环境，将商务知识和语言技能融合在一起，使学生的语言应用能力在更接近于真实的商务实践中得以提高。

2. 选材新，贴近时代

该系列教材在材料选择上参考了国内外最近几年出版的教材和其他相关材料，充分吸收

I

了国内外最新的教学科研成果，体现了国际商务活动不断变化的特点和商务领域专业性的特点，具有鲜明的时代特征。同时，该系列教材的许多文本、范例和研究材料均来自于近年来各类商务实践，体现了商务英语的真实性和实践性。

3. 练习形式多样，针对性强

该系列教材的练习将语言技能训练与商务环境较好地结合在一起，通过各种题型，对所涉及的商务环节和领域，有针对性地对学生进行训练。这不仅能够巩固学生所学的专业知识，而且还将提高他们的语言技能。

21世纪的中国更加开放，更加开放的中国在诸多方面都在与世界接轨。作为国际商务沟通的一个重要工具，商务英语的教学和研究理应跟上时代的发展和社会的需求。我们要更加重视并加强对商务英语教学的研究。该系列教材的编写是一次很好的探索，希望借此能进一步提高我国高校商务英语的教学和科研水平，为培养我国新型国际商务专业人才做出贡献。

中国国际贸易学会
国际商务英语研究委员会
原副主任
2016年3月

前言

这是一个信息化的时代,一个经济社会迅猛发展的时代。获取并准确地传递国际商务信息是个人、企业乃至整个国家参与国际竞争、进行经贸交流所必不可少的,而信息的获取和传递则离不开媒体。因此,如何从媒体中获取信息,并且提升阅读和应用这些信息的能力,对于商务工作者来说是十分重要的,而对于那些正在攻读经贸相关专业并有志于从事国际商务的学生来说,则显得尤为重要。为此,我们着手编写了《商务报刊选读》这本教材。

本书旨在帮助学生掌握阅读和理解商务报刊文章的方法和技巧,使他们熟悉当今经济贸易领域的专业知识、语言特色、惯用表达和句式,以提高其业务写作能力和商务交际能力。本书所选材料均来自英、美等国家或地区近年来主要的商业杂志和报纸。我们将这些文章按主题分为 9 个单元,包括:中国对外贸易与经济、地区经济与行业、金融与投资、企业发展与战略、营销与管理、人力资源、企业文化、企业家、贸易机构与合作会议等。各单元所选的文章内容新颖,风格多样,语言地道。

一、本书的特色

1. 时效性

本书的文章均选自英、美等国家或地区近年来有影响力的商业杂志和报纸,如《经济学家》《金融时报》《财富》《商业周刊》等。这些杂志和报纸有许多关于重大经济贸易的专题报道,其报道内容不仅涵盖面广、详尽深入,而且时效性很强,均是对新近的经济活动的迅速报道或有关专题的评论。阅读这些文章可以帮助读者了解近年来世界重大经济活动及专业人士对这些活动的独到见解,有助于形成全新的视角去阐释全球的经济发展。

2. 专业性

商务类新闻报道涉及内容之多是传统教科书所不能及的。不同内容具有不同的专业领域,因此也必然涉及反映该领域的专业词汇、新词语和独特的语言表达形式。接触这些材料无疑有助于读者接受语言发展的最新要素,使他们的语言运用更具专业性、职业性和时代特征。

3. 启发性

阅读不仅是获取信息的手段，更是提高分析能力的重要途径。孔子曰："学而不思则罔"。因此，如何引导学生在阅读中学会思考，尤其是培养他们在阅读西方报刊时如何"去伪存真，明辨是非"，避免"人云亦云"，这实际上对我们的英语报刊选读教学提出了更高的要求。鉴于此，我们在教材的结构设计上充分考虑了这一点，在每个单元均设置了"Group Discussion"，让学生就有关专题进行讨论；同时还提供了一个案例，供学生进行分析。这些讨论题的设计充满了启发性，能够较好地引导学生从不同的角度进行深入思考并展开讨论。

4. 细致性

无论是课文的选材和注解，还是练习的编写，都体现了编者的细致入微，尤其是注解和练习。课文的注解十分详尽，有时达 50 多条，不仅有语言难点的解释，更多的则是专业术语和背景知识的叙述。此外，每篇课文还附有"阅读小知识"，介绍商务英语报刊的相关知识、本单元的背景知识或进行专题说明，充分体现了"寓知识性于阅读"的编写理念。练习的编写则以辅助理解课文为目标，并在充分考虑如何提高学生翻译和语言概括等综合运用能力的基础上进行精心设计，合理搭配；题目涉及面广，语言程度较深，有一定的挑战性。

二、本书的教学安排

本书共 9 个单元，每单元包括 3 部分，即：Text A、Text B 和 Supplementary Reading。每一单元的篇幅较长，老师可根据实际情况用 4 学时来完成。其中，Supplementary Reading 可作为课外阅读让学生自行完成。此外，课堂上可留一部分时间让学生参与每一单元中"Group Discussion"和"Case Study"的讨论，以提高他们分析问题的能力。教师也可根据自身的教学实践，在每单元适当补充最新的报刊材料。

本书的主要读者对象为英语专业学生、商务英语专业学生及具有较好英语基础的其他经贸专业学生，同时也可用作外企白领阶层和其他商务英语爱好者的自学用书。

本书由束光辉担任主编，东刚担任副主编。其中，束光辉负责全书大纲的制定及大部分书稿的编写工作，东刚老师编写了课文的注释和词汇表。

本书的编写与出版得到北京交通大学语言与传播学院领导的大力支持及北京交通大学出版社张利军编辑的热情帮助，在此一并表示衷心的感谢。

编　者
2016 年 3 月

Contents

Unit 1　China's Foreign Trade and Economy ……………………………………（1）
中国对外贸易与经济

Unit 2　Regional Economy and Industry ………………………………………（24）
地区经济与行业

Unit 3　Finance and Investment …………………………………………………（54）
金融与投资

Unit 4　Corporate Development and Strategies ………………………………（86）
企业发展与战略

Unit 5　Marketing and Management …………………………………………（126）
营销与管理

Unit 6　Human Resources ………………………………………………………（172）
人力资源

Unit 7　Corporate Culture ………………………………………………………（204）
企业文化

Unit 8　Entrepreneur ……………………………………………………………（231）
企业家

Unit 9　Trade Organizations and Conferences on Cooperation ……………（268）
贸易机构与合作会议

参考文献 ……………………………………………………………………………（299）

Unit 1

China's Foreign Trade and Economy
中国对外贸易与经济

The Economy — A Bubble in Pessimism

"JUST the other day we were afraid of the Chinese," Paul Krugman recently wrote in the *New York Times*. "Now we're afraid for them." He is among a number of prominent commentators contemplating calamity in the world's second-biggest economy. Three measures seem to encapsulate their fears. Economic growth has slowed to 7.5%, from its earlier double-digit pace. The investment rate remains unsustainably high, at over 48% of GDP. Meanwhile, the debt ratio — ie, what China's firms, households and government owe — has risen alarmingly, to 200% of GDP, by some estimates.

Concerns about the first number were assuaged a little this month, when China reported strong figures for trade and industrial production (which rose by 9.7% in the year to July)[1] (see the chart). Yet beneath the cyclical ups and downs, China has undoubtedly seen its momentum slowing.

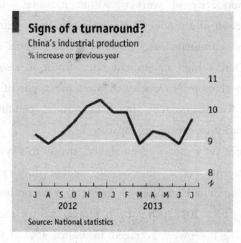

It is the combined productive capacity of China's workers, capital and know-how that sets a maximum speed for the economy, determining how fast it can grow without inflation. It also decides how fast it must grow to avoid spare capacity and a rise in the numbers without work.[2] The latest figures suggest that the sustainable rate of growth is closer to China's current pace of 7.5% than to the 10% rate the economy was sizzling along at.[3]

For many economists, this structural slowdown is inevitable and welcome. It marks an evolution in China's growth model, as it narrows the technological gap with leading economies and shifts more of its resources into services. For Mr. Krugman, by contrast, the slowdown threatens China's growth model with extinction.

China, he argues, has run out of "surplus peasants". Chinese flooding from the countryside into the factories and cities have in the past kept wages low and returns on investment high. The flood has slowed and, in some cases, reversed. So China can no longer grow simply by allocating capital to the new labour arriving from the fields. "Capital widening" must now give way to "capital deepening" (adding more capital to each individual worker). As it does so, investment will suffer "sharply diminishing returns" and "drop drastically".[4] And since investment is such a big source of demand — accounting for almost half of it — such a drop will be impossible to offset. China will, in effect, hit a "Great Wall".

The question is whether Mr. Krugman's concerns are justified. He is right about China running out of "surplus" labour. China's countryside is no longer so overmanned that people can leave without being missed. Now when they go, the job market tightens and wages rise in the places they leave behind. To tempt them away, wages must rise in the places to which they go.

Yet Cai Fang of China's Academy of Social Sciences believes that China ran out of surplus countryside labour as far back as 2003. If the economy were going to run into a wall, it would have done so a decade ago.[5] In fact, the economy has since enjoyed spectacular growth. For some time, the movement of workers from agriculture into industry and services has not been the chief source of China's success. From 1995 to 2012 this movement added only 1.4 percentage points to China's annual growth, says Louis Kuijs of the Royal Bank of Scotland. Instead, most recent growth has come from raising the productivity of workers within industry, not moving new ones in. Mr. Krugman fears the extinction of a model China is already doing without.

He and other respected commentators, notably Michael Pettis of Peking University, are certainly right to criticise China's high investment rate, for it is a source of great inefficiency. Investment should expand an economy's capacity to meet the needs of its consumers or its export markets. But in China, Mr. Krugman argues, much investment spending is Sisyphean: it is simply adding to the economy's capacity to expand its capacity.[6]

Yet over-investment is not yet a source of instability, thanks to a system that depends on captive savers. Because the government sets an interest-rate ceiling on deposits, the banks underpay depositors and undercharge corporate borrowers — in effect, a tax on household savers and a subsidy for state business.[7] According to a 2012 paper by Il Houng Lee of the IMF and co-authors, this transfer from households to big borrowers averaged an annual 4% of GDP in 2001 − 2011. The subsidy allows big firms to invest in projects that would otherwise be unviable. The authors reckon China's investment rate should be closer to 40% than 48%. But the distortion can be sustained while depositors continue to finance it — and, given also China's controls on capital outflows, they have little choice.

It is clear that China should lower its investment rate. But Mr. Krugman and others say that a lower investment rate could precipitate a crash. Their concern echoes a 70-year-old model of growth devised by Roy Harrod and Evsey Domar, in which the economy is balanced on a knife-edge between boom and bust.[8]

The model recognises that investment plays a dual role in an economy. It is, as Martin Wolf of the *Financial Times* puts it, both "a source of extra capacity" and a "source of demand". Sometimes these two roles work at cross purposes. If growth slows, then the economy will not need to add as much capacity. That implies less investment. But because investment spending is a source of demand, less of it also implies less demand, lowering growth still further. In avoiding excess capacity, the economy ends up creating more of it.

But how well does this model fit China? The country has both one of the world's highest investment rates and one of its most stable growth rates. That is presumably because investment is partly orchestrated by the government, which encourages more capital spending when other sources of demand are weak, and vice versa.[9] China's state-owned enterprises and local-government investment vehicles may not allocate capital to the right things. But at least they mobilise it at the right moments.

Indeed, the inefficiency of Chinese investment may be one reason why it will not create great instability. Mr. Lee and co-authors point out that China now requires ever higher investment to generate the same rate of growth (its incremental capital-output ratio, as economists call it, is rising). But a corollary is that the same rate of investment is consistent with China's slowing rate of growth.

Pessimists worry that slower growth will require less investment in capacity, which will, in turn, depress demand. But if the reason for slower growth is a reduction in the efficiency of investment, then slower growth will require just as much of it, precisely because it delivers less bang for the buck.[10]

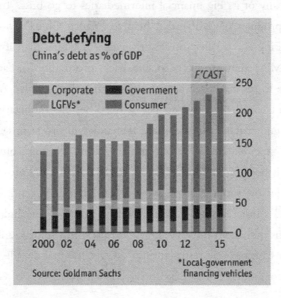

Critics of China's high investment worry not just about the redundant capacity it creates, but also about the debts it leaves behind. China as a whole is thrifty: its saving rate is even higher than its investment rate. But savers and investors are not usually the same. Standing between them is China's financial system, which transfers vast resources from the first to the second. The debts of China's firms amounted to 142% of GDP last year, according to Goldman Sachs, and investment vehicles sponsored by local governments had debts worth another 22.5% (see chart). Though impossible to calculate accurately, bad debts might amount to the equivalent of a quarter of the country's GDP.

The fat pipes of the financial system

A similar credit boom preceded America's crisis in 2008, and Japan's in the early 1990s. It is therefore natural to fear that China will suffer a similar fate. But a closer examination of their experience suggests that China is unlikely to repeat it.

Economists sometimes divide America's woes into two phases[11]: first the housing bust and then the Lehman shock[12]. America's house prices began falling as early as 2006, damaging household wealth. Housebuilding slowed sharply, weighing on growth, and many construction jobs disappeared. But for two years America's central bank, the Federal Reserve, was able to offset much of the harm to growth, while unemployment rose only modestly. (Economist, Sept, 3, 2013)

All that changed in September 2008 when Lehman Brothers[12] went bust, triggering acute financial panic. Nobody knew how big the losses from mortgage defaults might be, nor who might end up having to bear them. Creditors, shareholders, marketmakers and traders all rushed to make sure it was not them, by pulling credit lines, demanding collateral and dumping their securities.

In many ways, their dash for the exits proved to be more damaging for the economy as a whole than the danger from which they were seeking to escape. After the Lehman shock, a manageable number of mortgage insolvencies became a catastrophic liquidity problem. The lending mistakes of the past crippled the supply of finance in the present.

China may suffer something like the first phase of America's slowdown, but it should escape the second. It will not allow any of its big financial intermediaries to go bust. Investors may stop buying the wealth-management products (WMPs) that help to finance China's so-called shadow banking[13] system. But shadow banking is a smaller source of finance in China than it was in America. And if investors stop buying WMPs, they are likely to shift back into traditional bank deposits instead. The banks should thus be able to resist a credit crunch of the kind that crippled America's economy. And even then the government has plenty more scope, if need be, for monetary and fiscal stimulus.

Some economists argue that efforts to sustain demand will prove misguided. An unsustainable boom will leave workers stranded in the wrong jobs, making a painful bust necessary to reallocate them. Yet restructuring is not unique to a recession. Even in a steadily growing economy, plenty of upheaval is going on under the surface, as people are hired and fired, and as they hop between jobs of their own volition.[14] Just as busts push workers out of declining industries and into unemployment, so booms pull them out of sunset industries into sunrise ones.

China is no stranger to economic restructuring.[15] Over the past decade, the share of workers in agriculture fell from half to about a third. Exports have fallen from 38% of GDP in 2007 to 26% last year, while services now contribute as much to the economy as industry. And this enormous shake-up of employment and production took place in an economy that was growing by about 10% a year. China's economy can, it seems, evolve and expand at the same time.

New Words and Expressions

calamity	n.	灾难
encapsulate	v.	使……隔绝
assuage	v.	减轻（痛苦等）
cyclical	a.	循环的
sizzle	v.	发出嗞嗞声，高速发展
extinction	n.	灭绝，绝迹
captive	a.	受控制的
ceiling	n.	最高限制
unviable	a.	不可行的
precipitate	v.	促成，使发生
excess	a.	多余的
orchestrate	v.	统筹安排
incremental	a.	增长的
corollary	n.	推断，必然结果
buck	n.	美元
redundant	a.	多余的
thrifty	a.	节俭的
equivalent	n.	等同，相等量
precede	v.	发生在……之前
woe	n.	痛苦，忧伤
bust	a.	失败
default	n.	违约
collateral	n.	担保品
mortgage	n.	抵押，抵押品
insolvency	n.	无还债能力
liquidity	n.	资本流动性
crunch	n.	崩溃，危机
strand	v.	搁浅，陷于困境
upheaval	n.	动荡
volition	n.	意愿

ups and downs	波动
interest-rate ceiling	利率的上限
vice versa	反之亦然
redundant capacity	产能过剩
weigh on	对……产生影响
go bust	破产
mortgage insolvencies	抵押破产
shadow banking system	影子银行系统
credit crunch	信用危机
of one's own volition	自愿，主动地

Notes

1. Concerns about the first number were assuaged a little this month, when China reported strong figures for trade and industrial production. 对于第一种数据的担忧在本月可以稍稍舒缓一下了，因为本月中国贸易和工业生产的报告数据表现得较为强劲。

   句中的"assuage"指人们的担忧减轻的意思。

2. It also decides how fast it must grow to avoid spare capacity and a rise in the numbers without work.

   文中的"spare capacity"是指"产能过剩"，相当于"overcapacity"。

3. The latest figures suggest that the sustainable rate of growth is closer to China's current pace of 7.5% than to the 10% rate the economy was sizzling along at. 最近的数字表明，可持续增长率接近中国现有的7.5% 而不是经济高速发展的10%。

   其中，"sizzling"指（用油煎炸时）发出嗞嗞的响声，在这里指"经济高速增长"。

4. As it does so, investment will suffer "sharply diminishing returns" and "drop drastically". 这样做，投资回报率将急剧下降，投资额也迅速降低。

5. If the economy were going to run into a wall, it would have done so a decade ago. 如果中国的经济遭遇了困境，早在十年前就发生了。

   "run into a wall"与上文提到的"China will, in effect, hit a 'Great Wall'."均意为"中国经济发展遭遇了阻碍"。"Great Wall"在此意为"阻碍"。

6. But in China, Mr. Krugman argues, much investment spending is Sisyphean: it is simply adding to the economy's capacity to expand its capacity.

   句中的"Sisyphean"是"永远做不完，徒劳"的意思。

7. Because the government sets an interest-rate ceiling on deposits, the banks underpay depositors and undercharge corporate borrowers — in effect, a tax on household savers and a subsidy for state business.

   句中的"set an interest-rate ceiling"意为"设定了利率上限"。

Unit 1　China's Foreign Trade and Economy

8. Their concern echoes a 70-year-old model of growth devised by Roy Harrod and Evsey Domar, in which the economy is balanced on a knife-edge between boom and bust.　人们的这种担忧与 Yoy Harrod 和 Evesey Domar 七十年前提出来的增长模式是吻合的——经济的发展在繁荣和崩溃之间，就像在刀锋上保持平衡。
本句的意思是经济从繁荣走向崩溃，是很容易的。

9. That is presumably because investment is partly orchestrated by the government, which encourages more capital spending when other sources of demand are weak, and vice versa.
文中的"is partly orchestrated by the government"是指"由政府来统筹安排"。

10. But if the reason for slower growth is a reduction in the efficiency of investment, then slower growth will require just as much of it, precisely because it delivers less bang for the buck.
但是如果经济增长放缓的原因是投资效率下降，那么增长放缓需要增加投资，因为它会对货币产生较少的负面影响。
"buck"的本意是"美元"，此处指"货币"。

11. Economists sometimes divide America's woes into two phases...
句中的"America's woes"是指"美国金融危机"。

12. Lehman Brothers　雷曼兄弟公司
这是一家为全球公司、机构、政府和投资者的金融需求提供服务的全方位、多元化投资银行。雷曼兄弟公司自 1850 年创立以来，已在全球范围内建立起了创造新颖产品、探索最新融资方式、提供最佳优质服务的良好声誉。雷曼兄弟公司被美国《财富》杂志选为《财富》500 强公司之一。但是，2008 年 9 月 15 日，在次贷危机加剧的形势下，雷曼兄弟公司宣布申请破产保护。

13. shadow bank "影子银行"
又称为影子金融体系或者影子银行系统（Shadow Banking System），2011 年 4 月金融稳定理事会（FSB）对"影子银行"做了严格的界定："银行监管体系之外，可能引发系统性风险和监管套利等问题的信用中介体系。"对欧美来说，主要是围绕证券化推动的金融创新工具，这些工具在中国的金融市场里多数不存在。在中国，由于信托、理财等业务完全处于银监会的监管之下，与金融稳定理事会对影子银行的定义不符，因而不能将其视为影子银行。而对国内"影子银行"的概念至今没有一个明确的界定，只要涉及借贷关系和银行表外业务都属于"影子银行"。

14. Even in a steadily growing economy, plenty of upheaval is going on under the surface, as people are hired and fired, and as they hop between jobs of their own volition.
本句中的"upheaval"指"社会动荡，社会不稳定"。

15. China is no stranger to economic restricting.　中国对于经济结构调整是再了解不过了。
注意本句的意思，有些否定的比较结构实际上是肯定的意思。

阅读小知识（1）

英美主要经贸报刊简介

1. 美国的《商业周刊》（BusinessWeek）

它由 McGraw-Hill Companies Inc. 出版，是全球最大的商业杂志，每周发行量达 120 万册，读者人数超过 560 万人，遍及全球 130 个国家。美国《商业周刊》在亚洲和欧洲出版国际版。美国《商业周刊》提供深入独到的见解和细致详尽的信息，帮助专业人士在商业、财务及事业发展方面做出更明智的决定。通过美国《商业周刊》的报道，读者能掌握财经大事、金融趋势和预测、科技应用等方面的最新动向。

2. 英国的《经济学家》（Economist）

它是英国最大的综合性周刊。它与《金融时报》同属于皮尔逊父子公司所有。目前的发行量为 76 万多份，在全球 190 多个国家和地区拥有 300 万读者，是一本面向众多商界及政界决策者和精英的高端杂志。它具有 160 年的发展历史，至今仍保持着青春活力及旺盛的生命力。其内容已远远超出专业领域，成为涵盖世界政治、经济、商业、金融、科技、文化、艺术等内容的综合性杂志。

3. 英国的《金融时报》（Financial Times）

它于 1888 年 2 月 13 日问世于伦敦。这家报纸如今已发展成为世界最知名的金融、经济类报纸之一。该报着重报道财政、金融和工商等方面的消息、问题研究和动向，但也刊登政治、文化等方面的文章与评论。它是英国每天提供伦敦股票交易所全部行情的唯一日报。

4. 美国的《财富》（Fortune）

《财富》杂志于 1929 年由美国人亨利·卢斯创办，隶属于美国时代华纳公司（Time Warner）旗下的出版机构时代公司（Time）。它是以报道经济、商业为主要内容的大型刊物。此外，它有时还发表一些有分量的外交及军事方面的文章。它运营着两个杂志品牌——"财富论坛"和"世界 500 强排名"，在全球具有影响力。

5. 《远东经济评论》（Far Eastern Economic Review）

《远东经济评论》创办于 1946 年，是周刊，在香港出版。1997 年香港回归中国后，其业主易人，由道-琼斯公司（Dow Jones & Company, Inc.）出版。其主要报道和评论远东国家和地区的经济，但也发表政治、军事等方面的文章。该刊语言较《时代》周刊等浅显些。

6. 美国的《福布斯》（Forbes）

它是一份美国商业和金融杂志，于 1917 年由 B. C. Forbes 创立，总部设在纽约第五大道。它每年公布一次的 Forbes 500 排行榜，是根据销量、利润、资产、市值和雇员 5 个指标对美国公司的排名。此外，它还有世界公司的排行榜和个人财富的排行榜等。

Unit 1 China's Foreign Trade and Economy

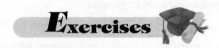

Exercises

I Decide the following statements are true (T) and false (F)

1. Economic growth has slowed down, the investment rate remains low, and meanwhile, the debt ratio has risen alarmingly. ( )
2. China experienced a 10% rate of growth in the last decades. ( )
3. Mr. Krugman thinks that the slowdown might terminate China's growth model. ( )
4. More and more people in the countryside tend to stay in their hometown because the job market tightens in big cities. ( )
5. The movement of workers from agriculture into industry and services has been the chief source of China's success. ( )
6. Investment should expand an economy's capacity to meet the needs of its consumers or its export markets. ( )
7. Depositors in China have little choice because China controls capital inflows tightly. ( )
8. China has one of the world's highest investment rates and one of its most stable growth rates as well. ( )
9. Since China's state-owned enterprises and local-government investment vehicles may not allocate capital to the right things, so they contribute very little to the economic growth. ( )
10. When investors stop buying the wealth-management products (WMPs) that help to finance China's so-called shadow banking system, they are likely to shift back into traditional bank deposits. ( )

II Choose one answer that best suits the following statements.

1. Some prominent commentators contemplate calamity in China's economy and their argument is supported by the following proofs EXCEPT: _____.
   A. Economic growth has slowed down
   B. The investment rate remains unsustainably high
   C. Figures for trade and industrial production are strong
   D. The debt ratio has risen alarmingly
2. Yet over-investment is not yet a source of instability, thanks to a system that depends on captive savers? The meaning of the underlined word is "_____".
   A. kept within bounds
   B. held under control of another person
   C. taken and held as or as if a prisoner of war
   D. being in a situation in which it is difficult to make a free choice

3. The banks underpay depositors and undercharge corporate borrowers, because _____.
   A. the government imposes taxes on depositors
   B. the government sets an interest-rate ceiling on deposits
   C. corporate borrowers can get loans from foreign financial institutions
   D. the interest rates are too low
4. What might be the results of high investment in China?
   A. Redundant capacity and debts.
   B. Inefficiency of investment.
   C. Growth in export.
   D. Increase of income.
5. When America's house prices began falling in 2006, the following phenomena followed EXCEPT: _____.
   A. Housebuilding slowed sharply
   B. Growth slowed down
   C. The banks bought a large number of houses
   D. Many construction jobs disappeared

III Translate the following passages into Chinese

1. The model recognises that investment plays a dual role in an economy. It is, as Martin Wolf of the Financial Times puts it, both "a source of extra capacity" and a "source of demand". Sometimes these two roles work at cross purposes. If growth slows, then the economy will not need to add as much capacity. That implies less investment. But because investment spending is a source of demand, less of it also implies less demand, lowering growth still further. In avoiding excess capacity, the economy ends up creating more of it.

2. Some economists argue that efforts to sustain demand will prove misguided. An unsustainable boom will leave workers stranded in the wrong jobs, making a painful bust necessary to reallocate them. Yet restructuring is not unique to a recession. Even in a steadily growing economy, plenty of upheaval is going on under the surface, as people are hired and fired, and as they hop between jobs of their own volition. Just as busts push workers out of declining industries and into unemployment, so booms pull them out of sunset industries into sunrise ones.

IV Write a summary of this text.

Unit 1　China's Foreign Trade and Economy

Can China Brave a US Downturn?

David Roche

　　How symbiotic are the Chinese and American economies? If the US economy catches cold, will China get the flu? At the first sight this might seem a simple question with a simple answer. Work out how much the US buys from China, cut the growth of US's imports from China in half and presto, see what is the hit to China's GDP.[1] The answer would be a 2% loss, if one assumes as a worse case scenario that US imports from China fall to a 5% annual growth rate from 20%. That would cut China's GDP growth to 8% from 10% — no big deal.[2]

　　But this would be the wrong answer. The real world is more complicated. A few of the more arcane considerations that cannot be ignored are: What could plug the hole in China's GDP made by a decline in export growth to the US? What would a US slowdown mean for other factors, such as foreign direct investment in China? What policy actions could China take to palliate the loss?

　　The analysis is only made more difficult by the fact that China's economic statistics don't add up. This provides a good starting point!

　　Let us ask ourselves the question: If Chinese exports were to weaken, could domestic demand make up the difference? According to China's economic statistics, the answer is, no way. Consumption in China is on a weakening trend as a proportion of GDP.

　　My own observation from working in China is that investment and savings is likely to be overstated, probably by inclusion in investment of a lot property transactions which are rightly transfers and not part of GDP, and therefore the contribution of the consumer is understated.[3] There is, of course, no way of proving this. But both rural and urban household incomes have been rising smartly, and China is a lot further down the road to creating a consumer society than the shrinking proportion of GDP that the statisticians attribute to the Chinese consumer would indicate.[4]

　　Bottom-up evidence tends to support this view. Passenger car sales have been rising at a steady 30% to 40% annual rate for much of 2006. Sales of household electronics were up 22% a year ago in November. China is the largest and fastest growing mobile phone market in the world. Most of China's sector reports for consumer products, which are more reliable than macro figures because they are based upon corporate reports, indicate a booming consumer sector that should be increasing as a proportion of GDP.[5]

　　This makes a difference! If China's consumer sector were in reality to account for 50% instead of the published 40% of GDP (still 20 percentage points of GDP less than in India), a 10% growth rate would add 5 percentage points to GDP growth every year, which is currently hidden, or double the maximum anticipated loss of growth from a 75% fall in export growth to the US.[6] This, by the way, is not a forecast! It is a sensitivity which demonstrates that an under-reporting of the size of the Chinese consumer sector and overstatement of investment may in reality greatly lessen the vulnerability of the Chinese economy to any slowdown in either of the latter sectors.[7]

Now let's extend further the analysis of investment. A hard landing for the US economy would hit US foreign direct investment in China. On average, China gets about $60 billion of FDI every year, of which 23% comes from the US. Let us assume this halves because of a US slowdown. The hit to China would come on three fronts. First the loss of FDI would subtract 0.4% from GDP. Then there would be the knock on effect of the loss of output from this highly productive source of investment. That could amount to an annual loss of production of around 0.8% of GDP. So falling US FDI would cause a total loss of 1.2% of China's GDP, coming as an additional loss on top of exports to the US that would constitute a total GDP cost of 3.2%.[8] This is a pretty serious hit. But it is less than the annual growth that may be hidden in the under-reported consumer sector.

Another vulnerability is investment by Chinese exporters, which would be hit by weakening US demand. This cannot be accurately quantified. But we do know that foreign-owned corporations and joint ventures account for 60% of exports. Therefore the additional impact on investment by domestic producers is quite likely to be small. It would be dwarfed by fast-growing infrastructure investments that China is currently undertaking and which would be boosted (see policy response below) if this scenario happened.[9]

Of course China's exports and inward FDI are very visible and relatively trustworthy figures. A downturn in both would set alarm bells ringing and generate headlines around the world. Even published Chinese GDP figures would look a bit dicey; annual growth could be reported as around 6% instead of 10% — the equivalent of declaring a recession in China, even though the reality might be a lot better than that.[10]

Nevertheless the news would trigger a policy reaction in Beijing. First, the tightening policy course of the People's Bank of China would be reversed. And second, the administrative freeze would come off investment in real estate and other sectors that the authorities have successfully jawed into a slowdown.[11]

But most importantly, China's fiscal accounts are in very good shape and could be used to stimulate the economy. The government savings rate (measured by receipts less current expenditure before public investment)[12] has risen by over 5% points of GDP to 11% in the last five years. This surplus could be spent in very visible and stimulatory ways.

China has another weapon to fight any downturn in demand. Its international reserves now stand at over $1 trillion. At most the Bank of China needs to hold about $600 billion as a safeguard against potential shocks. That would leave $400 billion, or more than 4% of GDP, that could be transferred to a sovereign fund and invested profitably — much as Singapore and many other reserve-rich states do.[13] Of course not all of this money should or would be invested in the domestic economy, but there is no doubt that using China's huge war chest is an attractive policy option for a rainy day.

Unit 1 China's Foreign Trade and Economy

In sum, China seems capable of withstanding the impact of even a quite dramatic slowdown, in both exports to the US and in the FDI that it receives from the US. China's vulnerability to such shocks is probably overstated by official statistics that may exaggerate investment but underreport the fast-growing consumer sector. A US downturn that impacted China would also elicit a fiscal and monetary policy response, which, at a rough guess, could offset between half and two-thirds of the growth loss from weakening exports and inward FDI.[14] Where China's economy really falls out of bed is if there is a global recession involving Japan and the EU, in addition to the US.[15] In my view this is very unlikely in the next year, but it is the nightmare scenario that China lacks the tools to deal with.

(*Far Eastern Economic Review*, January−February, 2007)

New Words and Expressions

brave	v.	勇敢面对
downturn	n.	低迷时期
symbiotic	a.	[生] 共生的
presto	ad.	赶快，立刻
scenario	n.	某一特定情节，情景
arcane	a.	神秘的，不可思议的
plug	v.	堵，塞，插上
palliate	v.	减轻，缓和
proportion	n.	比例，均衡
overstate	v.	夸大的叙述，夸张
transfer	n.	转账，过户，转让
understate	v.	保守地说，低估
smartly	ad.	大大地
shrinking	a.	萎缩的，收缩的
statistician	n.	统计员，统计学家
bottom-up	a.	颠倒的，自下而上的
electronics	n.	电子产品
reliable	a.	可靠的，值得信赖的
maximum	a.	最高的，最多的
anticipate	v.	预测，估计
forecast	n.	预测，估计
sensitivity	n.	敏感，灵敏（度）
demonstrate	v.	示范，证明，论证

under-reporting	n.	低报，申报不足
lessen	v.	减少，减轻
vulnerability	n.	弱点，易受攻击性
front	n.	面，方面
accurately	ad.	正确地，精确地
quantify	v.	确定数量，量化
dwarf	v.	（使）变矮小
infrastructure	n.	基础设施
trustworthy	a.	可信赖的
dicey	a.	不确定的，冒险性的
equivalent	n.	等价物，相等物
recession	n.	不景气，工商业衰退期
nevertheless	conj.	然而，不过
trigger	v.	引发，引起，触发
tightening	a.	紧缩的，收紧的
reverse	v.	颠倒，倒转
administrative	a.	管理的，行政的
freeze	n.	结冰，（工资、物价等的）冻结
jaw	v.	教训，推动
stimulatory	a.	刺激的，激励的
safeguard	n.	安全装置，安全措施
sovereign	a.	独立自主的，完全的
withstand	v.	抵抗，反抗，经得住
exaggerate	v.	夸大，夸张
elicit	v.	得出，引出，引起
offset	v.	弥补，抵消
nightmare	n.	梦魇，噩梦，可怕的事物
property transaction		财产交易，所有权交易
household income		家庭收入
sector report		部门报告，行业报告
be based upon		以……为基础
extend further the analysis of		进一步分析
knock on		敲击，结束
amount to		总计
fiscal account		财政账户
war chest		战争基金，（为竞争等）筹措资金

Unit 1 China's Foreign Trade and Economy

1. Work out how much the US buys from China, cut the growth of US's imports from China in half and presto, see what is the hit to China's GDP. 首先计算出美国从中国的购买总量，然后将美国从中国的进口增长率减半，就可以知道对中国GDP的影响了。
   句中的"work out"意为"计算出"。

2. The answer would be a 2% loss, if one assumes as a worse case scenario that US imports from China fall to a 5% annual growth rate from 20%. That would cut China's GDP growth to 8% from 10% — no big deal. 结果会降低2%，如果情况更为严峻，美国从中国的年进口增长率由20%下降到5%，那么中国的GDP增长将由10%降到8%，影响并不大。
   句中的"no bid deal"意为"没什么大不了的，影响不大"。文中的"that"引导定语从句修饰"scenario"。

3. ... investment and savings is likely to be overstated, probably by inclusion in investment of a lot property transactions which are rightly transfers and not part of GDP, and therefore the contribution of the consumer is understated. ……投资和储蓄可能被夸大了，大概因为计算时把大量的财产交易包含其中，这些财产交易只是转账过户而并非是GDP的一部分，因此消费者的贡献就被低估了。

4. But both rural and urban household incomes have been rising smartly, and China is a lot further down the road to creating a consumer society than the shrinking proportion of GDP that the statisticians attribute to the Chinese consumer would indicate. 但是城乡家庭收入大幅增长，中国更多的是在建设一个以消费者为中心的社会，而不是像统计人员对中国消费者的评价所显示的那样，他们在GDP中的比重越来越小。
   句中的"down the road"意为"沿着……方向，沿着……路"，"attribute to"的意思是"归因于，认为……所为"。

5. Most of China's sector reports for consumer products, which are more reliable than macro figures because they are based upon corporate reports, indicate a booming consumer sector that should be increasing as a proportion of GDP. 中国大部分行业的消费者产品报告因以公司报告为基础，比宏观数据更为可靠，这些行业报告显示出一个繁荣的消费领域，该领域应该会不断发展，成为GDP的一部分。

6. If China's consumer sector were in reality to account for 50% instead of the published 40% of GDP (still 20 percentage points of GDP less than in India), a 10% growth rate would add 5 percentage points to GDP growth every year, which is currently hidden, or double the maximum anticipated loss of growth from a 75% fall in export growth to the US. 如果中国的消费部门确实占GDP的50%，而不是所公布的40%（即使这样仍比印度低20个百分点），那么10%的增长率将会使GDP每年增长5%，这在目前是不明显的，或者是使因出口美国的增长率降低75%而导致的预期增长率的最大降幅翻倍。

句中的"which"引导非限制性定语从句,指前面整件事情。

7. ... an under-reporting of the size of the Chinese consumer sector and overstatement of investment may in reality greatly lessen the vulnerability of the Chinese economy to any slowdown in either of the latter sectors. ……低估中国消费部门的规模和夸大投资事实上都会缓解任何投资领域的减速而给中国经济带来冲击。

句中的"latter"是指投资领域。

8. So falling US FDI would cause a total loss of 1.2% of China's GDP, coming as an additional loss on top of exports to the US that would constitute a total GDP cost of 3.2%. 出口美国占GDP成本的3.2%,除此之外,美国的外国直接投资额的下降将会使中国的GDP再额外降低1.2%。

句中"coming"是现在分词短语作状语,引出结果。

9. It would be dwarfed by fast-growing infrastructure investments that China is currently undertaking and which would be boosted if this scenario happened. 如果这种情况出现,国内生产商的投资同目前中国正在进行并且将来会继续增加的基础建设投资相比,就显得渺小了。

本句中"if"引导的从句作全句的条件状语。

10. Even published Chinese GDP figures would look a bit dicey; annual growth could be reported as around 6% instead of 10% — the equivalent of declaring a recession in China, even though the reality might be a lot better than that. 甚至中国公布的GDP数字也会显得不确定,年增长率可能会是6%左右,而不是10%,其结果相当于宣布中国处于经济衰退,尽管实际情况会好很多。

11. ... the administrative freeze would come off investment in real estate and other sectors that the authorities have successfully jawed into a slowdown. 对房地产和其他领域投资的行政调控将有所松动,政府现在已成功地使这些领域的投资放缓。

句中的"the authorities"指的是政府当局。

12. The government savings rate (measured by receipts less current expenditure before public investment) ... 政府储蓄率(在公共投资之前,用收入减去流动支出)……

国民储蓄包括个人储蓄、企业储蓄和政府储蓄三部分。

13. That would leave \$400 billion, or more than 4% of GDP, that could be transferred to a sovereign fund and invested profitably — much as Singapore and many other reserve-rich states do. 那将会留下4 000亿美元,超过GDP的4%,这些外汇将会转给一家自主经营的基金进行投资以获取利润——这在很大程度上类似于新加坡等外汇储备充足的国家的做法。

14. A US downturn that impacted China would also elicit a fiscal and monetary policy response, which, at a rough guess, could offset between half and two-thirds of the growth loss from weakening exports and inward FDI. 影响中国的美国经济低迷将会引发财政金融方面的政策性反应,这些反应可能会抵消因出口疲软和流入的外国直接投资减少所造成的增长率降低幅度,这个比例大约在1/2至2/3之间。

文中的"at a rough guess"意为"大概猜测","which"引导定语从句修饰"response","weakening"意为"疲软的,越来越弱的,逐渐减少的"。

15. Where China's economy really falls out of bed is if there is a global recession involving Japan and

the EU, in addition to the US. 真正使中国经济产生问题的是发生包括欧盟、日本和美国在内的全球经济衰退。

文中的"fall out of bed"意为"出轨，出问题"，"where"引导一个主语从句，"if"引导的从句在句中作表语。

阅读小知识（2）

英美主要通讯社简介

（1）（美国）美联社（Associated Press, AP）：成立于1848年，总部设在纽约市，现在是世界上最大的通讯社。

（2）（美国）合众国际社（United Press International, UPI）：成立于1907年，它开创了一些重要的新闻报道业务，如于1925年开办了新闻图片等服务。在20世纪70年代末，该社就为100多个国家的4 503家客户提供服务。它有250多个分社对外提供新闻。

（3）（英国）路透社（Reuter's News Agency, Reuters）：1985年由路透（Paul Julius Reuters）创建，总部设在伦敦。它是一家商业性的通讯社。现在其业务已遍布全球150多个国家，有197个分社，用19种语言报道新闻。

（4）（英国）报纸联合社（Press Association, PA）：成立于1868年，它通过该社的新闻（PA News）、体育（PA Sport）和数据设计（PA Data Design）这三家公司而成为英国的全国新闻社，为报纸、广播电台和电视台提供全方位的新闻和信息服务，记者遍布全国。

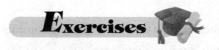

I Discuss and answer the following questions.

1. Why does the author think that China can withstand the impact of even a drastic downturn in its exports and FDI that it receives?
2. What are the effective weapons that China is equipped with in fighting downturn?
3. What makes the author think that the size of China's consumer sector is under-reported and investment overstated?
4. Do you think there are any other factors that can help explain China's strength in countering the impact by the downturn?

II Decide whether the following statements are true (T) or false (F).

1. China's economy can really withstand the downturn of the US unless there is a global recessions

that hit Japan, the EU and the US at the same time. (   )

2. It seems to the author that in China investment and savings is likely to be overstated, because investment of a lot of property transactions are only transfers and cannot be considered part of GDP. (   )

3. According to the author, China's sector reports for consumer products are more reliable than macro figures, for these report figures are collected in time by the State Statistics Bureau. (   )

4. The vulnerability of China's economy to any slowdown is exaggerated by overstatement of investment and under-reporting of the size of the consumer sector. (   )

5. Weakening US demand will not likely impact Chinese exports as expected, because foreign-owned corporations and joint ventures account for 60% of China's exports and in addition, fast-growing infrastructure investment in China can make up for such imports. (   )

6. It seems to the author that if a downturn in China's exports and inward FDI takes place, the world will be greatly affected and China will be in even worse situation. (   )

7. China has several weapons to fight any downturns in demand: the effective policies, rather sound fiscal accounts that can be used and large international reserves. (   )

8. China's economic growth will continue to maintain momentum, and can withstand the impact of even a quite drastic slowdown in exports to the US and in the FDI that it gets. (   )

9. The author predicts that China will not be vulnerable to the impact from a US downturn. Such a prediction is based merely on his empirical observations. (   )

10. The author is optimistic about China's economic strength against possible impact of a US downturn, because he is working in China. (   )

III Group discussion.

1. What do you think are the risks that face the Chinese companies in their business operations? Can you propose some effective cures to these problems?
2. Should China speed up the Yuan's rise? Please state your reasons.
3. What do you think of US-China trade relationship? What impact does it bring to people's lives of both nations?
4. Can you assess the impact of China's accession into the WTO and its efforts to open its economy?

Case Study

Is China too dependent on trade?

China's total trade volume has surged in recent years, and critics now often say that China's economic growth is overly dependent on foreign trade, warning that the ratio of trade to GDP — the foreign trade dependence ratio — is too high. Indeed, China's dependence on trade reached 80 percent in 2005, higher than that of many other countries, including the United States, Japan, and India, according to a study by the Chinese Academy of Social Sciences. China's reliance on exports has, in turn, caused friction with trading partners while potentially harming China's economic security, the critics note. Those on the other side of the domestic debate have questioned the calculation of the ratio: the size of China's GDP has largely been underestimated because it has only recently begun to take into account the service sector. Thus, China's dependence on trade is probably smaller than what critics suggest.

Supplementary Reading

China's Big Banks

Four of the world's biggest lenders must face some nasty truths.

"CHINA'S banks are not real banks," says Andrew Rothman of CLSA, a broker recently acquired by China's CITIC Securities. The country's biggest financial institutions are so closely held by the state that they are, in effect, arms of the treasury. Cosseted by rules that protect them from competition, they deliver huge profits in good times: bank profits as a share of China's economic output equalled nearly 3% last year, whereas the highest ratio achieved in recent decades by American banks was only 1% of GDP (in 2006). In bad times the state is there to clean up, just as it did during a surge in dud loans in 1990s.

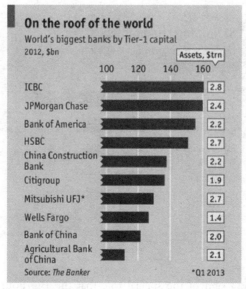

Chart 1

But the bargain that has driven China's "Big Four" banks to the top of the global league tables is breaking down. Profitable though they are now, another wave of non-performing loans will soon hit them. As the Chinese economy rebalances, the state is less willing than it was in the past to pour credit into state-owned enterprises (SOEs) at the expense of households and private firms. Mr. Rothman's epithet will not hold for ever. China's big banks are slowly becoming real institutions.

That will matter outside China as well as inside it. Its biggest lenders are giants of the banking world (see Chart 1). Industrial and Commercial Bank of China (ICBC), which showed a pre-tax profit of nearly $50 billion last year, was named recently by *The Banker*, a trade publication, as the world's largest bank measured by core capital. In 2000 ICBC's Tier-1 capital was just $22 billion; by the end of last year it had shot up to $161 billion, overtaking JPMorgan Chase and Bank of America. Three other Chinese banks have made it into the top ten: China Construction Bank (CCB), Bank of China (BOC) and Agricultural Bank of China (ABC).

The sheer size of these institutions is breathtaking. ICBC and ABC have over 400,000 employees each, nearly as many as Volkswagen, the world's biggest carmaker. ICBC has over 4m corporate clients. CCB has some 14,000 branches.

The Big Four were carved out of bits of the People's Bank of China (PBOC), the central bank, in the 1980s — though the original BOC dates back to the Qing dynasty. Ostensibly they were to be run like private commercial banks: all four have floated shares on the Hong Kong and Shanghai stock exchanges. But the state has maintained majority stakes in them as well as in the next-biggest bank, the Bank of Communications. The Big Four are led by senior figures in the Communist hierarchy, with bosses shuttling easily between banks and regulatory agencies. Wang Hongzhang, CCB's chairman, was previously a deputy governor at the PBOC and party secretary at its "discipline inspection commission". Xiao Gang, BOC's former chairman, now heads the China Securities Regulatory Commission, which supervises stockmarkets.

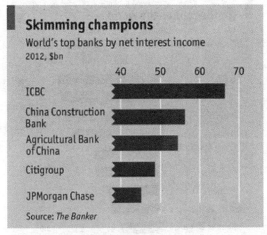

Chart 2

Such incestuous ties are a sign of the special role that the Big Four play in Chinese economic policy. Put bluntly, they are the chief instruments of financial repression. Because of the official ceiling on deposit rates, the big banks have a source of cheap funding that they can direct to favoured SOEs and other arms of government. ICBC, CCB and ABC enjoyed the highest net interest income of any banks around the world last year (see Chart 2).

But these headline figures hide a multitude of sins. China's use of its biggest banks to implement the 2009 economic stimulus has left a legacy of murky accounting, off-balance-sheet transactions and dodgy lending. Official data on non-performing loans put their level at just 1% of bank assets. No one believes that number. The banks' quarterly results released this week showed profits with little increase in provisions. But Morgan Stanley, an investment bank, reckons a more realistic figure may be 10% for all banks, and 6%-8% for the biggest. Things are worse in the many industries saddled with overcapacity: 17% of loans to the manufacturing sector, for example, could become duds if the economy sours, says Morgan Stanley.

The big banks have been here before. In the 1990s an elaborate bail-out was devised to recapitalise the Big Four and transfer dud loans to asset-management companies. It is improbable that a big Chinese bank would be allowed to go under if a similar situation arose again. Nevertheless their market share is rightly under threat.

Three changes in particular are weakening their position. The first is the stagnation of SOEs, which stands in sharp contrast with the dynamism of the "bamboo capitalists" in the private sector. Nicholas Lardy of the Peterson Institute for International Economics, a think-tank, calculates that over the past decade SOEs have destroyed so much value that, in the aggregate, they have produced negative real returns on capital employed. But private industrial firms, which create most jobs and much economic growth, have sharply positive returns.

As the economy slows, China's leaders have decided that resources should not be squandered in this way. Recent official proclamations threaten to cut investment in bloated state-run industries. China's big banks must therefore change how they do business, though they will still be tempted to lend to big firms that they suspect will not be allowed to fail.

Policymakers are also concerned about the rise of the shadow-banking sector. Because savers make little return on their bank deposits, they have sought riskier alternatives, anything from property to shadowy investment instruments known euphemistically as "wealth-management" products — some of them little better than Ponzi schemes. Charlene Chu of Fitch, a ratings agency, argues that shadow banking is pushing financial intermediation from a few big banks to tens of thousands of financing, leasing and guarantee firms and other less regulated, informal outfits. This, she thinks, is making financial data murky and less reliable.

If China's leaders ever did end the cap on deposit rates it would mean a revolution in banking. In the short term "the profits of almost all banks would shrink," says Oliver Rui of the China Europe International Business School. In the long term, though, he thinks the resulting competition would lead the better banks back to healthy margins. It might also gear them up to win back some market share from the shadow-banking sector, reckons Peter Williamson of Cambridge University's Judge Business School. A reported decision to allow banks soon to start issuing tradable certificates of deposit seems like another step towards preparing them for an end to the cap. But it would also expose them more to short-term funding risk.

The third force for change is China's long-awaited shift from an investment-led economy to one fired by domestic consumption. Over the past two years real consumption has contributed more to economic growth than has gross fixed capital formation; services oriented toward the domestic middle classes have grown more strongly than has export-oriented manufacturing. If this trend accelerates it will encourage the banks themselves to make more loans to small and medium-size enterprises and middle-class consumers.

The Winds of Change

That will force a cultural change at banks which in the past paid little attention to customer service or credit quality. Joseph Ngai of McKinsey, a consultancy, argues that "lending will no longer be a seller's market", in which firms ram credit down the throats of SOEs. His firm forecasts that loans to small companies and households, which together made up just 22% of the total in 2006, will soar to 57% of all loans (as measured by value) by 2021.

Put all of these trends together and the future looks less than rosy for the Big Four. Wen Jiabao, China's former prime minister, declared last year that they "make profits far too easily ... we have to break up their monopoly." Recent proclamations from the PBOC talk of boosting "private capital" in banking. On August 9th the China Banking Regulatory Commission, the industry's main regulator, unveiled draft rules for banking licences that are designed to encourage the entry of private capital into the industry.

Competition has already begun to dent the Big Four's monopoly. Smaller banks known as joint-stock commercial banks (JSCBs) were formed in the late 1980s and early 1990s by raising money from both the government and the private sector. The ambitious growth of JSCBs like China Minsheng and China Merchants has meant that the Big Four's share of banking assets had already shrunk to below 50% by 2010. As lending demand from small firms and households rises, the years of experience that JSCBs already have in this sector will count for even more.

Competition is also emerging from unexpected quarters. Alibaba and Tencent, two Chinese internet giants, are moving energetically into financial services. Tencent offers online payment services to fund managers, and wealth-management services to users of WeChat (a popular social-media app with more than 300m users). Alipay, Alibaba's online-payment arm, has introduced a service called Yu'E Bao ("remnant treasure") which offers e-commerce customers an easy way to divert leftover cash into high-interest funds. In just a few months it has attracted over $1 billion in investments.

These firms and smaller upstarts have a minuscule market share, but "this threat is all that any bank president here wants to talk about today," says a financial-industry specialist. *Caixin*, a Chinese financial magazine, reports that "several large banks have formed an 'Ali-bashing group' to fight what they see as Alibaba's invasion of their turf."

They are right to be worried. For one thing, punters actually like the products and services offered by the internet interlopers. What is more, unlike China's aloof bankers, these innovators already have volumes of proprietary data on the online purchasing habits and creditworthiness of consumers. The Big Four may yet be disrupted by Big Data.

With bad loans and competition rising, China's largest banks face tougher times ahead. ChinaScope Financial, a research firm partly owned by Moody's, a ratings agency, has analysed how declining net interest margins will affect China's banks. It estimates that the sector will need an injection of $50 billion −100 billion over the next two years just to keep its capital ratios at today's level. The managements of the Big Four realise this, and have won approval from their boards to raise over $40 billion in fresh capital over the next two years. But Andrew Sheng of the Fung Global Institute, a think-tank, reckons the sector will need to raise even more later: up to $300 billion over the next five years.

If the big banks rise to this challenge, greater transparency and more competition should follow. That would not just be good news for China. The once-parochial big banks are following their customers abroad. Nearly a quarter of BOC's assets are now overseas; ICBC's overseas assets grew by some 30% last year, more than double the rate of growth of the bank overall. They are also starting to invest in foreign banks. China's biggest banks are already world-beaters in terms of size. In time they may become world-class.

(*Financial Times*, Sept 12, 2013)

Answer and discuss the following questions:

1. What are roles of banks in our life? And what are their roles in economy?
2. How much do you know about China's banks? And how much do you know about other world leading banks? What are differences between China's banks and the banks in developed economies?
3. Should the big banks continue lending money to state-owned enterprises or switch to private industrial firms? Why? What are the risks for the banks if they make more loans to private companies?
4. What challenges are the large banks faced with? And what measures they can take to meet such challenges?

Unit 2

Regional Economy and Industry
地区经济与行业

Can Asians Innovate?

Henry S. Rowen

Clusters of craftsmen have existed as long as people have lived in substantial settlements — certainly since they have lived in cities. Modern examples include diamond cutters in Antwerp, knife makers in Sheffield, sock makers in Yiwu, and the cinematic entertainers in Mumbai.[1] This phenomenon is widely present in Asia's information technology (IT) industry.

Clusters form because firms benefit from having others in the same, or complementary, industries close by. There is a supply of skilled labor, specialized suppliers and buyers, and flows of knowledge among firms. This is the classic story told by the 19th century economist Alfred Marshall.[2] However, the story is a static one, and high tech industries are quintessentially dynamic. New firms can form new clusters.

As these examples suggest, market forces create them (with Silicon Valley[3] being the prime example), but governments often like to accelerate the process. They do this to enjoy the benefits of having a vibrant cluster sooner than the market might produce and from a belief, which might on occasion be warranted, of establishing a vibrant cluster before some other nation does, that is, to gain a first-mover advantage.[4] However, such initiatives imply that government officials know how to do this. The record on this is checkered.

Governments have used many methods to attract individuals and firms to the localities they pick: cheap financing, tax breaks, subsidized land and housing, special schools. If the conditions are favorable, such policies can successfully attract firms. However, has government done little more than cause firms that would form anyway to locate in a favored place instead of somewhere else in the country without substantial spillover benefits arising?[5] It can be hard to tell. One needs to consider the presence — or absence — of good public research organization in the region and, arguably even more, overall conditions for innovation and entrepreneurship in the country. These can vary greatly.

Beginning in the 1970s, a well-known cluster emerged in Taiwan's Hsinchu Science-based Industrial Park[6] (HSIP) that now contains several hundred companies, mostly in the IT industry. HSIP became noted for its fast-moving firms that were initially original equipment manufacturers (OEM)[7] for foreign firms before turning into original design manufacturers (ODM)[8]; presently some have become "orchestrators" of product designs offered to buyers worldwide. At its core were ITRC, the Industrial Technology Research Center, which took technologies in the pre-competitive state and developed them for commercialization by local companies. Its most famous firm was the pioneering chip foundry, TSMC, which was a spin-out from an ITRC lab.[9] HSIP and ITRC were founded by the government, which, together with powerful market forces, had led to a highly productive region.

Of Parks and Politics

Taiwan has pursued the "science-based park" model of Hsinchu with new parks in the south and in the center of the country. Since 2000, its IT companies have moved most of their manufacturing to mainland China where, unsurprisingly, they tend to cluster, notably in Kunshan, near Suzhou.

In the 1980s, clusters in software services began to develop in several Indian cities, firms in Mumbai, then in Bangalore, followed by New Delhi, Hyderabad, Chenai and Pune. In contrast to Taiwan, the government has long been a major obstacle to industry development through a host of restrictive regulations. Only when it began to seriously liberalize in 1991 did this industry take off. Foreign demand, notably in the US, was — and still — essential, and foreign firms have played a major role, but the leading Indian suppliers were domestic ones with some of them still growing. Governments can still be a problem; for example, the government of Karnataka state, whose capital is Bangalore, seems to be driving its thriving software industry away through inadequate investment in infrastructure.[10] Although the role of the government was not entirely negative (with, for instance, building a satellite ground station in Bangalore fairly early), the growth of Indian clusters has been essentially a market phenomenon.

China has many IT industry clusters, varying from strong to mediocre ones in performance. As is customary in China, the government has approached the cluster phenomenon from the top-down.[11] The Ministry of Science and Technology began its Torch Industrial Technology Program[12] in 1995 and as of 2005 had 83 groups in 16 provinces.

The three major high tech regions are Beijing, Shanghai and Shenzhen. The biggest is Beijing Zhongguancun Science Park[13], which contains China's leading universities, Academy of Science Institutes and thousands of companies. Legend Computer (now lenovo[14]) came out of the Chinese Academy of Sciences soon after economic liberalization began and is the leading firm in the cluster. Zhongguancun has the leading concentration of software firms and companies controlled by the state. Its cluster flourished with government assistance and support to these firms will likewise continue in the future.

Shanghai has the foremost integrated circuit-making cluster. The government subsidized the building of an IC foundry industry and, in turn, that industry led to the formation of many integrated circuit design houses. Shenzhen, in the South, specializes in manufacturing IT products; one firm, Foxconn[15] (from Taiwan), has 300,000 workers. In all three cases, the government and market forces play significant roles in support of developing clusters.

IT clusters are not universally present in Asia; Japan and South Korea, for example, are different. This is certainly not due to a shortage of excellent technologies or strong companies. It stems from having relatively few new high tech companies. Without them, clusters do not form.

Consider Japan's array of world-class consumer electronics, computers, and IT component companies, such as Matsushita[16], NEC[17], Fujitsu[18], Sony[19], Canon[20], Sharp[21] and many more. These long established companies have successfully renewed themselves. Already in place and with low labor mobility, the influences to form concentrations of IT firms in a few locations have been weak. A decade ago, the Ministry of International Trade and Industry[22] (MITI, now METI) began promoting more flexibility in industry. As a result, more startups have emerged but not yet much by way of IT clusters (with exception of a semiconductor concentration in Ksushu).

The pattern in Korea is similar to that in Japan. It also has large, successful IT companies but not many startups — hence the paucity of new clusters — with the exception of gaming and other internet content suppliers in Seoul. The Korean government is also changing the rules to encourage new firms; here, too, reveals evidence of a response from the market.

Japan and Korea have similarly created science parks, Japan in Tsukuba and Korea in Daeduk Science Town[23]. In both places good research was undertaken but neither has formed strong industry clusters due to national policies and customs favoring established firms over the newly created ones.[24]

All of the successful high tech clusters have various combinations of foreign involvement: downstream buyers, upstream sources of technology, professionals with foreign experience and direct investments by foreign firms. The sparser the set of such links the less vibrant the cluster is likely to be.[25]

The question of whether universities are a necessary ingredient comes up because of the prominence of good universities in the leading American clusters. The answer in Asia is "not really, so far." The main role for its universities, a vitally important one, has been to educate a growing number of talented scientists and engineers. This might seem surprising because of the high status, for example, of the Indian Institutes of Technology and of China's leading universities. In these cases the universities did not have major research missions before, but now they are beginning to do some serious research. This could influence the nature of new companies formed and their respective locations.

If the American experience is relevant for Asia, having good research universities is a necessary but not a sufficient condition for forming world-class clusters (with the US having more good universities spread around the country than it has high tech clusters).[26] It is also tricky to balance the requisites for academic excellence and a significant research contribution to industry. Even if they do a good job with the latter, and if the American experience is relevant, it is a mistake to expect universities on average to generate significant income from commercializing research findings.

Some government officials have assumed that it is a good idea to invite venture capitalists. There is nothing wrong with inviting them but will they come and do deals? Only if there are deals to be done and this, in turn, depends on the national and local entrepreneurial environments. Thus it is not surprising that the most developed Asian VC industry is in China's Taiwan with mainland and India coming along well, and Japan and Korea lagging.[27]

A natural question is what opportunities exist for new clusters to emerge? Are such spaces already occupied? The answer has to do with the emergence of new industries and where this phenomenon happens; this will be decided through a combination of private and government actions. The government of Singapore, for example, is making a big effort to create a bio-tech cluster. It is a safe bet that the clean energy ones will be emerging in many places. With fast-growing markets, clusters could emerge in new places, notably in China and India, as growth in established places is slowed by high costs of land and labor. Taiwan, faced with such constraints in the north, has developed new industry clusters in the south and central regions.

If there is a message in this story for the future of Asian clusters, it is to have natural rules that encourage entrepreneurship, openness to foreign connections of various kinds and support for research. Governments now widely recognize these needs, although translating them into actions still proves to be difficult. Creating strong research universities that foster commercialization of research results while also supporting high academic standards is an especially challenging task.

(*Far Eastern Economic Review*, July – August, 2007)

New Words and Expressions

cluster	n.	成群，成串，集散地，聚集地
settlement	n.	定居点，新建的居民点
Anterwerp	n.	安特卫普（比利时省份）
Sheffield	n.	谢菲尔德（英国英格兰北部城市）
Yiwu	n.	义乌（中国浙江省中部城市）
cinematic	a.	电影的，影片的
Mumbai	n.	孟买（印度最大的商业城市）
quintessentially	ad.	典型地，标准地
vibrant	a.	活泼的，生气勃勃的，有活力的
initiative	n.	主动，主动性，主动权
checkered	a.	多变的，不规则的

locality	n.	位置，地点
orchestrator	n.	管弦乐成员，组成人员
pre-competitive	a.	竞争前的
spin-out	n.	利用母公司的资源和技术成立的新公司
Bangalore	n.	班加罗尔（印度南部城市）
New Delhi	n.	新德里（印度首都）
Hyderabad	n.	海得拉（印度南部城市）
Chenai	n.	钦奈（印度南部城市）
Pune	n.	浦那（印度西部城市）
liberalize	v.	自由化
mediocre	a.	普通的
top-down	a.	从总体到细节的，综合的，自顶向下的
concentration	n.	集中物，集结物，密集（的东西）
foremost	a.	最先的，最初的，最重要的
startup	n.	启动
Ksushu	n.	九州（日本南部岛屿）
paucity	n.	极小量
Seoul	n.	首尔（韩国首都）
Tsukuba	n.	筑波（日本东京的卫星城）
Daeduk	n.	大田（韩国中部城市）
sparse	a.	稀少的，稀疏的
requisite	n.	必需品
entrepreneurial	a.	企业家的，创业者的
foster	v.	养育，培养，鼓励

information technology (IT) industry	信息技术产业（IT产业）
tax break	减税
chip foundry	芯片制造
Karnataka state	卡纳塔克邦（印度邦名）
Academy of Science Institute	科学研究院
IC foundry industry	智能卡制造工业
stem from	源自，起源于
downstream buyer	下游购买商
upstream sources of technology	上游技术资源
venture capitalist	风险投资家
VC industry	风险投资行业

Unit 2 Regional Economy and Industry

Notes

1. Modern examples include diamond cutters in Antwerp, knife makers in Sheffield, sock makers in Yiwu, and the cinematic entertainers in Mumbai.　当今的例子包括安特卫普的钻石切割、设菲尔德的刀具制造、义乌的袜子生产及孟买的电影制作等。
   安特卫普是比利时第二大城市、欧洲第二大港、世界第四大港、世界最大的钻石加工和贸易中心。设菲尔德位于英国南约克郡都市区，是英国重要的钢铁工业中心，以产优质钢及其制品著称，有英国最大的铸造厂，传统工业产品刃具、工具、餐具等颇负盛名。孟买是印度最大海港，也是印度人口最多的城市。孟买的电影业十分发达，印度电影大部分的外景都是在孟买电影城拍摄的，其以年出产1 000部电影的业绩傲视群雄，被称之为印度的"宝莱坞"。

2. Alfred Marshall　阿弗里德·马歇尔（1842—1924）
   当代经济学的创立者，现代微观经济学体系的奠基人，剑桥学派和新古典学派的创始人，19世纪末20世纪初英国乃至世界最著名的经济学家。他于1890年发表的《经济学原理》，被看做是与亚当·斯密的《国富论》和李嘉图的《赋税原理》齐名的划时代的著作，被奉为英国经济学的圣经。他的理论及其追随者被称为新古典理论和新古典学派，同时由于他及其学生，如J. M·凯恩斯、J. S·尼科尔森、A. C·庇古、D. H·麦格雷戈等先后长期在剑桥大学任教，因此也被称为剑桥学派。

3. Silicon Valley　（美国）硅谷
   硅谷位于加利福尼亚州的旧金山经圣克拉拉至圣何塞近50公里的一个狭长地带，是世界最为知名的电子工业集中地。其特点是以附近一些具有雄厚科研力量的美国一流大学，如斯坦福大学、伯克利大学和加州理工大学等为依托，以高技术的中小公司群为基础，并拥有思科、英特尔、惠普、朗讯、苹果等大公司，融科学、技术、生产于一体，所产半导体集成电路和电子计算机约占全美的1/3和1/6。20世纪80年代后，生物、空间、海洋、通信、能源、材料等新兴技术的研究机构纷纷出现，使该地区客观上成为美国高新技术的摇篮，也成为世界各国半导体工业聚集区的代名词。

4. They do this to enjoy the benefits of having a vibrant cluster sooner than the market might produce and from a belief, which might on occasion be warranted, of establishing a vibrant cluster before some other nation does, that is, to gain a first-mover advantage.　他们这样做是为了更早地享有一个有活力的聚集区域所带来的收益，而市场自发行为产生类似的结果会来得有些迟，同时这样做还基于一种观念，即赶在别国之前建立一个有活力的园区以抢占先机。
   句中的"from a belief"作状语修饰"do this"，"which"引导的非限制性定语从句修饰"belief"，"gain a first-mover advantage"意为"抢占先机"。

5. However, has government done little more than cause firms that would form anyway to locate in a favored place instead of somewhere else in the country without substantial spillover benefits arising?　但是，难道政府仅仅是让各种形式的公司建在有优惠待遇的区域而非其他地

方，然而却又不能产生大量附加收益？

句中的"spillover benefits"意为"额外收益，附带收益"。

6. Taiwan's Hsinchu Science-based Industrial Park　台湾新竹科技工业园

   新竹科技工业园是台湾高技术产业的摇篮，于 1976 年开始筹建，1980 年 12 月 15 日正式成立，是台湾第一科技园。园区规划面积 21 平方公里，是孕育台湾高新技术产业发展的基地，其 IC 产业更是台湾发展高新技术产业成功的典范，同时它也是全球第四大半导体产业基地。

7. original equipment manufacturers（OEM）　原始设备生产商

   这是一种按原单位（品牌单位）委托合同进行产品开发和制造，用原单位商标，由原单位销售或经营的合作经营生产方式。OEM 可简称为"代工生产"或贴牌生产，这种经营模式在国际上已运作多年并行之有效。OEM 与现代工业社会有着密切的关系。一些著名的品牌商品制造商，常常因为自己的厂房不能达到大批量生产的要求，或者又需要某些特定的零件，因此向其他厂商求助，这些伸出援手的厂商被称为原始设备生产商。

8. original design manufacturers（ODM）　原始设计制造商

   这是指委托方委托设计生产方按照自己提出的技术要求设计生产，产品由委托方收购的模式。设计生产方就称作 ODM，不仅要为品牌持有企业生产产品，还必须设计产品方案。OEM 和 ODM 两者最大的区别不单单是名称而已。OEM 产品是为品牌厂商度身订造的，生产后也只能使用该品牌名称，不能冠上生产者自己的名称再进行生产。而 ODM 则要看品牌企业有没有买断该产品的版权，如果没有，制造商有权自己组织生产，只要没有品牌企业的设计标识即可。

9. Its most famous firm was the pioneering chip foundry, TSMC, which was a spin-out from an ITRC lab.　它最著名的公司是芯片制造先驱 TSMC，该公司是利用 ITRC 实验室的资源技术成立的。

10. Governments can still be a problem; for example, the government of Karnataka state, whose capital is Bangalore, seems to be driving its thriving software industry away through inadequate investment in infrastructure.　政府仍是个问题，譬如以班加罗尔为首府的卡纳塔克邦政府就似乎因为对基础设施的投资不足而使繁荣的软件工业逐渐萎缩。

    句中的"drive away"原意是"驱走，赶走"，这里是指使软件行业逐渐萎缩。

11. As is customary in China, the government has approached the cluster phenomenon from the top-down.　对于聚集园区，政府通常从总体到细节上做出规划，这在中国已成惯例。

    句中的"as"指代后面的整个分句。

12. Torch Industrial Technology Program　火炬高新技术产业开发计划

    这是中国发展高新技术产业的指导性计划，于 1988 年 8 月经国务院批准，由科技部组织实施。火炬计划的宗旨是：实施"科教兴国"战略，贯彻执行改革开放的总方针，发挥中国科技力量的优势和潜力，以市场为导向，促进高新技术成果商品化、高新技术商品产业化和高新技术产业国际化。

13. Zhongguancun Science Park　中关村科技园

    中关村科技园是 1988 年 5 月经国务院批准建立的中国第一个国家级高新技术产业开发区。中关村科技园区覆盖了北京市科技、智力、人才和信息资源最密集的区域，包括海淀园、丰台园、昌平园、电子城科技园和亦庄科技园。

14. lenovo 联想集团

这是一家极富创新性的国际化的科技公司，由联想及原 IBM 个人电脑事业部所组成，拥有 19 000 多名员工，是全球个人电脑市场的领导企业。联想的总部设在纽约，同时在中国北京和美国北卡罗来纳州的罗利设立两个主要运营中心，研发中心分布在中国的北京、深圳、厦门、成都和上海，日本的东京及美国北卡罗来纳州的罗利。联想集团于 2004 年作为第一家中国企业成为国际奥委会全球合作伙伴。

15. Foxconn 富士康科技集团

它是台湾鸿海精密工业股份有限公司在大陆投资兴办的专业研发生产精密电气连接器、精密线缆及组配、电脑机壳及准系统、电脑系统组装、无线通信关键零组件及组装、光通信组件、消费性电子、液晶显示设备、半导体设备、合金材料等产品的高新科技企业，涉足电脑、通信、消费性电子等 3C 产业的多个领域。它是全球最大的计算机连接器、计算机准系统生产厂商，连续 7 年入选美国《商业周刊》发布的全球信息技术公司 100 大排行榜。

16. Matsushita 日本松下产业株式会社

它于 1918 年由松下幸之助创立，是知名的跨国公司，主要生产电子电器设备。其 2006 年全年的销售总额超过 710 多亿美元，2007 年《财富》500 强排名第 59 位。

17. NEC 日本电气株式会社

其总部位于日本东京，是世界 500 强企业之一。NEC 公司主要从事通信网络系统和设备、计算机软硬件及服务、集成电路及电子元器件等产品的研发、生产和销售，产品种类多达 15 000 多种。

18. Fujitsu 富士通公司

它是全球第三大 IT 服务公司，全球前五大服务器和 PC 机生产商，世界第二大企业用硬盘驱动器制造商和第四大移动硬盘制造商，是横跨半导体电子器件、计算机通信平台设备、软件服务等三大领域的全球化综合性 IT 科技巨人。

19. Sony 日本索尼公司

它是世界上民用及专业视听产品、游戏产品、通信产品、关键零部件和信息技术等领域的先导之一。它在音乐、影视、计算机娱乐及在线业务方面的成就也使其成为全球领先的电子和娱乐公司。2006 财年中的合并销售额约达 700 亿美元，2007 年《财富》500 强排名 69 位。

20. Canon 日本佳能公司

它是全球领先的生产影像与信息产品的综合集团，1937 年成立，总部位于日本东京，并在美洲、欧洲、亚洲及日本本土设有 4 大区域性销售总部。其产品系列共分布于三大领域：个人产品、办公设备和工业设备，主要产品包括照相机及镜头、数码相机、打印机、复印机、传真机、扫描仪、广播设备、医疗器材及半导体生产设备等。

21. Sharp 日本夏普公司

它是《财富》500 强企业之一，于 1912 年创立，成功研制了日本国产第一号收音机和电视机，在世界上首次推出电子计算器和液晶显示器，产品涉及电子信息、音响、通信、电化及电子零部件等领域。目前占有全球液晶电视市场的最大份额。

22. the Ministry of International Trade and Industry 日本国际贸易产业部

它是日本经济贸易产业部（the Ministry of Economy, Trade and Industry）的前身。日本经济贸易产业部是日本最重要的三个行政部之一，承担宏观经济管理职能，负责制订产业政策并从事行业管理，管辖国内工业、商业、资源能源、工业技术、专利权，以及对外贸易、对外经济合作等，是对产业界有很大影响的综合性政府部门。日本的流通产业振兴、调整政策和流通现代化等职能均由经济贸易产业部承担。

23. Daeduk Science Town　韩国大田科技园区
    大田是韩国科技研究机构云集的地区，24 个国家级科研机构中有 20 个落户大田，在大田市的大德科技园区内有近 800 个高科技企业，相当于中国的中关村科技园和美国的"硅谷"。

24. In both places good research was undertaken but neither has formed strong industry clusters due to national policies and customs favoring established firms over the newly created ones.　这两个地方的研究开展得不错，但没有形成很强的产业带，原因是国家政策和海关更多地支持大企业而非新成立的公司。
    句中的"favor"意为"支持，偏爱"，"over"表示比较。

25. The sparser the set of such links the less vibrant the cluster is likely to be.　这些联系越松散，产业带就越有可能缺乏活力。
    本句是"the more ... the more ..."句型的变形。

26. If the American experience is relevant for Asia, having good research universities is a necessary but not a sufficient condition for forming world-class clusters.　如果美国的经验对亚洲有所借鉴，那么拥有优秀的研究性大学对形成世界一流的产业群来说则是一个必要非充分条件。
    句中的"a necessary but not a sufficient condition"意为"必要非充分条件"。

27. Thus it is not surprising that the most developed Asian VC industry is in China's Taiwan with mainland and India coming along well, and Japan and Korea lagging.　这就不足为怪为什么亚洲最发达的风险投资产业首先是在台湾，其次是在中国大陆和印度，最后才是在日本和韩国。

阅读小知识（1）

新闻体裁

新闻体裁的划分众说纷纭，但英美等国有人认为除消息报道体裁外，专稿、评述、采访、杂文、传记等等都是特写（feature）体裁。然而，人们较多地倾向于将它分为消息、特写和社评 3 类。

1. 消息

消息报道分为两类：一类是通讯社的电讯或报道，短小精悍，内容最真实，被称之为"纯硬性新闻"（pure hard news），有的报纸将之辟为"Brief"栏目；另一类报刊的报道比通讯社的要详细得多，但有的由于夹杂着记者的推测和描绘，往往不如前者真实和经得起推敲。

2. 特写

新闻特写常指再现新闻事件、人物或场景的形象化报道。它吸取了一般新闻报道和文艺作品的长处，其结构则取两者之长。特写虽然也是一种新闻报道，但不少常常采取引人入胜的悬念式（suspended interest form）写作手法，将事件逐渐展开。英文的特稿写作也总要从一个具体的事件或人物展开，来表达一个人、一个社会现象。它是一种由小见大、从具体见整体的思路。从采访的对象来看，我们可以将特稿分为社会新闻特稿、人物新闻特稿和事件新闻特稿（或特写）。社会新闻特稿一般是从一个或一个事件入手表现社会发展的动态、趋势。人物新闻特稿（或称人物专访）是对具有新闻价值的人的描述。事件新闻特稿（或特写）则是对具有重大影响力的事件的特写或速写。

3. 社论和评论

社论是代表一家报纸或杂志的编辑部发表的权威性评论，所代表的是编辑部的观点。它常以第三者的口吻说话，或对人对事直接发表意见，表明立场、观点和倾向，或提出问题，或号召人们采取行动。评论是署名文章，往往在报道文章后就报道中提及的人和事发表评述，以启示读者。这是社论和评论所不同的。在文字上，报道类文章一般较简明，社论则较严肃，评论文章则较活泼，常借古讽今，因此后两类文章较难读懂。

社论和评论往往都开门见山，在第一段点出论题，类似引子，引导读者读下去。接着就逐段展开分析和评说。末段则为结论。

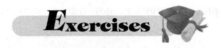

I Decide whether the following statements are true (T) or false (F).

1. Cluster of craftsman is present in Asia IT industry, because the IT industry is mainly developed in cities. (   )
2. High-tech industries may form, due to some conditions, which are somewhat different from the traditional industries. (   )
3. So long as government policies are favorable, IT clusters will emerge. (   )
4. The growth of Indian clusters has been in part a market phenomenon, although government grants much firm support to the IT industries. (   )
5. In the cities of Beijing, Shanghai and Shenzhen, China, the high-tech clusters flourish and are greatly supported by the government while the market role in these regions is very weak. (   )
6. One of the essential conditions for IT clusters to form is that there should be many new high tech companies. (   )
7. Japan has many large, successful IT companies, but few IT clusters, because the influences to form

concentrations of IT firms in a few locations have been insignificant. (   )

8. In Asia, IT clusters are mainly located around the leading universities, because they have been to educate a growing number of talented scientists and engineers. (   )

9. In Asia, to have good research universities is a necessary but not a sufficient condition for forming world-class clusters, because the universities on the average in those regions can produce research findings that are not highly commercialized. (   )

10. Governments should formulate rules and policies to effectively encourage entrepreneurship and openness to foreign connections of various kinds of support for research, but carrying them out to produce economic results is time-consuming. (   )

II Choose one answer that best suits the following statements.

1. Governments often like to accelerate the process of forming high-tech industry clusters because what they do is to _____.
   A. have a dynamic clusters soon
   B. fully take advantage of the market force
   C. gain more advantages than other nations
   D. get the benefits of establishing a dynamic cluster sooner and to obtain more advantages than other nations in moving the market of a certain line of products

2. The two nations of India and China have different approaches towards IT industry: _____
   A. The Indian government is playing a positive role while Chinese government is also greatly encouraging the development of IT industry.
   B. The Indian IT industry grows fast, which is propelled by the market force while in China, IT industry's development consists in government support and significant role of market forces.
   C. The Indian government adopts restrictive polices towards IT industry, but the Chinese government only lets the market have its role in spurring growth of IT industry.
   D. Both the Indian government and the Chinese government adopt encouraging policies to help IT industry to grow.

3. Japan does not have well-established clusters of IT industry, just because _____.
   A. many long-established companies have not updated their technologies
   B. the Japanese government does not pay adequate attention to the IT industry
   C. low labor mobility and rather scattered location of big companies prevent IT firms from forming clusters in a few places
   D. some world-class companies in Japan usually undertake R&D in IT industry

4. The record on this is <u>checkered</u>. (the third paragraph)
   The underlined word means: _____.
   A. examined by an authorized organ   B. censored by
   C. varied   D. examined and approved by the government

5. If the American experience <u>is relevant for Asia</u>, having good research universities is a necessary but

not a sufficient condition for forming world-class cluster ...

The underlined part means: _____.

A. having something to do with   B. applicable to
C. linked to   D. similar to

III Translate the following passages into Chinese.

1. The question of whether universities are a necessary ingredient comes up because of the prominence of good universities in the leading American clusters. The answer in Asia is "not really, so far." The main role for its universities, a vitally important one, has been to educate a growing number of talented scientists and engineers. This might seem surprising because of the high status, for example, of the Indian Institutes of Technology and of China's leading universities. In these cases the universities did not have major research missions before, but now they are beginning to do some serious research. This could influence the nature of new companies formed and their respective locations.

2. If the American experience is relevant for Asia, having good research universities is a necessary but not a sufficient condition for forming world-class clusters (with the US having more good universities spread around the country than it has high tech clusters). It is also tricky to balance the requisites for academic excellence and a significant research contribution to industry. Even if they do a good job with the latter, and if the American experience is relevant, it is a mistake to expect universities on average to generate significant income from commercializing research findings.

IV Write a summary of this text.

Market Meltdown Exposes Structural Weaknesses

Jo Johnson

The mini-meltdown in emerging markets has exposed a structural weakness[1] in India's economic fundamentals that will require some determined action on the part of government policy-makers. The challenge of increasing the meagre amount of foreign direct investment (FDI) India attracts is moving up the list of political priorities — an important development in a country where there are deemed to be few votes in economic reform.[2]

The drying up of global liquidity since the start of the year has been felt across emerging markets but particularly in India, the recipient of a disproportionate share of yield-seeking investment in recent years. While India accounts for only 6 per cent of the value of the Morgan Stanley emerging markets index[3], economists calculate that it has been attracting between 20 and 25 per cent of total emerging markets investment.

India's strong economic performance over the last three years has long led economists to warn against complacency. Real growth in gross domestic product reached 8.4 per cent in 2005−2006. It was led by strong domestic demand and, although the economy is expected to slow marginally in 2006−2007, India is still likely to log a good performance this year and next. The Asian Development Bank[4] expects growth of 7.6 per cent in 2006 and 7.8 per cent in 2007. Public finances are improving, with the federal fiscal deficit falling to 4.1 per cent of GDP.

One of the newly-exposed reefs is India's dependence on hot money — foreign institutional investment (FII) — for the financing of a growing current account deficit. In recent years, these volatile flows of money have dwarfed FDI, reflecting problems with the Indian business environment. In the last fiscal year, ending March 31, 2006, the flow of FII reached almost $11 bn, compared to just over $5.13 bn in the form of FDI.

The sharp equity market sell-off that began in India on May 12 has seen foreign institutional investors trim their exposures to Indian securities.[5] Foreign funds were net sellers to the tune of $2.4 bn in the 11 trading days that followed the Mumbai stock market[6] reaching an all-time high on May 11. Although foreign investors have returned somewhat gingerly in recent days, their total investment since January 1 stands at less than $3 bn. The rupee is weakening, with analysts predicting it will slip to 47.5 to the dollar by year-end.

"One of our key concerns with India's recent economic trends has been with the increasing dependence on potentially volatile capital inflows to fund the widening current account deficit[7]," says Rajeev Malik, a JPMorgan economist. India's export growth is in the range of 15 to 20 per cent — a remarkable turnaround in a country with a tradition of "export pessimism" — but surging domestic demand means the import bill is growing significantly faster.

Pushed upwards not just by mounting fuel prices but also by imports of capital goods and industrial raw materials, India's trade deficit in the year to March 31, 2006 reached a record-breaking $39.6 bn, with imports expanding by 33 per cent and exports by just 22 per cent.[8] The deficit in April and May — the first two months of this financial year — has reached $8 bn, up from $7.2 bn in the same period last year. JPMorgan expects the trade deficit to hit an all-time high of almost $70 bn — 8 per cent of GDP — in the current fiscal year[9].

Much of this is offset by India's large invisible surplus[10], composed of remittances from Indians living overseas and fast-growing software exports, which will account for approximately 4.3 per cent of GDP this fiscal year — or $34 bn — and will be boosted by the fall in the rupee. But with India's current account deficit still likely to reach 3.6 per cent of GDP in 2006−2007, equivalent to $30.4 bn, the government can ill afford a sharp fall-off in the inflow of foreign capital.[11]

In its 2006 outlook, the Asian Development Bank (ADB) noted that capital inflows in 2005 had been adequate to offset the current account deficit but warned of the growing importance of portfolio investment within total capital inflows and in relation to India's total foreign exchange reserves.[12]

"Given the potential volatility of these flows, this is causing some concern and points to the need to improve the environment for foreign direct investment," it says.

The Reserve Bank of India (RBI)[13], after marking a pause in its recent monetary tightening in April, appears to have been taken by surprise by the resurgence of concerns over higher inflation. It unexpectedly raised interest rates by 25 basis points between meetings on June 8, and further tightening was expected at the next quarterly monetary policy meeting on July 25. Concerns are building up over a potential slowdown in the growth of the real economy. Chetan Ahya, an economist at Morgan Stanley in Mumbai, predicts an end to the longest credit cycle[14] since the 1970s. Further weakening of the rupee on the back of the deteriorating current account deficit will compel the RBI to push up real interest rates further, reining back debt-funded growth and investment.[15] In the short term, the risk is therefore that India may struggle to maintain its current level of blistering 8 per cent-plus growth.

"Low real rates and a sharp rise in bank credit have been at the heart of India's growth acceleration story over the past three years," Mr. Ahya says. "Nominal bank credit growth[16] has accelerated from the bottom of 10.7 per cent in September 2003 to 31 per cent currently. The credit cycle is about to reverse. Debt-funded consumption growth, which has been at the heart of the above-trend GDP growth over the past three years, will be hit by the rise in the cost of capital."

Against such a macro-economic backdrop, addressing India's FDI deficiency can no longer be postponed. For the Congress-led government, this presages a further round of confrontation with the Left Front of Communist parties who make up the coalition's majority in parliament but have not themselves entered the government, preferring to "support" it from the outside.[17] The Left Front's opposition to more liberal FDI thresholds, to privatization and to labor reform, is visceral.

"It is amazing how much of the economic and political debate on future strategy is still conditioned by the colonial legacy[18]," notes Bimal Jalan, one of India's leading economists, in a recent essay. "The share of foreign direct investment is among the lowest in the world and relatively insignificant in relation to the size of the economy. India's industry and infrastructure are now largely owned by Indians. Yet policies to liberalize foreign investment continue to attract considerable political controversy."

Significant progress has been made towards liberalizing FDI, but the slow pace at which India has opened up important sectors such as banking, insurance, and retail has been a cause of endless frustration to foreign investors.

"Interest in India among investors remains very high — India rates among the top three destinations for FDI in a number of surveys — but actual FDI raised remains low relative to many other emerging markets[19]," the International Monetary Fund[20] says in a recent country report. The reasons India attracts less than one-tenth of the FDI that goes to China each year are not difficult to find. The World Bank[21] in its 2006 survey of the ease of doing business in 155 countries around the world ranks India a lowly 116th. "The country's overall investment environment has to be strengthened," the ADB says in its 2006 report, noting that entrepreneurs could expect to go through 11 steps to launch a business, taking more than 71 days, twice as long as the regional average.[22]

Whether measured in terms of the ease with which companies can hire and fire workers, the costs and procedures involved in importing or exporting a standardized shipment of goods, or the limited ability to enforce commercial contracts in a timely manner, India is a harder place to do business than other countries in the region.

If jitters about current account financing spook the markets, it may ultimately spur reforms that boost long-term investment.

(*Financial Times*, June 27, 2006)

New Words and Expressions

meltdown	n.	彻底垮台
meagre	a.	少量的，贫弱的
liquidity	n.	流动资金，流动性
disproportionate	a.	不成比例的
yield-seeking	a.	逐利的，谋求收益的
complacency	n.	自满，自鸣得意
marginally	ad.	不重要地，少量地
volatile	a.	可变的，变化的
sell-off	n.	廉价卖清
trim	v.	整理，修整，减少
gingerly	ad.	谨慎地，慎重地
rupee	n.	卢比（印度货币）
turnaround	n.	转变，转向
remittance	n.	汇款
portfolio	n.	有价证券（组合）
resurgence	n.	复兴，再起
deteriorating	a.	恶化的
blistering	a.	酷热的，起泡的
presage	v.	预示，预先警告，预言
privatization	n.	私有化，私人化
visceral	a.	出自内心的，肺腑的

liberalize	v.	自由化
frustration	n.	挫败，挫折，受挫
enforce	v.	执行，履行
jitter	n.	紧张不安，战战兢兢
spook	v.	使害怕，惊吓
economic fundamentals		经济基础
be deemed to		被认为
public finance		公共融资
current account deficit		经常账户赤字
to the tune of		达……之多
all-time high		空前最高纪录
rein back		抑止，使后退

1. structural weakness 结构性疲软
   这是指整个经济基础存在结构性问题，缺乏活力，具体表现为增长乏力，居民消费和企业投资双双不振，产品设备订单增长停滞，失业状况恶化，同时国家财政状况也不断亮起红灯。

2. The challenge of increasing the meagre amount of foreign direct investment (FDI) India attracts is moving up the list of political priorities — an important development in a country where there are deemed to be few votes in economic reform. 努力增加目前印度所吸引的外国直接投资，尽管数量较少，但正被提上政治日程。这对一个很少关心经济改革的国家来说是重大的进步。

3. Morgan Stanley emerging markets index 摩根士丹利新兴市场指数
   它是摩根士丹利公司提供的金融投资服务之一。摩根士丹利公司是一家成立于美国纽约的国际金融服务公司，提供包括证券、资产管理、企业合并重组和信用卡等在内的多种金融服务。摩根士丹利新兴市场指数选取全球新兴市场上代表公司的普通股股票，该指数涵盖的公司主要来自韩国、俄罗斯、巴西和中国，其他则来自阿根廷、智利、哥伦比亚、捷克、埃及、匈牙利、印度、印尼、以色列、约旦、马来西亚、墨西哥、巴基斯坦、摩洛哥、秘鲁、菲律宾、波兰、南非、泰国和土耳其等国家。

4. The Asian Development Bank 亚洲开发银行
   它是一个区域性国际金融机构，创建于1966年，总部设在菲律宾首都马尼拉，有来自亚洲和太平洋地区的成员，称作区域成员，此外还有来自欧洲和北美洲的非区域成员。建立亚洲开发银行的宗旨是促进亚洲和太平洋地区的经济发展和合作，特别是协助本地区发展中成员以共同的或个别的方式加速经济发展。亚洲开发银行自身开展业务的资金分为三部分：一是普通资金，用于亚洲开发银行的硬贷款业务；二是亚洲开发基金，用于亚洲开发银行的软贷款业务；三是技术援助特别基金，用于进行技术援助业务。此外，亚洲开发银行于1988年建立了日本特别基金，用于赠款性质的技术援助业务。亚洲开发银行对发展中成员的援助主要采取贷款、股本投资、技术援助和联合融资相担保四种形式。

5. The sharp equity market sell-off that began in India on May 12 has seen foreign institutional investors trim their exposures to Indian securities. 在印度证券市场上，开始于5月12日的快速清仓是外国机构投资者对印度证券产品的调整行为。

   句中的"equity market"指"证券市场"，"trim"意为"调整，整改"，"securities"意为"证券产品"。

6. the Mumbai stock market 孟买股票市场

   孟买股票市场主要指孟买证券交易所（Bombay Stock Exchange，BSE），成立于1875年，是亚洲最早的股票交易所，比东京股票交易所还早成立3年，目前已成为印度主要的股票交易市场。

7. One of our key concerns with India's recent economic trends has been with the increasing dependence on potentially volatile capital inflows to fund the widening current account deficit...
   对于印度最近的经济趋势，我们主要关心的问题之一是其越来越依赖于有风险的资本流入，以此来减少不断增长的经常账户赤字……

8. Pushed upwards not just by mounting fuel prices but also by imports of capital goods and industrial raw materials, India's trade deficit in the year to March 31, 2006 reached a record-breaking $39.6 bn, with imports expanding by 33 per cent and exports by just 22 per cent. 受油价增长及对资本货物和工业原材料进口的推动，截止2006年3月底，印度的贸易赤字达到创纪录的396亿美元，进口增长33%而出口则仅增长22%。

   句中的"with imports expanding..."是独立主格结构。

9. fiscal year 财务年度

   财务年度与日历年度（calendar year）相对应。如果企业的会计年度于12月31日终止，则称为日历年度。许多公司使用与自然经营年度相一致的会计年度，因此其会计年度常在淡季及存货量少、易于盘点时终止。选择这样的时间，完成年终会计程序的效率最高。不在12月份结束而是在别的月份结束的会计年度称为财务年度。一般公司以4月1日为财务年度的开始，而以来年的3月31日结束。

10. invisible surplus 无形资产盈余

    本文中的无形资产主要包括服务贸易及来自直接投资或投资组合的收入。

11. ...the government can ill afford a sharp fall-off in the inflow of foreign capital. ……政府将几乎不能承受外国资本流入急剧下跌的后果。

    句中的"ill"是副词，意为"几乎不，不够"，"fall off"意为"下跌，跌落"。

12. ...the Asian Development Bank noted that capital inflows in 2005 had been adequate to offset the current account deficit but warned of the growing importance of portfolio investment within total capital inflows and in relation to India's total foreign exchange reserves. ……亚洲开发银行指出，2005年的资本流入足以抵消经常账户赤字，但也提醒资本流入中投资组合不断增

长的重要性，并要和印度的外汇储备总额相对应。

句中"warned"的主语是"the Asia Development Bank"（亚洲开发银行）。

13. The Reserve Bank of India（RBI） 印度储备银行

    1935年成立，目前为印度中央银行，总部设在孟买。在成立时为私人所有，但在1949年实行国有化政策后改为印度政府所有。印度储备银行的主要职能包括制定、实施和监测货币政策，管理和监督银行金融系统的运营，进行外汇管制和管理及发行货币等。

14. credit cycle 信贷循环

    这里是指以信贷为支撑的经济循环模式。自20世纪70年代开始来，印度信贷成本比较低，许多经济活动可以通过信贷进行，而2007年6月利率提高25个基点则意味着信贷成本的提高。

15. Further weakening of the rupee on the back of the deteriorating current account deficit will compel the RBI to push up real interest rates further, reining back debt-funded growth and investment. 由于经常账户赤字不断恶化将会使印度卢比进一步贬值，这将迫使印度储备银行再度提高利率，以遏制借贷支撑的增长和投资。

    句中的"reining back"是现在分词作状语。

16. nominal bank credit growth 银行名义信贷增长率

    与实际信贷增长率相对应，名义信贷增长率扣除通货膨胀的影响之后即得出实际信贷增长率。

17. For the Congress-led government, this presages a further round of confrontation with the Left Front of Communist parties who make up the coalition's majority in parliament but have not themselves entered the government, preferring to "support" it from the outside. 对于一个议会主导的政府来说，这预示着与共产党左派阵线的又一轮对立，共产党左派阵线在议会中占有多数席位但并未进入政府，他们倾向于从外部施加影响。

    句中的"support"是反语。

18. the colonial legacy 殖民地影响

    在文中是指有些人担心印度重新被殖民化而不愿接受外国直接投资。

19. Interest in India among investors remains very high — India rates among the top three destinations for FDI in a number of surveys — but actual FDI raised remains low relative to many other emerging markets... 投资者对印度的兴趣很高，几项调查都显示印度是外国直接投资的前三大目的地，但同许多其他新兴市场相比，印度的实际外国直接投资额却仍然很低。

    句中的"interest in"意为"对……感兴趣"，"rates"意为"排名"。

20. International Monetary Fund（IMF） 国际货币基金组织

    根据1944年7月44个国家在美国新罕布什尔州布雷顿森林会议达成的《国际货币基金协定》，IMF于1946年3月正式成立。其宗旨是：促进成员国在国际货币问题上的磋商与协作；促进汇率的稳定和有秩序的汇率安排，从而避免竞争性的汇率贬值；为经常项目收支建立一个多边支付和汇兑制度，消除外汇管制；提供资金融通，缓解国际收支不平衡；促进国际贸易的发展，实现就业和实际收入水平的提高及生产能力的扩大。其职能为汇率监督、资金融通、提供国际货币合作与协商的场所。IMF 的最高决策机构是理事会，日常行政工作由执行董事会负责。基金组织的份额由特别提款权（Special Drawing Rights）表示，份额的多少同时决定了在 IMF 的投票权。1980 年 4 月 17 日，IMF 正式决定恢复中国的合法席位。

21. The World Bank 世界银行

    全称为国际复兴开发银行（The International Bank for Reconstruction and Development），隶属于联合国，是一个负责长期贷款的国际金融机构。它是根据 1944 年美国布雷顿森林会议上通过的《国际复兴开发银行协定》成立的。其宗旨是通过对生产事业的投资，资助成员国的复兴和开发工作；通过对贷款的保证或参与贷款等方式来促进私人投资，当成员国不能在合理的条件下获得私人资本时，则在适当条件下以银行本身资金或筹集的资金及其他资金给予成员国直接贷款，以补充私人投资的不足；通过鼓励国际投资，开发成员国的生产资源，提供技术咨询和提高生产能力，以促进成员国国际贸易的均衡增长及国际收支状况的改善。世界银行的主要业务活动包括对发展中成员国提供长期贷款，对成员国政府或政府担保的私人企业提供贷款和技术援助。世界银行与国际开发协会（International Development Association，IDA）、国际金融公司（International Finance Corporation，IFC）、多边投资担保机构（Multilateral Investment Guarantee Agency，MIGA）、国际投资争端解决中心（International Centre for Settlement of Investment Disputes，ICSID）共同组成了世界银行集团（World Bank Group）。

22. ... entrepreneurs could expect to go through 11 steps to launch a business, taking more than 71 days, twice as long as the regional average. ……要创建一家公司，企业家将要经过 11 道程序，花费 71 天，比该地区的平均时间高 1 倍。

阅读小知识（2）

新闻的标题

一、新闻标题的分类

新闻标题常用的有主题、副题、引题、提要题等几种形式。不过现在的英文报纸趋向采用主标题。标题是新闻的"眼睛"，也是报刊的"眼睛"，因此它应该是生动的、吸引人的。标题具有画龙点睛的作用。新闻标题可从以下几个方面来分类。

1. 从形式和内容方面分类

（1）摘要。这类标题提纲挈领，高度概括出新闻的主要内容，最简单易懂，并常用肯定句形式。例如：

East Asia Exposes the Limits of the Regional

（2）设问。它可表明未来可能发生某事或对某事的真实性表示怀疑。例如：

Can Asians Innovate?

Japan's Big Bang: Too Little, Too Late?

（3）说理。例如：

Why Drop the Computer?

（4）引语式标题。例如：

We Owe Our Lives to Our Pilot

（5）双标题。这种标题往往是一篇关于重大事件报道中的两部分标题。例如：

Japan's Lost Generation

Japan Inc. is back, but millions of young workers have been left behind

2. 从语言和文字技巧方面分类

（1）简练。例如：

Come Again

Broken Pottery

（2）冗长。例如：

China Should Speed Up the Yuan's Rise.

（3）平铺直叙，语言直白。例如：

How I Work

（4）引经据典。这类标题或直接引用、套用、改用文学名著之名、《圣经》典故，或运用名言、谚语、习语等。例如：

Farewell to Arms（Time）

注：该文章谈的是前苏联共产党总书记戈尔巴乔夫向前美国总统里根建议彻底销毁核武器的事。该标题引用了海明威的著名小说的书名——*A Farewell to Arms*。

（5）艺术加工。这类标题采用各种修辞手段，如使用比喻、押韵、反语、夸张、双关语等手段以追求生动、形象、幽默、讽刺等效果。例如：

Ballots, No Bullets（Time）

标题是编者和记者语言素养和文字技巧等综合水平的体现。据观察，美国报刊不如英国报刊那样讲究修辞手法，因而美国报刊的标题大多要比英国的容易读懂。

二、新闻标题的特点

1. 省略

（1）省略。从句法上讲，每个标题都是一个完整的句子，只是在标题上往往只标实义词而略去虚词。省略最多的虚词是冠词和动词"to be"。其次是介词、助动词、连词和代词。有时连实义词甚至主句也省略掉，但以不影响理解为前提。例如：

Japan's New Deal for Asia

（2）"and"常被逗号所取代，例如：

Thailand, Malaysia Ink Sea Treaty

＝Thailand and Malaysia Ink Sea Treaty

（3）动词"to be"有时被冒号所取代，例如：

Chinese Cooks: Masters at Turning a Turnip into a Flower

＝Chinese Cooks（Are）Masters at Turning Turnip into a Flower.

（4）动词"say"、"said"用冒号或引号代替，例如：

Mao: We Should Support Third World Countries

（5）以名词作定语替代形容词组成的标题常常既无动词也无连词，因而具有双重节省效果，例如：

Shotgun Death Riddle Drama（枪杀事件，扑朔迷离）

2. 时态

（1）几乎都用一般现在时，这是标题的另一个重要特点。新闻所述的事件多半是刚刚发生、正在发生或将会发生，按英语语法规则应用动词的相应时态。但为了让读者感到是"新闻"而不是"旧闻"，因此常用一般现在时。例如：

UK's Oldest Person Dies at 115

（2）用动词不定式表示将来时态，例如：

Iraq to Suspend Anti-Kurdish Campaign

（3）用过去分词表示，例如：

Case Probed

Brazil Elite Forced to Make Loans

Many Opportunities Missed in India

3. 缩略词

为了节省篇幅，编者在标题中使用缩略词，这是标题的第三个特点。

（1）机构。报刊中常用政治、军事、经济、文化、教育等重要机构的简称，例如：

EU's Future: The Vision and the Slog

NPC Drafts New Laws to Stem Corruption

（2）除了机构的首字母的缩略词外，标题也常用其他形式的缩略词，例如：

New Groups Boost Hi-tech Research（hi-tech ＝ high technology）

Shenzhen SEZ to Host Int'l Trade Meeting（int'l ＝ international）

4. 小词

标题中常用常见的小词或单音节短词，均为带有新闻体特色的标题词汇。例如：

Will She, Won't She?

Rich Man, Poor Man?

对初学者来说，要读懂标题，还必须要有国际知识，因此需要我们不断了解政治、经济、军事、外交、文化、体育、人物等方面的报道，积累这方面的知识。

Unit 2　Regional Economy and Industry

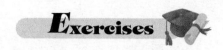

I Discuss and answer the following questions.

1. What are the newly exposed problems in India market?
2. What are structural problems in India? Can you describe them?
3. Compared with foreign institutional investment (FII), India's FDI is small. What do you think causes such a low level of FDI?
4. What do you think are the biggest risks for Indian economic growth?
5. According to the author, the slow pace at which India has opened up important sectors has something to do with its colonial legacy or its political system, do you agree?
6. What are the effective solutions to India's structural problems?

II Decide whether the following statement are true (T) or false (F).

1. The fact that FDI India gets is small has become the concerns of policy makers, but it seems to the author that the political system in India may pose a big challenge to the decision-maker first. (　)
2. In the past few years, India attracted very large amounts of yield-seeking investment, but since the start of the year, outflow of volatile capital begun to take place, which will immediately cause India's GDP to move down with a big margin. (　)
3. In India current account deficit is usually made up for by bank borrowings from overseas. (　)
4. India's trade deficit has hit a record high, which is caused by a large amount of imports of luxury goods and electric appliances, and increasing fuel prices. (　)
5. Although India's trade deficit can be offset by overseas remittances and fast-growing software exports, a sharp fall in the inflow of foreign capital can still place Indian government under a great pressure. (　)
6. In India, there arose a risk of higher inflation, and such a risk cannot be avoided in a short term. (　)
7. India's GDP growth over the past three years, which is underpinned by debt-funded growth and investment, can be changed by the credit cycle, but the rise in the cost of capital will affect the process. (　)
8. The Left Front of Communist Parties does not adhere to a conservative stance towards economic development in India. (　)
9. Because of its colonial legacy, India is a nation with low interests on investment. That is why India has always attracted low FDI in recent years. (　)
10. The cumbersome procedures for launching a business and a lengthy enforcement of commercial

45

contracts are among headaches of a business person in India, which calls for an immediate solution. (   )

III Group discussion.

1. India is a fast growing economy in recent years, and do you think that India can overtake China in its economic development?
2. What are the competitive advantages that India has, compared with China?
3. What are challenges that face India in its economic growth? Can you come up with measures to address those problems?
4. Can you make a brief comparison between India and China in its economic growth? Your comparison can focus on policies, government systems, natural resources, demographics, technological researches, etc.

Case Study

Can income inequality emerging in Asia stunt growth?

Growth with equality was the mantra of the Asian tigers during the three decades to the 1990s. Unlike Latin America, most of them combined speedy economic growth with relatively low and sometimes even falling income inequality, thereby spreading the economic gains widely. More recently, Asia economies have continued to enjoy the world's fastest growth, but the rich are now growing richer much faster than the poor.

According to a report by the Asian Development Bank (ADB), income inequality has increased over the past decade or so in 15 of the 21 countries it has studied. The three main exceptions are Thailand, Malaysia and Indonesia, the countries worst hit by the 1997 financial crisis. The biggest increases in inequality were in China, Nepal and Cambodia.

The ADB says that although poverty is falling, due to fast growth, it is still worrying to have rising inequality. The widening inequality can threaten growth, if it results in social unrest. High and rising inequality played a big role in Nepal's recent troubles. Rumblings of discontent across the region suggest government cannot afford to ignore such risks.

Populist measures to soak the rich are not the answer: they would impede growth. The ADB instead recommends governments to focus on policies that lift the incomes of the poor, such as improving rural access to health, education and social protection. More investment in rural infrastructure could boost productivity in farming and increase job opportunities for the poor.

But that is easier said than done.

(Adapted from *Economist*, August 11, 2007)

Supplementary Reading

Getting Worried Downturn

Whether or not it's an official recession, America's economy will feel grim

(Author Unknown)

In recent years, it has rarely paid to be pessimistic about America's economy. Time and again, worried analysts (including *The Economist*) have given warning of trouble as debt-laden and spendthrift consumers are forced to rein in their spending.

So far, that trouble has been avoided. The housing market peaked early in 2006. Since then home-building has plunged, dragging overall growth down slightly. But the economy has remained far from recession. Consumers barely blinked: their spending has risen at an annual rate of 3% in real terms since the beginning of 2006, about the same pace as at the peak of the housing boom in 2004 and 2005.

At the same time, rapid growth in emerging markets coupled with a tumbling dollar has provided the American economy with a new bulwark, one that strengthened even as financial markets seized up over the summer. Exports soared at an annual rate of 16% in the third quarter. Thanks partly to strong export growth, revised GDP figures due on November 29th are likely to show that America's output grew at an annual rate of around 5% between July and September. Never mind recession: that is well above the economy's sustainable pace of growth.

But the good news may be about to come to an end. The housing downturn has entered a second, more dangerous, phase: one in which the construction rout deepens, price declines accelerate and the wealth effect of falling prices begins to change consumers' behavior. The pain will be intensified by a sharp credit crunch, the scale of which is only just becoming clear. And, in the short term, it will be exacerbated by a spike in oil prices — up by 25% since August — that is extreme, even by the standards of recent years. The result is likely to be America's first consumer-led downturn in close to two decades.

Home Is Where the Rot Starts

The biggest source of gloom is housing. Despite almost two years of plunging construction, the collapse of the property bubble is far from finished and its impact on broader consumer behavior has barely begun. So far, the housing recession has been a builders' bust. Housing starts are down by 47% from their peak and residential building now accounts for 4.4% of GDP, down from a record of 6.3% in 2005. That is a big drop, but not yet unusually long or deep by historical standards. Nouriel Roubini and Christian Menegatti, of Roubini Global Economics, point out that the seven other housing recessions since 1960 lasted an average of 32 months and saw housing starts fall by 51%.

Judging by the large number of unsold homes and the pace at which buyers are canceling contracts (around 50% according to some homebuilders), it is clear that builders have further to cut back. Richard Berner, of Morgan Stanley, expects a further 25% decline, taking the pace of housing starts in 2008 to below 1m, the slowest since records began in 1959.

A builders' bust will not, by itself, drag the economy into recession. Most post-war construction busts have been followed by recession, but only because they were triggered by tighter monetary policy to head off inflation. The housing busts were a symptom of a forthcoming recession rather than the cause. This time, the source of trouble lies with the bursting of the housing bubble itself.

Since 1997, house prices have more than doubled in real terms. That increase has colored America's economy in ways that go far beyond the construction boom. In particular, rising house prices provide consumers with the collateral they need for a huge increase in borrowing.

Up to Their Necks

Relative to their incomes, consumers have been taking on more debt for decades, as America's increasingly sophisticated financial system allows more people more access to credit. But the pace of indebtedness has accelerated dramatically. The ratio of household debt to disposable income is now above 130%. Earlier this decade it was 100%; in the early 1990s it was 80% (See Chart 1).

That credit expansion was made possible by rising house prices. Now they are falling, credit conditions are tightening. Both shifts are just beginning. According to the S&P/Case-Shiller index, arguably America's most accurate national measure, house prices have fallen by around 5% in nominal terms since their peak, or 8% once inflation is taken into account. That is a tiny drop compared with the past decade's rise (See Chart 2).

Nor, judging by the pipeline of unsold homes, is it enough of a drop to bring demand in line with supplies. Unlike shares, whose prices change quickly, house prices are often "sticky" as homeowners are loth to acknowledge their houses are now worth less. But the coming months are likely to see a sharp jump in the supply of homes for sale under distressed conditions. More than 2m subprime borrowers face markedly higher mortgage payments over the next 18 months as their interest rates are adjusted to new levels. Many will be forced into foreclosure.

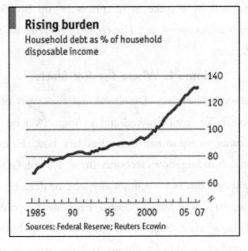

Chart 1

Unit 2 Regional Economy and Industry

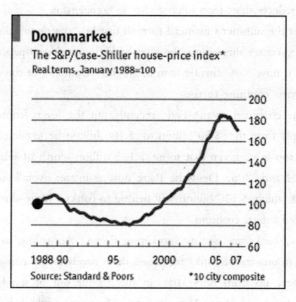

Chart 2

This constellation will drive house prices down. Most Wall Street seers expect a drop of around 10% in nominal terms over the next year or so, but price declines of 15% or even 20% are no longer regarded as outlandish. Economists differ on how, and by how much, falling house prices will affect consumers' spending. But empirical studies suggest that changes in house prices have a bigger effect on consumer spending in countries, like America, where credit markets are deepest.

The most recent research implies that changes in Americans' housing wealth affect their spending more than similar changes in their financial wealth, although the effect takes longer to emerge. A $100 fall in financial wealth is traditionally associated with a $3 - 5 decline in spending. An equivalent fall in housing wealth, it seems, eventually reduces spending by between $4 and $9.

Given that America's stock of residential housing is worth some $21 trillion (or almost one-third of all household assets), a 10% drop in house prices would make a discernible dent in consumption growth. If the spending response were at the top of economists' estimates, for instance, consumer spending would slow by almost two percentage points. The economists' studies, however, suggest that effect will be gradual: falling house prices will be an ongoing drag on consumer spending, rather than a sudden brake.

So far, this brake has been eased by strong gains in financial wealth. Thanks to higher stock prices, American households' overall assets have still been rising smartly. If the stock market loses momentum along with the economy, the wealth effect on consumer spending could appear quite quickly.

A wholesale credit crunch would make matters much worse. No one is yet sure how tight credit will get. It depends on how big the losses from the subprime-related mess turn out to be; who holds those losses; how far banks are forced to take troubled assets, such as those in structured investment vehicles, onto their balance sheets; by how much they cut back lending in response; and how far the Federal Reserve reduces short-term interest rates to compensate.

Three months after the summer's financial turmoil first hit, the omens do not look good. Entire markets for securitized assets are shriveling: the asset-backed commercial-paper market has shrunk for 13 weeks in a row and is now 30% smaller than in August. Estimates of the eventual losses from the subprime-related debt mess continue to rise.

Ben Bernanke, the chairman of the Fed, recently put the losses from bad mortgage loans at $150 billion, up sharply from the $50 billion to $100 billion he expected early in the summer. And even that may be too low, given that some $1.3 trillion-worth of subprime loans alone were originated between 2004 and 2006. Deutsche Bank now estimates overall subprime-related losses at up to $400 billion, of which $130 billion will belong to banks. Write-downs of that scale will eat into even the best-stuffed capital cushions.

By some measures, banks are already hunkering down. According to the Fed's most recent survey of loan officers, a quarter of banks tightened their standards on consumer loans (other than credit cards) in October, up from only 10% in July. Four out of ten banks demanded higher standards on prime mortgages, up from 15% in July. The pace at which banks are tightening their mortgage-lending standards rivals that of the early 1990s, when the banking sector as a whole was much weaker and less well capitalized (See Chart 3). But since tighter mortgage standards are themselves a response to the housing bust, they may overstate the extent of an economy-wide credit crunch.

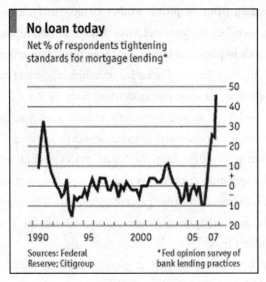

Chart 3

Shocked by Oil

Many Americans, however, will find credit harder to come by. And just as they do so, the third blow will come: that of higher fuel costs. Although it has fallen back this week, the benchmark price of crude oil is still above $90 per barrel, almost 25% higher than in August. This surge has not been fully reflected in American petrol prices, largely because refineries had unusually fat margins earlier in the year.

Average petrol prices are up 33 cents per gallon (or 12%) since mid-August. Unless crude prices fall dramatically, much dearer petrol lies ahead. If oil stays near to $100 per barrel, some analysts are talking about $4 per gallon by next summer.

Higher fuel costs are the equivalent of a tax on consumers, reducing the amount of money they can spend on other things. Jan Hatzius, of Goldman Sachs, reckons that a rise in petrol prices of one cent reduces consumers' overall disposable income by about $1.2 billion, and tends to drag consumer spending down by $600 m. Over the next few months, he reckons, higher fuel costs could reduce consumer spending by 1.2% at an annual rate. Overall, this drag will be smaller than the combination of tighter credit and falling house prices, but its impact will be concentrated over a shorter period.

A final cause for concern is the labor market. Low unemployment and solid wage growth have been a big reason for consumers' resilience thus far (See Chart 4). With unemployment at 4.7% and 166,000 new jobs in October, that strength looks intact. But careful inspection suggests that October's numbers mask a wider slowing. The pace of net job creation has fallen from a monthly average of 189,000 in 2006 to 118,000 in the past three months. Details from the household-based employment survey, which may be more accurate when the economy is slowing, are even darker. It shows very little net job growth in 2007, and an unemployment rate that is already up by three tenths of a point from its nadir.

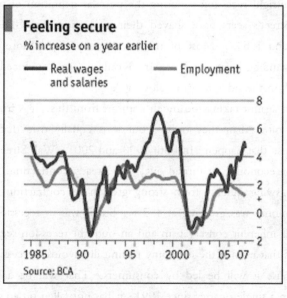

Chart 4

Add this all up and it is small wonder that consumers are feeling gloomy. Most gauges of consumer confidence have been plunging of late. The University of Michigan's index is at its lowest level in 15 years, leaving aside the aftermath of Hurricane Katrina. The latest evidence suggests spending is already weakening: core retail sales were flat in October.

Consumer spending, at around 70% of GDP, is by far the biggest determinant of the economy's fate. But it is not the only one. The odds of a downturn also depend on whether other engines reinforce — or counteract — consumers' weakness.

One wild card will be firms' investment. Corporate spending is historically volatile, often helping to tip an economy into a formal downturn. In America's last recession, in 2001, plunging investment was the source of trouble, as firms worked off the investment excesses of the late 1990s. Today, corporate America is in much stronger shape. Overall, balance sheets are healthy and profits strong. But as Martin Barnes, of Bank Credit Analyst, points out, domestic non-financial firms, the ones that do most capital spending, have been doing rather less well, with profits down by 9%, compared with a year earlier, in the first half of 2007. Corporate investment may not drag the economy down, but nor is it likely to offer a boost.

That role belongs elsewhere — to foreign trade. America's exports have been booming while import growth has slowed sharply. That has narrowed America's trade deficit and boosted output. Exports will not continue to grow at the torrid rates seen in recent months, but with the dollar showing scant signs of a turnaround and with emerging economies, in particular, looking remarkably resilient (see article), exports will remain an important prop. At 12% of GDP, they are now easily able to offset the drag from weaker construction.

Recession or Not?

Put all this together and do you get a recession? Many analysts expect a sharply slower economy, but not an outright recession — using the popular definition of two consecutive quarters of falling GDP. Wall Street's seers have shaved their projections for GDP growth in the fourth quarter of 2007 to around 1.5%. Most of them expect a couple more similarly weak quarters thereafter. A few long-standing bears, such as Mr. Roubini, are convinced recession is inevitable. But most forecasters reckon the odds remain below 50%.

Yet history cautions against taking too much comfort from this. It is true that pessimists tend to predict recessions more often than they occur, but it is equally true that mainstream forecasters usually fail to predict those that happen. In both 1990 and 2001, Wall Street's seers were predicting modest growth when the economy, it turned out, was already contracting. History also shows that America's economy can swing quickly from strong growth to contraction. During the first three months of 1990 the economy was growing at 4.7%, but it was in recession by July. Adjust Wall Street's forecasts for their inherent conservatism and an outright recession seems all too plausible.

The bigger point is that even if the economy technically avoids a recession, it will feel like one to most Americans because it will be led by consumers. That will be a big change. Consumer spending has not fallen in a single quarter since 1991; it has not fallen on an annual basis since 1980. Consumers barely noticed America's last recession — when low interest rates and high house prices kept them spending solidly (see Chart 5). Just how voters and politicians react to a consumer downturn in an election year is worryingly uncertain.

What's more, the squeeze on consumers will last longer than many expect because it involves the unwinding of an asset-price bubble and attendant financial excesses. Just as corporate spending stayed weak for years after the 2001 recession, so consumer spending will be crimped for more than

Unit 2 Regional Economy and Industry

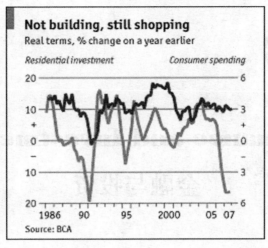

Chart 5

a few months. There seems little reason to expect, as many analysts seem to, that the housing bust will be history by the second half of 2008.

Finally, policymakers' responses may be more muted. In 2001, the economy was cushioned by a large fiscal boost, thanks to tax cuts and bigger spending, as well as much lower interest rates. A big tax cut now seems extremely unlikely. At the same time, the weak dollar and global economic strength that softened the downturn will also complicate the central bankers' ability to respond. Based on underlying inflation expectations, real interest rates are still above 2%. Central bankers often push short-term real rates to zero, or even below, in a downturn, suggesting there is plenty of room to cut, particularly since the housing glut means lower interest rates may pack less punch. But high oil prices and a falling dollar may preclude such an aggressive response, as Mr. Bernanke worries about rising inflation expectations. Recession or not, America faces a tricky road ahead.

(*Economist*, Nov. 15, 2007)

Answer and discuss the following questions:

1. What really sparked the downturn of the US economy?
2. Why is housing the biggest source of US economic gloom?
3. Do you think that the Fed's cut can save the situation? Why?
4. Do you agree that higher fuel costs have exacerbated the deteriorating situation of the US economy? Why?
5. Can you summarize the American labor market?
6. In what direction can you predict will American economy head for? Why?

Unit 3

Finance and Investment
金融与投资

Text A

Japan's Big Bang: Too little, Too Late?

Jean-Francois MinierWht

Twenty years ago the United Kingdom's financial system underwent an enormous transformation. The "Big Bang" propelled London from what had become a sleepy, domestic financial center to the world's most important financial hub — even ahead of New York. It also spurred job creation and nurtured the rebirth of the British economy, which had lost much of its competitive sparkle in the decades since World War II, and it helped the UK better prepare for an ageing society by resuscitating its almost collapsed pension system.

A decade later, Japan also had its own version of the Big Bang. But unlike the UK's, Japan did not result in wide-ranging reforms.[1] Today, much still remains to be done to make Tokyo a global financial center on par with New York or London — and even to ward off the mounting threat to its status as Asia's leading financial center posed by Hong Kong, Shanghai and Singapore.[2]

On Japan's things-to-do list for the financial industry: deregulation of cross-sector entry; development of genuine rule-based supervision; harmonization of accounting standards to global norms; increasing the reliability of the country's stock exchanges; improving the quality of its start-up markets; and forging stronger links with the financial systems of other Asian economies, especially with China.

Free, Fair and Global

When Japan's then prime minister, Ryutaro Hashimoto[3], launched his Financial Reform Initiative in November 1996, his objective was to produce a set of financial reforms — to be implemented by 2001 — that would shake up the Ministry of Finance and the Bank of Japan and allow Tokyo to become a "free, fair and global" financial market. Pension reform, as well as the clean-up of the banking sector's enormous bad loans problem, conveniently was left for subsequent administrations to tackle.[4] Yet even with this relatively narrow scope, the success of the reform initiative has been patchy, to say the least.[5] As the statistics show, of the 11 "must-do" objectives set by the Hashimoto administration, only eight have been completed. More importantly, given the phenomenal growth of global financial markets in recent years, the "must-do" list should probably be twice as long now.

At the September 2006 IMF/World Bank meetings in Singapore, I discussed funding flows and Asian financial centers with a senior executive of the World Bank. We marveled at the recovery of the region over these past 10 years and also agreed on just how important Japanese investors were to ensuring funding needs at reasonable cost to the World Bank. We were also puzzled, however, at why Japan had not managed to keep up with other global financial centers — London and New York in particular — and how it was being challenged by Singapore, Hong Kong and perhaps Shanghai in the future. We wondered if Tokyo markets would see the same fate as the harbors of Yokohama[6] and Kobe[7], which saw Hong Kong, Singapore and other Asian harbors overtake them in the past 20 years.

Singapore and Hong Kong, through a combination of tax incentives, infrastructure development and integration into the global financial flows passing through China, have managed to flourish in areas such as private banking, asset management and back office outsourcing.[8] This has attracted jobs that were previously performed in other financial centers around the globe and also has created new ones. Shanghai is less advanced and does not represent an immediate threat to Tokyo, but with China now possessing the largest foreign-currency reserves in the world (more than $1 trillion) and having already become the second-most important economy on the global agenda, it can only be expected that its growth will accelerate over the next few years.

Back in Tokyo later that week at a dinner attended by senior executives of Japanese securities firms, the conversation turned to the state of the country's bond market[9]. We agreed that, despite having the largest Treasury bond market in the world, Japan's bond markets were underdeveloped since all other segments (corporate, municipal, asset-backed and high-yield) were insignificant on an international scale. This in turn has contributed to the slow development of the domestic credit-derivatives[10] market as well. In conclusion, it was agreed that prior to focusing on the Asian bond markets through numerous government-sponsored initiatives, it would be prudent for Japanese financial institutions, supported by the government, to first develop the domestic bond market in a manner that does not rely on banks or the state to distribute credit to corporations and local authorities.[11]

While having benefited from product liberalization embedded in the Big Bang measures (especially securitization), the retail side is still below global norms due primarily to limited financing options faced by individuals and SMEs. The lack of a strong financing strategy by banks for smaller firms and individuals spurred the development of the less efficient and more expensive consumer-finance industry and even prompted regulators to dole out numerical targets to the megabanks for growing the proportion of their loans to SMEs — not exactly a market solution to financing needs.

The equity markets are not much better off. The infrastructure issues of the various exchanges (system breakdown, reputation issues with newly listed companies, etc.) are well documented. Less well-known is the fact that Tokyo has continued to slip in terms of trade volumes when compared to New York or Europe. Tokyo has also been unable to keep up with London in capturing listings from rapidly-developing economies, such as China and Russia.

And in foreign exchange, Tokyo has continued to lose volume and staff to Singapore and Hong Kong where most of the regional foreign-exchange teams are now located.

Missed Opportunity

At the inception, the Big Bang measures were expected to facilitate the shift from indirect financing driven by bank credit towards direct financing driven by securities markets. This would have allowed for more efficient distribution of fund towards well-managed and growth-generating companies, adding up to 0.3 percentage points to long-term potential GDP, according to 1997 estimates by the Ministry of International Trade and Industry (MITI). Given that actual GDP growth during the period 1996 to 2006 was a very modest 0.2% in real terms and 1.3% in nominal terms, Japan could have done with this much needed boost to its economic performance.[12] In addition, full implementation of these measures would have supported efficient management of the vast financial assets of the Japanese people, possibly even partially compensating for a pension and welfare system financially strained by a rapidly aging population.[13] Progress has taken place but to a degree much smaller than originally expected. As a result, only partial reforms of the pension system have been possible, making future reforms potentially more pressing and more painful.

Another consequence of Tokyo's inability to become a true global financial market is that Japanese companies will find increasingly difficult to thrive in the international business environment where global consolidation battles[14] have become more common. As seen in the recent takeover battle for Luxembourg-based steelmaker Arcelor[15] by India's Mittal Steel[16], increasingly, decision-making and opinion-shaping take place more in the global financial centers and not necessarily where companies are headquartered or have factories.[17] If Mittal's target had been Nippon Steel[18], for example, then for sure that Japanese steel maker's fate would have been decided in the board-rooms of pension funds[19], hedge funds[20] or investment banks[21] in London or New York, but certainly not in Tokyo.

Japanese financial institutions are being largely left out of global merger and acquisition activities, adding to their already low levels of competitiveness. A key factor in Japan's inability to compete effectively in the international financial sector is the lack of sophistication in the country's domestic financial sector. This has meant that Japan's financial institutions have little incentive to hone those skills necessary to compete internationally with their global peers in the most advanced markets. Furthermore, underdeveloped domestic markets means that Japanese financial firms lack the scale and profitability levels that would allow them to play an active role in global consolidation.

Why has Japan missed this opportunity to mold itself into a powerhouse of global finance? Is it, as some commentators would have it, due to some inherent inability of the Japanese to be successful in risk-taking activities?[22] Hardly. After all, it could be said that one of first types of financial derivatives originated in Japan when, in 1710, the Dojima Rice Exchange in Osaka[23] introduced rice warehouse receipts that could be actively traded against future deliveries. In addition, the underlying mathematical theory behind pricing of options[24] was introduced in Japan in 1942 by the Japanese mathematician, Kiyoshi Ito[25].

If not cultural, then the problem must be related to the action (or inaction) of other players in Japan's financial sector. For one, Japanese regulators surely must shoulder their share of responsibility. The stated Big Bang goal of furthering competition by promoting cross-sector entry among the various fields of banks, trust banks[26], securities companies[27] and insurance companies has yet to be realized. Today, the constraints between banking and insurance and between banking and securities remain considerable.

Neither are Japan's bureaucrats beyond reproach. The ministries have, in general, been too slow, overcautious and uncoordinated in their approach to implementing the reforms. Yet to be fair, the bureaucrats were often just answering to elected politicians and the political agenda of the day — agenda that were at times contrary to the spirit of the Big Bang.[28] Japanese politician's main failure has, in effect, been their inability to retain the grand vision that was set forth in 1996, and which should have been maintained as the guiding light when formulating new deregulation measures or when implementing regulations aimed at correcting perceived systemic weaknesses.[29] This breakdown stands in sharp contrast to the bipartisan ideological consistency that was sustained during the implementation of the British Big Bang.[30]

Finally, the media can also be faulted for its complete lack of perspective in embracing the cause for financial reform. It jumped on any phenomenon that could be seen as promoting the cause without much meaningful analysis, only to reverse course ostensibly when duped, deluding the general public to believe that the reform was the cause of all this chaos.[31] This was never more visible than during the recent scandals involving Takafumi Horie[32] and Yoshiaki Murakami[33], where both men went from zero to hero and back to zero in a very short period of time. Of course, a more appropriate starting point would be for the media to educate the public on development in finance — both the benefits and potential pitfalls. Perhaps even more importantly, the media should perform its true function by holding the country's politicians, bureaucrats and private-sector corporations accountable, and ensuring that all parties maintain momentum for reform.

Time Waits for No Man

In addition to the factors outlined above, there is one more point that cannot be stressed enough: The world does not stand still and any reform plan needs to reflect that reality. Clearly, Japan's financial reforms initiatives did not (and still do not). During these past 10 years, there has been explosive growth in the world's financial markets (despite the burst of the Internet bubble) on the back of increased globalization, and the emergence of new markets in China, Russia, India, Brazil, South Africa and the Gulf States. These forces, combined with an unprecedented funding need in the US to finance the war on terror, have contributed to a global reflationary situation which has fed all the world markets, especially commodities markets[34].

If Japan could only muster a lackluster, slow and merely partial reform packages in the context of a fast-changing world, then it is not surprising the package could never have been sufficient to ensure Japan a leadership role in global finance. Not just that, but the lack of proactive reform and ambition to set the global standards means that Japan may have to struggle just to retain its current position as Asia's leading financial hub in the face of mounting challenges from China, among others.

In the Five Year Plan covering 2006-2010, China's National Development and Reform Commission is planning to promote the displacement of manufacturing from the Eastern seaboard to deeper inland in order to minimize inequalities and bring the factory jobs closer to those rural areas with excess labor and to ensure better living standards in coastal regions.[35] As a result, China will need to develop its service industry in the same coastal regions if employment levels are to be maintained. Assuming a fully convertible yuan and further market liberalization, it is likely that the financial industry will enjoy exponential growth benefiting Hong Kong (the cross-border gateway) and Shanghai (for the domestic market).[36] From a regulatory perspective, these two markets could become joined at the back. Singapore will also benefit by providing offshore convenient private banking and asset management services for this growing Chinese wealth, becoming a kind of "Switzerland of Asia."[37]

In order for Japan to benefit from this trend, it needs a truly coordinated strategy by which all unachieved goals of the Big Bang (cross-sector entry, accounting harmonization, rules-based regulation, etc.) are swiftly implemented and by which a new set of ambitious objectives are set for the next five years. Failure to do this will probably mean that Japan will lose its regional leadership in the next 5 to 10 years. A faster adaptation to global change is also necessary, if Japan really wants to achieve global leadership status. This is, in my view, essential if Tokyo wants its voice heard on global harmonization talks and as it seeks parity with China when starting to forge greater economic and financial integration around China, with Japan reduced to a vassal role or left out completely as an outsider in the region.

Such are stakes for Japan that Prime Minister Abe should take direct leadership in formulating this new financial reform strategy and ensuring appropriate coordination.

(*Far Eastern Economic Review*, December, 2006)

New Words and Expressions

propel	v.	推进，驱使
hub	n.	中心
spur	v.	刺激，推动
nurture	v.	养育，给予营养物

rebirth	n.	新生,复兴
sparkle	n.	光彩,活力
resuscitate	v.	(使)复苏,(使)复兴
version	n.	样式,形式
deregulation	n.	缩小国家对经济干预的范围
harmonization	n.	校准,一致,调谐
start-up	a.	启动阶段的,开始阶段的
clean-up	n.	清除,获利
subsequent	a.	后来的,并发的
tackle	v.	处理,解决
patchy	a.	只是部分好的,不完整的
marvel	v.	大为惊异,觉得惊奇
flourish	v.	繁荣,兴旺
outsourcing	n.	外部采办,外购
accelerate	v.	加速,促进
underdeveloped	a.	不发达的
segment	n.	部分,片,段
high-yield	n.	高收益的,高产的
insignificant	a.	无关紧要的,可忽略的
credit-derivatives	n.	信贷衍生工具
prudent	a.	谨慎的
liberalization	n.	自由主义化,放宽限制
embed	v.	埋置,嵌入
securitization	n.	资产证券化
norm	n.	标准,规范
option	n.	选择
dole	v.	(常与out连用)施舍,少量给予
numerical	a.	数值的,表示数量的
megabank	n.	超巨大银行
listing	n.	上市
thrive	v.	兴旺,繁荣,茁壮成长
opinion-shaping	n.	观念引导,影响观点
board-room	n.	董事会会议室
sophistication	n.	使精致,使变得更好
hone	v.	用磨刀石磨,使更有效
scale	n.	规模
profitability	n.	收益性,利益率
powerhouse	n.	有影响的机构或国家

commentator	n.	评论员
originate	v.	起源，发生
warehouse	n.	仓库，货栈，大商店
receipt	n.	收条，收据
inaction	n.	无行动，不活动，无为
reproach	n.	责备，谴责
overcautious	a.	过度小心
uncoordinated	a.	不协调的
bureaucrat	n.	官僚主义者
retain	v.	保持，保留
grand	a.	壮观的，豪华的，重大的
formulate	v.	阐明，规划，设计
perceive	v.	感知，感到，认识到
systemic	a.	系统的，组织的
bipartisan	a.	两党的，代表两党的
ideological	a.	意识形态的
consistency	n.	一致性，连贯性
fault	v.	挑毛病，找……的岔子
perspective	n.	透视图，远景，观点，看法
reverse	v.	颠倒，倒转
ostensibly	ad.	表面上
dupe	v.	欺骗，坑害
delude	v.	迷惑，蛊惑
chaos	n.	混乱，混沌
scandal	n.	丑闻
pitfall	n.	未料到的危险（或困难）
accountable	a.	应负责的，有责任的
momentum	n.	动力，要素
burst	n.	迸发，爆发，突然出现
bubble	n.	泡沫，泡泡
unprecedented	a.	空前的，没有前例的
reflationary	a.	通货再膨胀
muster	v.	集合，召集，提起
lackluster	n.	无光泽，暗淡
proactive	a.	[心理] 前摄的
displacement	n.	移置，转移
inequality	n.	不平等，不同
excess	a.	过度的，额外的

convertible	a.	可改变的，自由兑换的
exponential	a.	指数的，幂数的
offshore	a.	离岸的，海外的
unachieved	a.	没有实现的，未曾达到的
swiftly	ad.	很快地，即刻
parity	n.	同等；平等
forge	v.	铸造，打造
integration	n.	成为整体，集成，一体化
vassal	a.	为臣的，仆从的
stake	n.	赌金，支撑，支柱

financial hub	金融中心
ward off	避开，挡住
rule-based supervision	依法监管
shake up	把……打散后重新组合，震动
funding flow	资金流动
tax incentive	税收激励
private banking	私人银行业务
asset management	资产管理
back office outsourcing	后勤服务外包
securities firms	证券公司
bond market	债券市场
Treasury bond market	国债市场
prior to	在前，居先
dole out	少量地发放，给予
equity market	产权投资市场
better off	状况好的
system breakdown	系统崩溃
pension funds	抚恤基金，退休基金
hedge funds	对冲基金
mold into	塑造成
jump on	扑向
the Gulf States	海湾国家
in the context of ...	在……的背景下

Notes

1. A decade later, Japan also had its own version of the Big Bang. But unlike the UK's, Japan did not result in wide-ranging reforms.　10年之后，日本也有了自己版本的"砰然重击"，但和英国不同，它的改革没有那么深远与广泛。

   句中的"the Big Bang"指的是英国20年前对金融系统大刀阔斧的改革。

2. Today, much still remains to be done to make Tokyo a global financial center on par with New York or London-and even to ward off the mounting threat to its status as Asia's leading financial center posed by Hong Kong, Shanghai and Singapore.　今天，要把东京建成纽约、伦敦一样的全球金融中心，仍有很多工作要做，此外还要面对香港、上海和新加坡对其亚洲金融中心地位日益增大的威胁。

   句中的"posed by Hong Kong, Shanghai and Singapore"是过去分词作定语，后置修饰前面的先行词"threat"；"on par with"意为"和……同等水平"。

3. Ryutaro Hashimoto　桥本龙太郎

   日本前首相，1937年7月29日生于冈山县的一个政治世家。1995年9月，桥本龙太郎当选为自民党总裁并出任副总理兼通产大臣。1996年1月11日，桥本龙太郎当选为第82任日本首相。在担任首相期间，他大力推行行政机构、财政、金融、税制等6大改革。1998年7月，自民党在参议院选举中失败，桥本辞去首相职务。2006年7月1日桥本龙太郎病逝于东京。桥本龙太郎喜爱剑道，爱好登山和摄影。

4. Pension reform, as well as the clean-up of the banking sector's enormous bad loans problem, conveniently were left for subsequent administrations to tackle.　养老金改革及银行系统巨额坏账的清理问题很自然地留给了下一届政府去解决。

   句中的"subsequent administration"指的是下一届政府。

5. Yet even with this relatively narrow scope, the success of the reform initiative has been patchy, to say the least.　即使在这样相对较小的范围内，至少可以说，改革也不是完全成功的。

   句中的"to say the least"是插入语，意思是"至少可以这样说，就是说得轻一些"。

6. Yokohama　横滨

   横滨是日本第二大城市，东临东京湾，南与横须贺等城市毗连，北接川崎市。横滨港是日本最大的港口，也是亚洲最大的港口之一。横滨地区是日本最大的工业地区，东京是世界金融中心之一，东京和横滨一起构成日本最大的工业带——京滨工业带。

7. Kobe　神户

   日本著名港口，兵库县首府，位于本州东南部，濒临大阪湾，背靠六甲山脉，距大阪约30公里，是日本著名的国际贸易港口之一。

8. Singapore and Hong Kong, through a combination of tax incentives, infrastructure development and integration into the global financial flows passing through China, have managed to flourish in areas such as private banking, asset management and back office outsourcing.　通过采取税收激

励措施，发展基础设施和融入流经中国的全球金融资本，新加坡和香港的私人银行、资产管理和内勤外部采购等行业蓬勃发展起来。

句中的"through a combination of..."作方式状语。"private banking"（私人银行业务）指银行针对私人客户所开发和提供的服务。"asset management"（资产管理）指委托人将自己的资产交给受托人，由受托人为委托人提供理财服务的行为。在文中指银行代客户进行投资的行为或提供的资产增值服务。"back office outsourcing"指后勤服务外包。外包是指企业在项目运作过程中的某些环节上借用外部资源，企业可以通过外包来提高核心竞争力、降低运营成本、巩固市场份额。"back office"即后勤办公室，就是为公司日常运作提供后勤服务的部门，通常是指信息技术、会计、人力资源等部门。这些后勤服务的外包就被称为后勤服务外包。

9. bond market   债券市场

    债券市场是发行和买卖债券的场所，是金融市场的一个重要组成部分。债券是政府、金融机构、工商企业等机构直接向社会借债筹措资金时，向投资者发行，并且承诺按一定利率支付利息并按约定条件偿还本金的债权债务凭证。债券的本质是债的证明书，具有法律效力。

10. credit-derivatives   信用衍生工具

    信用衍生工具是指通过非公开磋商达成的双边合约，用以控制信贷风险。信贷衍生工具包括远期合约、掉期、期权等价格取决于经济代理人（私人投资者或政府）信贷风险的金融资产。

11. In conclusion, it was agreed that prior to focusing on the Asian bond markets through numerous government-sponsored initiatives, it would be prudent for Japanese financial institutions, supported by the government, to first develop the domestic bond market in a manner that does not rely on banks or the state to distribute credit to corporations and local authorities.   总之，大家一致认为在政府推动关注亚洲债券市场之前，有政府背景的日本金融机构首先要在不依靠银行或国家向公司和地方政府摊派的前提下发展国内债券市场，这应该是比较审慎的做法。

    句中的"prior to"意为"在……之前"，文中引导时间状语；"that does not rely on banks or the state to distribute credit to corporations and local authorities"是定语从句，修饰先行词"manner"；"local authorities"指地方政府。

12. Given that actual GDP growth during the period 1996 to 2006 was a very modest 1.3% in real terms and 0.2% in nominal terms, Japan could have done with this much needed boost to its economic performance.   如果1996—2006年国内生产总值的实际增长率仅仅是1.3%，名义增长率是0.2%，那么日本就能够使经济有更好的表现。

    句中的"in real terms"意为"实际上"，"in nominal terms"意为"名义上"。以末期现行价格计算末期GDP，得出的增长率是名义经济增长率；以不变价格（即基期价格）计算末期GDP，得出的增长率是实际经济增长率；实际增长率＝（1＋名义增长率）/（1＋通胀率）－1。在计算经济增长时,一般都采用实际经济增长率。

13. In addition, full implementation of these measures would have supported efficient management of the vast financial assets of the Japanese people, possibly even partially compensating for a

pension and welfare system financially strained by a rapidly aging population. 此外，如果这些措施能够得以充分实施，将会有效管理日本人民的巨额金融资产，甚至可能会部分弥补因人口快速老化而导致的养老金和社会保障资金的不足。

句中的"strained"是过去分词作定语。

14. global consolidation battles 全球合并之争
    全球合并之争是指全球范围内的企业收购与吞并。

15. Arcelor 阿塞勒钢铁集团
    阿塞勒钢铁集团是全球钢铁工业改造的主导力量，是全世界最大的钢铁生产厂商，分布于60多个国家。在公司所有的主要市场，包括汽车业、建筑业、家用电器业、包装业，以至通用工业，都是市场的主导者。

16. Mittal Steel 米塔尔钢铁集团
    米塔尔钢铁集团隶属印度裔亿万富豪米塔尔麾下，在钢铁业内被誉为"世界上全球化程度最高"的公司。2005年4月，米塔尔钢铁集团以45亿美元收购美国国际钢铁集团，超过当时排名第一的欧洲阿塞洛钢铁集团，成为全球最大的钢铁生产企业。业界总结其成功秘诀为：在最合适的时机去收购与合并；用最精明的经营手法壮大那些被收购的企业。在美国《福布斯》杂志2004年公布的全球富豪排行榜上，米塔尔以250亿美元的身价名列第三，仅次于微软公司董事长比尔•盖茨和美国"股神"沃伦•巴菲特。

17. As seen in the recent takeover battle for Luxembourg-based steelmaker Arcelor by India's Mittal Steel, increasingly, decision-making and opinion-shaping take place more in the global financial centers and not necessarily where companies are headquartered or have factories. 正如最近米塔尔钢铁集团收购总部位于卢森堡的阿塞勒钢铁集团一样，越来越多的决策和谈判在全球金融中心内完成而没有必要是公司的总部或工厂所在地。

句中的"as"引导定语从句，指代后面的整个分句"increasingly, decision-making and opinion-shaping take place more in the global financial centers and not necessarily where companies are headquartered or have factories"；"increasingly"作后面分句的状语。

18. Nippon Steel 新日本钢铁公司
    新日本钢铁公司是一家日本跨国公司，是日本最大的钢铁公司，也是世界大型钢铁公司，总部在东京。新日本钢铁公司的前身是于1897年建成的官营八幡制铁所，1934年2月由官营的八幡制铁所和民间的轮西制铁、釜石矿山、富士制铁、东洋制铁、三菱制铁、九州制铁6家合并组成，1950年分成八幡制铁、富士制铁两家钢铁公司和日铁轮船公司及播磨耐火砖公司。1970年，八幡制铁、富士制铁两家公司合并，成立新日本钢铁公司，简称新日铁，当时该公司是世界上最大的钢铁公司。

19. pension funds 退休基金
    退休基金是指用来支付退休人员的养老退休金。基金是指专门用于某种特定目的并进行独立核算的资金。

20. hedge funds 对冲基金
    对冲基金意为"风险对冲过的基金"，起源于20世纪50年代初的美国。其操作的宗旨在于利用期货、期权等金融衍生产品及对相关联的不同股票进行实买空卖、风险对冲的操作技巧，在一定程度上规避和化解投资风险。在最基本的对冲操作中，基金管理者在购入一种股票后，同时购入这种股票的一定价位和时效的看跌期权（put option）。看跌期权的效用在于当股票价位跌破期权限定的价格时，卖方期权的持有者可将手中持有的股票以期权限定的价格卖出，从而使股票跌价的风险得到对冲。现在，对冲基金已成为一种新的投资模式的代名词，即基于最新的投资理论和复杂的金融市场操作技巧，充分利用各种金融衍生产品的杠杆效用，承担高风险、追求高收益的投资模式。

21. investment banks 投资银行

    投资银行是主要从事证券发行、承销、交易、企业重组、兼并与收购、投资分析、风险投资、项目融资等业务的非银行金融机构，是资本市场上的主要金融中介。投资银行是证券和股份公司制度发展到特定阶段的产物，是发达证券市场和成熟金融体系的重要主体，在现代社会经济发展中发挥着沟通资金供求、构造证券市场、推动企业并购、促进产业集中和规模经济形成、优化资源配置等重要作用。它属于金融服务业，主要服务于资本市场，是智力密集型行业。

22. Is it, as some commentators would have it, due to some inherent inability of the Japanese to be successful in risk-taking activities? 难道真的如一些人所评论的那样，是因为日本人在冒险活动领域天生缺乏能力？

    句中的"be due to"意为"归因于，归咎于"。

23. Dojima Rice Exchange in Osaka 大阪堂岛米市场

    大阪堂岛米市场成立于1730年，是大米的期货交易场所。

24. option 期权

    期权分为买入期权和卖出期权。买入期权是指它给予期权的持有者在给定时间或在此时间以前的任一时刻按规定的价格买入一定数量某种资产或期货合约的权利。卖出期权是指给予其持有者在给定时间或在此时间以前的任一时刻按规定的价格卖出一定数量某种资产或期货合约的权利。期权的持有者拥有该项期权规定的权利，他可以实施该权利，也可以放弃该权利，期权的出卖者则只负有期权合约规定的义务。期权的要素包括敲定价格（期权合同规定的购入或售出某种资产的价格）、到期日（期权合同规定的期权的最后有效日期为期权的到期日）、标的资产（期权合同规定的双方买入或卖出的资产为期权的标的资产）和权利金（买卖双方购买或出售期权的价格）。

25. Kiyoshi Ito 伊藤清

    日本数学家，其研究集中于概率论，特别是随机分析领域，2006年高斯奖得主。

26. trust banks 信托银行

    信托是信用委托的意思。它是指受他人委托，代为管理、经营和处理某项经济事务的行为。银行办理信托业务是以中间人身份所进行的一项银行业务，可将其归入中间业务范围。在信托业务中，拥有信托财产的人通常称为委托者，他们为达到一定目的，把财产委托给他人管理和处理；接受委托者的要求，按合同规定对信托财产进行管理和处理的人则为受托者。委托者把财产委托给受托者进行管理和处理时，双方需要签订合同或协议，这种行为就是信托行为。

27. securities companies 证券公司

    证券公司是指依照法律规定，经证券监督管理机构审查批准，从事证券经营业务的公司。证券公司是非银行金融机构的一种，是从事证券经营业务的法定组织形式。一般投资人必须透过证券公司买卖股票,但并不表示所有的证券公司都从事中介股票买卖的业务。根据经营项目的不同,证券公司可被划分为四类:第一,证券经纪商,也就是居间帮投资人买卖股票的证券公司;第二,证券承销商,帮助企业上市发行股票,如果投资人要买公司发行的新股票时,就必须找这种类型的证券公司;第三,证券自营商,他们如同一般投资人一样,也是股票的买卖者;第四,综合类证券商,就是同时经营以上三种业务的证券公司。

28. Yet to be fair, the bureaucrats were often just answering to elected politicians and the political agenda of the day-agenda that were at times contrary to the spirit of the Big Bang.   但公正地说,官僚们经常仅仅是对当选政客和目前政治日程的安排做出回应,而这些日程安排又经常是和"砰然重击"改革的精神相违背的。
    句中的"yet"表示转折。

29. Japanese politician's main failure has, in effect, been their inability to retain the grand vision that was set forth in 1996, and which should have been maintained as the guiding light when formulating new deregulation measures or when implementing regulations aimed at correcting perceived systemic weaknesses.   日本政府官员的失败事实上主要在于他们没有能力坚持 1996 年设立的宏伟蓝图,在制定新的政策减少国家干预或是执行那些旨在修正体制问题的规定时,那幅蓝图应该起指导作用。
    句中的"which"引导定语从句修饰"the grand vision";两个"when"引导的从句作定语从句中的状语。

30. This breakdown stands in sharp contrast to the bipartisan ideological consistency that was sustained during the implementation of the British Big Bang.   这种差异和英国实行"砰然重击"改革时两党在思想意识领域保持一致的情况截然相反。
    句中的 breakdown 指文中上句提到的日本政客不坚持 1996 年设定的目标。

31. It jumped on any phenomenon that could be seen as promoting the cause without much meaningful analysis, only to reverse course ostensibly when duped, deluding the general public to believe that the reform was the cause of all this chaos.   他们总是把焦点放在那些夸大原因的现象上面,而不做有意义的分析,当被蒙骗的时候仅仅简单地改变一下说法,使公众误以为改革是所有混乱的根源。
    句中的"promote"意为"放大,夸大"。

32. Takafumi Horie   崛江贵文
    日本网络新贵,"活力门"创始人,被指控操纵"活力门"股价,使东京证交所因股市剧烈动荡被迫暂时停止交易。他通过大笔收购挑战日本金融传统,曾是日本首相小泉纯一郎"刺客兵团"的尖兵。

33. Yoshiaki Murakami   村上世彰
    日本著名基金经理人,因违反日本内幕交易法,涉嫌股票内幕交易被捕。他管理的投资基金 MAC Asset Management 涉嫌在提前获知日本富士电视台 2005 年初即将提出公开收购日本广播公司的消息之后大量购入日本广播公司的股票,在短时间内牟取了暴利。该丑闻涉及日本央行行长福井俊彦。福井俊彦承认曾投资于村上世彰管理的基金,同时该事件也引发了日本各界对投资基金监管的反省。

34. commodities market　商品市场

　　一般商品市场指狭义的商品市场，如货物市场，包括消费品市场和工业品市场；特殊商品市场指为满足消费者的资金需要和服务需要而形成的市场，包括资本市场、劳动力市场和技术信息市场。近来商品市场出现了很多新特征，表现在消费品市场波动与生产资料市场波动、商品市场波动与投资波动、商品市场波动与货币供应量变化、商品市场波动与经济波动的互动关系等方面。

35. In the Five Year Plan covering 2006–2010, China's National Development and Reform Commission is planning to promote the displacement of manufacturing from the Eastern seaboard to deeper inland in order to minimize inequalities and bring the factory jobs closer to those rural areas with excess labor and to ensure better living standards in coastal regions.　在"十一五"规划中，中国发改委计划将制造业从东部沿海转移到内陆地区，希望以此实现国内差距最小化，使工厂更接近劳动力剩余的农村地区，同时保证沿海地区的生活水平。

　　句中的"in order to minimize ..."和后面的"to ensure ..."并列，引导目的状语。

36. Assuming a fully convertible yuan and further market liberalization, it is likely that the financial industry will enjoy exponential growth benefiting Hong Kong (the cross-border gateway) and Shanghai (for the domestic market).　如果人民币能够自由兑换，市场进一步放开，金融业很有可能会迅猛发展，而香港（国际交易的大门）和上海（国内市场）将从中收益。

　　句中的"cross-border"意为"跨国的，跨越边境的"；"it is likely ..."意为"有可能……"。

37. Singapore will also benefit by providing offshore convenient private banking and asset management services for this growing Chinese wealth, becoming a kind of "Switzerland of Asia."　新加坡也会从中国日益增长的财富中收益，他们可以提供便利的海外私人银行业务和资产管理服务，成为某种意义上的"亚洲的瑞士"。

　　句中的"a kind of"意为"有点，有几分"。"Switzerland"是瑞士，瑞士的金融业非常发达，瑞士共有600余家银行，分支机构5 070家，银行总资本达5 000多亿美元，纳税额占国家税收的20%，在国民经济中居重要地位。瑞士人均国外资产和投资占世界第一位，有"金融帝国"之称。

阅读小知识（1）

新闻的导语与主体

1. 新闻的导语

新闻的导语离不开5个"W"，即英语中的 WHO、WHAT、WHERE、WHEN、

WHY，译成中文为何人、何事、何地、何时、何故，有的还要加一个 HOW（怎样），这些看似深奥的东西其实与中学作文的写作原理基本类似。

导语一般有两个作用：第一，就是用精练、简洁的文字反映消息的要点或轮廓，使读者看了导语以后，就知道这条消息大体上告诉人们什么消息，从而引出主题，也就是把消息的主题引出来；第二，就是要唤起读者的兴趣，把读者吸引住，让读者情不自禁地把这条消息看下去。为了方便起见，我们把导语分为两种：直接式和延缓式。直接式导语要求记者在导语中把最重要的新闻主题以最简洁的方法告诉读者。它多用于对时效要求比较强的突发新闻等"硬"新闻。延缓式导语则要求记者调动自己驾驭文字的技术，使导语吸引读者。

不过，随着新闻事业的发展及传媒模式的变化，导语的写法也发生了变化，导语中所有要素不是一盘子全端出来，只是突出一两个要素，其余的则放在消息的展开部分或结尾去交代。

杂志文章的导语没有必要像新闻写作那样受字数的约束。按照英美报刊编排的习惯，一栏一般为 4 厘米宽，一般的消息导语要求在 35 个字以内。作为杂志采用的软新闻，导语可以完全长一些，可以 5 行，也可以 8 行或 10 行。但是，它的目的还是在于引导全文，引导读者。

2. 新闻的主体

新闻的主体结构最重要的莫过于"倒金字塔"。

"倒金字塔"（inverted pyramid）结构也叫"倒三角"结构。这一类型的特点是按照重要性递减的顺序来组织材料，把最新鲜、最重要的事实放在最前面，不太重要的往后放，最不重要的放在最后。"倒金字塔"结构的最大优点是"快"：从采写的角度讲，记者将最重要、最新鲜、最有趣、读者最关心的材料挑出来，写在消息最前面，很快组织一篇报道，不必在文章构思上多费斟酌；对后方编辑部门而言，收到这样的稿件后，处理也很快。

此外，还有"金字塔"结构，它与"倒金字塔"结构正好相反，它是按照新闻事实发展的本来顺序来写的。消息按照新闻事件的开头、发展、结尾的顺序进行，不像"倒金字塔"结构主体那样刻意按照新闻要素的重要性依大到小排序。目前，"金字塔"结构很少被使用。

新闻除了"倒金字塔"、"金字塔"等结构外，有时也能看到另外一种结构。这种消息往往是先在导语中写明主题，然后堆砌大量的事实来支撑这个主题。除了与导语呼应外，后面段落中每个事实之间都是平行并列关系，它们合起来共同说明导语阐述的问题。

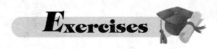

I Decide whether the following statements are true (T) or false (F).

1. The "Big Bang" program was originally launched in the UK to restore London to the World's most important financial hub and get rid of shadow cast by the almost-collapsed pension system. （   ）

Unit 3 Finance and Investment

2. Japan's version of the "Big Bang" was a successful one in that it initiated a series of profound reforms to make Tokyo a global financial center by deregulating cross-sector entry and increasing the reliability of the country's stock exchanges and etc. (　　)
3. It seems to the author that Singapore and Hong Kong have done an excellent job in such areas as private banking, asset management and back office outsourcing, and that Shanghai, backed by China's big foreign-currency reserves and the powerful presence of its economic development, will be on its way towards the financial hub in the area. (　　)
4. Japan's bond market was underdeveloped, because Japanese financial institutions developed the domestic bond market not through relying on banks or the state to distribute credit to corporations and local authorities. (　　)
5. In Tokyo's equity market, some problems with the system and some cases that are damaging to the image of newly listed companies have been uncovered, and what is even worse, Tokyo cannot raise adequate amounts of funds from emerging economies in Asia. (　　)
6. It seems to the author that Japan's failure to make efficient distribution of funds towards well-managed and growth-generating companies was the greatest contributor to the modest GDP growth in the past decade. (　　)
7. Japan's aging population generates great strains on a pension and welfare system, which can thoroughly be eased by rigorous implementation of financial measures. (　　)
8. According to the author, Japan has missed a good opportunity to develop itself into a powerhouse of global finance, which is partly due to Japanese bureaucrats' slow, overcautious and uncoordinated manner in implementing their reforms. (　　)
9. The author points out that the media is to blame for its insensible analysis and incomplete perspective in their story coverage of financial reforms. (　　)
10. The stakes for Japan to take direct leadership in mapping out this new financial reform strategy are to formulate a truly coordinated strategy and fast adapt itself to global changes and particularly to changes in China. (　　)

III Choose one answer that best suits the following statements.

1. Financial Reform Initiative launched by Japan's Prime Minister Ryutaro Hashimoto in November 1996 was considered by the author quite successful in that _____.
   A. a series of reforms not yet implemented were left for the next administration and in particular, rapid growth of global financial markets in recent years has rendered Japan out of pace
   B. no accomplishment was achieved in reform packages
   C. Japan's economic boom was hampered by this program
   D. the accounting standards in Japan's financial sector was not made compatible with global norms
2. Japan's bond markets were not well developed, mainly due to the fact that _____.
   A. Japanese financial institution was prudent to develop the domestic bond market
   B. the development of the domestic credit-derivatives market was slow and got no support from

the government

C. all other sectors in Japan were not well developed on an international scale, which exerted an adverse effect on the financial market

D. regulators in financial sector did not realize the importance of capturing listings from rapidly-developing economies

3. The author thinks that Japan has missed opportunity, and the possible consequences of which are: _____.

A. Japan's pension and welfare system will be more strained by a rapidly aging population

B. reforms of the pension system will be suspended

C. foreign trade volume will be on the drastic decline, particularly the trade volume with China

D. GDP growth slowed, and strains on pension and welfare system unrelieved, and even worse, Japanese financial institutions unable to obtain their global competitiveness

4. The reasons for Japan to miss the opportunity to become a global financial hub are that _____.

A. Japanese financial policy makers are unable to carry out the deep reforms in this sector while Japan's bureaucrats are slow and inefficient in their response to the changing situation. In addition, the media lack a sensible and complete perspective in their story coverage of financial reforms

B. Japanese culture has the element that inherently leads to being unable to succeed in risk-taking activities

C. Japanese financial sector lacks a coordinated strategy for its rapid development and there still remain considerable constraints between banking and insurance and between banking and securities

D. in the past decade, there has been explosive growth in the world's financial markets on the back of increased globalization, and the emergence of new markets in China, Russia, India, Brazil and etc

5. If Japan could only muster on a <u>lackluster</u>, slow and merely partial reform package in the context of a fast-changing world, then it is not surprising the package could never have been sufficient to ensure Japan a leadership role in global finance.

The underlined word in this sentence means: _____.

A. lockless   B. lack vitality   C. insufficient   D. bleak

III Translate the following passages into Chinese.

1. While having benefited from product liberalization embedded in the Big Bang measures (especially securitization), the retail side is still below global norms due primarily to limited financing options faced by individuals and SMEs. The lack of a strong financing strategy by banks for smaller firms and individuals spurred the development of the less efficient and more expensive consumer-finance industry and even prompted regulators to dole out numerical targets to the megabanks for growing the proportion of their loans to SMEs — not exactly a market solution to

financing needs.

The equity markets are not much better off. The infrastructure issues of the various exchanges (system breakdown, reputation issues with newly listed companies, etc.) are well documented. Less well-known is the fact that Tokyo has continued to slip in terms of trade volumes when compared to New York or Europe. Tokyo has also been unable to keep up with London in capturing listings from rapidly-developing economies, such as China and Russia.

2. If Japan could only muster a lackluster, slow and merely partial reform packages in the context of a fast-changing world, then it is not surprising the package could never have been sufficient to ensure Japan a leadership role in global finance. Not just that, but the lack of proactive reform and ambition to set the global standards means that Japan may have to struggle just to retain its current position as Asia's leading financial hub in the face of mounting challenges from China, among others.

IV Write a summary of this text.

It Isn't Easy

The world's central bankers have remained unruffled by the recent turbulence in the credit markets

(Author Unknown)

Call a man like Ben Bernanke[1] a pushover and you deserve a punch on the jaw. With a calm resolution that is beginning to mark his tenure, the Federal Reserve[2] chief and his colleagues left America's benchmark interest rate[3] unchanged at 5.25% after a meeting on August 7th and gave little indication that they were minded to cut rates in the near future.

The Fed acknowledged in a statement that financial markets had been volatile, that credit conditions had tightened (if only for "some" households and businesses) and that core inflation had "improved modestly".[4] But it stressed that America's economy was still on course for moderate growth, albeit with greater downside risks, and that inflation remains the main policy concern.[5]

Hopes of a bigger shift in tone, paving the way for a cut in interest rates later this year, were firmly dashed.[6] Before the Fed's statement, a cut by the end of the year had been fully priced into financial markets[7], with another expected by March. Once the market had digested the Fed's stance, it was only marginally less optimistic about the likelihood of lower rates.[8] But by stressing that policy will respond to economic developments, the Fed seemed at pains to quash any notion that it would ease policy to shore up financial markets.

If asset-market squalls do not merit a monetary response, worries about the wider impact of the housing slump in American economy may yet tip the balance. The downturn in the homebuilding industry has shaved nearly a percentage point off GDP growth in the past year, but the curtailment of new supply has not been enough to restore balance to the housing market.[9] The stock of lived-in houses for sale is already close to a 15-year high. The overhang of unsold homes is likely to grow, as more and more cheap introductory mortgages are reset to higher rates. Rising debt costs could force many overstretched homeowners to default and their lenders to foreclose.

Worryingly, the effects of the housing slump may be spreading. Consumer spending rose at an annualized rate of 1.3% in the second quarter, the smallest increase since the end of 2005. Car sales fell against in July and business surveys point to a recent softening of growth, particularly in services.

Weaker activity is starting to affect the job market too. The rise in the unemployment rate[10] to 4.6% last month was significant, says Jan Hatzius of Goldman Sachs[11], because it was entirely due to job losses, rather than an influx of jobseekers or a rise in the number leaving work voluntarily.

When demand stumbles, price pressures are likely to ease too. However, the recent bad news for America's economy might not be good news for inflation.

A lot depends on how revisions to GDP are judged. Late last month America's official statisticians cut their estimates of GDP growth by an average of 0.3 percentage points a year for the three years to 2006. These downgrades were incorporated this week into lower estimates for productivity growth and higher readings for unit labor costs, which rose by an alarming 4.5% in the year to the second quarter.

Downward revisions to GDP and productivity could imply that the economy's safe speed limit has dropped and that the short-term trade-off between output growth and inflation, already afflicted by high oil prices, had worsened.[12] Strong growth in unit wage costs against the backdrop of a tight-looking jobs market might limit the Fed's scope for rate cuts.[13]

Equally, however, the GDP revisions imply that there is less momentum behind the growth in demand. The downgrade was due mainly to lower growth in consumer spending. Stubbornly low unemployment, weak productivity growth and accelerating unit wage costs may simply be the results of firm's holding on to workers while demand is weak. David Rosenberg of Merrill Lynch[14] points out that there was a similar surge in unit wage costs at the end of 2000, on the eve of recession and big rate cuts.

If the Fed is inching closer to a neutral policy stance, other central banks are still looking to raise interest rates to temper growth and curb inflation. And some have even welcomed the markets' re-appraisal of risk. Jean-Claude Trichet, president of the European Central Bank[15] (ECB), said on August 2nd that strong vigilance was required to keep inflation in check. This was a signal that ECB is poised to increase its benchmark interest rate from 4% to 4.25% at its next meeting on September 6th. A few hours after the Fed meeting, Australia's central bank raised its key interest rate to 6.5%, the highest level for over a decade. The Bank of England's[16] quarterly Inflation Report, released on

August 8th, hinted that Britain's central bank may tighten the screw once more.[17] There is also a fair chance that the Bank of Japan will raise interest rates this month.

All of this is a reminder that the global economy is still strong. Indeed, America has the weakest year-on-year growth[18] rate of the 42 economies listed in the back pages of the Economist. Emerging-market economies are growing rapidly and in contrast to 1998, when the Fed was forced to cut rates by global market turmoil — are self-insured against the vagaries of market favor by current-account surpluses and huge foreign-exchange reserves. It is America that is most vulnerable to a drying-up of capital flows, which partly explains why the dollar is weak.

The Fed — quite rightly — is reluctant to signal rate cuts at the first sign of financial-market turbulence. An institution that has been criticized for not tightening sooner and faster during the housing boom will not want to encourage excessive risk-taking now.[19] Inflation is still the Fed's biggest worry, as it ought to be, although the concern about the housing downturn is increasing. The deepening economic gloom may well mean that it will eventually prove necessary to cut interest rates to arrest a sharper downturn. But for now, the right thing for Mr. Bernanke to do is to keep standing firm.[20]

(*Economist*, August 11, 2007)

New Words and Expressions

pushover	n.	<俚>容易打败的对手，容易做的事情
tenure	n.	（官职等的）保有，任期
benchmark	n.	基准
volatile	a.	可变的，不稳定的
albeit	conj.	虽然
downside	a.	底侧的，下降趋势的
shift	n.	移动，移位，变化
dash	v.	使破灭，使沮丧
digest	n.	消化，融会贯通
likelihood	v.	可能，可能性
marginally	ad.	在边上，边沿地
stance	n.	思维方式，立场，态度
quash	v.	取消，撤销，废除
notion	n.	概念，观念，想法
squall	n.	狂风吹袭，号啕，哇哇地叫嚷
merit	v.	应得，应受，值得
slump	n.	衰退，暴跌
shave	v.	剃，刮，削刮

curtailment	n.	缩减，缩短
overhang	n.	悬置，过剩，垂悬物
introductory	a.	初步的，开端的
mortgage	n.	抵押所借的款项，抵押
overstretch	v.	过度延伸，过度伸张
default	v.	缺席，拖欠
foreclose	v.	预先处理，取消抵押品赎回权
worryingly	ad.	焦虑地，烦恼地
annualized	a.	按年计算的
softening	n.	变安稳，减轻，减少
influx	n.	汇集，流动，流入
jobseeker	n.	求职者
stumble	v.	蹒跚，迟疑，踌躇
revision	n.	修订，修改，修正
statistician	n.	统计员，统计学家
downgrade	n.	下坡，退步
incorporate	v.	合并，具体表现
afflict	v.	使痛苦，使苦恼，折磨
trade-off	n.	比较评定，选择其一，交替换位
backdrop	n.	背景幕，(事件的) 背景
tight-looking	a.	看起来紧张的，收紧的
stubbornly	ad.	倔强地，顽固地
inch	v.	慢慢移动，慢慢前进
neutral	a.	中立的，中性的
temper	v.	(冶金) 回火、锻炼，调和，调节
re-appraisal	n.	重新估计，重新评价
vigilance	n.	警戒，警惕，警惕性
poised	a.	准备行动的，泰然自若的
year-on-year	a.	与上年同期数字相比的
turmoil	n.	骚动，混乱
self-insured	a.	自保的，自我保险的
vagary	n.	奇特行为，反复无常的行为
vulnerable	a.	易受攻击的，易受……的攻击
drying-up	n.	断流
gloom	n.	不利的局面，阴沉
be minded to		有意做（某事）
be on course for		向……航向不变

shore up	支持
tip the balance	失去平衡，打破平衡
lived-in houses	长时间有人居住的房屋
hold on to	坚持
keep ... in check	抑制，约束，制止，牵制
tighten the screw	拧紧螺丝，加强控制
be vulnerable to ...	易受……攻击的，易受……伤害的

Notes

1. Ben Bernanke 本·伯南克

   美国联邦储备委员会主席，1953 年出生于美国佐治亚州的奥古斯塔，1975 年获得哈佛大学经济学学士学位，1979 年获得麻省理工学院博士学位。在 2002 年被布什任命为美联储理事之前，伯南克主要从事学术工作，曾在普林斯顿大学工作 17 年，包括担任该校经济学系主任。2005 年 6 月，伯南克担任总统经济顾问委员会主席。伯南克学术成果丰硕，其中最有名的是他与合作者在一篇展望格林斯潘之后美联储政策的评论文章中，提出给通货膨胀设定目标的理论，即在一定时期内使通货膨胀率保持在特定的水平。

2. the Federal Reserve 美国联邦储备

   美国联邦储备负责履行美国中央银行的职责，这个系统是根据《联邦储备法》于 1913 年成立的，主要职责是制定并负责实施有关的货币政策、对银行机构实行监管、维持金融系统稳定和提供金融服务。这个系统主要由联邦储备委员会、联邦储备银行及联邦公开市场委员会等组成。联邦储备委员会（The Board of Governors of The Federal Reserve System）是联邦储备系统的核心机构，它是一个联邦政府机构，其办公地点位于美国华盛顿特区（Washington D. C.）。该委员会由 7 名成员组成（其中主席和副主席各一位，委员 5 名），须由美国总统提名，经美国国会上院与参议院批准方可上任，任期为 14 年（主席和副主席任期为 4 年，可连任）。联邦公开市场委员会（The Federal Open Market Committee，FOMC）是联邦储备系统中另一个重要的机构。它由 12 名成员组成，包括联邦储备委员会全部成员 7 名及纽约联邦储备银行行长，其他 4 个名额由另外 11 个联邦储备银行行长轮流担任。该委员会最主要的工作是利用公开市场操作（主要的货币政策之一），从一定程度上影响市场上货币的储量。另外，它还负责决定货币总量的增长范围（即新投入市场的货币数量），并对联邦储备银行在外汇市场上的活动进行指导。

3. benchmark interest rate 基准利率

   基准利率是在整个利率体系中起主导作用的基础利率。它的水平和变化决定其他各种利率的水平和变化。基准利率是金融市场上具有普遍参照作用的利率，其他利率水平或金融资产价格均可根据基准利率水平来确定。基准利率是利率市场化的重要前提之一。在利率市场化条件下，融资者衡量融资成本，投资者计算投资收益，以及管理层对宏观经济的调控，客观上都要求有一个普遍公认的基准利率水平作参考。所以，从某种意义上讲，基准利率是利率市场化机制形成的核心。市场经济国家一般以中央银行的再贴现率为基准利率；计划经济国家则由中央银行制定。在我国，中国人民银行对国家专业银行和其他金融机构规定的存贷款利率为基准利率。

4. The Fed acknowledged in a statement that financial markets had been volatile, that credit conditions had tightened (if only for "some" households and businesses) and that core inflation had "improved modestly".　美联储在一份声明中承认金融市场不太稳定，信贷吃紧（仅对"某些"家庭和公司而言），另外通货膨胀也得到了一定程度的控制。
   句中的3个"that"引导的从句并列作"acknowledged"的宾语。

5. But it stressed that America's economy was still on course for moderate growth, albeit with greater downside risks, and that inflation remains the main policy concern.　但也强调尽管存在经济下降的风险，美国经济仍然在朝着缓慢增长的方向前进，同时通货膨胀仍是政策主要关注的问题。
   句中的"albeit"引导让步状语。

6. Hopes of a bigger shift in tone, paving the way for a cut in interest rates later this year, were firmly dashed.　基调发生较大转变的希望彻底被粉碎，为年底降息铺路。

7. financial market　金融市场
   金融市场是经济生活中与商品市场、劳务市场和技术市场等并列的一种市场，它是进行资金融通的场所，在这里实现借贷资金的集中和分配，并由资金供给与资金需求的对比形成该市场的"价格"——利率。一般来说，现代金融市场有以下特点：交易主体及其关系的特殊性、交易方式的特殊性、交易场所的特殊性和交易工具的特殊性。金融市场的功能主要表现在资金筹集、宏观经济调节、信息反馈和产业结构优化等方面。

8. Once the market had digested the Fed's stance, it was only marginally less optimistic about the likelihood of lower rates.　一旦市场消化了美联储的政策，对市场低利率的趋势就比较乐观了。
   句中的"marginally"意为"少量地"，表示否定。

9. The downturn in the homebuilding industry has shaved nearly a percentage point off GDP growth in the past year, but the curtailment of new supply has not been enough to restore balance to the housing market.　房屋建筑行业的低迷导致去年GDP的增长下降了1个百分点，但新增供应的减少还不足以恢复房地产市场的平衡。
   句中的"shave...off"意为"削减，减少"。

10. unemployment rate　失业率
    失业率是指一定时期全部就业人口中有工作意愿而仍未有工作的劳动力数字。通过该指标可以判断一定时期内全部劳动人口的就业情况。一直以来，失业率数字被视为一个反映整体经济状况的指标，而它又是每个月最先发表的经济数据，所以外汇交易员与研究者们喜欢利用失业率指标来对工业生产、个人收入甚至新房屋兴建等其他相关的指标进行预测。在外汇交易的基本分析中，失业率指标被称为所有经济指标的"皇冠上的明珠"，它是市场上最为敏感的月度经济指标。

11. Goldman Sachs　美国高盛集团
    美国高盛集团是提供一体化服务的全球性投资银行，在投资、融资、收购兼并、股票债券研究等方面均处于世界领先地位。美国高盛集团创始于 1869 年，总部设于美国纽约，在伦敦、东京和香港分别设有地区总部，并在全球 19 个国家 41 个城市设有分公司或办事处，提供股票、债券、外汇和商品投资机会、融资、并购、房地产及其他咨询服务。

12. Downward revisions to GDP and productivity could imply that the economy's safe speed limit has dropped and that the short-term trade-off between output growth and inflation, already afflicted by high oil prices, had worsened. 国内生产总值和生产力向下修正意味着经济安全增长的速度限制下调，同时产值增长和通货膨胀之间的短期对冲，在受到居高不下的油价冲击之后，也进一步恶化了。

句中的两个"that"从句作"imply"的宾语。

13. Strong growth in unit wage costs against the backdrop of a tight-looking jobs market might limit the Fed's scope for rate cuts. 在就业市场看起来不太景气的情况下，单位工资成本的强劲增长可能会缩小美联储降息的空间。

14. Merrill Lynch 美国美林集团

美国美林集团是居于全球领导地位的财务管理及顾问公司之一，在 36 个国家与地区设有办事处，管理客户资产总值约 1.7 万亿美元。作为投资银行，它是全球领先的债券、股票承销商，以及世界各地公司企业、政府、机构组织和个人的策略顾问。公司属下的美林投资管理，是全球最大规模的金融资产管理人之一，管理资产约 5 240 亿美元。

15. European Central Bank 欧洲中央银行

有时也被简称为欧银，成立于 1998 年 6 月 1 日，是为了适应欧元发行流通而设立的金融机构，同时也是欧洲经济一体化的产物。其总部位于德国金融中心法兰克福。经济与货币联盟是欧共体建立的最终目标之一，从欧共体建立开始，成员国就在货币政策的事务上开展合作，当时有关欧共体的条约并没有将经济与货币联盟具体化，更无从进行授权，而央行行长委员会只是一个咨询性质的组织。管理委员会是欧洲中央银行的最高决策机构，负责制定欧元区的货币政策，并且就涉及货币政策的中介目标、指导利率及法定准备金等做出决策，同时确定其实施的行动指南。管理委员会由两部分人组成：一是欧洲中央银行执行委员会的 6 名成员，二是加入欧元区成员国的 12 名央行行长。

16. The Bank of England 英格兰银行

英格兰银行是英国的中央银行，是全世界最大、最繁忙的金融机构。它负责召开货币政策委员会，并对英国国家的货币政策负责。英格兰银行是世界上最早形成的中央银行，为各国中央银行体制的鼻祖。它现在隶属财政部，掌握着国库、贴现公司、银行及其余的私人客户的账户，承担政府债务的管理工作，其主要任务仍然是按政府要求决定国家金融政策。英格兰银行总行设于伦敦，职能机构分政策和市场、金融结构和监督、业务和服务三个部分。英格兰银行的领导机构是理事会，由总裁、副总裁及 16 名理事组成，是最高决策机构，成员由政府推荐，英王任命，至少每周开会一次。

17. The Bank of England's quarterly Inflation Report, released on August 8th, hinted that Britain's central bank may tighten the screw once more. 英格兰银行 8 月 8 日发布的季度通货膨胀报告暗示英国央行可能会再次采取紧缩政策。

句中的"tight the screw"本意为"收紧，上紧螺栓"，此处是比喻用法，指"采取紧缩政策，收缩银根"。

18. year-on-year growth 同比增长（逐年增长）

同比增长是指"与上年同期数字相比的"。

19. An institution that has been criticized for not tightening sooner and faster during the housing boom will not want to encourage excessive risk-taking now. 在房产泡沫时期被指责没有尽早尽快采取紧缩政策的机构现在不想过多地冒险了。

句中的"that has been criticized for not tightening sooner and faster during the housing boom"作定语，修饰"institution"；"an institution"是泛指。

20. But for now, the right thing for Mr. Bernanke to do is to keep standing firm. 但现在，伯南克要做的事情是站稳立场。

句中的"keep standing firm"意为"站稳立场"。

阅读小知识（2）

1. 道-琼斯平均指数（Dow-Jones Averages）

道-琼斯平均指数是美国用来反映股票市场行情变化的一种股票价格平均指数。它是美国历史最悠久的股票价格指数，取名于该公司的两位创始人查尔斯·道和爱德华·琼斯。

他们于1884年开始编制和公布股票价格平均指数以显示股票价格变动的基本趋势，由此诞生了道-琼斯指数。1896年5月26日，道-琼斯平均指数正式诞生。

1999年10月26日道-琼斯公司宣布从11月1日起更换4种成分股，以便该指数更能反映近20年来美国经济中技术成分的增加。该指数包括4组指数：30种工业股票平均指数，20种运输业股票平均指数，15种公用事业平均指数，65种以上股票的综合平均指数。

2. 纳斯达克（NASDAQ）

纳斯达克的全名为全国证券交易商协会自动报价系统，1971年才问世。它通过计算机网络将全国证券经纪商组织在一起，及时准确地向其提供场外交易行情。它最初专门让投资者交易一些资本额很小的新创企业股票，但经过短短20多年的发展，上市公司数目、上市的外国公司数目、月交易额都已超过纽约证券交易所。纳斯达克综合指数包括4 600多种股票，主要由美国的数百家发展最快的先进技术、电信和生物公司组成，包括微软、英特尔、美国在线、雅虎这些家喻户晓的高科技公司，因而成为美国"新经济"的代名词。

3. 纽约证券交易所（New York Stock Exchange, NYSE）

纽约证券交易所曾经是美国和世界上最大的证券交易市场。1792年5月17日，二十四个从事股票交易的经纪人在华尔街一棵树下集会，宣告了纽约股票交易所的诞生。1863年改为现名。自20世纪20年代起，它一直是国际金融中心，这里股票行市的暴涨与暴跌都会在其他资本主义国家的股票市场产生连锁反应,引起波动。现在它还是纽约市最受欢迎的旅游名胜之一。

纽约证券交易所目前是世界上第二大证券交易所。它曾是最大的交易所,直到1996年它的交易量被纳斯达克超过。

4. 欧元(Euro)

欧元源于1989年提出的道尔斯计划。1991年12月11日,马斯特里赫特条约启动欧元机制以来,到1999年初,大多数欧盟国家都把它们的货币以固定的兑换比例同欧元联结起来。根据马斯特里赫特条约,欧洲单一货币叫做"ECU"。1995年12月,欧洲委员会决定将欧洲单一货币改名为欧元"Euro"。2002年1月1日起,所有收入、支出,包括工薪收入、税收等都要以欧元计算。2002年3月1日,欧元正式流通后,欧洲货币的旧名称消失。欧元纸币由各参与国中央银行责成的欧洲中央银行负责发行,欧元硬币由各个参与国政府负责发行,但不同发行机构之间保持互相协调。欧盟政治家推动欧元的潜在意图就是要结束"美元的专制统治"。

1996年12月,设在德国法兰克福的欧洲货币局宣布1999年欧盟统一货币——欧元设计图案是经公开征选而评出的,奥地利纸币设计家罗伯特·卡利纳的方案中标。在该方案中,欧元共分7种面值,即5、10、20、50、100、200和500欧元,面值越大,纸币面积越大。

目前欧元区总共包括19个国家,它们分别是:奥地利、比利时、德国、希腊、法国、芬兰、爱尔兰、意大利、卢森堡、荷兰、葡萄牙、西班牙、斯洛文尼亚、塞浦路斯、马耳他、斯洛伐克、爱沙尼亚、拉脱维亚、立陶宛。

5. 期权(Option)

期权是指在未来一定时期可以买卖的权力,是买方向卖方支付一定数量的金额(指权利金)后拥有的在未来一段时间内(指美式期权)或未来某一特定日期(指欧式期权)以事先规定好的价格(指履约价格)向卖方购买或出售一定数量的特定标的物的权力,但不负有必须买进或卖出的义务。期权交易事实上是这种权利的交易。买方有执行的权利,也有不执行的权利,完全可以灵活选择。期权分场外期权和场内期权。场外期权交易一般由交易双方共同达成。

因此,拥有期权者也被认为是合约持有者。他有权利却无责任在指定时间或之前按指定价格向卖方买入或卖出合约订下的资产。故期权便是该资产衍生出来的产品,而此合约正是赋予期权买方一个"有期限"的权利去选择是否买卖相关资产。合约持有者是否行使其权利,视市场情况及相关资产的价格是否有利而定。

当持有者一旦行使期权后,期权沽出者则必须履行合约,以原来指定的价格买卖相关资产,承受于不利价格下买卖该资产的损失。既然期权买方拥有这么有利的条件,而相反卖方则处于被动及不利的位置,此买卖合约必不易成立。故此,买方须付出代价以换取无责任的选择权,而卖方则乐意地负起责任而收取金钱利益——亦即"期权金"。

期权可按其行使方式大致分为两类:美式期权和欧式期权。美式期权从买入之日起至到期日止的任何时间里都可被行使,而欧式期权则只能于到期日行使,所以美式期权在行使时间上具有较大的灵活性。

6. 国际清算银行（Bank for International Settlement, BIS）

国际清算银行是根据1930年1月20日签订的海牙国际协定，于同年5月由英国、意大利、法国、德国、比利时、日本等国的中央银行，以及代表美国银行界利益的3大银行（摩根银行、纽约花旗银行、芝加哥花旗银行）组成的银行团联合组成，后来其他国家的中央银行也加入了该行。其行址在瑞士的巴塞尔。

该银行成立之初是为了向第一次世界大战的战败国德国索取赔款，解决对德清算事宜。1944年后成为国际货币基金组织和世界银行的附属机构。

现在该银行是西欧多边清算制度的收付代理人，并接受各国中央银行的存款，代为买卖黄金、外汇，发行债券，办理国际性政府借款；促进中央银行之间的合作，为国际支付提供方便。

7. 艾伦·格林斯潘（Alan Greenspan）

艾伦·格林斯潘，1926年3月6日生于美国纽约，于1948年以优异成绩毕业于纽约大学并获得经济学学士学位，1950年获得经济学硕士学位，随后进入哥伦比亚大学继续深造，中途辍学，1977年获得经济学博士学位。

1954年到1974年和1977年到1987年，格林斯潘在他与威廉·汤森合作经营的汤森－格林斯潘经济咨询公司里担任副总裁、董事长、总裁。在1987年8月就任美联储主席后，格林斯潘关闭了这家设在纽约的公司。

1970年到1974年，格林斯潘担任总统经济顾问委员会成员，1974年到1977年担任该委员会主席。1981年到1983年，他担任全国社会保险改革委员会主席。1982年任总统国外情报顾问委员会成员。

此外，格林斯潘曾担任过财经结构与规则委员会委员、财政部顾问兼联邦储备委员会顾问、商务部经济顾问委员会成员、国会预算局顾问、总统国外情报顾问委员会成员等。他还曾担任过通用电缆等多家公司的董事。

1987年8月他被里根总统任命为联邦储备委员会主席。其后，他多次被任命为该委员会的主席，直至2006年1月31日卸任为止。格林斯潘担任美联储主席一职达18年5个月20天，任期之长仅次于在1951年至1970年担任这一职务的威廉·迈克切斯内·马丁。在格林斯潘担任美联储主席的18年多时间里，美国经济出现了创纪录的长达10年的持续增长期，中间只发生过两次温和的衰退。格林斯潘领导美联储应对了纽约股市大崩盘、亚洲金融危机、技术股泡沫破灭及"9·11"恐怖袭击事件等一系列重大危机。

1998年7月，格林斯潘因对美国经济发展做出的贡献被授予"和平缔造者"奖。2002年8月，英国女王授予格林斯潘"爵士"荣誉称号，以表彰他"对全球经济稳定所做出的杰出贡献"。2005年11月10日，格林斯潘被授予"总统自由勋章"

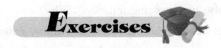

Exercises

I. Discuss and answer the following questions.

1. What happened to the American economy in 2007?
2. How does the housing slump in America affect consumer spending and job market?
3. What has caused the Fed not to make a cut in interest rates later this year? Do you think there is any justification in such a move?
4. Why do some major banks in the developed nations plan to raise their benchmark interest rate or interest rate while the Fed is reluctant to signal rate cuts at the first sign of financial market turbulence?
5. Is it expected that the Fed will raise its interest rate as the economic gloom is deepening in America?

II. Decide whether the following statements are true (T) or false (F)

1. In America, inflation is a big problem, which has put the US economy to halt. (   )
2. The Fed seems not to cut the interest rate to shore up financial market later this year, and this stance would sooner or later be understood and accepted by the market. (   )
3. The downturn in the house-building industry cut almost one percentage point off GDP growth in the past year, and such a downturn trend will continue, and may intensify the impact of the housing slump. (   )
4. The housing slump may contribute to a rise in consumer spending and affect the job market. (   )
5. According to the author, as American economic growth is slowing and the short-term balance between output growth and inflation is now lost, the labor cost will be greatly reduced. (   )
6. The author implies that with lower growth in consumer spending and lower employment rate, the market in the US will possibly be gripped by recession in the near future. (   )
7. The author thinks that it is an effective instrument to keep inflation in check by raising interest rates. (   )
8. As the US economy is experiencing a sluggish growth, many other developed nations in Europe as well as the nation of Australia are trying to temper growth and curb inflation. (   )
9. Many emerging-market economies are very prudent about and also vulnerable to financial risks. (   )
10. The author implies that although the Fed sticks to its firm stand of not cutting the interest rate for the time being, it will consider cutting the rate in the future if such a downturn trend persists in the US. (   )

III Group discussion.

1. Do you think China is also experiencing inflation? Why?
2. What are the effective recipes for curbing inflation within a nation?
3. Do you think raising interest rate is a good solution to overheated economy? What else can you suggest to check the inflation, if you think there is any?
4. Some economists argue that recessions are a process of creative destruction in which inefficient firms are weeded out and only by doing so, can capital be released from dying firms to new industries and can it leave the economy in a healthier state. Do you agree to this notion?

Case Study
Could Asian shares provide a safe haven for global investors?

It often seems that everything is made in China, but certainly not the latest turmoil in financial markets. Over the past four weeks, as world share prices have plunged, Chinese A-shares have leapt by over 20%. And as central banks elsewhere worry about a credit crunch, China's central bank this week raised interest rates for the fourth time this year.

Foreigners cannot buy A-shares, which means they cannot dump them either. The rest of Asia is less snugly insulated. Last week its markets suffered their biggest weekly fall for 17 years, and they remain 12% below their peak. Big financial losses in mortgage-linked securities have forced global investors to pull money out of emerging markets to raise cash and reduce the "risk" in their portfolios.

But the notion that all emerging market shares are risky is looking our of date. Based on fundamentals, Asian shares are now arguably less risky than many American ones. Although Asian financial firms have suffered some losses from securities linked to American subprime mortgages, their direct exposure is thought to be relatively small.

Moreover, Asian share prices look good value compared with those elsewhere. Despite a surge over the past few years, most markets are still below their mid-1990s peaks in dollar terms, including the Chinese shares that foreigners can buy. Yet profits have soared since then. One legacy of the 1997–1998 Asian crisis is that firms now focus on making money rather than maximizing market share or assets...

Most Asian economies are also much less vulnerable to capital outflows than they used to be, enjoying a current-account surplus and a large hoard of currency reserves. Foreign investors need worry less about an exchange-rate loss than in the past as many currencies are if anything undervalued. Asia also shows few signs of excess. Bank lending is growing much more slowly than a decade ago, and Asia is one of few parts of the world not experiencing a housing bubble. A recent study by the IMF finds that in most Asian countries house prices have kept pace with income since 1999.

The glaring exception to all of this is India, which unlike the rest of Asia has a housing bubble, a borrowing binge and a current-account deficit. By most measures, Indian shares also look pricier relative to their historical trend than anywhere else in Asia.

(Adapted from *Economist*, August 25, 2007)

Supplementary Reading

Credit Squeeze and Criticisms Deepen Crisis

Chris Giles

Rodrigo Rato bowed out as managing director of the International Monetary Fund at the weekend amid public plaudits, but some private criticism of his role and the fund's relevance to the global economy.

After the global credit squeeze that has stalked advanced economies since the summer the mood among central bankers and finance ministers was one of hope mixed with fear: hope that the world economy was sufficiently resilient to emerge with only a few scratches, and the twin fear that big problems still existed in the financial sector at the same time as the global outlook was highly uncertain.

The weekend's meetings certainly served their purpose in providing a forum for central bankers and finance ministers but little of substance emerged.

After Friday's meeting of the Group of Seven rich countries, finance ministers agreed on a tougher statement on currencies, stressing the need for China to allow an accelerated appreciation of its effective exchange rate. They also continued the now ritual statements on their own currencies, with the US repeating its mantra of a strong dollar policy; the continental Europeans (except the Germans) suggesting markets took note of these words; and the US pouring cold water on the significance of its words by later insisting markets should determine currency levels.

One G7 insider said that, for all the noise afterwards, currencies had not actually been discussed at all.

At Saturday's IMF meeting, the communiqué made it clear that despite the turmoil in markets, the participants could agree only to repeat previous statements that the risks to the world outlook were a shared responsibility requiring increased saving in the US, reform in Europe and Japan, boosts to domestic demand in Asia, and more currency flexibility.

Many of the fund's most powerful members were angry that the IMF was so feeble just at the time it should be centre stage. The global credit squeeze was, after all, truly transnational, having its roots in the US subprime mortgage sector, but its consequences spreading worldwide.

The fear, privately expressed by central bankers, is that the credit squeeze is the first of many disorderly episodes that will result from the huge global trade imbalances that emerged over the past decade. These have kept interest rates artificially low worldwide and encouraged reckless lending.

Many international officials believe that the IMF remains in serious trouble.

Bank of Canada Governor's Parting Shot

The failure of the IMF to agree reform increased the risk of a "huge" global economic "crisis" brought about by the disorderly unwinding of global economic imbalances, says David Dodge.

It is in the middle of a dispute with China over its new policies on scrutinizing member countries' economies and exchange rates. And after the Europeans stitched up the new managing director's job and the chair of its most powerful committee, its reform efforts have stalled.

This leaves its legitimacy in emerging markets at a new low, without the ability to devise co-ordinated solutions and hold member countries to their commitments.

"We're disappointed that we haven't moved forward more quickly," Robert McCormick, US undersecretary to the Treasury, said. The US, however, strongly supports the IMF's new surveillance policy brought in by Mr. Rato.

David Dodge, the outgoing Canadian central bank governor, was able to say publicly what others said behind the scenes. "This is precisely the time we need the fund's ability and skills to deal with global imbalances."

He added that the breakdown in reform efforts had decreased the "chance of coming to a common view across the fund's membership" on currency policy.

"The longer the imbalances go on, the greater risk that we will end with a rather messy denouement."

Instead of dealing with the big issue for the global economy — how to deal with frictions and trade imbalances that arise from many big countries operating market-based exchange rates while others have pegged rates — sideshows were the order of the weekend.

The G7 and IMF agreed to study best practice for sovereign wealth funds in terms of transparency and accountability but, as Ted Truman of the Peterson Institute of International Economics said, it was "stupid" for anyone to believe the IMF or any rich country finance minister could tell countries with huge surplus reserves and a sovereign wealth fund how it should operate.

By contrast, the World Bank appeared to be regaining its footing under the new leadership of Robert Zoellick.

All these troubles leave Dominique Strauss-Kahn, the next IMF managing director, who takes office at the beginning of November, with a huge challenge to make it relevant.

Whether blame lies within the fund or member governments is a difficult question. These annual meetings were its moment to be in the spotlight — and it was found not up to the job.

(*Financial Times*, October 21, 2007)

Unit 3 Finance and Investment

Answer and discuss the following questions:

1. What did many central bankers and financial ministers fear about the world economic situation at the IMF meeting?
2. According to the communiqué released by IMF meeting, what did participants agree to do with the risks to the world outlook?
3. What differing opinions did Fund's members and central bankers hold towards the economic situation?
4. What were the biggest challenges that faced the IMF in dealing with the world economic problem?

Unit 4

Corporate Development and Strategies

企业发展与战略

How Microsoft Conquered China

Or is it the other way around? Fortune's[1] David Kirkpatrick goes on the road to Beijing with Bill Gates[2], who threw his business model out the window.[3]

David Kirkpatrick

Mr. Bill Gates! Mr. Bill Gates! a young woman shrieks as the black car pulls up. A pallid student in a nylon windbreaker pushes his way through the security line and hands the world's richest man a small envelope with a floral design. "It's very important," he pants.

Another day in China, another round of talks. Today the Microsoft[4] (Fortune 500[5]) chairman is being named an honorary trustee of Peking University. Yesterday it was an honorary doctorate from Beijing's Tsinghua University — the 13th in the school's 82-year history. Gates, wearing the same lopsided grin he has had on his face for the past few days, takes the envelope from the young man. For him this is a triumphant visit to China, a victory lap of sorts, on which I've been invited to tag along.[6] The country is his.

No other Fortune 500 CEO gets quite the same treatment in China. While most would count themselves lucky to talk with one of China's top leaders, Gates will meet with four members of the Politburo on this four-day April trip. As one government leader put it while introducing Gates at a business conference, the Microsoft chairman is "bigger in China than any movie star." Last spring President Hu Jintao toured the Microsoft campus in Redmond[7], Wash., and was feted at a dinner at

Gates' home. "You are a friend to the Chinese people, and I am a friend of Microsoft," Hu told his host. "Every morning I go to my office and use your software."

It was not always so. Microsoft bumbled for years after entering China in 1992, and its business was a disaster there for a decade. It finally figured out that almost none of the basic precepts that led to its success in the US and Europe made sense in China. There Microsoft had to become the un-Microsoft — pricing at rock bottom instead of charging hundreds of dollars for its Windows operating system and Office applications; abandoning the centerpiece of its public-policy approach elsewhere, the protection of its intellectual property at all costs; and closely partnering with the government instead of fighting it as in the US, a stance that has opened the company to criticism from human rights groups.

"It took Microsoft 15 years and billions of dollars of lost revenue to learn how to do business in China," says Sigurd Leung, who follows the company at research firm Analysys International in Beijing.[8] "We were a naive American company," concedes Gates in an interview in his car as he is driven to yet another meeting with government leaders. "You've got to just keep trying and trying and trying." But now, he says, snacking on Pringles[9] and Diet Coke[10], "we have a wonderful position in China, and we're going to see great growth every year for the next five years."

Gates says he's certain China will eventually be Microsoft's biggest market, though it may take ten years. Projected sales this year are already three times what they were in 2004, yet still less than annual revenue in California. (Microsoft will not disclose figures, but Fortune estimates China revenue will exceed $700 million in 2007, about 1.5% of global sales.) Now Microsoft even has its own five-year plan in China, formulated to match up with the government's. Says Robert Hormats, a longtime China watcher at Goldman Sachs: "It's a great turnaround story with wonderful lessons for other companies."

False start

The story begins 15 years ago, when Microsoft sent a couple of sales managers into Chinese mainland from Taiwan. Their mission? Sell software at the same prices the company charged elsewhere. Says Craig Mundie, the top Microsoft executive who now guides its China strategy: "It was the classic model — hang out a shingle and say, 'Microsoft: Open for business.'" But the model didn't work.

The problem wasn't brand acceptance; everyone was using Windows. It's just that no one was paying. Counterfeit copies could be bought on the street for a few dollars. As Ya-Qin Zhang, who heads Microsoft's Chinese R&D, puts it: "In China we didn't have problems with market share. The issue is how we translate that into revenue."

Microsoft fought bitterly to protect its intellectual property. It sued companies for using its software illegally but lost regularly in court. Its executives, who often disagreed with the strategy, failed in its implementation. Country managers came and went — five in one five-year period. Two of them later wrote books criticizing the company. One, Juliet Wu, whose "Up Against the Wind[11]" became a local bestseller, wrote that Microsoft heartlessly sought sales by any means, that its anti-piracy policy was needlessly heavy-handed, and that her own efforts to help bosses in Redmond understand China had been rebuffed.

Then a different form of resistance emerged. Beijing's city government started installing free open-source Linux operating systems on workers' PCs. (The Chinese Academy of Sciences[12] promoted a version called Red Flag Linux[13].) Meanwhile security officials were troubled that government and military operations depended on Microsoft software made in the US. Could the technology be spying on China?

In 1999, Gates sent Mundie, who heads the company's public-policy efforts, to figure out why Microsoft was so reviled. On the trip he had an epiphany: "I remember going back to Redmond and saying, 'Our business is just broken in China,'" Mundie recalls. He concluded that the company was assigning executives too junior and that selling per se was overemphasized. "But where we were most broken," he says, "was that our business practices and our engagement did not reflect the importance of having a collaborative approach with the government."

Mundie started visiting China four or five times a year. He brought 25 of the company's 100 vice presidents for a week-long "China Immersion Tour." He hired former Secretary of State Henry Kissinger[14] to advise him and open doors. And he told leaders that Microsoft wanted to help China develop its own software industry, an urgent government priority. The company even commissioned a McKinsey[15] study for Chinese officials in 2001 that, among other things, recommended improving the protection of intellectual property.[16]

Mundie also began talks with Chinese security officials to convince them that Microsoft's software was not a secret tool of the US government. As a result, in 2003 the company offered China and 59 other countries the right to look at the fundamental source code for its Windows operating system and to substitute certain portions with their own software — something Microsoft had never allowed in the past.[17] Now when China uses Windows in President Hu's office or for that matter in its missile systems, it can install its own cryptography.

But it was a relatively small step in 1998 — the opening of a research center in Beijing — that proved a turning point. "We just started it here because we thought they'd do great research," says Gates, who raves about the quality of the country's computer scientists. The lab was what Gates calls a "windfall" for Microsoft's image. It began accumulating an impressive record of academic publications, helped lure back smart émigré scientists, and contributed key components to globally released products like the Vista operating system[18]. The lab soon became, according to polls, the most desirable place in the country for computer scientists to work.

By 2001, Microsoft executives were coming to the conclusion that China's weak IP-enforcement laws meant its usual pricing strategies were doomed to fail. Gates argued at the time that while it was terrible that people in China pirated so much software, if they were going to pirate anybody's software he'd certainly prefer it be Microsoft's.

Today Gates openly concedes that tolerating piracy turned out to be Microsoft's best long-term strategy. That's why Windows is used on an estimated 90% of China's 120 million PCs. "It's easier for our software to compete with Linux when there's piracy than when there's not," Gates says. "Are you kidding? You can get the real thing, and you get the same price." Indeed, in China's back alleys, Linux often costs more than Windows because it requires more disks. And Microsoft's own prices have dropped so low it now sells a $3 package of Windows and Office to students.

Gates in China

In 2003, Mundie and Gates took a quantum leap forward in China by hiring Tim Chen, who had been running Motorola's[19] China subsidiary. Chen was a superstar, but when he was hired, articles in the Chinese press asked if he, too, would fall victim to the Microsoft "curse."[20]

Chen arrived with entrée to the corridors of power and a practiced understanding of how a Western company could succeed in China. He kept up the blitz of initiatives. Microsoft made Shanghai a global center to respond to customer e-mails. It began extensive training programs for teachers and software entrepreneurs. It worked with the Ministry of Education to finance 100 model computer classrooms in rural areas. "So with all this work," says Chen, "we start changing the perception that Microsoft is the company coming just to do anti-piracy and sue people. We changed the company's image. We're the company that has the long-term vision. If a foreign company's strategy matches with the government's development agenda, the government will support you, even if they don't like you."

Microsoft put its money on the line, even inviting officials to help decide in which local software and outsourcing companies it should invest. So far Microsoft has spent $65 million, and it recently committed to an additional $100 million. Says Chen: "There was synergy, which we formalized, between the need of the Chinese economy to have local software capability and our need for an ecosystem of companies around us using our technology and platform.[21]"

At the same time, the Chinese government started thinking more like Microsoft: It required central, provincial, and local governments to begin using legal software. The city of Beijing completed its portion of the project late last year and now pays for software its employees — most of whom never adopted Linux — had previously pirated. (Microsoft won't say how steep a discount it offered the government.)

In another boost for Microsoft, the government last year required local PC manufacturers to load legal software on their computers. Lenovo, the market leader, had been shipping as few as 10% of its PCs that way, and even US PC makers in China were selling many machines "naked."[22] Another mandate requires gradual legalization of the millions of computers in state-owned enterprises. In all, Gates says, the number of new machines shipped with legal software nationwide has risen from about 20% to more than 40% in the past 18 months.

Win-win?

So did Microsoft conquer China, or is it the other way around? Toward the end of Gates' trip, on the sidelines of China's Boao Forum[23], I sat down again with the Microsoft founder. One of the things I wanted to ask him was how he squares the company's "alignment" in China with its leaders' suppression of free speech on the Internet.[24] Our conversation, which had been flowing freely, ground to a halt. He said nothing. His silence lasted so long I found myself piping up out of discomfort. "That's a very pregnant pause," I said. "I don't think I want to give an answer to that," he finally replied.

Mundie, however, gamely ventured an answer in a separate interview. He started by talking about the challenges of transforming a socialist planned economy into one based on the market, and noted that never before have leaders anywhere attempted such a huge transition. "Whether it's running a global company or a government," he says, "people have to sit there and make their own value judgments against what they deem to be the greater good all the time.[25] I personally have found the Chinese leaders to be fairly thoughtful about these things. Each society makes choices to protect the rest of society. There are some aspects of that that happen here and in other countries that people would prefer didn't happen. But in the grand scheme of things, they're what people think is required to keep stability.[26]" When I asked him if he had discussed any of this with China's leaders, he answered, "No. It's not what they consider to be my field of expertise. Nor do I."

Many multinational companies would love to be in Microsoft's shoes. Says Carl Bass, CEO of Autodesk[27], the $2-billion-a-year design-automation company: "To do business in China you have to work closely with government." Sean Maloney, who heads marketing at Intel[28] (Fortune 500), agrees: "You can't do too many investments in China that the government doesn't approve of. You might as well ask them."

Microsoft's China strategy is clearly paying off. More than 24 million PCs will be sold this year, adding to the 120 million already in place. Although the company's China revenues average no more than $7 for every PC in use (compared with $100 to $200 in developed countries), Gates says those figures will eventually converge. "What we have here is not about me, and it's not about where President Hu went to dinner or anything like that," he says. "It's an institution-to-institution relationship, where we've really found a win-win way of doing things together that will generate a substantial part of Microsoft's growth in the next decade. I don't know any company in the IT industry where things have worked out as well as they have for Microsoft.[29]" And not badly for China either.

(*Fortune*, July 23, 2007)

New Words and Expressions

shriek	v.	尖叫,尖声喊叫
pallid	a.	苍白的,暗淡的
nylon	n.	尼龙
windbreaker	n.	防风上衣
floral	a.	植物群的,花似的,花的
pant	v.	喘着气说,气喘
honorary	a.	荣誉的,名誉的

Unit 4 Corporate Development and Strategies

trustee	n.	理事或董事，托管理事或董事
doctorate	n.	博士头衔
lopsided	a.	倾向一方的，不平衡的
triumphant	a.	胜利的，成功的
Politburo	n.	政治局
fete	v.	宴请，招待，给予……巨大的荣誉
bumble	v.	拙劣地做，弄糟
centerpiece	n.	中心装饰品，位于中心的东西
concede	v.	勉强，承认，退让
projected	a.	预计中的
formulate	v.	规划，设计
watcher	n.	观察者，注视者
turnaround	n.	转变，转向，（经济、营业等的）突然好转
shingle	n.	小招牌
counterfeit	a.	伪造的，假冒的
bitterly	ad.	苦苦地，悲痛地
anti-piracy	n.	反盗版
heavy-handed	a.	重击的，出手重的
rebuff	v.	回绝
revile	v.	辱骂，斥责
epiphany	n.	（对事物真意的）领悟
collaborative	a.	合作的，协作的
immersion	n.	沉浸，专心，热衷
commission	v.	任命，委托，委托制作
cryptography	n.	密码使用法，密码系统
rave	v.	叫嚷，发狂地说
windfall	n.	被风吹落的果子（尤指苹果），横财
lure	v.	引诱
émigré	n.	流亡者，出走的人
poll	n.	民意测验，调查
enforcement	n.	执行，强制
alley	n.	胡同，通道
subsidiary	n.	子公司
superstar	n.	超级明星
entrée	n.	入场许可，进入
corridor	n.	走廊
blitz	n.	闪电攻势，闪电战
perception	n.	理解，感知，感觉

outsourcing	n.	外部采办，外购
synergy	n.	协作，企业合并后的协力优势
formalize	v.	使具有形式，使定形
ecosystem	n.	生态系统
platform	n.	平台
steep	a.	陡峭的，急剧升降的
sideline	n.	界外区域，侧道
square	v.	使与……一致，符合
alignment	n.	调准，定线，合作，结盟
pregnant	a.	重要的，富有意义的
gamely	ad.	游戏般地
venture	v.	冒昧，斗胆去……
converge	v.	聚合，集中于一点

figure out		解决，断定，领会到
snack on		以……为快餐
projected sales		预计销售额
match up with		调整与……相一致，符合
intellectual property		知识产权
source code		源代码
be doomed to		注定（失败的、毁灭的、死亡的）
corridors of power		势力走廊，政府机构外围势力圈
outsourcing companies		外包公司
pipe up		开始吹奏，跟……的调子

Notes

1. **Fortune** 《财富》
   《财富》杂志由美国人亨利·鲁斯于1930年创办，主要刊登经济问题研究文章。现隶属美国时代华纳集团，《财富》杂志自1954年推出"全球500强排行榜"，是"全球500强排行榜"评估体系的建立者。该体系是世界知名企业用来判断自身实力、规模和国际竞争力的重要指标，影响巨大。《财富》杂志举办了一系列引人注目的财经论坛，如著名的《财富》全球论坛，即世界500强年会便是其中之一。《财富》全球论坛开始于1995年，其中1999年、2001年和2005年年会分别在中国的上海、香港和北京举办。

2. **Bill Gates** 比尔·盖茨
   1955年出生，是全球个人计算机软件的领先供应商——微软公司的创始人、前任董事长和首席执行官。盖茨曾就读于西雅图的公立小学和私立湖滨中学。在那里，他开始了自己个人计算机软件的职业生涯，13 岁开始编写计算机程序。1973 年进入哈佛大学，在哈佛期间，盖茨为第一台微型计算机——MITSAltair 开发了 BASIC 编程语言。三年级时从哈佛退学，全身心投入其与童年伙伴 Paul Allen 一起于 1975 年组建的微软公司。盖茨有关个人计算机的远见和洞察力一直是微软公司和软件业界成功的关键。

3. Fortune's David Kirkpatrick goes on the road to Beijing with Bill Gates, who threw his business model out the window. 《财富》杂志的大卫·凯帕瑞克陪同比尔·盖茨一同前往北京，在中国市场上比尔·盖茨放弃了他原来的商业模式。

   句中的"out the window"是习惯用语，意为"突然失去，浪费了某样东西"。

4. Microsoft （美国）微软公司

   微软公司创建于 1975 年，总部设在华盛顿州的雷德蒙德市，是全球最大的计算机软件提供商。作为全球最大的软件公司，微软公司一直是新技术变革的领导者。微软公司为各种计算机安装设备驱动程序，提供一系列软件产品的开发、制造、授权和支持。微软公司的 7 类主要产品是：客户端、服务器平台、信息工具、商业解决方案、MSN、移动应用系统及嵌入式设备和家庭消费及娱乐。

5. Fortune 500　财富 500 强

   这是国人对美国《财富》杂志每年评选的"全球最大五百家公司"排行榜的一种约定俗成的叫法，其评选的唯一依据是年营业收入。《财富》杂志还评选"美国最大五百家公司"（也称为"财富五百强"）、美国和全球最受赞赏的公司、美国青年富豪排行榜、全球商界最具权势 25 位企业家等一系列排名。

6. For him this is a triumphant visit to China, a victory lap of sorts, on which I've been invited to tag along. 这次中国之行，我全程陪同，对他来说，这次行程是成功的。

   句中的"on which"引导非限制型定语从句，修饰"visit to China"; "of sorts"意为"某种"。

7. Redmond　（美国）雷德蒙德市

   美国城市，隶属华盛顿州，濒临太平洋，人口约 5.7 万，是微软公司总部所在地。

8. ... who follows the company at research firm Analysys International in Beijing.

   这部分是定语从句，修饰前面的"Sigurd Leung"，意为"就职于北京易观国际，一直对微软公司进行跟踪研究"。句中的"Analysys International"指易观国际，它是中国领先的咨询集团企业之一，易观国际所属易观咨询、易观研究、易观顾问、易观数据为客户提供咨询、研究、顾问和数据服务解决方案。易观国际在加拿大及我国的香港、北京和上海均设有分支机构。

9. Pringles　"品客"薯片

   "品客"薯片隶属宝洁公司。1970 年，宝洁公司"品客"薯片在美国诞生，是宝洁公司最独特的产品之一，可口的味道、松脆的口感和弧形片装三大独特之处帮助"品客"薯片从美国起步，在短短三十年间风靡全球。在美国，"品客"薯片是最受欢迎的休闲食品之一。

10. Diet Coke　健怡可口可乐

    健怡可口可乐隶属可口可乐公司（Coca-Cola Company）。可口可乐公司是举世闻名的汽水大王，它在全球各地有 500 余种产品销售，其中可口可乐、健怡可口可乐、雪碧、芬

93

达四大品牌在全球最畅销汽水前 5 位中独占 4 位。

11. Up Against the Wind 《逆风飞飏》
作者吴士宏，讲述一个从"生而自卑"到"个性飞扬"的传奇色彩故事，具有自传体性质。尤其是她在微软的经历，从辞职的理由到微软的市场功夫、人治方式、管理秘诀，以及微软的灵魂和掌舵人——她所知道的盖茨和总裁鲍尔等均描写得精彩独到。作者从 IBM 从一个蓝领勤务到 IBM "南天王"，又到中国渠道总经理的升迁之路，告诉读者杰出管理者的历练过程。

12. The Chinese Academy of Sciences 中国科学院
中国科学院于 1949 年 11 月在北京成立，是国家科学技术方面的最高学术机构和全国自然科学与高新技术综合研究发展中心。

13. Red Flag Linux 红旗 Linux 操作系统
属于 Linux 系统，比起 Windows，用户可以对电脑有更多的控制，但需要学会一些命令，该系统是基于 UNIX 的基础开发出来的，其源代码全球公开。另外，与 Windows 相比，该系统在浏览网页的时候安全性更高些。

14. Henry Kissinger 亨利·基辛格
德国出生的犹太人，1973 年至 1977 年任美国国务卿，1973 年获得诺贝尔和平奖，担任了一个外国移民在美国所能取得的最高政治位置——国务卿。三十多年前，中美之间的一次秘密接触，启动了两个伟大国家改变世界的进程，亨利·基辛格博士由此获得了极高的名望。随后，他明智地推动美国走出越南战争的泥潭。1977 年 1 月，基辛格离开共和党执掌了 8 年的白宫。

15. McKinsey 麦肯锡公司
麦肯锡公司是世界级领先的全球管理咨询公司，1926 年成立，主要目标是帮助领先的企业机构实现显著、持久的经营业绩，改善并打造能够吸引、培育和激励杰出人才的优秀组织机构。麦肯锡公司采取"公司一体"的合作伙伴关系制度，业务涉及公司整体与业务单元战略、企业金融、营销/销售与渠道、组织架构、制造/采购/供应链、技术、产品研发等领域。

16. The company even commissioned a McKinsey study for Chinese officials in 2001 that, among other things, recommended improving the protection of intellectual property. 2001 年，公司甚至还为中国官员委托安排一项麦肯锡研究，并建议加强知识产权保护。
句中的"that"引导定语从句，修饰"study"；"among other things"在定语从句中作状语。

17. As a result, in 2003 the company offered China and 59 other countries the right to look at the fundamental source code for its Windows operating system and to substitute certain portions with their own software — something Microsoft had never allowed in the past.
因此，2003 年公司向中国和其他 59 个国家公开了 Windows 操作系统的源代码，允许他们用自己的软件替换某些部分，这在过去微软是从不允许的。
句中的源代码就是源程序，是指未编译的文本代码，是一系列人类可读的计算机语言指令。在现代程序语言中，源代码可以书籍或者磁带的形式出现，但最为常用的格式是文本文件，这种典型格式的目的是为了编译出计算机程序。计算机源代码的最终目的是将

Unit 4 Corporate Development and Strategies

人类可读的文本翻译成为计算机可以执行的二进制指令，这种过程叫做编译，通过编译器完成。

18. Vista operating system Vista 操作系统

    Vista 操作系统是微软下一代操作系统，以前叫做 Longhorn，后来微软对外宣布正式名称是 Windows Vista。作为微软的最新操作系统，Windows Vista 第一次在操作系统中引入了"Life Immersion"概念，即在系统中集成许多人性的因素，一切以人为本。

19. Motorola 摩托罗拉公司

    摩托罗拉公司创立于 1928 年，是世界财富百强企业之一，是全球通信行业的领导者，为客户提供无缝移动通信产品和解决方案。其业务范围涵盖宽带通信、嵌入式系统和无线网络等领域。摩托罗拉公司有四大业务集团，分别是移动终端事业部、网络事业部、政府及企业移动解决方案事业部和宽带联网事业部。

20. Chen was a superstar, but when he was hired, articles in the Chinese press asked if he, too, would fall victim to the Microsoft "curse." 陈是个超级明星，但当他上任的时候，中国媒体有文章置疑他是否同样也会沦为微软"诅咒"的牺牲品。

    句中的"fall victim to"意为"沦为……的牺牲品"。

21. There was synergy, which we formalized, between the need of the Chinese economy to have local software capability and our need for an ecosystem of companies around us using our technology and platform. 中国经济需要提高国产软件能力，而我们则需要一个使用微软技术和平台的企业生态系统，在这两者之间，我们形成了一种配合和默契。

    句中的"which"引导定语从句修饰"synergy"，而"between ... and ..."是介宾短语作定语，和"which"引导的从句修饰同一个先行词。

22. Lenovo, the market leader, had been shipping as few as 10% of its PCs that way, and even US PC makers in China were selling many machines "naked." 过去市场的领导者——联想集团仅仅给 10% 的个人电脑产品安装正版软件，甚至一些美国个人电脑商销售的也只是"裸机"，即没有安装正版软件。

    句中的"naked"是比喻用法，指没有安装正版软件。

23. China's Boao Forum 中国博鳌论坛

    又名博鳌亚洲论坛，是一个非政府、非营利的国际组织，目前已成为亚洲及其他大洲有关国家政府、工商界和学术界领袖就亚洲及全球重要事务进行对话的高层次平台，并致力于通过区域经济的进一步整合，推进亚洲国家实现发展目标。2001 年 2 月，博鳌亚洲论坛正式宣告成立。论坛的成立获得了亚洲各国的普遍支持，并赢得了全世界的广泛关注。从 2002 年开始，论坛每年定期在中国海南博鳌召开年会。

24. One of the things I wanted to ask him was how he squares the company's "alignment" in China with its leaders' suppression of free speech on the Internet. 我想问他的一个问题是，在中国他是如何调整来应对中国领导层对网络自由言论的压制的。

    此处作者依据西方的某些标准来看待中国对网络的管理，对中国的某些政策存在偏见，事实上中国对网络管理是遵循中国的国情、文化传统、价值观念和国家政治稳定等各方面因素而进行的。譬如，色情网站在很多国家是合法的，而在中国则是被限制的。

25. ... people have to sit there and make their own value judgments against what they deem to be

the greater good all the time. ……人们要坐下来，针对他们认为的较大利益，始终做出自己的价值判断。

句中的"what they deem to be"是插入语；"all the time"意为"始终"。

26. But in the grand scheme of things, they're what people think is required to keep stability. 但在各种重要事情的安排中，这些就是人们所要求的保持稳定。

句中的"what people think is required to keep stability"是表语从句，其中的"people think"作表语从句的插入语。

27. Autodesk 欧特克公司

欧特克公司是世界领先的设计和数字内部创建资源提供商。公司提供软件和 Internet 门户服务，借助设计的威力，推动客户的业务，并向工程和设计领域及电影、广播和多媒体领域提供服务。美国境内的《财富》500 家工业和服务公司，有 90% 是欧特克公司的客户。

28. Intel 英特尔公司

英特尔公司是全球最大的半导体芯片制造商，成立于 1968 年。1971 年，英特尔公司推出了全球第一个微处理器，它所带来的计算机和互联网革命，改变了整个世界。英特尔公司为计算机工业提供微处理器、芯片组、板卡、系统及软件等产品。

29. I don't know any company in the IT industry where things have worked out as well as they have for Microsoft. 在 IT 行业里，据我所知，没有公司能像微软那样顺利地开展业务。

句中的"as well as"引导同级比较。

阅读小知识（1）

新闻英语的语言特点

新闻语言的特色是语句简洁，力求精练，以最少的字写出最多的内容。

1. 句法特点

多用名词短语，少用从句，以便于行文的简洁。有时只是在职业、头衔或人名前加用某类形容词。例如：

No longer are the swarming peoples of Asia and Africa sunken, as for centuries past, in a passive acceptance of their lot.

A quiet, tubercular physicist named Robert Goddard appeared before a board of military-weapons experts.

2. 用词特点

（1）新词是新闻用语的一个显著特征，例如：e-commerce, cyber-economy, Websurfing。

（2）旧词新义。旧词新义也可被视为一种新词，在报刊中常见，这样衍生出的新义有两种。

① 第一种是旧词词义赋予新的含义，例如：

For most large foreign companies, a Chinese presence is only a small part of world investments.

这里的"presence"是"投资经营"的意思。

Mr. Bush is encouraging a different chemistry with the man who has taken his place.

此处的"chemistry"不是"化学"的意思，而是"人际关系"的意思。

② 另一种是一些行业用词被吸收、改变为新闻用语，例如：

The single most striking change has been the official recognition that the flagship of the third term, the poll tax, was the error.

"flagship"为"旗舰"的意思，在此被喻为头等大事。

I have no present intention of endorsing candidates for other offices in the November 7 election. We are all running independent campaigns. I've never believed in a package deal.

"a package deal"意为一揽子交易。

（3）创造新词，例如：

What counts is what flits by on the tube and pulses through the headphones of your Discman.

随着科学生产技术的不断改进，新一代的 Walkman 已经问世，现代英语词汇里又增添了一个新词，即"Discman"。再如"infoport"（信息港）、"cybersurfing"（网上冲浪）等。

（4）采用外来语。报刊英语词汇的显著特点之一就是经常掺用外来语，而且正呈现日益增多的趋势，例如：bloc，集团（法语）；glasnost，公开性（俄语）；per capita，人均（拉丁语）；en masse，总体上（法语）；tatami，榻榻米（日语）；Zeitgeist 时代精神（德语）等。

（5）俚语。俚语是英语中生动活泼、多姿多彩的一种语言形式，富有语言魅力和感染力，尤其是在多元、勤变、务奇、趋俗的新闻文体中更是备受青睐。俚语作为一种非正式用语，其最显著的特点在于非正式性，在语体正式程度上可以大大低于正规语或普通体语言，甚至比口语（colloquialism）更不正式。报刊中出现了各类俚语。俚语有军事俚语、体育俚语、黑人俚语、校园俚语等。比如："He is sort of heavyweight in the rag trade.", 这儿的 heavyweight 本是体育俚语，在这儿被用来指"显赫人物"。再如，"... the night he and other breakers showed up ... ready to boggie."中的"breaker"是黑人俚语"霹雳舞手"的意思。青年学生是俚语产生、传播、使用的主要群体之一。纵览英文报端，便可信手拈来数例：boodle（拥抱，接吻）、cake（容易）、hit the book（发奋读书）、pull an all-nighter（熬夜）。

（6）委婉语。为了使听者顺耳、读者舒服等原因，人们就造出一些具有安慰或美化作用的委婉语。例如越南战争时，美国为攻打越南北方而入侵了柬埔寨，美国官方不用"invasion"而用"incursion"；"大败"不用"rout"或"heavy defeat"，而用"strategic withdrawal"；再如"comfort women"（慰安妇）、"air support"（空中支援，实指轰炸）、"strategic village"（战略村，实际上是集中营）、"welfare mother"（福利母亲，其实就是失业母亲）等。

（7）采用借喻词和提喻词。借喻是指借一事物的名称指代另一事物，例如"the Crown"喻指"皇室事务"。以局部代表全体，或以全体喻指部分，这称为提喻，如"Washington"代表美国。

在英美报刊中，这两种喻义词尤其多，例如"Capitol"（国会山）、"Donkey"（美国民主党）、"Elephant"（美国共和党）、"Silicon Valley"（美国高科技集中地）、"Fleet Street"

（英国报业）、"Madison Avenue"（美国广告业）等。

Exercises

I Decide whether the following statements are true (T) or false (F).

1. No other Fortune 500 CEO gets quite the same treatment in China, because they are not as rich as Bill Gates. (　　)
2. Microsoft was inept at its market in China almost for a decade, just due to the fact that the company did not adjust its strategies in the US and other developed nations to China's market successfully. (　　)
3. Microsoft's strategies in China get criticism from human rights groups, because the group members think that Microsoft allows piracy to infringe on its intellectual property rights. (　　)
4. China will be Microsoft's biggest market, as Gates predicts with confidence, but now its market share in China is not very large, compared with its global sales. (　　)
5. Microsoft fought bitterly to protect its intellectual property, which had effectively prevented the piracy of its software. (　　)
6. It seemed to Mundie that Microsoft's unsuccessful practices were attributed to its not so good collaboration with Chinese government. (　　)
7. Microsoft changed its previous strategies, i. e. it commissioned a Mickinsey study for Chinese official, recommended improving the protection of intellectual property, and even allowed its fundamental source code for its Windows operating system to be looked at by China, with some of its portion substituted with China's own software, all of which had played a pivotal role in its business development in China. (　　)
8. Microsoft sponsored its extensive training programs for software entrepreneurs in order to produce IT professional for its future business operation only. (　　)
9. The nation required central, provincial and local governments to use legal software, but the PC manufacturers are encouraged to load more pirated softwares. (　　)
10. Many other multinational companies followed the example of Microsoft in their business development in China — to be cooperative with the Chinese government. (　　)

II Choose one answer that best suits the following statements.

1. Microsoft did not succeed in promoting its business as it entered China's market, because _____.

    A. it priced too high

    B. its operating system was not compatible with China's Office applications

    C. its business principle did not suit China's specific situation

D. it did not effectively protect its intellectual property rights
2. As Microsoft started its business 15 years ago, it adopted its classic model elsewhere in that _____.
   A. it priced the same as elsewhere and cracked down on illegal use of its software
   B. it set up training centers to develop well qualified IT professionals
   C. it invested large amounts of money in advertisement and other promotional activities.
   D. it fought bitterly with its rivals by constantly introducing the latest products through R&D
3. Microsoft adopted the following strategies to turn around its business in China: _____.
   A. it adopted a cooperative stance with Chinese government to dispel their mistrust
   B. it opened some research centers to produce scientists for its own, and changed its pricing strategies
   C. it replaced sales managers and executives in China with the personnel who were pragmatic about business operation
   D. it invited officials to help decide in which local software and outsourcing companies it should invest
4. In 1999, Gates sent Mundie, who heads the company's public-policy efforts, to figure out why Microsoft was so reviled . . .
   The meaning of underlined word is: _____.
   A. revolted   B. exposed   C. getting high approval   D. unwelcome
5. Although the company's China revenues average no more than $7 for every PC in use (compared with $100 to $200 in developed countries), Gates says those figures will eventually converge . . .
   The meaning of the underlined word is: _____.
   A. become the same   B. diverge further
   C. differ greatly   D. conflict with each other

III Translate the following passages into Chinese.

1. It was not always so. Microsoft bumbled for years after entering China in 1992, and its business was a disaster there for a decade. It finally figured out that almost none of the basic precepts that led to its success in the US and Europe made sense in China. There Microsoft had to become the un-Microsoft — pricing at rock bottom instead of charging hundreds of dollars for its Windows operating system and Office applications; abandoning the centerpiece of its public-policy approach elsewhere, the protection of its intellectual property at all costs; and closely partnering with the government instead of fighting it as in the US, a stance that has opened the company to criticism from human rights groups.

2. In 2003, Mundie and Gates took a quantum leap forward in China by hiring Tim Chen, who had been running Motorola's China subsidiary. Chen was a superstar, but when he was hired, articles in the Chinese press asked if he, too, would fall victim to the Microsoft "curse."
Chen arrived with entrée to the corridors of power and a practiced understanding of how a

Western company could succeed in China. He kept up the blitz of initiatives. Microsoft made Shanghai a global center to respond to customer e-mails. It began extensive training programs for teachers and software entrepreneurs. It worked with the Ministry of Education to finance 100 model computer classrooms in rural areas.

IV Write a summary of this text.

Will She, Won't She?

(Author unknown)

Having bought Gillette[1] and focused on big brands, the world's largest consumer-goods company is betting that scale is the way to success.

In the corner of a meeting room next to the bosses' office at the headquarters of Procter& Gamble (P&G)[2], a large sculpture of a woman in a hat watches over proceedings with a serene smile. "She is at the center of all our decisions," says Richard Antoine, head of human resources and confidant of Alan Lafley[3], the company's chief executive.

Founded in 1837 by William Procter, a candlemaker, and James Gamble, who made soap, P&G is the world's biggest consumer-goods company. It sold $76.5 billion worth of them in the year to June 30th. And it probably knows more about consumer marketing[4] than any other firm on the planet. Interestingly, many people at P&G do not use the word "consumer". Nor might they ask if a "customer" or "shopper" would buy a putative new product. They are more likely to ask: "Would 'she' buy it?"

Women have long accounted for four-fifths of P&G's customers. Over the years, the way P&G sells to them has changed dramatically. In the 1930s it sponsored radio shows — the original soap operas — to encourage women (usually housewives) to buy its detergent. Now radio has been surpassed by television and the internet as a means of promotion, and "she" has become ever more independent, demanding and fickle. The variety of products on offer has exploded, not just from makers of branded goods, like P&G, but also from the big supermarket chains that now dominate the retail end of the business and sell their own labels alongside the big brands.[5]

"She is in control now," says Mr. Antoine. The consumer-goods giant is spending lots to find out what she actually wants. Staff from its Consumer and Market knowledge division tour the world and spend entire days with women to observe how they shop, clean, eat, apply their make-up or put nappies on their babies. They try to understand how a woman reacts in the first three to seven seconds after she sees an item in a shop (the "First Moment of Truth"[6], in P&G-speak) and when she tries it at home (the "Second Moment of Truth").

At first P&G struggled in the new world of empowered she-consumers. In 2000, after a big drop in profits, its share price took a tumble. Mr. Lafley, a company veteran, took over that year (P&G is a great believer in promoting from within). The company he leads has such a reputation for insularity that employees are known as "proctoids", but Mr. Lafley has been trying to open up more to the outside world and to streamline P&G's notorious bureaucracy.[7] He also needed a clear strategy for the company's growth. That, he concluded, lay in investing more in the power of brands: the strongest brands, he reasoned, would be sought out by consumers everywhere.

Mr. Lafley began with the acquisition of Clariol[8], a hair-dye company, in November 2001. Two years later he paid $6.9 billion for Wella[9], a family-owned German beauty firm. But the biggest deal, in January 2005, was the $57 billion purchase of a company known for serving men rather than women: Gillette, which controls three-quarters of the world market for razors and shaving foam.[10]

Has the huge Gillette purchase paid off? Mr. Lafley admits that he took a big risk. Four out of five mergers don't work out, he says, and big deals fail more often than small ones. But he has a list of five reasons why mergers fail. On all counts he says P&G is now doing fine.

Strategy is first on Mr. Lafley's list. Mergers of companies that are either not at all complementary or pursue completely different strategies tend to fail.[11] But both P&G and Gillette are strong companies, and their brands and international coverage match each other well. P&G is good at innovation, understands consumers and knows how to nurture brands. Gillitte's strengths are technology and the ability to roll out new products within a few weeks. And of course there is the chance to learn about marketing to the other sex. This year Gillette launched Pure Divine[12], a body wash for women. P&G is working harder to sell High Endurance[13], which it claims is America's first body wash for men. New Gillette products for women and new P&G products for men are on the way.

Next comes company culture. Though they have their similarities, these two old American companies also had important differences in style. Management at P&G is consensus-driven whereas Gillette's was hierarchical. To ease unification Mr. Lafley set up a special team to work out how to take the best from the two cultures. The chief of P&G North America is a Gillette man. Mr. Lafley managed to keep around 95% of Gillette staff who were asked to stay. Still, many top Gillette people chose to go, their decision eased by the large payoffs specified in their employment contracts should the firm be taken over.[14]

Bosses are third. Gillette and P&G made such an obvious strategic fit that their chiefs had already talked a couple of times in the 1990s. In the end James Kilts, the head of Gillette, made the first move because he wanted to avoid a takeover by Colgate-Palmolive[15], run by Reuben Mark, his arch-rival. Mr. Kilts stayed on for a year after the merger to ease the transition. He and Mr. Lafley seemed to get along well.

Fourth, mergers often fail to produce the cost savings that companies promise. P&G and Gilette said that their union would yield efficiencies in manufacturing, marketing and distribution of some $1.2 billion annually by the end of the third fiscal year after the merger.

Fifth, what about revenue? Clayt Daley, P&G's chief financial officer, admits that a merger can truly be called a success only when the new entity hits its revenue targets too. P&G and Gillette promised about $750 m annually by the end of the third year. Mr. Daley says the merged company is on track to meet both cost and revenue targets, but is not there yet.

On August 3rd the company said that net sales were 8% higher in the fourth quarter (April to June) than a year before, and rose by 12% in the whole year. Organic growth — stripping out the effects of acquisions — was only 5% in 2006-2007, compared with 8%-9% in the couple of years before the Gillette deal. The pre-merger figure was atypical, insists Mr. Daley. The company's long-term goal is organic growth of 4%-6% a year.

Extra, Extra Large

Though Mr. Lafley says he is meeting his chosen criteria, investors have not been grateful: in the past year P&G shares have underperformed the S&P 500 stock market index[16], although the gap has narrowed in recent weeks. This may explain P&G decision, also revealed on August 3rd, to boost its share-repurchase program to $24 billion-30 billion, or 12%-15% of its capitalization, at a rate of $8 billion-10 billion a year for the next three years.[17]

Analysts, though, generally say favorable things about Mr. Lafley's spending spree. William Schmitz, who follows consumer-goods industries for Deutche Bank, is one who thinks that size can become an inhibitor of growth. "The company raised the bar very high by needing to increase sales by some $6 billion annually just to meet its targets for growth," argues Mr. Schmitz, who thinks that without its big mergers P&G would probably grow faster now. But even Mr. Schmitz has a "buy" recommendation on the shares.

Scale looks more likely to be a help than a hindrance in today's consumer-goods industry. One reason is that it saves costs in procuring commodities, the prices of which have risen sharply in recent years, pushing up the cost of the foodstuffs, packaging, chemicals and energy that go into the industry's products.[18] In the old days such price increases could be passed on to consumers, but today P&G and its peers are under pressure from gigantic retailers to keep prices low. The biggest of all, America's Wal-Mart[19], alone gobble up one-fifth of P&G sales. Several hundred proctoids are stationed in Bentonville[20], Wal-Mart's home town, and the relationship has deepened since the Gillette takeover. Hence a second advantage of scale: as P&G gets bigger, it is becoming less dispensable for Wal-Mart.

Retailers have increased their power by developing their own brands, or privates' labels[21]. In the markets where this has gone furthest, such as Britain, retailers' own brands account for 40% of grocery sales. In many countries the growth of private labels is spilling over from food to household goods and personal-care products. According to a recent report by the Boston Consulting Group (BCG)[22], retailers' own brands are also expanding to online sales and convenience stores. And the most sophisticated own-brand producers have begun to "out-innovate" makers of branded consumer goods, says BCG, by using the insights into consumer behavior gained through their loyalty programmes and research. By evaluating sales data and test-driving innovations in their shops, they are able to adapt their innovations more quickly to consumers' needs than makers of branded goods can.

Those marketing techniques are getting more and more sophisticated. In May, Wal-Mart and P&G started the rollout of Prism, a system of infrared sensors that counts the number of times shoppers are exposed to product displays, banners and televisions, in order to measure the effectiveness of in-store marketing. Typically obsessive, P&G also sends out staff to trail round after other customers' trolleys, double-checking the sensor system. "We depend on them as much as they depend on us," explains Jeff Weedman, of P&G's external-business development team.

For retailers and makers of consumer goods alike, the complexity and cost of advertising and marketing have increased. As the world's biggest advertiser, P&G has tremendous clout in adland. It spent $6.8 billion in 2005—2006 and at least 10% more in 2006—2007 (*Advertising Week*[23], a trade publication, reckons $7.5 billion). It has often been a pioneer of new marketing techniques. This year Publics[24], a French advertising firm, and Dassault Systémes[25], a French software company, turned to P&G for advice before launching a digital-marketing joint venture in June. The scheme allows consumer-goods companies to create and adapt new products online with the input of consumers.

Mr. Lafley's quest for big, valuable brands means he is prepared to sell tired ones. He got rid of Sunny Delight[26], an American soft-drink range, and Punica[27], a German juice brand, as well as Jif[28] (peanut butter), Crisco[29] (pastry shortening), Pert Plus[30] (shampoo), Sure[31] (deodorant) and P&G's towel business in South Korea. He also shed five detergents: BIZ[32], Milton[33], Sanso[34], Rei[35] and Oxydol[36]. Soon he may take a critical look at underperformers in the Gillette stable too. Growth at Duracell[37], its battery business, and Braun, which makes electrical appliances, has been disappointing — but "purposefully disappointing", claims Mr. Lafley, because of a focus on Gillette's razors and blades.

These disposals have made P&G more reliant on a smaller number of leading brands. Today it has 23 with annual sales of more than $1billion. The biggest Pampers[38] nappies collected more than $7 billion last year. Gain[39], a detergent, is the latest to cross the $1 billion mark. It has a strong scent and is aimed mainly at Hispanics and African-Americans, who according to P&G research attach more importance to a good smell of cleanliness.

The other effect of selling off underperformers is a sharper focus on beauty and health products, which have higher margins and are less under threat from retailers' own labels.[40] The sales helped to finance the acquisitions of Wella and Clairol, which made P&G one of world's biggest beauty companies. Beauty accounts for $21 billion in sales, more than one-quarter of the group's global total. Seven of its beauty brands — Olay[41] (skin care), Pantene[42] and Head & Shoulders[43] (shampoo), Wella (hair-care), Always[44] (feminine hygiene), March 3[45] (shaving blades and razors) and Gillette (shaving blades, razors, gels, creams and deodorants) — all bring in sales of more than $1 billion a year. As a reward for her success as boss of the beauty business, Susan Arnold was made head of all global business-units in May: she runs beauty and household goods as well as health and well-being.

Innovation is the second area where Mr. Lafley has shaken things up. Inventing new products and brands is hard in an industry that, like many of its customers, is well into middle age. According to a study by Deloitte[46], a consulting firm, the number of new consumer goods and product extensions increased by 80% between 2002 and 2005, but less than one-quarter of them had sales of $7m or more in the year after they were launched.

Until Mr. Lafley took over, P&G made all its inventions in-house and the company's expenses for research and development were higher than those of rivals. Proctoids used to say that the phrase "not invented here" was, well, invented here. In 2001 Mr. Lafley started the "Connect and Develop" programme to open up his company's innovation model. In addition to 9,000 researchers in 11 research centers around the world, P&G has 75 technology scouts who travel the globe in search of new ideas that P&G might take up and develop. He also pushed for more collaboration between the various bits of the P&G empire. For instance, when developing Crest[47] White-strips, a tooth-whitener, P&G drew on the knowledge of people in the toothpaste business and those in R&D drew on the knowledge of people in the toothpaste business and those in R&D working on a novel film technology, as well as experts in bleach from fabric and home care.

After five years of "open innovation" half of the company's inventions come from outside. One-third of new patents are issued to individuals and small companies, says Nabil Sakkab, head of corporate R&D; 30 year ago most were issued to big companies. So it makes a lot of sense to reach out. The company's R&D has become more productive, partly as a result of this. P&G says that its sales per R&D employee have roughly doubled since 2000.

Mr. Lafley has also developed joint ventures, such as the one set up in 2002 with Clorox[48], a maker of household products, to produce food-storage wraps. In addition to the use of its cling-film technology, P&G brought 20 full-time employees to the enterprise, while Clorox contributed its bags, containers and wraps business. In May, Inverness Medical Innovations[49] and P&G formed a 50-50 joint venture for consumer diagnostics. The new company, Swill Precision Diagnostics[50], based in Geneva, is the largest pregnancy-test business in the world. Its brands include Clerblue[51] and Accu-clear[52].

To continue to build up its superbrands, P&G needs to focus more on emerging economies, where the scope for growth in sales of basic consumer goods is far greater than in rich countries. Already more than 40% of P&G's growth comes from emerging markets, which contribute more than one-quarter of its sales. That is a good portion, but Unilever and others sell up to half of their wares in developing countries. Gillette could be useful. It is strong in India, where P&G has long been outgunned by Unilever. China, Russia and Ukraine are already big markets with sales of some $3 billion annually in each country.

P&G has learned that it is a mistake to take a product designed for a developed market into a developing country without proper consideration of the needs and means of women without much to spend. Naturella[53], for instance, is a panty liner first sold in Mexico that has become popular in Russia, Poland and other east European countries with women on similar average incomes. Downy Single Rinse[54], a fabric softener, was designed for parts of the world where water is scarce and rinsing clothes several times is costly or impossible. A laundry detergent called Vizir[55] has become

Poland's number one.

Still lagging its rivals, P&G forecasts that by 2010 emerging economies will account for 30% of the group's sales. Continuing to tune its products to the budgets and aspirations of local shoppers will surely be of the essence. And knowing what consumers want — and creating wants — is still one of the things P&G does best. In the past it used this skill mainly for women in Western countries with relatively high incomes. But in future years P&G will target women, rich and poor, everywhere — as well as the other half of humanity.

(*Economist*, August 11, 2007)

New Words and Expressions

sculpture	n.	雕像，雕塑
proceeding	n.	会议录，学报，进行
serene	a.	平静的，安详的
confidant	n.	心腹朋友，知己
candlemaker	n.	蜡烛制造商
putative	a.	推定的，假定的
sponsor	v.	发起，主办，赞助
detergent	n.	清洁剂，去垢剂
surpass	v.	超越，胜过
demanding	a.	过分要求的，苛求的
fickle	a.	变幻无常的，浮躁的，薄情的
dominate	v.	支配，占优势
giant	n.	巨人，天才
make-up	n.	化妆品
nappy	n.	尿布
empower	v.	授权与，使能够
veteran	n.	老手，富有经验的人
insularity	n.	与外界隔绝的生活状况
notorious	a.	声名狼藉的
bureaucracy	n.	官僚，官僚作风
razor	n.	剃刀
coverage	n.	所包括的范围（程度、区域、数额）
nurture	v.	养育，给予营养物，发展
divine	a.	上帝的，天赐的
endurance	n.	忍耐（力），持久（力），耐久（性）

consensus	n.	一致同意，多数人的意见
hierarchical	a.	分等级的
unification	n.	统一，一致
payoff	n.	报酬，支付，偿清
arch-rival	n.	主要竞争对手
distribution	n.	分配，分发，销售
entity	n.	实体
organic	a.	组织的，建制的
atypical	a.	非典型的
underperform	v.	（股票等）运作差于（一般市场价格）
capitalization	n.	股本，资本总额
spree	n.	狂欢，无节制的狂热行为
inhibitor	n.	抑制者
hindrance	n.	妨碍，障碍
procure	v.	获得，取得
foodstuff	n.	食品，粮食
dispensable	a.	不是必要的，可有可无的
out-innovate	v.	在创新方面胜过
insight	n.	洞察力，见识
test-drive	v.	试驾，试用
rollout	n.	首次展示
prism	n.	分光光谱，棱镜
infrared	n.	红外线
sensor	n.	传感器
obsessive	a.	强迫性的
trail	v.	跟踪，追踪
trolley	n.	手推车
double-check	v.	仔细检查，再次确认
tremendous	a.	极大的，巨大的
clout	n.	敲，猛击，影响
adland	n.	广告业
reckon	v.	计算，估计
quest	n.	寻求
pastry	n.	面粉糕饼，馅饼皮
deodorant	n.	除臭剂
battery	n.	电池
blade	n.	刀刃，刀片
reliant	a.	信赖的，依靠的
gel	n.	凝胶体，冻胶
extension	n.	附加部分

Unit 4 Corporate Development and Strategies

tooth-whitener	n.	牙齿增白产品
novel	a.	新奇的，新颖的
bleach	n.	漂白，漂白法，漂白剂
cling	n.	粘紧，附着
cling-film	n.	食品薄膜
diagnostics	n.	诊断学
swill	n.	涮，冲洗
precision	n.	精确，精密度，精度
pregnancy-test	n.	妊娠试验，妊娠诊断试验
superbrand	n.	超级品牌
portion	n.	一部分，一分
wares	n.	商品，货物
outgun	v.	胜过，超越
softener	n.	软化剂，柔软剂
lag	v.	落后于
humanity	n.	人类

soap operas		肥皂剧
share price		股票价格
shaving foam		修面泡沫，剃须膏
roll out		大量生产
body wash		沐浴露
be on track		在轨道上，在路上
strip out		去除，剥除
gobble up		大口吞咽，占据
private label		私人标签
personal care products		个人护理产品
online sales		网上销售
convenience stores		便利店
infrared sensors		红外线感应器
electrical appliance		家用电器
sell off		廉价卖清
shake up		把……打散后重新组合
take up		吸收
home care		居家护理
food-storage wraps		食品储藏包装
panty liner		卫生棉，卫生护垫
tune . . . to . . .		调整以适应……

Notes

1. Gillette 吉列公司
   吉列公司的总部设于波士顿,成立于1901年,主要生产剃须产品、电池和口腔清洁卫生产品。2005年在《商业周刊》评出的世界品牌100强中位列第15位,品牌价值175.3亿美元。2007年与宝洁公司合并。

2. Procter & Gamble（P&G） 宝洁公司
   宝洁公司始创于1837年,是世界最大的日用消费品公司之一,总部位于美国俄亥俄州辛辛那提市。2007年,在《财富》杂志最新评选出的全球500强中,排名第74位。宝洁公司全球雇员近10万,在全球80多个国家设有工厂及分公司,所经营的300多个品牌的产品畅销160多个国家和地区,其中包括织物及家居护理、美发美容、婴儿及家庭护理、健康护理、食品及饮料等。

3. Alan Lafley 阿伦·雷富礼
   阿伦·雷富礼是宝洁公司总裁兼CEO。他自2000年起担任宝洁CEO,在执掌宝洁公司后,致力于服务消费者的承诺,从而重新唤起宝洁一度在20世纪90年代曾失去的生机与活力。雷富礼倡导高管团队来源地的多样化,力图改变过去管理团队中的保守作风,再造了企业文化,重新燃起了宝洁的创新精神。同时,雷富礼还进行了一系列的收购兼并活动,使宝洁公司变得更为强大。

4. marketing 市场营销
   根据美国市场营销协会的定义,市场营销是对思想、产品及劳务进行设计、定价、促销及分销的计划和实施的过程,从而产生满足个人和组织目标的交换。产品概念不仅包括产品或劳务,还包括思想；市场营销活动不仅包括营利性的经营活动,还包括非营利组织的活动；营销强调交换过程,突出市场营销计划的制订与实施。

5. The variety of products on offer has exploded, not just from makers of branded goods, like P&G, but also from the big supermarket chains that now dominate the retail end of the business and sell their own labels alongside the big brands. 所提供产品的种类爆炸性地增长,不仅有来自诸如宝洁等大企业的名牌产品,还包括来自大超市连锁店的产品,它们控制着商业的零售终端,可以把自己的标签同知名品牌放在一起。
   句中的"not just ... but also ..."意为"不仅……而且……",后面的"from"引导的短语作定语,修饰"the variety of products"；"that"引导定语从句修饰前面的"big supermarket chains"；"labels"指超市自己的品牌标签。

6. the "First Moment of Truth" and the "Second Moment of Truth" 第一关键时刻和第二关键时刻
   "Moment of Truth"意为"关键时刻,真理瞬间",在这里指消费者对产品的反应和所采取的行动。

7. The company he leads has such a reputation for insularity that employees are known as

"proctoids", but Mr. Lafley has been trying to open up more to the outside world and to streamline P&G's notorious bureaucracy. 他所领导的公司与外界联系不多而名声在外，以至于员工们都被专门称为"宝洁员工"，但雷富礼一直致力于对外开放，并对公司名声不好的机构进行精简。

句中的"streamline"意为"使（企业、组织等）简化并更有效率，整顿"，"open up to the outside world"意为"对外开放"。

8. Clariol　伊卡璐

    著名染发品牌，2001 年被宝洁公司收购。

9. Wella　（德国）威娜公司

    该公司成立于 1880 年，是欧洲第二大美发和护发公司，2003 年被宝洁公司收购。

10. But the biggest deal, in January 2005, was the ＄57 billion purchase of a company known for serving men rather than women: Gillette, which controls three-quarters of the world market for razors and shaving foam. 但最大一笔交易却是 2005 年 1 月花费 570 亿美元收购吉列公司。吉列公司以生产男用产品闻名于世，控制着全球剃须刀和修面泡沫市场四分之三的份额。

    句中的"which"引导定语从句，修饰"Gillette"；"known for"是过去分词作定语。

11. Mergers of companies that are either not at all complementary or pursue completely different strategies tend to fail. 合并的公司如果不能互补或是同追求的战略完全相背，那么这种合并往往是失败的。

    "that"引导的从句作定语，修饰"companies"；"tend to"意为"往往，趋向"。

12. Pure Divine　沐浴露品牌

    该品牌于 2007 年由吉列公司专为女性消费者推出。

13. High Endurance　沐浴露品牌

    该品牌由宝洁公司专为男性消费者推出。

14. Still, many top Gillette people chose to go, their decision eased by the large payoffs specified in their employment contracts should the firm be taken over. 但是，很多吉列高级管理人员仍然选择离开，他们这么轻松地做出决定是因为就业合同中规定一旦公司被收购，他们就可以获得大额赔偿。

    句中的"eased"和"specified"都是过去分词作定语，修饰前面的先行词；"should the firm be taken over"引导条件状语。

15. Colgate-Palmolive　高露洁棕榄公司

    它是全球顶尖的消费品公司之一，总部在美国纽约，有近二百年的历史。公司在口腔护理、个人护理、家居护理和宠物食品等方面为消费者提供高品质的消费品，其中有很多是广大消费者耳熟能详的全球著名品牌，如高露洁、棕榄、洁齿白、Ajax、Protex、Fab、Irish Spring、Mennen 和 Science Diet，等等。

16. the S&P 500 stock market index　标准普尔 500 指数

    标准普尔 500 指数是记录美国 500 家上市公司的一个股票指数。这个股票指数由标准普尔公司创建并维护。标准普尔 500 指数覆盖的所有公司都是美国主要交易所，如纽约证券交易所、纳斯达克交易所的上市公司。与道－琼斯工业平均指数相比，标准普尔 500

指数具有采样面广、代表性强、精确度高、连续性好等特点，被普遍认为是一种理想的股票指数和期货合约的标的。

17. This may explain P&G decision, also revealed on August 3rd, to boost its share-repurchase program to ＄24 billion－30 billion, or 12%－15% of its capitalization, at a rate of ＄8 billion－10 billion a year for the next three years. 这可以解释为什么宝洁公司像 8 月 3 日披露的那样决定继续推进它的股票回购计划，在未来 3 年内以每年 80 亿～100 亿美元的速度回购 240 亿～300 亿美元的股票，相当于其股本的 12% ～ 15% 。

 句中的"also revealed on August 3rd"是过去分词作定语，修饰前面的先行词。

18. One reason is that it saves costs in procuring commodities, the prices of which have risen sharply in recent years, pushing up the cost of the foodstuffs, packaging, chemicals and energy that go into the industry's products. 其中一个原因是：它可以节省日用品采购的成本。最近几年日用品价格急剧上涨，进而提高了食品、包装、化学制品和能源的成本，而这些都是生产行业产品所必需的。

 句中的"commodities"指日用品，"go into"意为"加入，进入"，"the prices of which"引导非限制性定语从句。

19. Wal-Mart　沃尔玛百货有限公司

 它由美国零售业的传奇人物山姆·沃尔顿先生于 1962 年在阿肯色州成立。经过四十余年的发展，沃尔玛百货有限公司已经成为美国最大的私人雇主和世界上最大的连锁零售商。沃尔玛一直奉行"人才本地化"的政策。2007 年，沃尔玛以 3 511.39 亿美元的年营业收入排名世界 500 强榜首。

20. Bentonville　本顿维

 美国阿肯色州西北部城市，是全球最大零售商沃尔玛的总部所在地。

21. privates labels　私人标签

 这是指销售时产品品牌由再销售商或零售商而非制造商拥有。在少数情况下，销售商就是生产商。私人标签产品一般是没有做过广告、知名度很低的产品，多为地方品牌。

22. Boston Consulting Group（BCG）　波士顿咨询集团

 它是一家著名的美国企业管理咨询公司，成立于 1963 年，在战略管理咨询领域被公认为先驱。该公司的最大特色和优势在于公司已经拥有并还在不断创立的高级管理咨询工具和理论，管理学界极为著名的"波士顿矩阵"就是由该公司于 20 世纪 60 年代创立的。BCG 的四大业务职能是企业策略、信息技术、企业组织、营运效益。

23. Advertising Week　广告周刊（美国杂志 300 强之一）

24. Publics　阳狮广告集团

 法国最大的广告集团，目前是世界六大广告集团之一。

25. Dassault Systémes　法国达索系统公司

 它是全球产品生命周期管理（PLM-Product Lifecycle Management）应用软件的第一开发及供应商，是法国达索飞机公司的子公司，自 1981 年以来达索系统一直是 3D 软件的先驱。它的解决方案使企业能够创造并数字化地模拟其产品，以及这些产品的制造和维护工序及所需资源。其核心特点是以三维立体形式提供一种现实的可视化功能，让使用者可以明白无误地沟通并真正实现协同工作。

26. Sunny Delight　阳光心情

    美国软饮料品牌，2004 年由宝洁公司出售给总部位于波士顿的投资公司 J. W. Childs。

27. Punica　普尼卡

    德国果汁品牌，1984 年被宝洁公司收购，2004 年被出售给一家私募股权集团（Private Equity Group）。

28. Jif　杰夫

    世界著名花生酱品牌，2001 年由宝洁公司出售给果冻制造商 J. M. Smuckers 公司，此次交易被认为是经典的收购案例。

29. Crisco　点心用酥油品牌

    该品牌由宝洁公司推出，2002 年出售给 J. M. Smuckers 公司。

30. Pert Plus　飞柔

    洗发水品牌，由宝洁公司开发，1987 年进入美国，1989 年进入中国，更名为飘柔（Rejoice），后飞柔品牌被出售。

31. Sure　宝洁旗下除臭剂品牌

    该品牌于 2006 年被宝洁出售给 Innovative Brands 公司。

32. BIZ　清洁剂品牌

    该品牌于 2000 年被宝洁公司出售给 Redox Brands 公司。

33. Milton　宝洁旗下清洁剂品牌（后被出售）

34. Sanso　清洁剂品牌

    1965 年被宝洁公司收购，2000 年出售给 Fit 公司。

35. Rei　清洁剂品牌

    2000 年被宝洁公司出售给 Fit 公司。

36. Oxydol　奥克多

    洗衣粉品牌，2000 年被宝洁公司出售给 Redox Brands 公司。

37. Duracell　金霸王

    著名家庭用电池品牌，1964 年正式被采用，1996 年被吉列公司收购。

38. Pampers　帮宝适

    世界纸尿裤领导品牌，1961 年由宝洁公司开发推出。

39. Gain　格尼

    洗衣粉品牌，由宝洁公司设计开发。

40. The other effect of selling off underperformers is a sharper focus on beauty and health products, which have higher margins and are less under threat from retailers' own labels.

    出售表现一般品牌可以更好地集中发展美容和保健产品，因为它们的利润更高，而且受零售商自有品牌的威胁较小。

    句中的"which"引导定语从句，修饰前面的"beauty and health products，margins"在这里指利润。

41. Olay　玉兰油

    国际护肤品品牌，1985 年被宝洁公司收购，目前玉兰油全球销售额近 10 亿美元，成为世界上最大、最著名的护肤品品牌之一。

42. Pantene   潘婷

    洗护发产品品牌，1947年在欧洲诞生，不久之后登陆美国市场，1986年被宝洁公司收购。其产品的关键因素是维生素原B5。目前，潘婷已经成长为一个价值3.1亿美元的品牌，是世界上最大的洗护发产品品牌，也是欧洲及北美最大的美发造型产品品牌，在全世界超过165个国家销售。1992年潘婷品牌登陆中国。

43. Head & Shoulders   海飞丝

    洗护发产品品牌，由宝洁公司拥有，该品牌主要针对去屑市场。

44. Always   好自在

    妇女卫生用品品牌，与护舒宝（Whisper）同是宝洁公司旗下的孪生品牌，亚洲地区叫护舒宝，非亚洲地区叫Always，但后来宝洁公司把Always也经营到了亚洲。

45. March 3   锋速3

    国际剃须刀和剃须刀片品牌，由吉列公司开发。

46. Deloitte   德勤咨询公司

    它是德勤集团主管咨询业务的子公司，由德勤集团咨询部门发展而来。德勤咨询分支机构遍布全世界，涉及的行业领域包括消费品行业、制造业、通信媒体业、金融服务业、医药业、教育保健及公共事业等，客户关系管理是它的一大长项。

47. Crest   佳洁士

    牙齿护理产品品牌，由宝洁公司于1955年设计开发，佳洁士牙膏是世界上第一种含氟并经临床证实能预防龋齿的牙膏。

48. Clorox   高乐氏

    世界著名家庭与个人日用消费品公司，属世界500强企业。

49. Inverness Medical Innovations   美国英凡尼医学科技公司

    它是世界上最大的验孕产品公司，为妇女健康市场制造和销售快速诊断产品，并从事获取、制造和营销先进医疗设备技术的业务，总部位于马萨诸塞州的沃尔瑟姆。

50. Swiss Precision Diagnostics   快速诊断产品公司

    2007年由IMI与宝洁公司合资成立，公司总部位于瑞士日内瓦，并在英国贝特福德设有分支机构，该公司结合IMI的研发能力和P&G的市场销售能力，全力推进针对个人用户的肿瘤和心血管疾病的快速诊断产品。

51. Clerblue   妊娠检测产品设备品牌

    该品牌由Inverness Medical Innovations公司设计开发。

52. Accu-clear   妊娠排卵检测产品设备品牌

    该品牌由Inverness Medical Innovations公司设计开发。

53. Naturella   卫生巾品牌

    该品牌由宝洁公司于2003年在墨西哥推出。

54. Downy Single Rinse   衣物柔顺剂品牌

    该品牌由宝洁公司针对缺水地区推出，产品可以和洗衣粉剂一起使用，降低衣物洗涤所需水量。

55. Vizir   洗涤剂品牌

    该品牌由宝洁公司针对欧洲市场推出，在欧洲占有很大的市场份额。

Unit 4 Corporate Development and Strategies

阅读小知识（2）

美国部分著名企业介绍

1. 思科系统公司

思科系统公司（Cisco Systems Inc.）是全球领先的互联网解决方案供应商。其设备和软件产品主要用于连接计算机网络系统，使人们能够在任何时间、任何地点，通过任何计算机都能实现对信息的访问。由思科系统公司提供的互联网商业解决方案已为众多用户提供了快捷有效的信息交换途径，降低了用户开销，提高了工作效率，并拉近了用户与其客户、商业伙伴和公司职员之间的距离。

目前，思科系统公司已成为公认的互联网解决方案的领先厂商，其提供的互联网解决方案是世界各地成千上万个公司、大学、企业和政府部门建立网间网的基础，用户遍及电信、金融、服务、零售等行业，以及政府部门和教育机构等。市场研究公司 Dataquest 的一项调查结果显示，思科系统公司已在 1996 年跻身世界十大电信公司行列，是全球增长最快的电信产品供应商，年增长率达 87%。同时，思科系统公司也是建设互联网的中坚力量，目前互联网上 80% 以上的骨干路由器是思科公司的产品。

2. 埃克森－美孚公司（Exxon Mobil）

埃克森－美孚公司是总部设在美国的大跨国公司，也是世界最大的综合性石油公司（排在荷兰皇家/壳牌公司之前）。1999 年 11 月 30 日，埃克森公司和美孚公司正式合并成为埃克森－美孚公司，总部设在得克萨斯州达拉斯市附近的爱文市。埃克森－美孚公司经营石油天然气的探索、生产、供给、运输及向全世界行销业务。埃克森－美孚公司的炼油厂每天可以处理 600 多万桶石油，公司在世界 118 个国家拥有 4 万多个以埃克森、埃索和美孚为商标的服务站（包括在美国的 1 万 6 千多个）。埃克森－美孚公司还生产并出售石油化工产品，同时也涉足煤矿、采矿及发电业。

3. 惠普公司（Hewlett-Packard）

惠普公司（简称 HP）是在 1939 年由美国两位年轻的发明家比尔·休利特（Bill Hewlett）和戴维·帕卡德（David Packard）创建的。

60 多年来，HP 从未停止过创新和变革的步伐。这种精神使 HP 从一家年收入 4 000 美元的公司发展成为今天在全球拥有 150 000 名员工、分支机构遍及 170 多个国家和地区、2006 财政年度营业收入达 917 亿美元的信息产业巨擘，业务范围涵盖 IT 基础设施、全球服务、商用和家用计算及打印和成像等领域。目前全世界有超过 10 亿人正在使用 HP 技术。如今的 HP，作为全球领先的高科技公司，在美国财富 500 强中名列第 11 位，并在美国《商业周刊》"全球最具价值品牌"中排名第 13 位。

113

4. IBM 公司

IBM 即国际商业机器公司。公司总部位于美国纽约州阿尔蒙克,1914 年创建于美国,是世界上最大的信息工业跨国公司,同时也是全球最大的硬件公司(362.8 亿美元)、信息技术服务(193 亿美元)及信息技术租赁和融资(37.8 亿美元)公司。目前拥有全球雇员 30 余万人,业务遍及 164 个国家和地区。

在长期的发展过程中,IBM 始终不渝地坚持三个基本的信念:

第一,尊重个人,重视机构内每一个成员的尊严和权利,充分调动员工的工作积极性;

第二,注重客户服务,力争百分之百的用户满意;

第三,精益求精,无论做哪一项业务都追求尽善尽美。

所有这些形成了 IBM 的企业精神,同时也使 IBM 与世界融为一体,深入人心。

5. 美国电话电报公司(American Telephone & Telegraph Company)

美国电话电报公司是美国电信业公司,简称 AT&T,创建于 1885 年,公司总部设在纽约,原为贝尔电话公司的子公司,经营长途电话业务。1900 年接管了贝尔公司的全部资产,成为母公司,改名为美国电话电报公司。1909 年,将其业务扩大到电报领域。

美国电话电报公司有 8 个主要部门:贝尔实验室、商业市场集团、数据系统公司、通用市场集团、网络运营集团、网络系统集团、技术系统集团、公司国际集团。其主要业务是:① 为国内国际提供电话服务,利用海底电缆、海底光缆、通信卫星,可联系 250 个国家和地区,147 个国家和地区可直接拨号;② 提供商业机器、数据类产品和消费类产品;③ 提供电信网络系统;④ 提供各种服务及租赁业务。它还为政府提供产品和服务。该公司非常重视科研和开发新产品。

美国电话电报公司在泰国、德国、新加坡等地设有工厂。在意大利、韩国、日本等国设有子公司或者合资公司。1995 年 9 月,该公司解体为三个独立的公司:通讯服务公司、通讯设备公司、电脑信息服务公司,并且退出个人电脑领域。

6. 福特汽车公司(Ford)

福特汽车公司是世界最大的汽车企业之一。由亨利·福特先生于 1903 年创立。1908 年福特汽车公司生产出世界上第一辆属于普通百姓的汽车——T 型车,世界汽车工业革命就此开始。1913 年,福特汽车公司又开发出了世界上第一条流水线,这一创举使 T 型车一共达到了 1 500 万辆,缔造了一个至今仍未被打破的世界纪录。亨利·福特先生为此被尊为"为世界装上轮子"的人。

福特汽车公司旗下拥有的汽车品牌有阿斯顿·马丁(Aston Martin)、福特(Ford)、捷豹(Jaguar)、路虎(Land Rover)、林肯(Lincoln)、马自达(Mazda)、水星(Mercury)和 Volvo。此外,它还拥有世界最大的汽车信贷企业——福特信贷(Ford Credit)、全球最大的汽车租赁公司——赫兹(Hertz)及汽车服务品牌(Quality Care)。这些都是人们耳熟能详的品牌。同时,由于福特汽车公司多年的苦心经营,这些品牌本身都具有巨大的价值。

7. 波音公司(Boening)

波音公司是世界上最大的航空航天公司。1996 年,波音公司收购了罗克韦尔防务及空间系统分部；1997 年，波音与麦道合并；2000 年，波音公司收购了休斯航天和通讯业务分部。波音公司的历史映射出一部世界航空航天发展史。波音公司不仅是全球最大的民用飞机和军用飞机制造商，而且是美国航空航天局（NASA）最大的承包商。

40 多年来，波音公司一直是世界民用飞机市场的领导者，其主要民用飞机产品包括 717、737、747、757、767、777、MD-80、MD-90、MD-11 和波音公务机。目前，全球正在使用中的波音喷气客机达 1.1 万架。波音公司的客户支持部门通过无与伦比的技术支持帮助用户维持飞机的最佳使用状态。

在军用飞机和防御产品的研制生产方面，波音公司也处于全球领先地位。波音公司的战斗机和攻击机产品包括：F/A-18E/F 超级大黄蜂、F/A-18 大黄蜂、F-15 鹰、F-22 猛禽、AV-8B 鹞、JSF 联合攻击战斗机等。联合攻击机无疑将是未来 20 年处于核心地位的战术飞机项目。

作为美国航空航天局最大的承包商，波音公司的未来与航天飞行、宇宙探索和日益增多的商业航天项目密切相关。波音公司制造了航天飞机轨道飞行器和主发动机，为航天飞机的有效载荷做了准备，完成了整个航天飞机系统的集成。

在商业航天方面，波音公司制造了首批 40 颗全球定位系统（GPS）卫星，使精确导航发生了革命性的变化。之后，波音又签订了制造 33 颗新一代 GPS 卫星的合同。波音公司与俄罗斯、乌克兰和挪威等伙伴公司一起组成一个海上发射合资公司，在太平洋的移动平台上发射卫星。波音公司还制造了"德尔塔"Ⅱ型、Ⅲ型运载火箭，并正在开发"德尔塔"Ⅳ型运载火箭。

8. 通用电气公司（GE）

通用电气公司是世界上最大的多元化服务性公司，同时也是高质量、高科技工业和消费产品的提供者。从飞机发动机、发电设备到金融服务，从医疗造影、电视节目到塑料，通用电气公司致力于通过多项技术和服务创造更美好的生活。

通用电气公司在全世界 100 多个国家开展业务。通用电气公司的历史可追溯到托马斯·爱迪生，他于 1878 年创立了爱迪生电灯公司。1892 年，爱迪生通用电气公司和汤姆森－休斯敦电气公司合并，成立了通用电气公司。通用电气公司是自道－琼斯工业指数 1896 年设立以来唯一至今仍在指数榜上的公司。

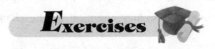

I Discuss and answer the following questions.

1. Why do many people at P&G not use the word "customer", but more likely to ask: "Would 'she' buy it?"
2. Why does P&G change its marketing strategies dramatically nowadays? Does it succeed in its new endeavor? Why?
3. What measures did Mr. Lafley adopt to change the situation of P&G?

4. Do you agree to such a statement in the text: "Scale looks more likely to be a help than a hindrance in today's consumer-goods industry"? Why?
5. What can you learn from P&G's corporate development strategies?

II Decide whether the following statements are true (T) or false (F).

1. P&G has changed its way of selling goods dramatically mainly because women have become more demanding and fickle. (   )
2. Mr. Lafley made a series of acquisition of some famous brands including Gillette, and this strategy has already proved to be successful now. (   )
3. Scale does not always be promoter of growth, but in today's consumer-goods industry, it holds truth. (   )
4. To counter the fierce competition, many retailers developed their own brands or private labels. (   )
5. The marketing techniques of retailers are getting more and more sophisticated because consumers have higher demand for product variety. (   )
6. P&G is the world's biggest advertiser and each year it also earns big revenue by producing heavy amounts of advertisement. (   )
7. P&G started selling off underperformers so that it could focus on beauty and health products, which could bring the company more profits and were more competitive. (   )
8. In 2001, Mr. Lafley's "Connect and Develop" program aimed to open up his company's innovation model which meant a shift from in-house innovation to open innovation — drawing on expertise and knowledge from the other related industries. (   )
9. Unilever has the powerful presence in India where P&G is expected to defeat the company in the near future. (   )
10. P&G learned that it was of essence for its strategies to suit the needs of the emerging markets in the world. (   )

III Group discussion.

1. What are the most valuable things we can learn from the corporate development in P&G?
2. Do you think that it is important to pay attention to the changing environment for a market? Why?
3. How can a company best accommodate the specific needs of a market?
4. What can we learn from Mr. Lafley's "Connect and Develop" program?
5. What do you think of the development of corporate culture?

Unit 4 Corporate Development and Strategies

Case Study

What teaches us Colgate-Palmolive?

Few chief of executives nowadays manage to dominate a company for as long as Reuben Mark has, let alone leave at a time for their own choosing and with an intact reputation. Mr. Mark, who confirmed on January 30th that he will step down as boss of Colgate-Palmolive this year has headed the consumer-products giant for 23 of his 68 years and worked there for more than 40. During his tenure total shareholder returns have exceeded 4,000%, almost three times those of the American stock market.

The higher the note on which Mr. Mark departs, however, the tougher the job will be for his successor, Colgate's 54-year-old president and chief operating officer, Ian Cook. The impact of a big restructuring program (a rare event at Colgate) which helped to lift profits last year, and should add some \$300m to the bottom line in 2007, will fade thereafter. Rapid expansion in Latin America, which accounts for nearly a third of profits and where sales are growing by 14% a year, may slow as the region's economies cool. Some analysts expect Colgate's earnings growth to drop to the mid-single digits from 2008.

It is hard to see what could rev it up again. The legacy of Mr. Mark's disciplined and highly focused style is a culture that is conservative — some would say overly conservative. Colgate's last big innovation, its range of "Total" toothpastes to fight tooth decay, was introduced in the 1990s. It was late to the newer craze for whitening strips, which was spotted first by Crest, its archrival, owned by Procter&Gamble (P&G). Colgate's copycat product — a paint-on whitener — was a flop. And most of Colgate's recent new products, though slickly promoted by celebrities such as Brooke Shields, are brand extensions: toothpastes flavored with mint or cinnamon, or enriched with Vitamin C.

"Colgate is not strong on big innovation," says Jason Gere, an analyst at AG Edwards in New York. "The business is in great shape now, but my biggest question is about future growth." By contrast, P&G has gambled on entire new product categories and has created billion-dollar hits such as its Swiffer anti-static mops.

In addition to its relative lack of innovation, Colgate has also eschewed big acquisitions. Mr. Mark reportedly once dreamt of a merger with Gillette, a company snapped up by P&G in 2005. Last year Pfizer's consumer-health division, including Listerine mouthwash — a brand Mr. Mark said he would love to own — was bought by Johnson & Johnson. Either multi-billion dollar deal would have been risky. But by passing them up, Colgate has closed off potential routes to long-term growth and allowed two of its larger rivals to become even more threatening.

Once P&G combines the clout of its own Crest brand with Gillette's Oral-B franchise, Colgate could find its core earnings from toothpaste being squeezed. And Colgate's heavy reliance on a few categories (it is in about one-fifth as many product markets as P&G) in a relatively small number of regions (in some Latin American countries its market share in toothpaste approaches 80%) makes it vulnerable to a price war or a determined marketing push by a rival.

Today such risks look theoretical, and Colgate's healthy near-term growth and fat share-price are very real. Yet corporate fortunes can change rapidly and it is worth asking how quickly a culture as conservative as Colgate's would adapt. Mr. Cook is a reserved, rather unflamboyant British marketing manager, making Mr. Mark look feisty by comparison. Like Mr. Mark he is also a company lifer, having been at Colgate for over three decades. Not only has he risen under Mr. Mark, he will also have his former boss remaining as chairman, at least for a while — which fall short of best practice in corporate governance. The rest of the board of eight non-executive directors has an average age of more than 66 and six have each served for more than 10 years — which under British standard would throw their independence into doubt.

Investors rarely question a company's corporate governance when all is going well, but they swiftly turn into critics if things change.

(Adapted from *Economist*, Feb. 3, 2007)

Supplementary Reading

Cisco's Display of Strength

Rik Kirkland

Cisco fell hard, went through a wrenching period of reinvention, and is now stronger than it has ever been, reports Fortune's Rik Kirkland.

Sipping Diet Coke in a suite at New York's Mandarin Oriental hotel after a day that began with a joint interview with Microsoft CEO Steve Ballmer conducted by PBS's Charlie Rose, followed by a quick march through a luncheon speech, some one-on-ones with the trade press, and a dozen customer meetings, John Chambers doesn't look or act the way you or I would — exhausted.

As the shadows lengthen over the Hudson River, Cisco's ever ebullient 58-year-old CEO is just getting warmed up. "This is the most excited I've been in ten years," he'd said earlier during his taping with Charlie and Steve. Now in his soft, 90-mph drawl he's explaining why: "I believe a new wave of innovation is coming that will make the first wave of the Internet seem small."

My, that does sound exciting. Example? "This will shock you," he says, leaning forward. "The other day I started the morning with my top staff in India. Then I went to Japan and a meeting with Fujitsu, then on to Cleveland, then London and a meeting with BT. The whole trip took only 3.5 hours, and I was far more effective in the calls."

The reason: Chambers was traveling, of course, over Cisco's latest gee-whiz product: telepresence, a high-def, life-sized, Internet-based communications system that is to traditional video-conferencing what the latest big-screen surround-sound plasma extravaganza would be to Grandma's black-and-white set with rabbit ears. "When I asked the team to design this," he recalls, "I said, 'Make it like Star Trek. You know, Beam me up, Scotty.'"

Giving companies the ability to beam the CFO into meetings or link virtual teams of engineers across the globe already looks like a winner. Telepresence, notes Marthin De Beer, senior vice president in charge of Cisco's emerging technologies group, is "our fastest-ramping internally developed new business in history."

But it's just one part of Chambers' strategy to ensure that as video, voice, and data converge on the Internet and at the same time go mobile, Cisco is selling one-click solutions that tie it all together. "Unified communications" is the buzzword for the fast-growing corporate piece of this puzzle — a piece that Microsoft also wants. But Cisco's ambitions don't stop there. In "the next big market transition," which Chambers believes is fast unfolding, the Internet will become the delivery medium of all communications — and eventually everything from security systems and entertainment to health care and education. Essentially, Cisco wants to be the world's biggest tech company, period — hardware, software, services, everything. "My biggest challenge is not growth but how well we prioritize," he says.

Let's pause to acknowledge that not everyone buys this vision. "When I heard a few weeks ago that John Chambers was excited again, I got excited too," says Fred Hickey, author of a respected tech stock newsletter. "I said to myself, 'The end must be near!'" Hickey isn't singling out Chambers. Like other tech bears, he simply doubts that talking up potent concepts — "video as the killer app" or the rise of "the network as platform" — will boost Cisco's stock, not to mention higher fliers like Google (Fortune 500) and Apple (Fortune 500), once the recession that he believes is coming pushes consumer and corporate spending off a cliff. Hickey also hasn't forgotten Chambers' role as the pied piper of the last tech bubble, in particular his insistence, as the carnage mounted, that Cisco could continue to grow at a 30% to 50% annual clip. It couldn't.

Chambers doesn't deny that a downturn in the economy would be "a hurdle." But one reason his exuberance remains irrepressible is that "this is a movie we've seen before." He's not referring to the horror show at the turn of the millennium but to a less frenzied era — the early to mid-1990s. Back then Cisco famously pioneered using the Internet for automation — it closed its financial books in record time, did remote manufacturing, and so forth. That success helped persuade customers to buy tons of routers and switches in hopes that they too could strike gold. Chambers wants Cisco to serve as its own best sales tool once again, this time by becoming among the first to master a new generation of collaborative technologies-telepresence, unified communications, and corporate versions of social networks like Facebook and MySpace — and then use them to deliver an even bigger productivity payoff. Only now, he says, Cisco (Fortune 500) will be able to do "in one year what took us four years in the first movie."

Cisco dazzled Wall Street a few months back when it reported its numbers. Sales jumped 23%, to nearly $35 billion, while profits climbed 31%, to $7.3 billion. Setting aside the growth generated by acquisitions, including its $6.9 billion purchase of cable set-top box maker Scientific Atlanta, its biggest deal ever, revenues still rose 17% — not bad for an outfit that by now should be subject to the law of large numbers. Chambers reinforced the hope that Cisco can keep defying that law by raising his guidance for future sales increases from the 10% to 15% range to 12% to 17%.

The organization posting those fine numbers, however, is very different from the growth monster that briefly (two days in spring 2000) held the title of World's Most Valuable Company. Think of the company from its IPO in 1990 to 2000 as Cisco 1.0, and the company from 2001 to 2006 as Cisco 2.0.

Cisco 1.0 was a two-hit wonder: It sold routers and switches to FORTUNE 500 companies and made rapid-fire acquisitions to scoop up technology it needed. Cisco 2.0 built a more diversified customer base (cable companies, telcos, smaller businesses along with the big boys) and a much broader range of products, many of which it developed internally — IP telephones, data storage, digital media, and, to use a favored Chambers-ism, "end-to-end-architected solutions" (which sounds like "Indian-architected solutions" when he says it). Version 1.0 was a "plumbing" company called Cisco Systems and invisible to the public beyond its high-wattage stock; in the 2.0 phase it dropped the "Systems" and became just Cisco, and started doing product placements in hit TV show's like Fox's 24. (Whenever the President yells at the Russians? Cisco telepresence.)

The roots of all this were planted in the dark winter of 2001. Once Chambers and his team faced what hit them, they moved with alacrity, laying off 8,500 employees and taking a $2.2 billion write-off. They also asked tough questions about where they'd gone wrong. The conclusion was obvious but difficult to implement: Cisco had to innovate faster.

The first step was to reorganize the company into "probably the world's biggest functionally aligned organization," as Charlie Giancarlo, Cisco's chief development officer, puts it. Translation: Unlike GE (Fortune 500) or 3M or Citigroup (Fortune 500) or pretty much any huge corporation you can think of, Cisco has no divisional presidents or country chiefs with permanent separate armies, all backed by their own support staffs (sales, marketing, engineering, and so on). Instead, at Cisco those functions are all centralized. Whenever the company tackles new markets or geographical areas, the folks responsible for business units must assemble teams drawn from troops controlled by the functional heads.

Why reinvent the standard org chart? One reason is to save money. During the go-go years of 100% annual growth and ceaseless acquisitions (23 in 2000 alone!), Cisco garnered a nickname in Silicon Valley, "the Borg" — after the aliens in Star Trek who expand across the universe by absorbing new species into a hive mind. But by 2001 the hive mind had developed a bad migraine. Cisco's operating expenses soared above 50% of sales as groups charged with entering new markets, such as telecommunications, threw money and bodies at the problem. The new setup instantly cleared away things like overlapping sales and marketing groups. Better still, it continues to enable

Cisco to run remarkably lean. Though the company has nearly doubled in size since 2002, operating expenses today are only 39% of sales.

India's Firms Outpace China's in the Race to "Go Global"

Reorganizing around functions also forced Cisco's brutally competitive culture to learn a new way to grow. The old method, says VC and consultant Geoffrey Moore, who delved into Cisco in his recent book Dealing With Darwin, was to hand an executive fearsome financial targets and tell him to make like a Spartan — "You know, either come back with your shield, or on it." The new Cisco would keep the goals but demand collaboration. Compensation changed too: Instead of getting paid just for meeting targets, top people got rewarded based on how peers rated them on their teamwork. "It's no longer about doing the diving catch," Chambers says.

It wasn't an easy transition. Everyone hated the new way at first. Executives didn't like sharing resources; joint strategy-setting and decision-making was cumbersome. "Things ground to a halt," says Giancarlo. "The first two years were very painful," admits Chambers. Some of the most successful people in the old regime left after their bonuses went poof, thanks to the new compensation system. Others were asked to leave. Overall, Chambers estimates, about 10% of his top team "couldn't make the transition."

Today Cisco operates through six business "councils," each formed around potential $10 billion markets (e.g., consumer, enterprise, and emerging markets). Reporting to the councils are some 30 "boards" that zero in on newer markets with at least $1 billion in possible sales (connected homes, mobility, sports and entertainment). Most of the leadership serves on three councils or boards, so it pays to be flexible.

Case in point: Treasurer Dave Holland, who is also the unlikely co-head of Cisco's new sports and entertainment board. He started out negotiating the sale of some company-owned land to the Oakland A's; next thing you know, he and his team are planning the construction of what will be the A's "Cisco Field" and courting folks from the NFL, NBA, and NASCAR to consider what Cisco technology might do for them. Quick: Name any other big company that would give its treasurer oversight of a potential growth business.

This year Chambers began pushing his company into its next incarnation, which he calls Cisco 3.0. That's shorthand for a range of things Cisco is doing to spur even more teamwork and innovation. Take telepresence: 50 big companies, among them Verizon, Aflac, McKesson, BT, and SAP, have bought systems since the launch last winter. (List price: $299,000 for three 65-inch plasma screens in a special conference room and $71,000 for a single-screen setup.) "It was phenomenal," says Wal-Mart CIO Rollin Ford, who saw a demonstration recently. "I believe it's a technology we will embrace." P&G is installing more than 40 telepresence rooms worldwide over the next nine months. "We are rocking and rolling here," says CIO Filippo Passerini. "To have a breakthrough in the way we operate, we needed a big leap." But no one is more excited about the productivity potential than Cisco itself. Since December, Chambers has rolled out 120 telepresence centers across the company (paid for by ordering every department to cut its travel budget by 20%).

Cisco to Buy WiMax Startup Navini for $330 Million

Another tool is social networking, that new-time religion that Cisco has embraced with a convert's fervor. In September it launched a website that is a microcosm of everything evoked by the phrase "Web 2.0." There's a Ciscopedia, where people can build an evolving body of lore about anything fellow Ciscans might want to know. There are text blogs and video blogs, discussion groups, and "problems and solutions links." There's an internal version of MySpace, which provides not only title and contact info but also personal profiles, job histories, interests, and videos. Soon it will show whether a person is reachable by, say, office phone, cell, IM, or telepresence, and offer a one-click connection.

And there's more. "We're going to use social bookmarking to allow us to take the pulse of the organization," says Jim Grubb, who built the website (and whose day job is putting together John Chambers' demos). They'll do that by aggregating the tags employees create into "tag clouds" when they click on sites. Tracking these will allow a Cisco honcho to get a snapshot of the current hot-button issues for marketing or finance. If an employee is tagged as the go-to person for virtualization, say, he could earn a bonus for this previously unacknowledged expertise. That's down the road. Asked for a here-and-now example, Cisco marketing head Sue Bostrom laughs (proudly) and recounts the six-month online campaign to develop and select a five-note "Cisco sound" for TV and Internet ads. "Ten thousand employees voted," she says, "and 1,200 partners also participated."

Ah, yes, partners. More than most businesses, Cisco relies on outsiders — "the ecosystem," as they call it — to purvey its goods and services. "Channel partners account for some 92% of our sales," says Paul Mountford, who managed those relationships for years before moving to head emerging markets in 2006. One tool for husbanding the ecosystem among smaller businesses is WebEx, the online-meeting hosting service Cisco bought for $3 billion last May. Of the roughly 600 telepresence sessions now held each week within Cisco, roughly one-third involve big customers and partners. Those connections should proliferate as more systems get sold and as Cisco and others eventually lower prices and develop ways to take telepresence down to smaller screens (like the desktop), all connected using open Internet standards.

The best proof that all this team building can pay off comes from Marthin De Beer's emerging-technologies group. Charged three years ago with cooking up $1 billion businesses from scratch, his team's first project was to develop the telepresence system. But that had been Chambers' baby. In search of second acts, De Beer a year ago set up an internal Wiki called I-Zone that has so far generated 400 business ideas. "Better still," he says, "another 10,000 people have added to those ideas." His team measures which notions draw the most activity and cherry-picks a handful to unveil at Cisco's quarterly leadership-development program. Normally at such gatherings, promising up-and-comers from across a company hear lectures, bond, and ponder case studies. But De Beer decided to use these sessions to take the most promising I-Zone ideas and pound them into real-world business plans. Three of the nine notions so tested are now in active development.

This whole process has been an eye opener even for Chambers. He used to tell his staff, "I do strategy; you do execution." "He was amazed," says Ron Ricci, a former consultant who since

2000 has served as Cisco's internal culture keeper. "He said, 'We just did three billion-dollar market opportunities without my knowing about it.'"

Tech's Time of Tumult

The human embodiment of Cisco 3.0 may be Wim Elfrink, head of the company's new Globalization Center East in Bangalore, India, which officially opened at the end of October. Though he occupies a typical Cisco cubicle, the nerve center of his working life lies a few miles away, in a spacious second-floor office overlooking the pool at his California-style home. There he travels around the world on a 65-inch Cisco telepresence screen. "Without this, I don't know if I would have taken this job," he says.

That job, like most things Cisco, isn't easy to explain. Elfrink is one of 13 executives who make up the company's operating committee. (This is the group that sits right below Chambers and into which all the councils report.) He also runs Cisco's service business, which last year generated more than \$5.5 billion in revenue. Since moving to India a year ago, he's taken on responsibility for expanding Cisco's business in the region, for turning the new Globalization Center into a worldwide "intelligent back office," and for ensuring that by 2010 the Indian operation employs 10,000 people and is a base for roughly 20% of the company's "top talent." Though Elfrink has recruited 20 senior executives within Cisco to come east and join his mission, only four people in Bangalore report to him directly. (Remember, most work for functional heads back in San Jose.)

So if your job is to manage 8,000 people scattered around the world, help lead a \$35 billion company based in California, supervise a now 3,200-person, \$1 billion investment in India, build new businesses across a dozen times zones — and the only way you can get it done is by networking like crazy with external partners and internal allies — well, you can see why the guy likes being able to telecommute.

"I'm learning to work in batches," he says. On a typical day in Bangalore, Elfrink starts at 6 AM with a couple of hours of home telepresence back in the United States, where the workday is ending. At his other office he spends the day with customers or visiting delegations from abroad before getting home for dinner and some family time with his wife and two boys. And then it's back onto telepresence to spend a few more hours with his fellow San Jose brass or perhaps partake in a virtual breakfast with a key partner. "And then I have a beer," he says with a laugh.

Beyond the size and rising wealth of the potential market in Asia and the rest of the developing world — "70% of the world's population and 70% of our future growth are within a four-hour flight from Bangalore," Elfrink points out — what's exciting for Cisco is the chance to innovate here on a scale that the West can't match.

With Saudi Arabia building six cities the size of Manhattan in the desert over the next decade and skyscrapers rising like mushrooms in places like Dubai, real estate developers out here have the opportunity to erect "connected" buildings that use the Internet to control security, lighting, and elevators, as well as offer digital entertainment and services that have yet to be invented. "The reason God was able to create the world in seven days," says Elfrink, "is because there was no installed base."

Whatever comes next, Cisco has a hard act to follow itself. So far no company in history has ever achieved what it did in the 1990s: going from IPO to a $500 billion market cap in one decade. Consider this: The one candidate with a shot is Google, which went public three years ago and then zoomed to a market cap around $200 billion (right above where Cisco stands today). But for GOOG to match CSCO and break the $500 billion mark — and this is not even adjusting for inflation — its share price still has to rise from today's roughly $650 level to over $1,600.

Anything can happen, but that's a steep hill for any company to climb or reclimb. Looking ahead, it's easy to list threats, though most come with countermeasures. What about the rise of a hungry, low-cost new competitor like China's Huawei? Its sales have grown from $2.5 billion to $15 billion in five years, a pace more akin to the Cisco of the 1990s. But as Paul Mountford, senior VP for emerging markets, points out, "While they're the only competitor we see everywhere, we never really go head-to-head with them" because Cisco is selling high-value applications and not just boxes. Anyway, he notes, whatever Huawei is doing in emerging markets hasn't kept Cisco from growing 2.5 times faster there than in the US — while maintaining the same plump margins.

What about open source? Google is reportedly using Linux-like routers and switches to stitch together its networks. If that trend spreads, it could reduce demand for Cisco's high-priced wares. Still, most big companies seem to prefer the security that comes with buying Cisco. "Remember, we service 170 million customers a week," says Wal-Mart (Fortune 500) CIO and big Cisco customer Ford (Fortune 500). "And I never want to be accused of not being able to take people's money."

Chambers even ticks off a couple more threats: The broadband build-out in the United States stagnates at its current world-lagging pace and the tech industry as a whole "fails to solve some of the security problems." Still, he'd prefer to dwell on the upside. If Cisco is right about the payoff from the new video and Web 2.0 technologies, he says — and if it succeeds in its own transformation — then "this will transform every government and company in the world." In which case, he goes on to note, "Any of our peers who don't do it won't survive." (You gotta admit: Nobody mixes aw-shucks humility with barely contained cockiness quite like John Chambers.)

Will they pull it off? All we'll hazard is that if anybody has a shot, these guys do. What may be most impressive about Cisco is its capacity to display what F. Scott Fitzgerald defined as a first-rate intelligence: "The ability to hold two opposed ideas in the mind at the same time and still retain the ability to function."

You see that flexibility in Chambers, a control freak trying to spur a bottom-up reinvention. You see it in how his managers practice teamwork while retaining a measure-everything mentality. ("To this day the way you manage at Cisco is through targets called weekly commits," says consultant Moore. "So John can push all this collaboration stuff while knowing his people are still going to have those weekly commit meetings.") Most of all, you see it in how Cisco is absorbing different business models — companies with lower margins, mass customer bases, and distinct organizational structures, such as Linksys and Scientific Atlanta.

Don Proctor, head of the company's new collaboration software group, describes Cisco's evolution as a three-stage process. "We have been focusing for our whole history on product innovation," he says. "Over the past five years we've put a lot of focus on process innovation. Now we're entering a new phase focused on business model innovation. That's a necessary step for us because as we go forward we're going to be in businesses that are even further from our roots than the businesses we are in today."

Well said. To restate that in Star Trek terms: Captain's log, Stardate 11. 2007. Bad news. The Borg lives! Worse news. It's teaching itself new tricks.

(*Fortune*, October 31, 2007)

Answer and discuss the following questions:

1. What is Cisco's ambitious plan for the development in the near future?
2. What contributes to the success of the Cisco business?
3. How does Elfrink manage his company?
4. What are biggest challenges facing Cisco in its development?
5. What can we learn from Cisco's story of corporate growth?

Unit 5

Marketing and Management
营销与管理

Text A

Wal-Mart's Midlife Crisis

Anthony Bianco

Declining growth, increasing competition, and not an easy fix in sight[1]

John E. Fleming, Wal-Mart's newly appointed chief merchandising officer, is staring hard at a display of $14 women's T-shirts in a Supercenter a few miles from the retailer's Bentonville (Ark.) headquarters. The bright-hued stretch T's carry Wal-Mart's own George label and are of a quality and stylishness not commonly associated with America's über-discounter.[2] What vexes Fleming is that numerous sizes are out of stock in about half of the 12 colors, including frozen kiwi and black soot.

Fleming may be America's most powerful merchant, but a timely solution is beyond him even so. Wal-Mart failed to order enough of these China-made T-shirts last year, and so they and other George-brand basics will remain in short supply in most of its 3,443 US stores until 2007's second half, depriving the retailer of tens of millions of dollars a week it sorely needs.[3] "The issue with apparel is long lead times," says the quietly intense Fleming, who spent 20 years at Target Corp. (TGT) before joining Wal-Mart Stores Inc. (WMT) "We will get it fixed."

For nearly five decades, Wal-Mart's signature "everyday low prices" and their enabler — low costs — defined not only its business model but also the distinctive personality of this proud, insular company that emerged from the Ozarks backwoods to dominate retailing.[4] Over the past year and a half, though, Wal-Mart's growth formula has stopped working. In 2006 its US division eked out a 1.9% gain in same-store sales — its worst performance ever — and this year has begun no better.[5] By this key measure, such competitors as Target[6], Costco[7] (COST), Kroger[8] (KR), Safeway[9]

(SWY), Walgreen's[10] (WAG), CVS[11], and Best Buy[12] (BBY) now are all growing two to five times faster than Wal-Mart.

Wal-Mart's botched entry into cheap-chic apparel is emblematic of the quandary it faces. Is its alarming loss of momentum the temporary result of disruptions caused by transitory errors like the T-shirt screwup and by overdue improvements such as the store remodeling program launched last year? Or is Wal-Mart doing lasting damage to its low-budget franchise by trying to compete with much hipper, nimbler rivals for the middle-income dollar? Should the retailer redouble its efforts to out-target Target, or would it be better off going back to basics?

If Wal-Mart seems short of answers at the moment, it might well be because there aren't any good ones. Increasingly, it appears that America's largest corporation has steered itself into a slow-growth cul de sac from which there is no escape. "There are a lot of issues here, but what they add up to is the end of the age of Wal-Mart," contends Richard Hastings, a senior analyst for the retail rating agency Bernard Sands[13]. "The glory days are over."

Simple mathematics suggest that a 45-year-old company in an industry growing no faster than the economy as a whole will struggle to sustain the speedy growth rates of its youth. In Wal-Mart's case, this difficulty is exacerbated by its great size and extreme dominance of large swaths of the US retail market. Wal-Mart already controls 20% of dry grocery, 29% of nonfood grocery, 30% of health and beauty aids, and 45% of general merchandise sales, according to ACNielsen[14].

However, the expansion impulse is as deeply embedded in Wal-Mart's DNA as its allegiance to cut-rate pricing. Wal-Mart was able to boost total US revenues by 7.2% last year by opening new stores at the prodigious rate of nearly one a day. According to Wal-Mart CEO H. Lee Scott Jr., the company plans to sustain this pace for at least the next five years. In fact, he is on record saying that room remains in the US for Wal-Mart to add 4,000 Supercenters — the largest of its store formats by far — to the 2,000 it now operates.

Does Scott, 58, recognize any limits whatsoever to Wal-Mart's growth potential in the US, which accounted for 78% of its $345 billion in sales last year? "Actually, and I know it's going to sound naive to you, I don't," he replies. "The real issue is, are (we) going to be good enough to take advantage of the opportunities that exist?"

Too Close for Comfort

Wall Street does not share Scott's bullishness, to put it mildly. Wal-Mart shares are trading well below their 2004 high and have dropped 30% in total since Scott was named CEO in 2000, even as the Morgan Stanley (MS) retail index[15] has risen 180%. "The stock has been dead money for a long time," says Charles Grom, a JPMorgan Chase & Co.[16] (SPM) analyst.

Even money managers who own Wal-Mart's shares tend to see the retailer as a beaten-down value play, not a growth company. "I'd be surprised if true growth-oriented investors were involved at this point," says Walter T. McCormick, manager of the $1.2 billion Evergreen Fundamental Large Cap Fund[17], which began buying the stock a year ago. "The issue the Street has is market saturation: We may be in the seventh inning of a nine-inning game.[18]"

One can argue that the deceleration of Wal-Mart's organic growth is a function of the aging of its outlets, given that same-store sales rates slow as stores mature.[19] Outlets five years or older accounted for 17% of all US Supercenters in 2000 and 44% in 2006, and will top 60% in 2010, according to HSBC[20] (HBC) analyst Mark Husson. "There's an inevitability of bad middle age," he says.

Meanwhile, the underlying economics of expansion have turned against Wal-Mart, even as it relies increasingly on store-building to compensate for sagging same-store sales. On balance, the new Supercenters are just not pulling in enough sales to offset fully the sharply escalating costs of building them. Part of the problem is that many new stores are located so close to existing ones that Wal-Mart ends up competing with itself. All in all, the retailer's pretax return on fixed assets, which include things such as computers and trucks as well as stores, have plunged 40% since 2000.

Even many analysts with a buy on Wal-Mart want it to follow the lead of McDonald's Corp.[21] (MCD) and cut way back on new-store building to concentrate instead on extracting more value from existing stores, which vary wildly in their performance.[22] Wal-Mart disclosed a year and a half ago that same-store sales were rising 10 times, or 1,000%, faster at the 800 best-managed outlets than at the 800 worst-run ones. Equally shocking was its admission that 25% of its stores failed to meet minimum expectations of cleanliness, product availability, checkout times, and so on.

Scott is acutely aware of the Street's discontent. "We have to find a way to give our shareholders back the returns that they need through some mechanism," he acknowledges. In March, Wal-Mart boosted its dividend 31%. Apparently, the board also is considering spinning off Sam's Club, the warehouse club division that is a perennial also-ran to Costco.

Wal-Mart announced late last year that it would trim its customary 8% annual addition to US square footage to 7% in 2007. At the moment, though, slamming on the brakes is out of the question. Says Scott: "If you stop the growth at Wal-Mart, you'd be silly to think that (alone) means you're going to have better stores."

Wal-Mart's "home office" has taken a series of steps to improve the performance of its far-flung store network. Last year it implemented a whole new supervisory structure that required many of its 27 regional administrators to move out of Bentonville and live in the districts they manage. In April, Scott removed the executive in charge of US store operations and put her in charge of corporate personnel instead.

The number of stores falling below the threshold of minimum customer expectations has declined but remains "more than would be acceptable," says Scott, who is surprisingly philosophical about the persistence of mediocrity. Asked why it has been so difficult to fix bad stores, he replies: "That's a very good question. It's a question I ask all the time."

The polite, self-deprecating Scott is no Robert L. Nardelli, whose ouster as Home Depot Inc.'s[23] (HD) chief had as much to do with his abrasive personality as the chain's business problems.[24] That said, Wal-Mart's stock has performed worse under Scott than Home Depot's did under Nardelli. "The Street is going to look to the back half of 2007 for evidence of improvement," says an adviser to a large, longtime Wal-Mart shareholder. "If that doesn't happen, you're going to see a tremendous amount of pressure."

Scott & Co. already is struggling to cope with mounting sociopolitical backlash to Wal-Mart's size and aggressive business practices. Over the past decade, dozens of lawsuits were brought by employees claiming to be overworked and underpaid, including the mother of all sex discrimination class actions.[25] Organized labor set up two Washington-based organizations to oppose the antiunion employer at every turn (see BusinessWeek.com, 4/9/07, "Stop the Bullying, Wal-Mart"). And hundreds of municipalities across the country erected legal obstacles of one kind or another.

Wal-Mart's initial reaction to the gathering storm of opposition was to ignore it and maintain the defiant insularity that is a legacy of its Ozarks origins. "The best thing we ever did was hide back there in the hills," Sam Walton, the company's legendary founder, declared shortly before his death in 1992.

In the past few years, Scott has reluctantly brought Wal-Mart out from behind its Bentonville barricades. Virtually from scratch, this famously conservative company has built a large public and government relations apparatus headed by Leslie A. Dach, a veteran Washington political operative of pronounced liberal bent. Few CEOs have embraced environmental sustainability as avidly as has Scott, who also broke with the Republican orthodoxy of his predecessors by advocating a hike in the federal minimum wage.

It's not just rhetoric: Wal-Mart has indeed made substantive reforms in some areas. It has struck up effective working relationships with many of the very environmental groups it once disdained. No less dramatically, the company has added three women (one is Hispanic) and two African American directors to its board and also tied all executive bonuses to diversity goals.

It turns out, though, that there is a dark, paranoid underside to Wal-Mart's visible campaign of outreach. What began as an attempt by Wal-Mart's Threat Research and Assessment Group to detect theft and pro-union sympathies among store workers grew into surveillance of certain outside critics, consultants, stockholders, and even Wal-Mart's board.[26] Bruce Gabbard, a security technician fired for allegedly unauthorized wiretapping of a New York Times reporter, has described himself as "the guy listening to the board of directors when Lee Scott is excused from the room."

Wal-Mart's spreading Spygate scandal is perhaps the most damaging in a long sequence of PR disasters, including last year's conviction of former No. 2 executive Thomas M. Coughlin on fraud and tax evasion charges stemming from embezzlement of company funds. Coughlin, a Walton protégé who had been Scott's leading rival for the CEO post, is serving a sentence of 27 months of house arrest.

There is no way of measuring how much business Wal-Mart is losing to competitors with more benign reputations. According to a recent survey conducted by Wal-Mart itself, though, 14% of Americans living within range of one of its stores — which takes in 90% of the population — are so skeptical of the company as to qualify as "conscientious objectors."[27]

But the Arkansas giant's fundamental business problem is that selling for less no longer confers the overwhelming business advantage it once did. Low prices still define the chain's appeal to its best customers, the 45 million mostly low-income Americans who shop its stores frequently and broadly. But the collective purchasing power of these "loyalists," as Wal-Mart calls them, has shriveled in recent years as hourly wages have stagnated and the cost of housing and energy have soared.

More affluent shoppers also walk Wal-Mart's aisles in great numbers, but they tend to buy sparingly, loading up on toothpaste, detergent, and other "consumables" priced barely above cost while shunning higher-margin items such as clothes and furniture. To the selective middle-income shopper, quality, style, service, and even store aesthetics increasingly matter as much as price alone. "Here's the big thought Wal-Mart missed: Price is not enough anymore," says Todd S. Slater, an analyst at Lazard Capital Markets[28].

Backwoods Knowhow

At first, Wal-Mart management blamed its loss of momentum mostly on rising gasoline prices — a theory undercut when same-store sales kept falling even as the cost of gas receded during the latter half of 2006. Today, Wal-Mart executives are more willing to acknowledge the X factor of intensified competition. Says Fleming: "We're now up against world-class competitors that are each taking a slice of our business."

Wal-Mart not only was slow to recognize this threat but also responded haphazardly once it did. The nub of the problem was that the discounter had relied for so long on selling for less that it did not know any other way to sell. Wal-Mart did not begin to build a marketing department worthy of the name until Fleming was named to the new position of chief marketing officer in spring, 2005, an appointment Scott hailed as "an extraordinary move for us."

Founded in 1962, Wal-Mart rose to dominance on the strength of its mastery of retailing's "back-end" mechanics. Forced by the isolation of the Ozarks to do for itself what most retailers relied on others to do for them, Wal-Mart built a cutting-edge distribution system capable of moving goods from factory loading dock to store cash register faster and cheaper by far than any competitor.[29] It added to its cost advantage by refusing to acquiesce to routine increases in wholesale prices, continually pressing suppliers to charge less.

Walton, who was both a gifted merchant and a born tightwad, also pinched pennies in every other facet of business, from wages and perks (there were none) to fixtures and furnishings. Aesthetics counted for so little that when the retailer finally put down carpet in its stores it took care to choose a color that matched the sludgy gray-brown produced by mixing dirt, motor oil, and the other contaminants most commonly tracked across its floors. To Wal-Mart, the beauty of its hideous carpet was that it rarely needed cleaning.

Low costs begat low prices. Instead of relying on promotional gimmickry, Wal-Mart sold at a perpetual discount calculated to make up for in volume what it lost in margin. Walton's philosophy was price it low, pile it high, and watch it fly. His belief in everyday low prices made him a populist hero even as he built America's largest fortune. (His descendants still own 40% of Wal-Mart's shares, a stake worth $80 billion.) Regulators forced "Mr. Sam" to modify his slogan of "Always the lowest price" to the hedged "Always low prices!" But hundreds of retailers went broke trying to compete with Wal-Mart on price just the same.

In many ways, Wal-Mart has remained reflexively tight-fisted under Scott, a 28-year company veteran who trained at Walton's knee and rose to the top through trucking and logistics. Last year,

Wal-Mart began remodeling the apparel, home, and electronics sections in 1,800 stores, replacing miles of that stain-colored carpeting with vinyl that looks like wood. To Fleming, the new "simulated wood" floor is all about aesthetic improvement. His boss takes the classical Wal-Mart view. "The truth is that vinyl costs less," Scott says. "And the maintenance on the vinyl costs less than the maintenance on the carpet."

Yet Wal-Mart is neither as low-cost nor as low-price a retailer as it was in Walton's day, or even when Scott moved up to CEO. Most dramatically, overhead costs jumped 14.8% in 2006 alone and now amount to 18.6% of sales, compared with 16.4% in Scott's first year — a momentous rise in a business that counts profit in pennies on the dollar.

The imperatives of reputational damage control have prompted Bentonville to add hundreds of staff jobs in public relations, corporate affairs, and other areas that the company happily ignored when it was shielded by the force field of Walton's folksy charisma. And as the nation's largest electricity consumer and owner of its second-largest private truck fleet, Wal-Mart was hit doubly hard by the explosion of energy costs.

Wal-Mart also has purposefully, if not entirely voluntarily, inflated its cost base in expanding far beyond its original rural Southern stronghold. It is far more expensive to buy land and to build, staff, and operate stores in the large cities that are the final frontier of Wal-Mart's expansion than in the farm towns where it began. Then, too, the company is encountering mounting resistance as it pushes deeper into the Northeast, Upper Midwest[30], and West Coast, requiring it to retain legions of lawyers and lobbyists to fight its way into town.

Narrowing the Gap

Under Scott, Wal-Mart even blunted its seminal edge in distribution by letting billions of dollars in excess inventories accumulate at mismanaged stores. A dubious milestone was reached in 2005 as inventories rose even faster than sales. "You'd see these big storage containers behind stores, but what was more amazing was that (local) managers were going outside Wal-Mart's distribution network to subcontract their own warehouse space[31]," says Bill Dreher, a US retailing analyst for Deutsche Bank[32] (DB).

Over the past decade, top competitors in most every retailing specialty have succeeded in narrowing their cost gap with Wal-Mart by restructuring their operations. They eliminated jobs, remodeled stores, and replaced warehouses, investing heavily in new technology to tie it all together. Unionized supermarkets even managed to chip away at Wal-Mart's nonunion-labor cost advantage, signaling their resolve by taking a long strike in Southern California in 2003–2004.[33] The end result: Rival chains gradually were able to bring their prices down closer to Wal-Mart's and again make good money.

Consider the return to form of Kroger Co., the largest and oldest US supermarket chain. Cincinnati-based Kroger competes against more Wal-Mart Supercenters — 1,000 at last count-than any other grocer. That is why until recently the only real interest Wall Street took in the old-line giant was measuring it for a coffin. Today, though, a rejuvenated Kroger is gaining share faster in the 32 markets where it competes with Wal-Mart than in the 12 where it does not.

A recent Bank of America[34] (BAC) survey of three such markets — Atlanta, Houston, and Nashville — found that Kroger's prices were 7.5% higher on average than Wal-Mart's, compared with 20% to 25% five years ago. This margin is thin enough to allow Kroger to again bring to bear such "core competencies" as service, quality, and convenience, says BofA's Scott A. Mushkin, who recently switched his Kroger rating to buy from sell. "We're saying the game has changed, and it looks like it has changed substantially in Kroger's favor," he says.

While Wal-Mart vies with a plethora of born-again rivals for the trade of middle-income Americans, it also must contend on the low end of the income spectrum with convenience and dollar-store chains and with such "hard discounters" as Germany's Aldi Group[35]. These no-frills rivals are challenging Wal-Mart's hold over budget-minded shoppers by underpricing it on many staples.

To right Wal-Mart's listing US flagship division, Scott installed Eduardo Castro-Wright as its president and CEO in fall, 2005. The Ecuador-born, US-educated Castro-Wright, now 51, worked for RJR Nabisco[36] and Honeywell International Inc[37]. (HON) before joining Wal-Mart in 2001. In Castro-Wright's three years as CEO of Wal-Mart Mexico, revenues soared 50%, powered by sparkling same-store sales growth of 10% a year.

To date, Castro-Wright has fallen so far short of replicating the miracle of Mexico that in January he had to publicly deny rumors that he was about to be transferred back to international. Instead, Scott shifted the vice-chairman over Castro-Wright to new duties. That the US chief now reports directly to Scott both solidifies Castro-Wright's status and ups the pressure on him to show results.

Castro-Wright can point to progress on the cost side of the ledger. By tightening controls over the stores, headquarters has halved the growth rate of inventories to 5.6% from 11.5% two years ago. Wal-Mart also has squeezed more productivity out of its 1.3 million store employees for eight consecutive quarters. This was done by capping wages for most hourly positions, converting full-time jobs to part-time ones, and installing a sophisticated scheduling system to adjust staffing levels to fluctuations in customer traffic.[38]

Wal-Mart has found other new ways to economize, notably by cutting out middlemen to do more contract manufacturing overseas. The company's much publicized green initiatives have tempered criticism from some left-leaning opponents but are perhaps best understood as a politically fashionable manifestation of its traditional cost-control imperative.

By any conventional measure, Wal-Mart remains a solidly profitable company. Rising overhead costs have cut into net income, which in 2006 rose a middling 6.7%, a far cry from the double-digit increases of the 1990s. Return on equity continues to top 20%, however, and US operating margins actually have widened a bit under Castro-Wright, as costs have risen a bit slower than Wal-Mart's average selling price.

Evidently, though, it is going to take a lot more than Castro-Wright's workmanlike adjustments to revive Wal-Mart's moribund stock. In the end, Scott's aversion to a McDonald's-style strategic about-face leaves Wal-Mart no alternative but to try to grow its way back into Wall

Street's good graces. But if opening a new Wal-Mart or Sam's Club almost every day can't move the dial, what will?

Foreign markets present an intriguing mix of potential and peril for Wal-Mart, which first ventured abroad in 1992. Although the company now owns stores in 13 countries, the lion's share of those revenues comes from Mexico, Canada, and Britain. In 2006 international revenues rose 30%, to $77 billion. At the same time, though, Wal-Mart's long-standing struggles to adapt its quintessentially American low-cost, low-price business model to foreign cultures was underscored by the $863 million loss it took in exiting Germany.

Wal-Mart is the rare US company that is more politically constrained at home than abroad in angling for outsize growth opportunities. In March it withdrew its application for a Utah bank charter[39] just before a congressional committee was set to convene hearings. The retreat marks an apparent end to its decade-long campaign to diversify into consumer banking[40].

Although Wal-Mart regularly makes sizable acquisitions abroad, it is in no position to respond in kind to such domestic dagger thrusts as CVS's $26.5 billion acquisition of pharmacy benefits manager Caremark Rx. "That deal is a real threat, but Wal-Mart would have huge antitrust problems if it made an acquisition of any size," says a top mergers-and-acquisitions banker. "They are kind of stuck."

In the end, Wal-Mart seems unlikely to regain its stride unless it can solve what might be the diceyest conundrum in retailing today. That is, can it seduce tens of millions of middle-income shoppers into stepping up their purchases in a major way without alienating its low-income legions in the process?

Largely because of the pressing need to differentiate itself from Wal-Mart, Target began grappling with this very puzzle more than a decade ago and gradually solved it with the cheap-chic panache that transformed it into "Tar-zhay." Says the president of a leading apparel maker: "Target has an awareness of what's happening in fashion equal to a luxury player, maybe greater. They have set the bar very high."

Scott acknowledged as much in making former Target exec Fleming chief marketing officer, reporting to Castro-Wright. Fleming, who had been CEO of Wal-Mart. com, went outside to fill every key slot in building a 40-person marketing group from scratch. He supported Wal-Mart's move into higher-priced, more fashionable apparel and home furnishings with the splashiest marketing the retailer had ever done, buying ad spreads in *Vogue*[41] and sponsoring an open-air fashion show in Times Square[42].

Wal-Mart's top management all the way up to and including Scott presumed that Wal-Mart could run like Tar-zhay before it had learned to walk. "What Wal-Mart tried to do smacks of a kind of arrogant attitude toward fashion — that you can just order it, put it down, and people will buy it," says Eric Beder, a specialty retailing analyst at Brean Murray, Carret & Co.[43]

Crash Course

Wal-Mart did everything at once and precipitously, introducing ads even as it was flooding stores with new merchandise and before it could complete its store remodeling program. Bentonville was learning marketing on the fly and did not even attempt to adopt the sort of formal, centralized merchandise planning at which Target and many big department-store chains excel. Instead, Wal-Mart relied on dozens of individual buyers to make critical decisions as it pushed hard into unfamiliar product areas.

How else to explain why a retailer whose typical female customer is thought to be a size 14 loaded up on skinny-leg jeans? Or why Wal-Mart's cheap-chic Metro7 line got off to a flying start in 350 stores only to crash and burn as it was rolled out to 1,150 more? Or why Wal-Mart not only severely misread demand for George-brand basics but also is unable to replenish its stocks for months on end while "fast-fashion" chains such as H&M[44] easily turn over entire collections every six weeks?

Scott loved Wal-Mart's bold new direction until he hated it, his enthusiasm diminishing in sync with same-store sales throughout much of 2006. "We are going to sell for less," Scott says now, emphasizing a return to Wal-Mart's first principles. "I believe that long after we are gone, the person who sells for less will do more business than the person who doesn't."

Yet Scott also signaled his continuing commitment to the pursuit of the middle-income shopper by promoting Fleming to yet another new post, chief merchandising officer, as part of a January shakeup of the senior ranks. Although Wal-Mart no doubt has sponsored its last glitzy runway show, Fleming insists that the company is sticking with its underlying strategy of "customer relevance"—that is, of moving beyond a monolithic focus on price to try to boost sales by targeting particular customers in new ways.[45] "We're not going to back off," he vows. "We've learned certain lessons. Some things we'll build on, some things we won't."

While the look of its stores is primarily a function of how much Wal-Mart chooses to spend on them, the retailer is unlikely ever to come up with an ambience conducive to separating the affluent from their money without changing its whole approach to labor.[46] The chain's dismal scores on customer satisfaction surveys imply that it is understaffing stores to the point where many of them struggle merely to meet the demands of its self-service format.

It is entirely possible even so that Wal-Mart in time will figure out how to sell vast quantities of dress-for-success blazers, 400-thread-count sheets, laptop computers, and even prepackaged sushi. But as Wal-Mart closes in on $400 billion in annual revenues, it is going to have to overachieve just to get same-store sales rising again at 3% to 5% a year.

The odds are that Scott, or his successor, will have to choose between continuing to disappoint Wall Street or milking the US operation for profits better reinvested overseas.[47] Only by hitting the business development equivalent of the lottery in countries like China, India, or Brazil can the world's largest retailer hope to restore the robust growth that once seemed like a birthright.

(*BusinessWeek*, March 5, 2007)

New Words and Expressions

fix	n.	困境
supercentre	n.	（尤指郊区的）大商店区，特大购物中心
hue	v.	染色的，有颜色的
stylishness	n.	时髦，流行，漂亮
über	a.	特级的，极大的
discounter	n.	廉价商店，折扣商店
basics	n.	生活必需品
sorely	ad.	强烈地，非常
apparel	n.	衣服，装饰
intense	a.	热切的，热情的
enabler	n.	推动者，推动力
insular	a.	孤立的，超然物外的，保守的
backwoods	n.	边远地区，远离城镇的森林区
formula	n.	公式，规则，模式
eke	v.	补充，增加
botch	v.	修补得不好，做得拙劣
cheap-chic	a.	廉价时尚
chic	a.	别致的，时尚的
emblematic	a.	象征（性），标记的
quandary	n.	困惑，窘境，进退两难
momentum	n.	动力，势头
disruption	n.	中断，分裂，瓦解
transitory	a.	短时间的，暂时的
screwup	n.	事情弄糟
overdue	a.	迟到的
remodel	v.	重新塑造，改造，改变
hip	a.	熟悉内情的
nimble	a.	灵活的，敏捷的，思路敏捷的
redouble	v.	加倍，加强
steer	v.	朝……前进
cul de sac	n.	死胡同
exacerbate	v.	恶化，增剧，使加剧
swath	n.	狭长的条或片

nonfood	a.	非食物的，与食物无关的
allegiance	n.	忠贞，效忠
prodigious	a.	巨大的
whatsoever	a.	无论什么
bullishness	n.	看涨人气，牛市
beaten-down	a.	被摧毁的，减价的
saturation	n.	饱和（状态）
inning	n.	一局，（棒球、板球的）盘，局
deceleration	n.	减速
outlet	n.	销路，市场
inevitability	n.	必然性
sagging	a.	下垂，下沉
escalate	v.	逐步升高，逐步增强
plunge	v.	下降，急降
extract	v.	拔出，榨取，析取
checkout	n.	（超级市场等的）收款处，付款处
acutely	ad.	尖锐地，剧烈地
discontent	n.	不满
perennial	a.	长期的，永久的
trim	v.	整理，修整
footage	a.	总长度
fling	v.	猛投，抛，掷
philosophical	a.	哲学的
persistence	n.	坚持，持续
mediocrity	n.	平常，平庸
deprecate	v.	抗议，抨击，反对
ouster	n.	驱逐，夺取
abrasive	a.	恼人的，粗糙的
sociopolitical	a.	社会政治的，同时涉及社会和政治的
backlash	n.	（政治或社会上的）对抗性反应
overwork	v.	（使）工作过度
antiunion	a.	反对工会的
municipality	n.	市政当局，自治市
erect	v.	树立，建立
defiant	a.	挑战的，挑衅的，目中无人的
insularity	n.	（思想、观点等的）偏狭，僵化
legendary	a.	传说中的，传奇（式）的
barricade	n.	有激烈争论的领域或主题

Unit 5 Marketing and Management

virtually	ad.	事实上，实质上
apparatus	n.	机构，组织
operative	n.	工人，技工
pronounced	a.	显著的，断然的，明确的
liberal	a.	自由主义的
bent	n.	倾向，爱好
sustainability	n.	持续，支撑
avidly	ad.	贪心地，热心地
orthodoxy	n.	正统，信奉正统
predecessor	n.	前辈，前任
hike	n.	增加，提高
rhetoric	n.	浮夸与修饰，浮夸的言语
disdain	v.	蔑视，鄙弃
diversify	v.	使多样化，使不同
paranoid	a.	像患偏执狂的
underside	n.	荫蔽面，阴暗面
outreach	n.	伸出，延展
detect	v.	侦查，探测
pro-union	a.	支持工会的
surveillance	n.	监视，监督
allegedly	ad.	涉嫌，有嫌疑
unauthorized	a.	未被授权的
wiretapping	n.	窃听
embezzlement	n.	盗用，侵占，挪用
protégé	n.	门徒，受到影响或支持的人
benign	a.	良好的，良性的
skeptical	a.	怀疑性的，好怀疑的
conscientious	a.	凭良心的，谨慎的，尽责的
objector	n.	反对者，提出异议的人
Arkansas	n.	阿肯色州（美国中南部的州）
overwhelming	a.	压倒性的，无法抵抗的
shrivel	v.	枯萎，（使）失效
sparingly	ad.	节俭地，保守地
shun	v.	避开，避免
aesthetics	n.	美学，审美
undercut	v.	削弱（力量、地位）
haphazardly	ad.	偶然性，随意性
nub	n.	要点，核心

hail	v.	拥戴，欢呼
mastery	n.	掌握
acquiesce	n.	默许，勉强同意
tightwad	n.	吝啬鬼
pinch	v.	掐，挤，捏
perk	n.	额外津贴
sludgy	a.	泥泞的，淤泥多的
contaminant	n.	致污物，污染物
track	v.	追踪，留下足迹
hideous	a.	丑陋的，丑恶的
beget	v.	招致，产生，引起
gimmicky	n.	噱头，巧妙手法
perpetual	a.	永久的
populist	n.	（美国的）人民党党员
hedge	v.	躲闪，说话做事留余地，避免正面答复
reflexively	ad.	反射（性）地，折转地
vinyl	n.	[化] 乙烯基，乙烯树脂
simulate	v.	模拟，模仿，仿制
imperative	n.	需要，必要，命令
folksy	a.	和气的，友好的，无拘束的
charisma	n.	超凡魅力，感召力
stronghold	n.	中心地，大本营
legion	n.	军团，大批的人，队伍
lobbyist	n.	活动议案通过者，说客
blunt	v.	使变钝
dubious	a.	不可靠的，可能有问题的
milestone	n.	里程碑，里程标，重要事件
subcontract	v.	转包合同
unionize	v.	统一，成立工会
nonunion	a.	不属于工会的，不承认工会的
Cincinnati	n.	辛辛那提（美国俄亥俄州西南部城市）
coffin	n.	棺材
rejuvenate	v.	使复原，使恢复精神，使恢复活力
plethora	n.	过剩，过多
spectrum	n.	范围，领域，系列
no-frill	n.	未成装饰，不摆架子
staple	n.	主要产品（或商品）
flagship	n.	旗舰

Unit 5 Marketing and Management

sparkle	v.	使闪耀，使产生活力
replicate	v.	复制
solidify	v.	（使）团结，巩固
ledger	n.	分类账，分户总账
middleman	n.	中间人
initiative	n.	主动，积极性
temper	v.	调和，调节
left-leaning	a.	左倾的
manifestation	n.	显示，表现
workmanlike	a.	精巧的，技巧熟练的
moribund	a.	濒死的，即将消灭的，呆滞的
aversion	n.	厌恶，讨厌的事和人
about-face	n.	向后转，大改变，彻底改变
intriguing	a.	迷人的，有迷惑力的
peril	n.	危险
quintessentially	ad.	典型地，标准地
underscore	v.	画线于……下，强调
dagger	n.	短剑，匕首，敌意
thrust	n.	插，戳，刺
pharmacy	n.	配药业，制药业
dicey	a.	不确定的，冒险性的
grapple	v.	抓牢，抓紧，格斗
panache	n.	羽饰，华丽，炫耀
exec	n.	执行，实行
splashy	a.	惹人注目的
open-air	a.	户外的，露天的
smack	v.	带有……风味
precipitously	ad.	突然地，急转直下地，轻率地
replenish	v.	补充存货
sync	n.	同时，同步
shakeup	n.	重组，摇匀
glitzy	a.	闪光的，耀眼的
monolithic	a.	单一的
ambience	n.	周围环境，气氛
conducive	a.	导致……的；有助于……的
blazer	n.	颜色鲜明的运动夹克
prepackage	v.	出售前预先包装
sushi	n.	寿司，生鱼片冷饭团

overachieve	v.	（在学业等方面）超过预期的成就
birthright	n.	与生俱来的权利

frozen kiwi	冰冻猕猴桃色
black soot	烟黑色
lead time	提前时间
business model	商业模式
growth formula	增长模式
eke out	弥补……的不足，竭力维持
same-store sales	单店销售收入
store remodeling	店面改建
steer . . . into . . .	驾驶进入，向……前进，与……接轨
dry grocery	干货店
health and beauty aids	保健美容品
cut rate	减价
pretax return	税前回报
cut way back	减少，削减
spin off	分立，创造新事物而不影响原物
square footage	面积，平方英尺
slam on	猛击，撞击
corporate personnel	公司人事
strike up	建立起，开始
house arrest	（本宅）软禁
load up on	大量储存
worthy of the name	名副其实的
back end	后端
motor oil	电动机润滑油
overhead cost	营业成本，总开支
truck fleet	卡车车队
core competency	核心竞争力
vie with	与……竞争
move the dial	起作用，有效果，达到目的
lion's share	最大份额
grapple with	尽力解决某困难问题
build . . . from scratch	白手起家，从一无所有建起
on the fly	匆忙地，忙碌地
on end	连续地
in sync with . . .	与……同步
back off	后退
thread count	纱密度

Unit 5 Marketing and Management

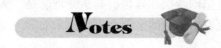

1. Declining growth, increasing competition, and not an easy fix in sight.　增长减速，竞争加剧，面临一个不容易解脱的困境。
   句中的"fix"意为"困境，困难"。

2. The bright-hued stretch T's carry Wal-Mart's own George label and are of a quality and stylishness not commonly associated with America's über-discounter.　这些颜色鲜艳的 T 恤衫印有沃尔玛自己的乔治标签，其质量和风格同美国的大型廉价超市联系不起来。
   句中的"associated"是过去分词作定语。

3. Wal-Mart failed to order enough of these China-made T-shirts last year, and so they and other George-brand basics will remain in short supply in most of its 3,443 US stores until 2007's second half, depriving the retailer of tens of millions of dollars a week it sorely needs.　由于去年没有订购到足够的中国产 T 恤，因此 2007 年下半年前，在沃尔玛全美 3 443 家的多数店里，T 恤及其他乔治牌日常用品将供应不足，这会导致零售商每周损失急需的几千万美金。
   句中的"depriving"是现在分词作状语，"it sorely needs"作定语修饰前面的"tens of millions of dollars"，"deprive...of..."意为"剥夺，丧失"。

4. For nearly five decades, Wal-Mart's signature "everyday low prices" and their enabler — low costs — defined not only its business model but also the distinctive personality of this proud, insular company that emerged from the Ozarks backwoods to dominate retailing.　近 50 年来，沃尔玛"天天低价"的标志和低成本推动所代表的不仅仅是其商业模式，同时还有这个骄傲并且与众不同的公司的鲜明个性，它源于偏僻的山野乡村，进而控制了零售业。
   句中的"that"引导的是定语从句。

5. In 2006 its US division eked out a 1.9% gain in same-store sales — its worst performance ever — and this year has begun no better.　2006 年其美国店面的同店销售额增长率仅为 1.9%，达到历史最低，而今年年初情况仍没有什么好转。

6. Target　塔吉特公司
   美国第四大零售商，位于明尼苏达州的明尼阿波利斯市，在美国 47 个州设有 1 330 家商店，为客户提供当今时尚前沿的零售服务。塔吉特物美价廉，并将自己的顾客群 80% 定位于女性。和沃尔玛的"天天低价"相比，塔吉特对于低价的承诺有适度的保留，它的广告词是："期待更多，花费更少"。

7. Costco　好市多公司
   美国第 6 大零售商，是一家仓储会员式企业，是会员制仓储批发俱乐部的创始者。自成立以来该零售商即致力于以尽可能低的价格提供给会员高品质的品牌商品，它提供给会员的不仅仅是众多的商品选项，而且还有许多特别的会员专享的服务与权益。目前公司在全世界经营有数百家卖场。

8. Kroger　克罗格公司

美国第三大零售集团，是美国具有百年历史的名店之一，创造了世界零售百年史上的若干个第一。该公司一直把创新摆在首位，其指导理念是"人无我有，人有我新"。许多美国商业法规都是根据克罗格公司的发展而制定出来的。

9. Safeway　西夫韦公司

北美最大的食品和药品零售商之一，其战略是薄利多销，信念是1915年提出的"一切为了顾客"。

10. Walgreen　沃尔格林公司

美国第二大药房连锁店，是药品、食品零售连锁企业，主要经营药品和食品百货的零售。

11. CVS

美国最大的药品零售商，在美国的36个州和哥伦比亚特区运营着超过5 400家零售药店和专用药品店，其经营理念是以客户为中心，第一经营目标是以杰出的服务、客户价值、最方便的购物体验满足每一位消费者的健康保健需求。

12. Best Buy　百思买集团

它是全球最大的家用电器和电子产品的零售和分销及服务集团。集团包括 BEST BUY 零售、音乐之苑集团、未来商场公司、Magnolia Hi-Fi 及热线娱乐公司，其发展宗旨是以物美价廉、易于使用的高科技娱乐产品提高生活品质。

13. Bernard Sands　柏沙信用顾问公司

该公司是一家信用评级及服务机构，位于纽约，是美国最权威的零售评级机构之一，该机构还同时提供信用咨询服务。

14. ACNielsen　AC 尼尔森市场研究公司

它是全球领先的市场研究、资讯和分析服务的提供者。AC 尼尔森是荷兰 VNU 集团属下公司，公司总部位于美国纽约，在全球超过 100 个国家提供市场动态、消费者行为、传统和新兴媒体监测及分析服务。客户依靠 AC 尼尔森的市场研究、专有产品、分析工具及专业服务，以了解竞争环境，发掘新的机遇和提升他们市场及销售行动的成效和利润。

15. retail index　零售指数

零售指数主要用于反映当前社会消费状况。调查对象为各种形态和规模的零售业，包括汽车零售商、超级市场、药品和酒类经销商等。因为零售业范围太广，因而采用随机抽样的方式，以求取较具代表性的数据资料。零售指数的提升，代表个人消费支出的增加，经济情况好转。

16. JP Morgan Chase & Co.　摩根大通公司

它是全球历史最长、规模最大的金融服务集团之一，总部位于纽约，为3 000多万名消费者及企业、机构和政府客户提供服务，业务遍及50多个国家，是投资银行业务、金融服务、金融事务处理、投资管理、私人银行业务和私募股权投资方面的领导者。

17. Evergreen Fundamental Large Cap Fund　长荣基本面大型股基金

著名基金，管理着12亿美元资金，专门投资大型股，其资产组合主要包括价值型及成长型股票。

18. We may be in the seventh inning of a nine-inning game.　我们可能已经处于游戏的结束阶

段了。

本句采用的是比喻的表达方式，用9局游戏中的第7局来表示游戏快结束了，暗示对投资沃尔玛不是很有信心。

19. One can argue that the deceleration of Wal-Mart's organic growth is a function of the aging of its outlets, given that same-store sales rates slow as stores mature. 如果同店销售增长率随着店面经营时间的延长而减缓，人们可能会认为沃尔玛内生增长率的下降是其销售网络老化的表现。

    句中的"function"意为"函数"，引申为"表现"；"given that"引导条件状语从句。

20. HSBC 汇丰集团

    汇丰集团是全球最大规模的银行及金融服务机构之一，总部设于伦敦，在欧洲、亚太地区、美洲、中东及非洲等地区拥有约9 500家附属机构，提供广泛的银行及金融服务，包括个人金融业务、工商业务、企业银行、投资银行、资本市场及私人银行等。

21. McDonald's Corp. 麦当劳公司

    它是全球规模最大、最著名的快餐集团，总部位于美国伊利诺伊州的Oak Brook，是拥有数十亿美元资产的国际性公司。从1955年创始人麦当劳兄弟和雷·克洛克在美国伊利诺伊州开设第一家餐厅至今，它在全世界的120多个国家和地区已开设了数万家餐厅，现在仍以快速的趋势迅猛发展。在很多国家，麦当劳代表着一种美国式的生活方式。其经营理念为"麦当劳不仅仅是一家餐厅"。

22. Even many analysts with a buy on Wal-Mart want it to follow the lead of McDonald's Corp. (MCD) and cut way back on new-store building to concentrate instead on extracting more value from existing stores, which vary wildly in their performance. 即使很多推荐买入沃尔玛的分析师也想让它学习麦当劳公司，减少新开店的数量，把重点放在如何从现有店面中获取更多收益，这些店面的经营情况彼此差别很大。

    句中的"buy"指的金融理财分析师推荐买入的评级。

23. Home Depot Inc. 家得宝公司

    它是世界上最大的家庭家居用品零售商，在美国50个州拥有2 042家零售店，同时还是美国家居领域最大的综合性批发中心，在美国及加拿大有900多处批发中心，为顾客及商家提供建筑房屋、家居改进设备、维护设备、市政基础部件。

24. The polite, self-deprecating Scott is no Robert L. Nardelli, whose ouster as Home Depot Inc.'s (HD) chief had as much to do with his abrasive personality as the chain's business problems. 礼貌、低调的斯科特不是罗伯特·L. 纳德里，纳德里被家得宝公司解除首席执政官的职位，除了公司的商业问题以外，这还和他难以与人相处的个性有关。

    句中的"whose"引导定语从句；"abrasive"原意是"摩擦"，此处指难以与人相处。

25. Over the past decade, dozens of lawsuits were brought by employees claiming to be overworked and underpaid, including the mother of all sex discrimination class actions. 在过去的10年里，公司雇员以工作过度和报酬过低为由提起了几十起诉讼，包括性别歧视的集体诉讼。

26. What began as an attempt by Wal-Mart's Threat Research and Assessment Group to detect theft and pro-union sympathies among store workers grew into surveillance of certain outside critics,

consultants, stockholders, and even Wal-Mart's board. 沃尔玛威胁研究和评价部门一开始用来侦测盗窃及雇员中支持工会活动的措施,逐渐变成了某些外部批评者、顾问、股东甚至董事会的监督手段。

句中的"what"引导主语从句。

27. According to a recent survey conducted by Wal-Mart itself, though, 14% of Americans living within range of one of its stores — which takes in 90% of the population — are so skeptical of the company as to qualify as "conscientious objectors." 但是沃尔玛最近的一次调查显示,在其分店辐射范围的居民中,14% 的美国人对公司表示怀疑而成为"有良心的反对者",而沃尔玛零售店的辐射范围占到了美国总人口的 90%。

句中的"which"引导定语从句,修饰前面的"Americans";"conscientious objectors"指基于良心、道德或宗教的原因而反对某些事项的人。

28. Lazard Capital Markets 拉扎德资本市场
美国著名市场研究公司,于 2005 年由拉扎德公司资本重组成立,向客户提供咨询、资产管理、可转换票据销售及承销等服务。

29. Forced by the isolation of the Ozarks to do for itself what most retailers relied on others to do for them, Wal-Mart built a cutting-edge distribution system capable of moving goods from factory loading dock to store cash register faster and cheaper by far than any competitor. 因为当初奥沙克与外界联系较少,沃尔玛必须自己做许多其他零售商可以让别人去做的事情,这促使沃尔玛建立了一套很有竞争力的分销体系,能够以比竞争对手更快、价格更低的方式把商品从工厂手中转换成现金。

句中的"cash register"意为"收银台",此处引申为把商品销售出去变现。

30. Upper Midwest 美国中西部的北部
这一区域包括密歇根州部分地区、爱荷华州、印第安纳州和伊利诺伊州,也有人把密苏里州以及俄亥俄州的部分地区归入其内。

31. You'd see these big storage containers behind stores, but what was more amazing was that (local) managers were going outside Wal-Mart's distribution network to subcontract their own warehouse space. 你会看到店面后面巨大的仓储仓库,但令人诧异的是分店经理们却在沃尔玛销售网络之外转包他们自己的仓储空间。

句中的"what"引导主语从句。

32. Deutsche Bank 德意志银行
全世界最大的综合性银行之一,在全球 74 个国家建立了分支机构,共有员工 65 000 多名。该银行成立于 1870 年,目前资产总额已达到 9 720 亿欧元,在欧洲乃至世界金融领域扮演着举足轻重的角色。德意志银行的企业银行和证券服务、交易银行、资产管理及私人财富管理服务,均在全球市场上首屈一指,其私人和商业银行服务在德国和部分欧洲国家更是占据领先地位。

33. Unionized supermarkets even managed to chip away at Wal-Mart's nonunion-labor cost advantage, signaling their resolve by taking a long strike in Southern California in 2003 – 2004. 有工会组织的超市甚至成功地抵消了沃尔玛因没有工会所带来的成本优势,2003—2004 年间加州南部的长时间罢工表明了他们的决心。

句中的"unionized"意为"有工会组织的","non-union"意为"没有工会组织的"。

34. Bank of America   美国银行

    美国第二大银行,全称是美洲国民信托储蓄银行,是加利福尼亚财团控制的一家单一银行持股公司,创建于1968年,总部设在旧金山。其业务收入的85%来自于美国本土,该银行拥有美国最大的全国性零售网络,有超过5 700个零售银行办事处,它庞大的分支机构网络几乎覆盖了所有人口众多的大城市。该银行还是美国头号小型企业信贷银行和头号向少数族裔开办的小型企业提供贷款的银行,并与几乎所有的美国财富500强企业和80%的世界500强企业建立了业务关系。

35. Germany's Aldi Group   德国阿尔迪集团

    德国著名连锁超市。据一项调查显示,89%的德国居民在阿尔迪超市购物,平均每2.5万人口就配有一个阿尔迪超市;德国的食品消费支出中,平均每4欧元就有1欧元进了阿尔迪的钱袋。沃尔玛败走德国的最主要的原因是受竞争对手阿尔迪超市的影响。阿尔迪超市号称是"贫民的超市"。

36. RJR Nabisco   雷诺士－纳贝斯克集团

    1985年9月,雷诺工业公司收购了当时全美最大的饼干食品制造商纳贝斯克食品有限公司,改名为雷诺士－纳贝斯克集团,1985年集团总销售额195亿美元,成为当时全球最大的消费品公司。1988年11月,RJR Nabisco与Kohlberg Kravis Roberts & Co.（KKR）签订合并协议,合并于1989年4月完成,金额达到250亿美元,是当时美国历史上最大的合并案。

37. Honeywell International Inc.   （美国）霍尼韦尔国际公司

    其总部位于新泽西州莫里斯镇,成立于1999年,由原世界两大著名公司——美国联信公司及霍尼韦尔公司合并而成。霍尼韦尔国际公司是一家年收入超过200亿美元,在多元化技术和制造业方面占世界领导地位的跨国公司,连续50年位列《财富》500强排行榜。在全球,其业务涉及航空产品及服务、住宅及楼宇控制和工业控制技术、自动化产品、特种化学、纤维、塑料、电子和先进材料及交通和动力系统等领域。

38. This was done by capping wages for most hourly positions, converting full-time jobs to part-time ones, and installing a sophisticated scheduling system to adjust staffing levels to fluctuations in customer traffic.   这是通过给大多数计时工作报酬设置上限、把全职工作改为兼职及采用一套完善的根据顾客流量不同而调整雇员数量的调度体系来实现的。

    句中的"cap"意为"为……设置上限","customer traffic"在这里指"顾客流量"。

39. Utah bank charter   犹他州银行执照

    这里反映的是美国的银行监管体制,由于历史原因,美国的银行监管体制相当复杂。首先,由于银行实行国法银行和州法银行（"国法银行"亦称"国民银行",指依照联邦法律登记注册的银行；"州法银行"指按依照各州法律登记注册的银行,而并非州立银行）并存的双重银行体制,因此法律不仅赋予联邦政府以监管商业银行的职能,而且也授权各州政府行使监管职责。因此,除美国财政部下设的货币监管总署（OCC）以外,各州政府均设立了银行监管机构,形成了联邦和州政府的双线监管体制。

40. consumer banking   消费者银行业务

    又称银行零售业务（retail banking）,包括个人储蓄、信用卡、分期付款贷款（个人融资、教育贷款、汽车贷款和租赁)、循环信贷（如透支、家庭股权抵押贷款)、住宅抵押及小企业信贷便利等业务。

41. *Vogue* 《时尚》
该杂志隶属于康泰纳仕有限公司，成立于 1892 年，是世界上历史悠久且广受尊崇的一本时尚类杂志。《时尚》介绍世界妇女时尚，包括美容、服装、服饰、珠宝、保健、健美、旅行、艺术、待客、名人轶事和娱乐等方面的内容。到现今为止，已经在 16 个国家和地区发行出版，全世界各个不同版本的《时尚》均聘用了本地最有能力和创造力的编辑、写手及摄影师来呈现出各个国家不同的文化。在中国，由康泰纳仕有限公司与人民画报社合作出版的《VOGUE 服饰与美容》，已在 2005 年 8 月 15 日正式在中国发行面市，这是《时尚》在全球进入的第 16 个市场。

42. Times Square 美国纽约时代广场
又称为世界十字路口（Crossroads of the World），位于曼克顿市的心脏地带，以 One Times Square 大厦为中心，附近聚集了近 40 家 Broadway Show 及 Off-Broadway Show 剧院，加上多间大型电影院，每天都吸引逾万人前来欣赏，是繁盛的娱乐及购物中心。纽约通常称公园为"广场"，而这里既不是公园，也不是四方形的广场，而是一块三角地带，名称的由来是因 1904 年《纽约时报》的总社迁移至此，因而得名。如今，纽约时报总社虽已移到第 43 街 8 号和 7 号之间，但时代广场的名称仍然沿用至今。

43. Brean Murray, Carret & Co. 美国飞利凯睿证券有限公司
该公司成立于 1973 年，是一家提供全系列服务并以研究为导向的证券公司，公司专注于为小型价值型与成长型企业提供优越的投资机会，服务内容包括资产净值调查、投资银行业务、机构销售与贸易、企业联合与资产管理，公司客户包含机构投资者、高资产净值人士和公司。

44. H&M 海恩斯·莫里斯
世界著名的服装和化妆品连锁专卖店，第一家店于 1947 年由 Erling Persson 在瑞典创立，销售服装和化妆品。其商业理念是"以最优价格，提供时尚与品质"。H&M 还销售自己品牌的化妆品；H&M 自身没有任何工厂，它主要与位于亚洲及欧洲的约 700 家独立供应商进行合作，在全世界有 20 多家生产办事处。

45. Although Wal-Mart no doubt has sponsored its last glitzy runway show, Fleming insists that the company is sticking with its underlying strategy of "customer relevance"— that is, of moving beyond a monolithic focus on price to try to boost sales by targeting particular customers in new ways. 毫无疑问，沃尔玛成功地组织了上一次炫目的时尚秀，但弗莱明还是认为公司应该坚持其"顾客相关性"的基本战略，也就是不仅仅靠价格，而是靠通过用新的方式定位特殊顾客群来提高销量。
句中的"runway show"意为"时尚秀"，"of moving beyond..."和前面的"strategy"搭配。

46. While the look of its stores is primarily a function of how much Wal-Mart chooses to spend on them, the retailer is unlikely ever to come up with an ambience conducive to separating the affluent from their money without changing its whole approach to labor. 尽管店面外观是沃尔玛装修投入的主要标志，但如果不改变其用工方式，零售商还是不能创造出一种氛围

使富人轻易地把钱掏出来。

句中的"conducive"意为"有助于",在此处作定语修饰前面的先行词。

47. The odds are that Scott, or his successor, will have to choose between continuing to disappoint Wall Street or milking the US operation for profits better reinvested overseas.

斯科特或者他的继任者必须做出两难选择:要么继续让华尔街失望,要么从美国本土经营中获利,而将从美国本土经营中获取的利润用于海外再投资将是更好的选择。

句中的"the odds"意为"可能,机会","better reinvested"是过去分词作定语。

阅读小知识(1)

新闻用语(journalistic terms)是通讯社、杂志、报社的专用语,现将一些主要的用语总结如下:

gazette 公报	express paper 快报
bulletin 新闻简报	broadsheet paper 大报
Sunday news 星期日报	clipping 剪贴报
organ 机关报	review news 评论报
press office 报社	journalist 新闻工作者
managing editor 主编	managing director 社长
associate editor 副主编	ace reporter 名记者
staff reporter 撰稿人	correspondent 驻外记者
press correspondent 摄影记者	training newsman 见习记者
freelancer 自由撰稿人	contributor 投稿人
special dispatch 专电	flash 快讯
soft news 软新闻	exclusive news 独家新闻
titbit news 花絮	spot news 现场报道新闻
breaking news 突发性新闻	hearsay news 传说新闻
headline news 头条新闻	running stories 滚动报道
monograph 专论	criticism 评论
leaderette 短评	news release 新闻稿
press notice 宣传稿	special publicity 特宣稿
profile 人物特写	social event feature 社会新闻特写
supplement 副刊	book page 书评版
opinion page 言论版	editor's notes 编者按
deck/subtitle/subhead 副标题	agony column 读者问答栏
wanted column 招聘栏	the opening number 创刊号
periodical 定期刊	memorial 纪念刊

Exercises

I. Decide whether the following statements are true (T) or false (F).

1. "Everyday low prices" is not only the business model of Wal-Mart, but also is of the distinctive personality of this company, which has proved successful even today. (　)
2. Wal-Mart sought to dominate the retailing by expanding its size constantly and cut-rate pricing. (　)
3. Wal-Mart's shares at the stock market were not appealing to investors, because Wal-Mart was undergoing the aging of its outlets and slow growth. (　)
4. Wal-Mart decided to slow its annual addition to US square footage, a move aiming to cope with the credit squeeze of the Feds. (　)
5. The retailer under Scott was strain on its relations with its employees, but was on good terms with the environmental groups, because it needed to tarnish its reputation among the consumers. (　)
6. The "selling for less", Wal-Mart's operation principle which helped secure overwhelming business advantages, is past, but now such principle has changed because more high-incomer buy some kinds of high-end goods. (　)
7. The trouble with Mal-Mart was that it always held on to the business policy of offering attractive discounts and was not fiercely engaged in systematic marketing undertakings to cope with the changing situation. (　)
8. Under Scott, the retailer has remained tight-fisted in its operation, but recently the company changed its stain-colored carpeting with a new carpet of more attractive aesthetic value to appeal to consumers so that its sales could be boosted. (　)
9. Kroger Co., the largest and oldest US supermarket chain, as well as other no-frills rivals was challenging Wal-Mart's hold over budget-minded shoppers. Wal-Mart, for keeping its low prices, reformed its wage and labor systems and cut out middlemen to contract more manufacturing overseas. (　)
10. It seems to the author that Wal-Mart can get likely out of entrenchment by expanding its operation to the emerging markets. (　)

II. Choose one answer that best suits the following statements.

1. The cul de sac in the expansion of business of Wal-Mart was _____.
   A. lack of funds for further investment
   B. market saturation and the rising cost of expansion
   C. big discount offers

D. declining service performance.
2. The retailer's reputation was affected by its _____.
   A. environment pollution
   B. worsening government relations
   C. labor disputes and a few PR scandals
   D. indecent ways of competition with its opponents
3. It seems to the author that Wal-Mart is encountering the mounting difficulties, mainly because the retailer _____.
   A. ignored the high-incomer's purchasing power
   B. only focused on low-price strategies to appeal to consumers
   C. overlooked the importance of marketing work and did not take any effective overall marketing steps
   D. was tightwad and did not invest heavily in improving the shopping environment
4. The polite, self-deprecating Scott is no Robert L. Nardelli, whose ouster as Home Depot Inc.'s (HD) chief had as much to do with his abrasive personality as the chain's business problems.
   The meaning of the underlined word is: _____.
   A. self-cheating, headstrong   B. self-disapproving, harsh and hurtful
   C. self-deceiving, obstinate   D. self-restraining, aberrant
5. Scott loved Wal-Mart's bold new direction until he hated it, his enthusiasm diminishing in sync with same-store sales throughout much of 2006.
   The meaning of the underlined part is: _____.
   A. keeping pace with   B. in proportion to
   C. equivalent to   D. on the equal footing with

III Translate the following passages into Chinese.

1. Wal-Mart's botched entry into cheap-chic apparel is emblematic of the quandary it faces. Is its alarming loss of momentum the temporary result of disruptions caused by transitory errors like the T-shirt screwup and by overdue improvements such as the store remodeling program launched last year? Or is Wal-Mart doing lasting damage to its low-budget franchise by trying to compete with much hipper, nimbler rivals for the middle-income dollar? Should the retailer redouble its efforts to out-Target Target, or would it be better off going back to basics?

2. If Wal-Mart seems short of answers at the moment, it might well be because there aren't any good ones. Increasingly, it appears that America's largest corporation has steered itself into a slow-growth cul de sac from which there is no escape. "There are a lot of issues here, but what they add up to is the end of the age of Wal-Mart," contends Richard Hastings, a senior analyst for the retail rating agency Bernard Sands. "The glory days are over."

IV Write a summary of this text.

Why Toyota Is Afraid of Being Number One

It's overtaking Detroit[1]— with trepidation. Now, the carmaker is relying on ever-savvier PR to avoid the US backlash it dreads.

(Author Unknown)

Ask consumers why Toyota[2] may soon be the largest automaker in the world, and they will point to the Camry[3]. Or the Prius[4]. Or the RAV4[5]. Ask manufacturing geeks, and they'll tell you it's about just-in-time production and a maniacal focus on constant improvement.

But there's another drama behind the carmaker's tire-squealing momentum. It's a story that might be called: How Toyota is winning the hearts and minds of America.

With a deft combination of marketing, public relations, and lobbying, Toyota has done a remarkable job over the past 20 years of selling itself as an American company. That drives the Big Three to distraction. Here's Chrysler[6] communications chief Jason Vines: "The thing I resent is Toyota wrapping themselves in the American flag," he says. "We still employ more people and contribute more to the economy."

Who cares what Detroit thinks? Well, strange as it sounds, Toyota does. Its executives may privately relish victory at the expense of General Motors[7] (GM), Ford[8] (F), and Chrysler (DCX), but here's the truth: Toyota is afraid to be No. 1 — or at least what that implies. And not just because one of its slogans is "Run scared."; it's because the extra scrutiny could undo much of the hard work of the past 20 years. "We constantly need to think about the potential backlash against us," Toyota CEO Katsuaki Watanabe tells *BusinessWeek* in an exclusive interview. "It's very important for our company and products to earn citizenship in the US. We need to make sure we are accepted."

A 17.4% retail market share should signal acceptance. But Toyota is not admired from sea to shining sea. Yes, the company has won the coasts. But one-third of car buyers are biased against imports, says Harris Interactive. And most of those Ford- and Chevy-loving holdouts live in the Midwest and Texas. In those precincts, Toyota still has a lot of persuading to do. Which explains why it launched the full-size Tundra[9] pickup — a red state vehicle from its aggressive hood to its brawny haunches — and is building it in San Antonio[10].

Here's the thing: The Tundra amounts to an assault on the last redoubt of Big Three profits. But Toyota doesn't want to be seen as the one that pushes Detroit over the edge. So to prevent a backlash, the company is amping up the charm — launching literacy programs in San Antonio, vowing to share technology with Ford, and pouring money into lobbying, more than doubling since

2002 the amount it spends each year, to $5.1 million.[11] Says Jim San Fillippo, an analyst with Automotive Marketing Consultants Inc.[12]: "Toyota is the best at going native."

In the early '80s, Toyota sold nine models and had 6% of the market. But the company was winning converts with fuel-efficient, reasonably priced cars like the Toyota Corolla[13]. Detroit, meanwhile, was beginning to endure the agonies that continue to this day. Japan was ascendant, and xenophobia was in full cry.

Toyota scion Shoichiro Toyoda needed to boost sales in the US but feared angering consumers and Washington polls. So in 1984, he hired a Ford pr guy named James Olson. Dr. Toyoda summoned Olson to Nagoya and exhorted him to undertake genchi genbutsu ("go and see").

What Olson found wasn't terribly surprising: With just one US factory — and a joint venture with GM, at that — Toyota was widely viewed as a foreign interloper. At Olson's urging, the company began playing to local sentiment. In 1986, Toyota announced a new plant in Kentucky[14]. In the same year, it rehired many of the 3,000 laid-off GM workers to staff the joint-venture plant in Fremont[15], Calif. George Nano ran the United Auto Workers local at the time, and recalls company executives and plant bosses eating in the same cafeteria as the rank and file. That never happened when GM was running the factory.

That same year, a Ron Howard[16] comedy called Gung Ho appeared; it contrasted the American and Japanese work ethic at a car plant operated by an Asian company called Assan Motors. (Toyota later used the film as an example of how not to manage Americans.)

Toyota escalated the pr offensive. In 1991, it started funding the National Center for Family Literacy[17] and other do-good works. It was textbook corporate philanthropy. But Toyota also did something few American corporations would consider: dispatching efficiency gurus to companies like Viking Range Corp.[18] and Boeing Co. (BA) and to local hospitals. All this was an effort to help make these places work smarter — and build goodwill.

Beating the Tax

But even the savviest gestures were of little use against rising trade tensions. In 1993, Big Three executives won a sit-down with President Bill Clinton. Why, they wanted to know, could the likes of Toyota flood the US with cars, while domestic automakers were mostly locked out of Japan? "It was clear Detroit was having trouble," recalls Mickey Kantor, who was then Commerce Secretary. So Clinton threatened a 100% tax on luxury car imports.

That would have mauled Toyota's five-year-old Lexus[19] brand. It was time for some Kabuki[20]. In those days, Toyota had no game in Washington. But Toyoda was a friend of Walter F. Mondale, then ambassador to Japan. They made a deal: Toyota would build three plants in the US if Clinton nixed the tax. It seemed like a concession at the time. But one Toyota executive says the company planned to open the factories all along.

Detroit's lobbying had come to naught. Toyota was about to establish a beachhead from which it would double US market share over the next decade. With each new plant, Toyota won friends in Congress, where it began building clout.

Toyota executives have a name for politicians they deem friendly: the Toyota Caucus. These are people who represent the states — California, Indiana, Kentucky, Texas, and West Virginia — where Toyota builds cars and trucks. One of the club's charter members, if you will, is Jay Rockefeller, the junior Democratic senator from West Virginia. The Rockefellers and the Toyotas go way back; Jay studied in Japan and speaks the language.

While most states set up their lobbying offices in Tokyo, West Virginia's headquarters is in Nagoya[21], near Toyota's headquarters. Few have worked harder than Rockefeller to persuade Toyota to build a plant in his state. In 1996, not long after the Clinton luxury tax was quashed, the state got a $400 million engine plant in Buffalo, W. Va. Today 1,000 people work there, and the investment has swelled to $1 billion.

In 2001 Toyota gave $1 million to the Blanchette Rockefeller Neurosciences Institute at West Virginia University, a medical research center named after the senator's mother. About the same time, Toyota and Honda Motor Co.[22] (HMC) began backing a push for tax credits for consumers who bought hybrids. The Prius was selling at a premium over conventional cars and Toyota wanted a marketing tailwind. Four years later, Congress passed a credit for up to $3,150. One of the bill's sponsors was Rockefeller. He denies Toyota directly lobbied him over the hybrid sweetener. But Toyota did talk to his staff about the bill, and Rockefeller acknowledges that "maybe I learned something from Toyota" about automotive technology.

Few automakers have a more unassailable environmental pedigree than Toyota (its closest rival is Honda). And no car better represents the company's green creed than the Prius. To hear Toyota tell it, the hybrid was simply so trendy and well-engineered it practically sold itself. There's more to the story than that.

Just before Toyota was about to launch the Prius in 1999, it called Dan Becker, director of global warming initiatives at the Sierra Club[23]. The company wanted the group's seal of approval for the Prius. Becker persuaded his superiors to create an award for the best hybrid technology. The idea was controversial, and Becker says some Sierra Clubbers called him a "whore for the auto industry." In the end, Honda's hybrid Insight won the Sierra Club Award for Excellence in Environmental Engineering; the Prius won the following year.

The Toyota-Sierra Club dance didn't end there. In 2001, the group borrowed a half-dozen Priuses and drove them from Maine to Florida, stopping in cities along the way and letting people drive them. The group also held a cross-country trek along Route 66, hitting towns and cities from Chicago to Los Angeles. The drive-and-tell seemed to work wonders. Says Becker: "Someone at Toyota told me that a phenomenal percentage of people who tested the car bought one." By 2004, Toyota had passed Honda and had the greenest image. "They just blew past us in the surveys," says John German, manager for environment and energy analysis for American Honda Motor Co. "They're in first place now."

Meanwhile Toyota turned to its point man in celebrity-ville: Mike Sullivan, who owns Toyota of Hollywood[24]. Sullivan got hold of 26 Priuses and took them to the 2003 Oscars. Before long, such stars as Cameron Diaz[25] and Leonardo DiCaprio[26] were being photographed ("Look, we're so green!") with their Priuses. "It became the cool thing to do," says Sullivan. Now, every

November, Toyota sponsors the annual Environmental Media Assn[27]. Awards in Los Angeles. TV shows and movies that feature environmental causes get a trophy. Celebrities enter the ceremony along a green carpet, Sullivan is a sponsor, and the Toyota image is omnipresent.

Heading for the Heartland

Today, Toyota is the most respected car company in America. And yet to become the biggest-selling carmaker in the US, it needs to make serious inroads into the heartland, where imports are often considered un-American and the pickup truck rules the road.[28] Nationally, Toyota has a 17.4% retail share. But once you break down the numbers by region, a more nuanced picture emerges. In the Midwest Toyota has just 11%, according to R. L. Polk & Co.[29], which tracks car registrations. And in Texas, Toyota has a meager 5% share of the pickup market. Mike Foster will proudly tell you why. A 50-year-old homebuilder from San Antonio, he has 195,000 miles on his Ford F-150. "I've never owned a Japanese car of any kind," says Foster. "I believe in supporting American jobs. I know Toyota creates jobs here, but the money goes back to Japan."

Knowing what it's up against, Toyota has rolled out a $300 million marketing campaign for the Tundra. It is sponsoring livestock shows, bass-fishing tournaments, and made its NASCAR[30] debut on Feb. 18. Toyota has a campaign, internally dubbed "Prove It," involving free test drives at Bass Pro Shops[31], a national chain of outdoor sports shops, and 84 Lumber stores. Its TV ads feature a narrator, complete with Texas drawl, promoting the Tundra as "the all-new, built-in-America, Toyota truck."

Meanwhile, Toyota is out winning hearts and minds in San Antonio's south side, where the factory is. In late January, the company brought its 16-year-old literacy program to Sky Harbor Elementary School. There, in the Toyota Family Literacy Program Room, Hispanic families are learning to read and write English. "The south side had not been receiving much attention," says Jada Pitman, who runs the program. "But now you have homes and roads being built to accommodate Toyota. Their presence is really being felt in the community."

In Washington, too. Toyota's chief lobbyist, Josephine Cooper, who formerly told Detroit's story on the Hill[32], has been busy. At her behest, Toyota has amped up its advertising efforts inside the Beltway[33]. Its latest campaign has been running on TV and in such publications as Roll Call[34], Washingtonian[35], Congress Daily[36], and Congressional Quarterly[37]. It reminds politicians that Toyota has spent $17 billion over 20 years on new plants and that it directly employs 38,000 Americans.

Five decades after selling its first cars in America, Toyota still feels the need to apologize for—or at least justify — its success. Now, the company's relentless expansion is bringing unwanted attention. A series of recalls has hurt Toyota's reputation for quality. Environmentalists complain that the automaker's move into the big-truck market makes it look more and more like the Big Three all the time. And James E. Press, who runs the North American operations, acknowledges that Toyota is under greater scrutiny now that it's closing in on GM as the world's No. 1 automaker.[38] Yet among Toyota's US leaders, at least, there is the feeling that the humility has gone far enough. During a recent meeting at the North American headquarters in Torrance, Calif., executives agreed

商务报刊选读

Toyota should stop worrying about being loved and learn to accept industry leadership. Are you listening, Watanabe-san[39]?

(*BusinessWeek*, March 5, 2007)

New Words and Expressions

trepidation	n.	震颤，发抖，（心的）动摇
savvy	a.	精明的，能干的，有见识的
automaker	n.	汽车制造商
geek	n.	做低级滑稽表演的人，伪装者
maniacal	a.	发狂的，狂乱的
squealing	n.	啸声，振鸣声
momentum	n.	动力，要素
deft	a.	敏捷熟练的，灵巧的
relish	v.	爱好，喜欢
scrutiny	n.	详细审查
holdout	n.	坚持（者），坚持不合作者
precinct	n.	区域，围地，范围
pickup	n.	小型货运汽车
haunch	n.	腰，腰部
assault	n.	威胁，伤害
amp	v.	放大，扩大
ascendant	a.	居支配地位的，占优势的
xenophobia	n.	仇外，惧外者
scion	n.	后裔，子孙
exhort	v.	劝诫，忠告
interloper	n.	闯入者，（为图私利）干涉他人事务者
sentiment	n.	情感，情绪，观点
philanthropy	n.	慈善事业
guru	n.	头面人物，专家，权威
maul	v.	抨击，伤害，损害
Kabuki	n.	歌舞伎（日本传统剧种）
nix	v.	禁止，拒绝
naught	n.	零
beachhead	n.	滩头阵地，登陆场，据点
caucus	n.	核心小组会议

Unit 5 Marketing and Management

quash	v.	取消
swell	v.	（使）膨胀，增大
unassailable	a.	攻不破的，无懈可击的
pedigree	n.	血统，家谱，出身
cred	n.	美好形象，声誉
whore	n.	出卖信仰（才能）者
phenomenal	a.	显著的，现象的
celebrity	n.	名声，名人
ville	n.	城市，村
trophy	n.	战利品，奖品
inroad	n.	侵袭，侵入
nuance	a.	有细微差别的
meager	a.	贫乏的，不足的
homebuilder	n.	住宅建筑（或设计）者
livestock	n.	家畜，牲畜
debut	n.	初次登场，开张
drawl	n.	慢吞吞的说话
behest	n.	命令，吩咐，要求
relentless	a.	无情的
humility	n.	谦恭，谦逊

just in time production	及时生产，及时制造
tire squealing	轮胎摩擦
from sea to shining sea	从美国西海岸到东海岸
amp up	放大，扩大，增加
rank and file	普通成员，士兵
work ethic	工作的伦理道德
do-good work	好事，善事
come to naught	成为泡影
tax credits	税款扣除数，税收抵免
at a premium	超过票面价值
well-engineered	工程设计精良
cross-country trek	越野长途旅行
celebrity ville	名人区，名人别墅区
pickup truck	小型货运汽车
roll out	铺开，展开
close in on	逼近，遮蔽

1. Detroit 底特律
   美国密歇根州最大城市，是世界闻名的汽车城，位于密歇根州境东南部，底特律河西岸，东濒圣克莱尔湖，与加拿大汽车城温莎隔河相望。汽车业是其主导产业部门，现代化生产水平高，年产量约占全美的27%，美国最大的3家汽车公司通用、福特、克莱斯勒公司总部均设于此。

2. Toyota 丰田汽车公司
   世界十大汽车工业公司之一，日本最大的汽车公司，创立于1933年。早期的丰田牌、皇冠、光冠、花冠汽车名噪一时，近来的克雷西达、凌志豪华汽车也极负盛名。丰田汽车公司的三个椭圆的标志是从1990年初开始使用的，标志中的大椭圆代表地球，中间由两个椭圆垂直组合成一个T字，代表丰田汽车公司，象征丰田汽车公司立足于未来，对未来的信心和雄心。

3. Camry 凯美瑞（丰田汽车品牌）

4. Prius 普锐斯
   丰田汽车品牌，世界上最早实现批量生产的混合动力汽车。

5. RAV4 小公主
   丰田汽车品牌，是丰田公司微型多功能越野车家族中的基本型车，开创了"城市休闲运动车"的新市场。

6. Chrysler 克莱斯勒公司
   美国第三大汽车公司，由沃尔特·克莱斯勒创立于1925年，该公司在全世界许多国家设有子公司，是一个跨国汽车公司，总部设在美国底特律。公司以经营汽车业务为主，也涉足游艇、钢铁、艇外推进器等业务和军用物资生产，以及出口、运输、金融、信贷、租赁和保险领域。公司在美国国内拥有36家汽车制造厂和汽车零部件厂，22家零部件仓库及10家国防和宇航工业工厂。公司产品分为汽车产品和金融业务两类，此外还提供汽车租赁服务。

7. General Motors 通用汽车公司
   全球最大的汽车公司之一，其核心汽车业务及子公司遍及全球。通用汽车公司是由威廉·杜兰特于1908年9月在别克汽车公司的基础上发展起来的，成立于美国的汽车城底特律。现总部仍设在底特律。通用汽车公司迄今在全球33个国家建立了汽车制造业务，其汽车产品销往200多个国家。通用汽车公司旗下的轿车和卡车品牌包括：别克（BUICK）、凯迪拉克（Cadillac）、雪佛兰（Chevrolet）、GMC、通用大宇（GM DAEWOO）、霍顿（Holden）、悍马（Hummer）、欧宝（OPEL）、庞蒂亚克（PONTIAC）、萨博（Saab）、土星（Saturn）和富豪（VOLVO）。

8. Ford 福特汽车公司
   世界最大的汽车企业之一，1903年由亨利·福特创立于底特律市。现在的福特汽车公司是世界超级跨国公司，总部设在美国密歇根州迪尔伯恩市。1913 年，福特汽车公司开发出了世界上第一条流水线，这一创举使 T 型车一共达到了 1 500 万辆，缔造了一个至今仍未被打破的世界纪录，福特为此被尊为"为世界装上轮子"的人。福特汽车公司旗下拥有的汽车品牌有阿斯顿·马丁（Aston Martin）、福特（Ford）、捷豹（Jaguar）、路虎（Land Rover）、林肯（Lincoln）、马自达（Mazda）、和水星（Mercury）。

9. Tundra　冻原
丰田皮卡汽车品牌，是丰田主打美国市场的轻型皮卡汽车。

10. San Antonio　圣安东尼奥
位于美国最南部，是得克萨斯州的三大城市之一（其他两个是休斯敦和达拉斯），美国第八大城市。圣安东尼奥被著名旅游杂志《柯尼旅行家》（Conde Nast Traveler）誉为"全美第二位，全球第九位最受喜爱的旅游城市"。

11. So to prevent a backlash, the company is amping up the charm-launching literacy programs in San Antonio, vowing to share technology with Ford, and pouring money into lobbying, more than doubling since 2002 the amount it spends each year, to $ 5.1 million.　为了防止产生对抗性反应，公司努力采取措施改善自己的形象，包括在圣安东尼奥市启动扫盲项目，许诺同福特公司共享技术，并拨出更多的钱用于游说议员，从 2002 年开始，每年用于该项的花费成倍增长，达到 510 万美元。
句中的"launching""vowing""pouring"引导的短语是并列关系，后面的"doubling"引导的分词短语作状语，修饰前面的"pouring money into lobbying"；"amp up"意为"提高，提升，扩大"。

12. Automotive Marketing Consultants Inc.　美国汽车营销咨询公司
它是美国著名汽车咨询业公司，主要业务包括消费者驾驶相关服务、经销商培训、车辆检测及员工培训等。

13. Corolla　花冠
丰田汽车品牌，第 10 代之后在中国翻译为卡罗拉。从 2000 年开始，以"最畅销汽车"称号载入《吉尼斯世界纪录》，更于 2003 年以 2 800 万辆的成绩刷新了汽车单一品牌累计销量的世界纪录。

14. Kentucky　（美国）肯塔基州
位于美国中东部，昵称为"blue grass state"，首府是法兰克福（Frankfort），主要城市与乡镇有路易斯维尔（Louisville）、柯芬顿（Covington）、莱克星顿（Lexington）、欧温斯波洛（Owensboro）及草坪市（Bowling Green）等。州中主要景观包括坎伯兰瀑布、猛犸洞国家公园（世界遗产，具有世界最大的洞穴系统）、红河谷、湖间路、伯尔尼森林和林肯出生地。

15. Fremont　弗里蒙特
美国加州城市，是美国硅谷的一部分，计算机软件行业的许多大公司总部都位于此地。

16. Ron Howard　罗恩·霍华德
著名演员和导演，他创造了一部又一部的票房大片，为好莱坞的电影工业做出了杰出贡献。凭借《美丽心灵》一片，他荣获第 74 届奥斯卡最佳导演奖。

17. National Center for Family Literacy　美国国家家庭识字中心

为强化家庭的作用，进一步加强少数民族家庭儿童和贫困家庭儿童的识字工作，1989年由美国联邦政府组织成立，其主要任务是开展和领导全国各州的家庭识字工作。

18. Viking Range Corp. 维京股份有限公司（美国著名家庭厨具制造商）
19. Lexus 雷克萨斯

丰田汽车品牌，该品牌名是丰田花了3.5万美元请美国一家取名公司命名的，"雷克萨斯"（Lexus）的读音与英文"豪华"（Luxury）一词相近，能够给人以豪华轿车的印象。雷克萨斯汽车商标采用车名"Lexus"首字母"L"的大写形式，并在外面用一个椭圆包围的图案。椭圆代表着地球，表示雷克萨斯轿车遍布全世界。

20. Kabuki 歌舞伎

歌舞伎是创始于17世纪的日本传统剧种，后来常常比喻诡秘的、错综复杂东西。此处指丰田公司需要采取些措施，找些关系渠道来解决问题。

21. Nagoya 名古屋

日本爱知县首府，是仅次于东京、大阪和横滨的第四大城市。名古屋因其发达的工商业而举世闻名，是综合性的大工业城市，纺织业和造船业非常发达，也是日本三大批发商之一。

22. Honda Motor Co. 本田汽车公司

世界著名的汽车公司，1948年以生产自行车助力发动机起步，目前公司在小型通用发动机、踏板摩托车及跑车等各领域都拥有独创技术，并不断研发生产新产品。除日本之外，本田公司在全世界29个国家拥有120个以上的生产基地，生产摩托车、汽车和通用产品。本田技术研究所是当今日本乃至世界汽车业的佼佼者。

23. Sierra Club 塞拉俱乐部

美国自然资源保护组织，总部设在旧金山，是美国最大、历史最久、最有影响力的草根环境保护组织，是由约翰·缪尔（John Muir）于1892年与其他182位志同道合者共同创建的。塞拉俱乐部是一个美国公民就环境问题发表自由言论和提出他们自己观点、声音的组织。

24. Toyota of Hollywood 丰田汽车公司好莱坞分公司

它是第一家获得丰田经销权的公司。

25. Cameron Diaz 卡麦隆·迪亚兹

好莱坞著名演员，1994年首次不经意出演了《变相怪杰》，大获成功，从而改变了卡梅隆的一生。之后她步入影坛，曾主演影片《新娘不是我》和《霹雳娇娃》。

26. Leonardo DiCaprio 莱昂纳多·迪卡普里奥

好莱坞著名影星，在《外星通缉者3》之中扮演了一个角色，标志着他的电影生涯的开端。1991—1992年，拍摄电视剧《成长的烦恼》。其主演的电影包括《罗密欧与朱丽叶》、《泰坦尼克号》、《铁面人》、《纽约黑帮》和《飞行者》等。

27. Environmental Media Assn 环境媒体协会

美国非营利组织，其使命是在全球范围内动员媒体娱乐界人士普及环境保护知识，并鼓励引导人们采取实际行动保护环境。

28. And yet to become the biggest-selling carmaker in the US, it needs to make serious inroads into the heartland, where imports are often considered un-American and the pickup truck rules the

road. 但要成为美国销量最大的汽车制造商,它需要慎重考虑进入美国腹地,因为在那里进口被认为是非美国化,公路上跑的也都是皮卡。
句中的"where"引导非限制性定语从句,修饰前面的先行词。

29. R. L. Polk & Co.　波尔卡有限公司
这是一家私营性质的全球性公司,为汽车行业和相关产业提供汽车信息和市场解决方案。

30. NASCAR　全国赛车联合会
NASCAR 是 The National Association for Stock Car Auto Racing 的缩写,它将赛车运动带入了一个革命性的时代。现代意义上赛车的成功应该归功于比尔·弗朗斯。1938 年,比尔·弗朗斯成功举办了代托那海滩赛车赛,并成立了自己的组织机构,经过不断的策划和完善,NASCAR 于 1948 年 2 月 15 日正式成立,并经过半个多世纪之后,获得了巨大的成功。NASCAR 每年组织约 2 000 场比赛。NASCAR 的成员人数超过 50 000 人,其中包括一部分全世界最出色的车手、机械师和车队老板,每年超过 150 000 000 名观众观看其组织的比赛。

31. Bass Pro Shops　巴斯超级商店
美国最大的户外用品连锁店,是一家专业出售渔具(Fishing)、野外及户外(Outdoors)装备的商店。

32. on the Hill　在国会里
这里的"Hill"指"Capitol Hill",即国会。

33. inside the Beltway　在国会环路内
这里的"Beltway"指国会环路,此处引申为在国会活动的相关领域之内。

34. Roll Call　《点名报》(美国国会日报)

35. Washingtonian　《华盛顿人》
美国著名时政杂志,杂志定位很高,目标读者为城市高收入、高学历的精英。

36. Congress Daily　《国会日报》
由《国家杂志》(National Journal)出版,每日两次覆盖国会山的新闻。

37. Congressional Quarterly　《国会季刊》
它是美国国会季刊公司在华盛顿出版的期刊,专门报道美国国会和政府的活动及国会投票情况分析。

38. And James E. Press, who runs the North American operations, acknowledges that Toyota is under greater scrutiny now that it's closing in on GM as the world's No. 1 automaker.　负责北美运营的詹姆士·E. 普瑞斯承认丰田公司正受到越来越详细的审查,因为它正步步逼近通用汽车公司而有望成为世界上最大的汽车制造商。
句中的"close in on"意为"逼近,遮蔽","now that"引导原因状语从句。

39. Watanabe-san
此处指丰田 CEO 渡边捷昭。

商务报刊选读

阅读小知识（2）

欧洲部分著名企业介绍

1. 英国石油（BP）

英国石油是世界第一大综合石油公司（位于埃克森－美孚之前），其前身是英国石油阿姆科（BP Amoco），由英国石油和阿姆科公司于1998年合并而成。阿姆科公司收购了大西洋富田公司（ARCO）之后有了长足的增长。英国石油（其中包括阿拉斯加大量控股）的石油储量为184亿桶。它是美国最大的石油及天然气生产商，也是最大的炼油（日产量340万桶）、石油化工、专业化工产品的制造商。

2. 壳牌（Royal Dutch/Shell Group）

荷兰皇家/壳牌集团公司简称壳牌公司，其组建始于1907年壳牌运输和贸易有限公司与荷兰皇家石油公司股权的合并。以众多标准衡量，其均堪称全球领先的国际油气集团。此后，该集团逐渐成为世界主要的国际石油公司，业务遍及大约130个国家，雇员人数约10万人。其合作伙伴也非常广泛。

它是国际上主要的石油、天然气和石油化工的生产商，在30多个国家的50多个炼油厂中拥有权益，而且是石油化工、公路运输燃料（约5万个加油站遍布全球）、润滑油、航空燃料及液化石油气的主要销售商。同时，它还是液化天然气行业的先驱，并在全球各地大型项目的融资、管理和经营方面拥有丰富的经验。

壳牌集团是世界上最大的跨国投资商，其品牌是世界上最著名的品牌之一。

3. 德国安联保险集团（Allianz）

该集团于1890年始创于德国柏林，而今总部位于慕尼黑，业务遍及欧洲、北美、南美、非洲、中东及亚太地区的70多个国家，拥有700多个子公司。其管理的资产总额高达11 720亿欧元，为全球三大资产管理公司之一（仅次于瑞士银行）。

该集团历史上著名的承保工程有：1906年美国旧金山大地震、1912年"泰坦尼克号"沉船事件、2001年美国"9·11"事件、2002年欧洲水灾。其目前是中国唯一可综合开拓个人/团体寿险、财产保险、责任保险等所有保险业务的外资保险集团。

4. 安盛（AXA）

法国安盛集团是全球最大的保险集团，亦是全球第三大国际资产管理集团。安盛集团首家公司于1816年在法国成立，通过多项收购及合并活动，其业务网络覆盖全球五大洲逾60个国家及地区，全球职员及保险代理人约11万名。安盛集团的主要业务为保险及资产管理。2006年，公司年收入为720亿欧元，管理资产10 640亿欧元，净收入33亿欧元。

安盛集团分别在巴黎证券交易所和纽约证券交易所上市，集团的数家公司也在其经营地上市,包括香港、纽约、法兰克福、伦敦、布鲁塞尔及都柏林等。

1997 年,安盛集团获中国政府批准在上海筹建中外合资寿险公司。1999 年 6 月,在中国上海成立了由法国安盛集团和中国五矿集团合资组建的金盛人寿保险有限公司。

法国安盛集团在 2006 年美国《财富》杂志评选的全球 500 强企业排行榜中位居 15 位。

5. 大众汽车(Volkswagen)

世界十大汽车公司之一,创建于 1938 年德国的沃尔斯堡,创始人是世界著名的汽车设计大师波尔舍。大众汽车公司经营汽车产品占主要地位,是一个在全世界许多国家都有业务的跨国汽车集团。大众汽车顾名思义是为大众生产的汽车。1934 年 1 月 17 日,波尔舍向德国政府提出一份为大众设计生产汽车的建议书。随之,建议被批准,后来由波尔舍组建了一个由 34 万人入股的大众汽车股份公司,年产量为 100 万辆。

在沃尔斯堡的"大众汽车城"里,第一批"甲壳虫"问世,但仅仅生产了 630 辆就因二次世界大战而停产。

继"甲壳虫"后,大众汽车公司在 1980 年实现了四轮连续驱动大客车的大批量生产,推出 80 年代世界最畅销的高尔夫汽车,从而成为欧洲最大的汽车商。

大众汽车公司在全世界有 13 家生产性子公司,海外有 7 个销售公司,23 个其他公司。其主要品牌有斯柯达、桑塔纳、帕萨特、柯拉多、奥迪、奥迪科贝等。整个汽车集团产销能力在 300 万辆左右。

6. 德国西门子公司(Siemens)

西门子公司是世界上最大的电气工程和电子公司之一。其业务遍及全球 190 多个国家,在全世界拥有大约 600 家工厂、研发中心和销售办事处。公司的业务主要集中于 6 大领域:信息和通信、自动化和控制、电力、交通、医疗系统和照明。西门子的全球业务运营分别由 13 个业务集团负责,其中包括西门子财务服务有限公司和西门子房地资产管理集团。

西门子的中国业务是其亚太地区业务的主要支柱,并且在西门子全球业务中起着越来越举足轻重的作用。

7. 家乐福(Carrefour)

法国家乐福集团成立于 1959 年,是大型超级市场(Hypermarket)概念的创始者,于 1963 年在法国开设了世界上第一家大型超市。1999 年 8 月 30 日家乐福兼并普罗莫代斯组成世界第二大零售集团。如今家乐福已发展成为欧洲最大、全球第二的零售商。该企业在 2007 年度《财富》全球最大五百家公司排名中名列第 32 位。

家乐福于 1995 年进入中国后,采用国际先进的超市管理模式,致力于为社会各界提供价廉物美的商品和优质的服务,受到广大消费者的青睐和肯定,其"开心购物家乐福"、"一站式购物"等理念已经深入人心。

8. 瑞士雀巢集团(Nestle)

雀巢是食品业的领头羊,是当今世界消费性包装食品和饮料行业最为成功的经营者之一。1867 年,公司以婴儿麦片产品起家,并在进入 20 世纪后与英瑞炼乳公司及三家巧克力公司合并。1938 年，雀巢首创了速溶咖啡，迅速风靡世界。此后雀巢并购或投资了多家企业，公司规模不断扩大，最终成为横跨饮品、巧克力和糖果、烹饪制品、冷冻食品和冰淇淋、宠物食品、药品和化妆品等多领域的综合性企业，旗下拥有雀巢咖啡、美极、美禄等大量著名品牌。2006 年年销售额达到 477 亿美元以上，其中大约 95% 来自食品的销售，因此雀巢可谓是世界上最大的食品制造商，也是最大的跨国公司之一。公司以生产巧克力棒和速溶咖啡闻名遐迩，目前拥有适合当地市场与文化的丰富的产品系列。

9. 法国标致汽车公司（Peugeot）

该公司是世界十大汽车公司之一，法国最大的汽车集团公司，创立于 1890 年，创始人是阿尔芒·标致。1976 年标致汽车公司吞并了法国历史悠久的雪铁龙公司，从而成为世界上一家以生产汽车为主，兼营机械加工、运输、金融和服务业的跨国工业集团。标致汽车公司的总部在法国巴黎，汽车厂多在弗南修·昆蒂省，雇员总数为 11 万人左右，年产汽车 220 万辆，汽车总产量超过雷诺汽车公司而居法国第一。标致汽车公司拥有 92 家国内公司和 84 家海外公司，海外公司以商业公司为主，工业公司不多，其中最大的海外工业公司有英国塔尔伯特汽车公司和西班牙塔尔伯特汽车公司。

20 世纪 80 年代，标致汽车公司和中国合作在广州建立合资企业，将标致 504、505 型汽车输入到中国。标致汽车产品从微型到豪华型都有，最受欢迎的是中型汽车。标致汽车的特点是寿命长、质量好，它的 205 及 309 型汽车在历年的汽车拉力赛中独占鳌头。该公司下属 2 个品牌：标致和雪铁龙。

10. 麦德龙（METRO Group）

麦德龙股份公司（Metro AG）常称作"麦德龙超市"，是德国最大、欧洲第二、世界第三的零售批发超市集团，是德国股票指数 DAX 的成分公司，世界 500 强企业之一，分店遍布 31 个国家。公司由奥托·拜斯海姆（Otto Beisheim）创建，目前总部位于杜塞尔多夫的麦德龙集团是全球批发市场的领头羊，在麦德龙和万客隆（仅限欧洲）品牌旗下拥有多家麦德龙现购自运商场。集团在 30 个国家拥有员工大约 270 000 名。2006 年麦德龙集团的销售额达 600 亿欧元，50% 的集团销售额来自麦德龙现购自运。

麦德龙是世界第一的现购自运制商业集团。"现购自运"是指专业顾客在仓储式商场内自选商品，以现金支付并取走商品。与传统的送货批发相比，现购自运的优势在于较好的性价比、食品和非食品分类范围广、即时获得商品、更长的营业时间。商场提供 17 000 种以上食品，30 000 种以上的非食品。特别是在生鲜食品的供应上，包括水果、蔬菜、活鱼、肉制品、奶制品。麦德龙现购自运的目标顾客包括餐饮业、酒店业、食品、非食品贸易服务商及机构采购，在这里他们可以找到大包装以满足特殊需求。

11. 汇丰控股有限公司（HSBC Holding）

该公司总部设于伦敦，是世界上规模最大的银行及金融服务机构之一。汇丰控股有限公司的国际网络横跨全球 77 个国家和地区，办事处超过 9 800 个，覆盖欧洲、亚太地区、美洲、中东和非洲。

汇丰控股有限公司的股份在伦敦、香港、纽约、巴黎及百慕达证券交易所挂牌买卖，股东大约 200 000 名,来自全球 100 多个国家和地区。汇丰控股有限公司为超过 1.1 亿名客户提供全面的金融服务,主要有:个人理财、消费融资、工商业务、企业银行、投资银行和资本市场,以及私人银行。

12. 菲亚特(Fiat)

菲亚特于 1899 年创立,是当今世界主要工业集团之一,在 190 个国家有常设机构,包括 654 家公司、189 座工厂、120 所研究中心,员工约 17 万名。

作为世界汽车工业的创始者之一,从成立伊始,菲亚特就奉行着双重的发展战略:集中创新和走向外国市场。这主要表现为产品的高技术含量及先进的工业系统和组织结构。

菲亚特于 1979 年在北京首次设立了常驻代表处。1999 年,菲亚特和南京汽车集团在乘用车领域共同成立了一家合资公司——南京菲亚特。如今,菲亚特在中国拥有 4 家代表处、6 家合资企业和 9 家独资企业,总投资额超过 10 亿美元,年营业额逾 9 亿美元,拥有员工近 8 000 名。在中国,菲亚特不仅是意大利最大的投资者,也是最大的国际汽车制造商之一,它促进了投资地区的就业和经济发展。

13. 特易购(Tesco)

特易购公司成立于 1932 年,是英国最大的零售公司,也是世界三大零售商之一,已有 80 年的历史。在英国,英国人每 8 英镑的消费中,至少有 1 英镑花在特易购的连锁店里。在超市领域,特易购排名在美国沃尔玛和法国家乐福之后,属世界 500 强企业。

特易购除了在英国本土的 691 家大型购物中心外,该公司 42% 的店铺分布于中欧与东南亚各国,是一个国际化的超市巨人。

14. 苏黎世金融服务集团(Zurich Financial Services)

苏黎世金融服务集团创建于 1872 年,总部位于瑞士苏黎世,是瑞士第一家跨国性的保险公司。

苏黎世金融服务集团是以保险为核心业务的金融服务机构,全球网络的分支机构和办事处遍布北美、欧洲、亚太、拉丁美洲和其他市场。苏黎世金融服务集团是《财富》杂志(Fortune)全球 500 强企业中排名前 100 位的企业。1998 年,苏黎世集团与英美烟草金融服务公司合并,组成苏黎世金融服务集团,并先后成功地合并了 British American Financial Services 及美国的 Farmers 等国际知名的金融服务机构,使本集团更加壮大,成为世界最著名十大金融保险集团之一。

苏黎世金融服务集团拥有下述知名品牌与公司:联合邓巴、鹰星集团、农夫保险集团、特莱尼德等,总资产 4 240 亿美元,保费收入 490 亿,客户 3 500 万,雇员 70 000 人。苏黎世金融服务集团是一家居世界领先地位、获国际公认从事金融保险服务的全球性集团,核心业务为非寿险、寿险、再保险和资产管理,业务遍及 50 多个国家和地区。

苏黎世金融服务集团在中国的发展可以追溯到 1993 年,是第一家在中国设立代表处的欧洲保险公司。苏黎世金融服务集团目前在北京和上海均设有办事处。

15. 德意志银行(Deutsche Bank)

德意志银行 1870 年成立于德国柏林,是德国最大的银行和世界上最主要的金融机构之一，总部设在莱茵河畔的法兰克福。它是一家私人拥有的股份公司，其股份在德国所有交易所进行买卖，并在巴黎、维也纳、日内瓦、巴斯莱、阿姆斯特丹、伦敦、卢森堡、安特卫普和布鲁塞尔等地挂牌上市。

德意志银行与集团所属的德国国内和国际的公司及控股公司一起，提供一系列的现代金融服务，包括吸收存款、借款、公司金融、银团贷款、证券交易、外汇买卖和衍生金融工具。历年来，德意志银行一直被穆迪评级公司、标准普尔评级公司和IBCA评为为数极少的几家AAA级银行之一。在亚洲及太平洋地区，德意志银行是分支机构最多的欧洲银行。

1981年，德意志银行作为第一家德国银行在北京建立了代表处。1993年，其广州代表处成立，不久又升格为分行。1995年又开设了上海代表处。

16. 联合利华公司（Unilever）

该公司为英、荷合资企业，成立于1930年，是世界著名的日用及食品化工集团，在世界500家大型企业中名列第35位。公司在荷兰鹿特丹和英国伦敦各有一个总部。荷兰部分主要生产食品，英国部分则主要生产日用化工产品。公司现有员工30.6万人，分布在世界上70多个国家和地区。该公司的国际品牌，从多芬、力士、旁氏、奥妙到立顿、家乐、和路雪，所有产品都拥有产品配方和品牌塑造方面的国际优势。

在1923年，联合利华就在上海建立了第一家企业，生产并销售阳光牌和力士牌香皂，很快该企业就成为当时远东最大的香皂生产商。1986年，改革开放使联合利华重新进入中国，并在上海成立了第一家合资公司——上海利华有限公司。2000年，联合利华在上海成立研究发展中心。2002年，中国成功加入WTO，联合利华又在上海成立了全球采购中心。

17. 宝马（BMW）

宝马是驰名世界的汽车企业，也被认为是高档汽车生产业的先导。宝马公司创建于1916年，总部设在德国的慕尼黑。80年来，它由最初的一家飞机引擎生产厂发展成为今天以高级轿车为主导，并生产享誉全球的飞机引擎、越野车和摩托车的企业集团，名列世界汽车公司前20名。宝马也被译为"巴依尔"。

宝马公司的业务遍及全世界120个国家。宝马汽车主要有3、5、7、8系列汽车及双座篷顶跑车等。1994年宝马公司收购了英国陆虎汽车公司（RoverGroup）；1998年，宝马公司又购得了劳斯莱斯汽车品牌；宝马公司在美国南卡罗来纳州的新厂也落成投产，这是在美国的第一家外国高档汽车生产厂。

宝马公司致力于推动中国汽车工业在高科技应用方面的发展。1994年4月，宝马公司在北京设立了代表处。

18. 雷诺（Renault）

雷诺汽车公司是世界十大汽车公司之一，法国第二大汽车公司，创立于1898年，创始人是路易·雷诺。而今的雷诺汽车公司已被收为国有，是法国最大的国有企业，也是世界上以生产各种类型汽车为主，涉足发动机、农业机械、自动化设备、机床、电子、塑料、橡胶等领域的垄断工业集团。

雷诺汽车公司的汽车产品十分齐全，除小客车和载货车外，各种改装车、特种车应有尽有，在十大汽车公司也是独此一家。雷诺汽车公司下分小客车、商用车、自动化设备及工业产品 4 个部，统管国内外所有的子公司。

公司总部设在法国比扬古，雇员总数为 22 万人，全年可生产汽车 205 万辆。其最新的小汽车产品有雷诺 Cilo、雷诺 19、雷诺 25 型等。

19. 巴斯夫（BASF）

该公司是全球领先的化工公司。BASF 在德国与 Bayer，Hoechest 并列驰名，是德国三大化工厂之一。该公司创立于 1865 年，现已成为全球性的企业集团，其工厂分布于欧洲、北美洲、中美洲、南美洲、亚洲及澳洲等地。BASF 企业集团在德国有直属公司和分布于全球的 270 个附属公司。它是中国化工领域最大的外国投资商之一，目前在大中华区有 4 000 多名员工，拥有 16 个全资子公司和 8 个合资公司。为了适应当地市场的需求，公司还在香港、北京、上海、广州、南京、青岛、成都和台北共设有 8 个办事处。

BASF 的产品范围包括化学品、塑料、特性化学品、农用产品、精细化学品及原油和天然气。作为各行各业值得信赖的合作伙伴，BASF 的智能解决方案和高价值产品帮助客户取得了更大的成功。

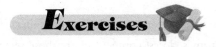

Exercises

I Discuss and answer the following questions.

1. Why is Toyota afraid of being number one?
2. Do you think Guanxi should be one of the key components in marketing mix in China? Why?
3. What approaches does Toyota adopt to win big shares in the US market?
4. When Toyota encountered resistance that came from Clinton Administration's threatened a 100% tax on luxury car imports, how did Toyota successfully get over the obstacle?
5. How did Toyota launch the Prius in the US?
6. What can we learn from Toyota's immense efforts made in environment causes?
7. What challenges do you think will lie ahead for Toyota?
8. Has Toyota really won the minds and hearts of the US auto consumers? Why?

II Decide whether the following statements are true (T) or false (F).

1. Toyota did a good job over the past 20 years of selling its autos to the US consumers mainly by setting up JVs in the United States. (   )
2. Toyota kept itself from being arrogant in its business operation in the US to avoid possible hostilities from the US consumers. (   )
3. Toyota's strategies were so successful that they met with no negative responses from the auto

buyers. (　)

4. Toyota's endeavor was mainly focused on winning friends in Congress to increase its lobbying power in its favor. (　)

5. The green image of Toyota was greatly enhanced by its "drive and see" activities in many American cities, in addition to inviting Hollywood celebrities to join the environmental campaigns and to other related activities. (　)

6. Toyota has become the most respected car company and the biggest-selling carmaker already in the US. (　)

7. Toyota has been carrying out its long-term literacy program in many ethnic group elementary schools to expand its influence in the US. (　)

8. A series of recalls of Toyota and its move into the big-truck markets have caused some outcries of consumers, making them think that this auto-maker was only profit-driven. (　)

9. There are some challenges awaiting Toyota, but the company will proceed along with its policies to win the hearts and minds of American people. (　)

10. It seemed to the author that PR endeavor was the only component for Toyota's success in the US. (　)

III Group discussion.

1. What do you think is the effective green marketing in China?
2. Do you agree that a company's closest competitors are those seeking to satisfy the same customers, needs and making similar offers? Why?
3. How should a company identify the needs of its product and in what ways can the needs be best satisfied in China?
4. Do you think that PR is very important to a foreign company based in China? How can its PR work be done to promote the operation of the company?
5. If a company wants to improve its image in China, what work should be done by the company?

Case Study

How an Indian company plans to woo America's heartland with it fuel-efficient SUVs and pickups

Engineers from India design advanced jet engines, write some of the world's most sophisticated software, and run massive global computer networks. But can they make a pickup truck that will sell in America's heartland?

Mahindra & Mahindra, a conglomerate based in Mubai, intends to find out. In spring, 2009, the company plans to launch two-and four-door pickups and a sport-utility vehicle in the US. This trio of diesel-powered trucks will compete against a big pack of aggressively promoted offerings from GM, Ford, Dodge, Nissan, and Toyota. All of these manufacturers have been warring over a domestic pickup market that is shrinking and a SUV market that's overcrowded.

Skepticism abounds. Trucks in the US are sold with imagery of waving flags, macho companionship, and brawny workers showing off feats of towing strength to the sound of John Mellencamp anthems. Buyers tend to be loyal, practical traditionalists.

Considering that established players such as Toyota, Nissan, and Honda have already had their share of trouble attracting this crowd, some experts wonder whether a little-known company from a country that has no history of selling vehicles to American consumers has a prayer. They are also skeptical that buyers will flock to diesel — a technology that many US consumers associate with the belching big rigs. "It looks like an impossible marketing play," says auto industry consultant Dan Gorrell of AutoStrategem in Tustin, Calif.

But at a time of soaring gas prices, Mahindra's vehicles are going to have one big thing in their favor: superior fuel economy. Despite diesel's historic brown image, it is emerging as a green technology. New low-sulfur fuel, federally mandated in 2006, can produce mileage figures that nearly equal those of more fashionable hybrids. Mahindra estimates that its compact SUV, the Scorpio, and pickups, one of which will be called the Appalachian, will get about 30 miles per gallon in the city and as much as 37 on the highway. That compares with 30 city/34 highway for the $27,000 Ford Escape SUV hybrid and 21 city/27 highway for the gas-powered $23,000 Toyota RAV4.

Although Mahindra is unknown to most American consumers, the company has made cars in India for more than 50 years. The $4.5 billion company also has financial services, information technology, telecommunications, and agricultural equipment businesses. Over the past decade, it has sold more than 50,000 tractors in the US.

Well aware of the image problems confronting an Indian pickup, Mahindra has conducted extensive consumer research in America. At a recent meeting at the Alpharetta (Ga.) offices of Global Vehicles, the company that will distribute the brand in the US, interviews with potential buyers were projected on a big screen. "I don't see them (Mahindra) entering the market and immediately competing with more established brands," said one thirty something male. "Can it really be made well if it comes from India?" asked another.

Given these attitudes, the company has made a key strategic decision: It is not going to waste energy trying to persuade the unpersuadables. Instead, Mahindra is going to target the three groups it believes will be the most receptive to its vehicles-consumers who identify themselves as "green," people who have bought Mahindra tractors, and the close to 3 million Indian expatriate households in the US. The plan is to generate buzz with these buyers, then hope the word spreads to the mainstream.

Rather than unrolling a big image-building marketing campaign, which would be drowned out by the thunder of other truck promotions, Mahindra plans to start small. It will spend only about $20 million on marketing in 2009, less than 10% of what Toyota spent to launch the Tundra pickup. Almost none of this money is expected to be devoted to television or glossy print ads. Instead, it will purchase carefully selected search terms and banner ads on Web sites popular with its target consumers. These links will steer potential buyers to detailed information about Mahindra's trucks. The green consumers whom the company is courting relentlessly research the products they buy, and then frequently promote them to friends.

Mahindra has set modest sales targets for its American operation. In the second six months of 2009, it plans to sell just 18,000 vehicles, followed by 45,000 in 2010. Mahindra will ship its SUV whole from India, but the pickup trucks will be transported in pieces. They will be assembled at one of three plant sites Global is scouting in the Southeast. Worried that any quality problems could quickly stigmatize the Mahindra brand, Global Vehicles CEO John A. Perez is working hard with Mahindra to keep the number of defects to a minimum. "We don't want to be Kia or Hyundai and have to apologize after we launch," says Perez.

So far, Perez has attracted 263 dealers to distribute Mahindra trucks. One of them is Steven Taylor, a Cadillac dealer who's invested more than $1 million in a Mahindra franchise in Toledo despite all of the obvious risks. "Trucks and an SUV that get over 30 mpg is a market niche that will get noticed," Taylor says.

(Adapted from *BusinessWeek*, November 5, 2007)

Supplementary Reading

Korea's Path to Brand Creation

Dae Ryun Chang

As the so-called bric countries like China and India rush to gain acceptance as viable economic entities, a key business engine for sustainable growth will be the development of global brands. Both countries may boast remarkable economic success, but there is still a notable absence of recognizable Chinese and Indian brands especially in the foreign marketplace.

For instance, not a single brand from either country rated mention in *Interbrand* and *BusinessWeek*'s list of the top 100 Global Brands by value in 2006. Of course, this list was dominated by the "usual suspects" such as Coca Cola, Microsoft, Louis Vuitton and Toyota. Recently, however, brands from one Asian country, namely South Korea, have begun to join this elite club. Samsung, LG and Hyundai are now fully entrenched among the "big boys", and their rankings are steadily climbing.

For China and India, Korean brands serve as good role models, because their winning formula is much easier to emulate compared to Western brands. Many of the current issues facing Chinese and Indian brands mirror the early experiences of those Korean brands. Whereas many US, European and Japanese companies have spent decades managing their brands, Korean firms see brand management as a relatively new concern. Thus the "footsteps" that Korean brands have made on their path to success can still be readily traced and followed. So what are the key lessons?

Companies invariably follow an evolution in terms of how they understand brand management. In stage one, firms in developing countries commonly conceive of a brand as just a name for the product. This view is not entirely misplaced because the "brand name" itself is important, but of course brands are more than just a "name."

In Korea, as recently as 20 years ago a cottage industry of old-school name experts located in Seoul's Tongindong neighborhood used to apply *fengshui* principles to choose names for company products, just as if they were choosing names for children. Companies would then pre-register hundreds of these "good" names to make sure they preempted their competition from using such "fortune-laden" brands. This practice is now all but dead.

In stage two, companies begin to attain a sense of brand and corporate identity. This is when companies first appreciate the physical look and meaning of a brand. They begin to hire corporate identity consulting firms to align the brand design and brand concept.

For Korean brands, a key mantra has been to globalize their corporate identity. For instance, in the early 1990s Korea Explosives made itself over as Hanwha, which is a shortened version of its original name. It exchanged its old corporate logo, which literally had a smokestack symbol, for one that was softer and brighter. This strategy reflected Hanwha's diversification from heavy industry alone to consumer retailing and resorts management. Last year, Hanwha hired a leading Egyptian-British designer, Karim Rashid, to remake the company yet again because of Hanwha's entry into the global financial industry.

Similar changes in branding philosophy are taking place in China and India. When Legend Computer acquired IBM's Thinkpad, it transformed itself into "Lenovo."

Lenovo's strategy echoes the 1990s move by Goldstar, which renamed itself LG (short for its Korean name Lucky Goldstar). LG coincidently also acquired a famous US brand, Zenith, at the time of its name change. This two-fold maneuver had mixed results: The new name was successful and its friendly logo became instantly pronounceable and familiar all around the world, but Zenith never regained its past glory. Lenovo and LG are in different industries but the latter's experience points to the need for self-reliance. More specifically, there are not short-cuts to branding success, and Lenovo must make sure that Lenovo is accepted in its major markets and not just depend on the namesake of its more recognized acquisition.

The last stage is acceptance of the brand as a key corporate asset. The brand equity concept means that brands are worth monetary value to companies. As such, brands can be considered just as valuable as any other item on a corporate balance sheet. Good brand valuation models are able to attribute the key drivers of brand equity. Asian companies that are serious about brand equity should therefore avail themselves of qualified brand consulting to sort out the variables that help or deter brand building and maintenance.

Be Patient

People of ten forget that for a long time all Korean brands were at the bottom of the branding "totem pole." Korean firms suffered from a very negative country-of-origin bias. Consumers associated Korean products and brands with being inexpensive, mass-produced and inferior quality. The key message therefore is that it takes a long time to build strong brands. The most expensive outdoor advertising space in Hong Kong is overlooking Victoria Harbor. As people cross the ferry from Hong Kong Island to Kowloon, world-renowned brands are readily seen during the day and at night. For a very long time, the two key spaces have been occupied by Motorola and Samsung. Perhaps the most expensive outdoor advertising space in the world is on Times Square in the heart of Broadway in New York City; Samsung and LG long ago taken prominent spaces there. In Paris and in airports in the major cities of the world, Korean companies in the past nearly monopolized push carts advertising. All these efforts paid off many years later.

China is expecting a big "bounce" for its brands after the 2008 Olympics, just as Korea did after the 1998 Olympics. It is safe to say that Korean brands did not immediately obtain the expected effect after 1988; nevertheless that year is commonly seen as a milestone, after the Korean market became liberalized to foreign competition. As more and more international firms entered Korea, local companies began to study how their foreign counterparts nurtured their brands.

Procter and Gamble is renowned for its brand management system, and it is not coincidence then that legions of former P&G managers are now chief marketing officers and, in some cases, CEOs of the best brand managed outfits in Korea. A similar branding technology transfer can be expected in China as their nationals become trained not only in China but also abroad in top multinational marketing companies. As for India, in some respects the history of brand management is longer since their most famous marketing concern, Hindustan Lever, has enjoyed a long association with Unilever. But like China, the India market was not liberalized until the early 1990s. And now, more importantly, the two countries have a budding middle class that demands and appreciates good brands regardless of whether they are local or foreign.

Be Flexible

Brand management is a very fragile business. Even though it may take a manager's lifetime to build a successful global brand, it can be easily ruined in a short period of time, as new brands are always waiting in the wings and consumers themselves are ceaselessly looking for the next "big brand." It is imperative therefore for all brands to continue to appear consumer-friendly.

AmorePacific is a Korean company that has set its sights on becoming a top 10 global cosmetics company in the next decade. What makes AmorePacific's success most noteworthy is that it competes in the global "high touch" industry as opposed to the "high tech" industry. Its strategy does not conform to any conventional global brand model. In each market, the company has been careful to adapt to the local branding conditions.

For instance, in China, AmorePacific has taken advantage of the widespread appeal of the

Korean wave and used Jeon JiHyun, star of the popular movie "My Sassy Girl" as its main advertising spokesperson. In the US it has initially relied on public relations and buzz created by editorial mentions in fashion magazines such as Vogue and W. It also has a flagship store that doubles as a day spa located in SoHo, New York City, where its clientele can experience the brand in a holistic manner. In Korea, the firms still relies on door-to-door distribution for some of its most luxurious brands since it realizes that local consumers demand more personalized cosmetic consultation.

Samsung has recently become the jersey sponsor of the Chelsea football team in the English Premiership. This partnership with current FA Cup champion has brought unprecedented marketing side benefits to Samsung. Chelsea's multinational team includes star players from the United Kingdom, the Ivory Coast, Ghana, Germany, the Ukraine, the Netherlands and France, just to name a few. The games are televised back to these countries and along with them the Samsung logo, creating great visibility for the Korean electronics giant among not only existing markets but also future ones.

These endeavors create a more consumer-friendly "touchpoint" for the brands. Conventional communication media such as mass advertising are cost efficient but limited in terms of their ability to evoke personal interaction with consumers. In contrast, on-site brand touchpoints can engage both loyal and new consumers.

The ultimate lesson that even Korean companies are still in the process of learning is that brand management is hard. To join the exclusive "A-list" of global brands, companies must invest time, money and the best people to build and maintain their brands.

(*Far Eastern Economic Review*, July and August, 2007)

Answer and discuss the following questions:

1. How did firms in the developing countries conceive of a brand as just a name for the product in the very beginning of their brand path?
2. What can we learn from Lenovo and LG's brand-building experience?
3. What made Korea value the importance of brand building in its development?
4. Do you think that Beijing's 2008 Olympics will speed up local brand building up of those famous producers in China? Why?
5. Do you think that cases of AmorePacific and Samsung are instructive to our Chinese entrepreneurs for their creation of successful global brand? And in what way?
6. Do you think that conventional communication media such as mass advertising are cost efficient but limited in terms of their ability to evoke personalized interaction with consumers? Why?
7. What are the effective means to help an entrepreneur to enhance the public awareness of his brand?

Unit 6

Human Resources
人力资源

 Text A

Fear of Firing

Michael Orey

How the threat of litigation is making companies skittish about axing problem workers

Would you have dared fire Hemant K. Mody?

In February, 2003, the longtime engineer had returned to work at a General Electric Co. (GE) facility in Plainville, Conn., after a two-month medical leave. He was a very unhappy man. For much of the prior year, he and his superiors had been sparring over his performance and promotion prospects. According to court documents, Mody's bosses claimed he spoke disparagingly of his co-workers, refused an assignment as being beneath him, and was abruptly taking days off and coming to work late.[1]

But Mody was also 49, Indian born, and even after returning from leave continued to suffer a major disability: chronic kidney failure that required him to receive daily dialysis. The run-ins resumed with his managers, whom he had accused flat out of discriminating against him because of his race and age.[2] It doesn't take an advanced degree in human resources to recognize that the situation was a ticking time bomb.[3] But Mody's bosses were fed up. They axed him in April, 2003.

The bomb exploded last July. Following a six-day trial, a federal court jury in Bridgeport, Conn., found GE's termination of Mody to be improper and awarded him $11.1 million, including $10 million in punitive damages. But the award wasn't for discrimination. The judge found those claims so weak that Mody wasn't allowed to present them. Instead, jurors concluded that Mody had been fired in retaliation for complaining about bias. GE is seeking to have the award overturned, and a spokesman said, "We feel strongly there is no basis for this claim." Through his attorney, Mody declined to discuss the case with *BusinessWeek*.

If this can happen to GE, a company famed for its rigorous performance reviews, with an HR operation that is studied worldwide, it can happen anywhere.[4] It has never been easier for US workers to go to court and allege that they've been sacked unfairly. Over the past 40 years federal, state, and local lawmakers have steadily expanded the categories of workers who enjoy special legal protection — a sprawling group that now includes women, minorities, gays, whistleblowers, the disabled, people over 40, employees who have filed workers' compensation claims, and workers who have been called away for jury duty or military service, among others.[5] Factor in white men who believe that they are bias victims — so-called reverse-discrimination[6] lawsuits — and "it's difficult to find someone who doesn't have some capacity to claim protected status," observes Lisa H. Cassilly, an employment defense attorney at Alston & Bird in Atlanta.

These workers wield a potent weapon: They can force companies to prove in court that there was a legitimate business reason for their termination. And once a case is in court, it's expensive. A company can easily spend $100,000 to get a meritless lawsuit tossed out before trial. And if a case goes to a jury, the fees skyrocket to $300,000, and often much higher. The result: Many companies today are gripped by a fear of firing. Terrified of lawsuits, they let unproductive employees linger, lay off coveted workers while retaining less valuable ones, and pay severance to screwups and even crooks in exchange for promises that they won't sue.[7] "I've seen us make decisions (about terminations) that in the absence of this litigious risk environment, you'd have a different result," acknowledges Johnny C. Taylor, Jr., head of HR at IAC/Inter ActiveCorp[8] (IACI), the conglomerate that runs businesses such as Match. com and Ticketmaster.

The fear of firing is particularly acute in the HR and legal departments. They don't directly suffer when an underperformer lingers in the corporate hierarchy, but they may endure unpleasant indirect consequences if that person files a lawsuit. Says Dick Grote, an Addison[9] (Tex.) talent management consultant: "They don't get their bonuses based on the number of lawsuits they win. They get their bonuses based on the number of lawsuits they don't get involved in."

This set of divergent incentives puts line managers in a tough position. When they finally decide to get rid of the underperforming slob who plays PC solitaire all day in her cubicle, it can be surprisingly tough to do. And that, in turn, affects productive workers. "Few things demotivate an organization faster than tolerating and retaining low performers," says Grant Freeland, a regional leader in Boston Consulting Group's organization practice.

But it's often the supervisors themselves who bear much of the blame when HR says someone can't be shown the door. That's because most fail to give the kind of regular and candid evaluations that will allow a company to prove poor performance if a fired employee hauls them into court.[10] Honest, if harsh, reviews not only offer legal cover, but they're also critical for organizations intent on developing top talent. "There were definitely a lot of situations where a supervisor got fed up with somebody and wanted to terminate them, but there's no paperwork," says Sara Anderson, who worked in HR at Perry Ellis International[11] (PERY) and Kenneth Cole Productions Inc.[12] (KCP) in New York. Frequently, the work that the manager suddenly claims is intolerable is accompanied by years of performance evaluations that say "meets expectations." Says Anderson: "You look in the file, and there's nothing there to prove (poor performance), so it's like it didn't happen."

When Mody signed GE's job application in 1998, the form said his employment was "at will" and "the Company may terminate my employment at any time for any reason."

Well, not exactly.

The notion that American workers are employed "at will" — meaning, as one lawyer put it, you can be fired if your manager doesn't like the color of your socks — took root in the laissez-faire atmosphere of the late 19th century, and as an official matter is still the law of the land in every state[13], save Montana. The popular conception of at-will employment is exemplified by the television show *The Apprentice*, which features Donald Trump[14] pointing a finger at an underling and ousting him or her on the spot. That dramatic gesture makes great television, but it isn't something that happens very frequently anymore in the American workplace.

The rise of unions was the first development to put a check on summary dismissal. Collective-bargaining agreements outlined the specific kinds of infractions that could lead to termination, and set up procedures for discipline and review that a company must follow before a worker can be fired.[15] But unions generally didn't deal with the problem of discrimination, and in some cases perpetuated it.

For most American workers now, their status as at-will employees has been transformed by a succession of laws growing out of the civil rights movement in the 1960s that bar employers from making decisions based on such things as race, religion, sex, age, and national origin. This is hardly controversial. Even the legal system's harshest critics find little fault with rules aimed at assuring that personnel decisions are based on merit. And most freely acknowledge that it is much easier to fire people in the US than it is in, say, most of Western Europe. Mass layoffs, in fact, are a recurring event on the American corporate scene. On Apr. 17, for example, Citigroup Inc. announced it will shed some 17,000 workers.

Yet even in these situations, RIFs (for "reduction in force") are carefully vetted by attorneys to assess the impact on employees who are in a legally protected category. And these days the majority of American workers fall into one or more such groups. Mody, for example, belonged to three because of who he was (age, race, and national origin) and two more because of things he had done (complained of discrimination and taken medical leave). That doesn't mean such people are immune from firing. But it does mean a company will have to show a legitimate, nondiscriminatory business reason for the termination, should the matter ever land in court.

As it happens, the judge in Mody's case tossed out his discrimination claims. But the retaliation allegation did go to the jury — a development that is increasingly blindsiding businesses. Plaintiffs are winning large sums not because a company discriminated against them, but because the company retaliated when they complained about the unproven mistreatment.

The rules surrounding retaliation may sound crazy, but they are one of the big reasons why the fear of firing is so prevalent. Retaliation suits are a hot growth area in employment law. In 2005 and

2006, retaliation claims represented 30% of all charges individuals filed with the Equal Employment Opportunity Commission[16], a required first step before most discrimination cases can go to federal court. That's up from about 20% just 10 years ago. "Even if there isn't a good discrimination claim, the employee has a second bite at the apple," notes Martin W. Aron of defense firm Edwards Angell Palmer & Dodge[17] in Short Hills, N. J. Last year the US Supreme Court increased the legal risk to business by ruling that improper retaliation can involve acts far short of firing or demoting someone.[18] So even excluding an employee from meetings, relocating his or her office, or other intangible slights could lead to liability.

Of course, prohibitions against retaliation exist for a good reason. Without them, many workers would find it too risky to come forward with even legitimate complaints. Yet defense attorneys are deeply suspicious that some workers abuse the protection. Fearing their jobs may be in jeopardy, they may quickly contact HR with an allegation of discrimination or call a corporate hotline to report misconduct, thereby cloaking themselves in the protection of anti-retaliation law.[19] "That's a fairly common fact scenario," says Mike Delikat of Orrick Herrington & Sutcliffe[20] in New York, a law firm that represents businesses. "The best defense is a good offense."

After 1991, when congress allowed punitive damages and jury trials in job discrimination cases, litigation in the area exploded. In 2006, 14,353 employment cases were filed in federal court, up from 8,273 in 1990, though down from a peak of 20,955 in 2002. It should be noted that these statistics, which include both unlawful termination cases and other types of claims, dramatically understate the frequency with which companies deal with these issues. For every case that's filed in court, several more are quietly settled well beforehand.

Many of the lawsuits may seem ridiculous. IBM is currently defending a case filed by James C. Pacenza, a plant worker it dismissed for visiting an adult Internet chat room while on the job. In his lawsuit, Pacenza claims that his propensity to such behavior stems from post-traumatic stress disorder, which he suffers as a result of military service in Vietnam, and that IBM violated the Americans with Disabilities Act. He also alleges that two other employees who had sex on an IBM desk were "merely transferred," so he was treated with undue harshness. Pacenza's attorney, Michael D. Diederich Jr. , says his client "didn't violate any of IBM's policies regarding computer usage."

Even when employers beat back silly suits, it often doesn't feel like much of a victory. That's because meritless cases can still tie up companies in burdensome and expensive proceedings for years. In October, 2002, Southview Hospital in Dayton fired Karen Stephens, a nurse who worked in a unit for premature babies and other at-risk newborns. Six other nurses had reported that Stephens was abusive to infants, according to court filings, spanking them when they were fussy, wagging their noses until they screamed in pain, pinching their noses shut to force-feed them, and calling them "son of a bitch." Stephens, who was 60 at the time, sued Kettering Adventist Healthcare Network[21], which operates Southview, denying "inappropriate" conduct and alleging that the real reason she was let go was age discrimination.

Only after a year and a half of legal dueling did a federal district judge in Dayton toss out Stephens' claims in April, 2005. But then she appealed, and it took another year — and an additional round of legal briefing — before the US Court of Appeals for the Sixth Circuit[22] upheld the dismissal, noting that "Stephens has offered no evidence to indicate that she did not mistreat the infants," or that Kettering did not have a "legitimate, nondiscriminatory reason for discharging her." Kettering declined to comment on the case. "I never lost a baby in 25 years," Stephens said in an interview.

The cost and distraction of lawsuits lead many employers to engage in contortional, and at times perverse, litigation avoidance. Defense attorney Cassilly offers the story of one of her clients, a hospital in the Southeast forced to reduce its ranks because of budget cuts. The head of one department elected to let go a female employee in favor of keeping a more junior male, whom he had spent a great deal of effort to recruit and whom he felt was more valuable. But the hospital overrode that choice and laid off the man out of concern that it would be more exposed in a lawsuit by the woman.

Another of Cassilly's clients, a manufacturer, acquired a new facility and quickly identified one worker as having "a variety of performance problems." But the woman, an African American, had nothing in her personnel file indicating prior trouble, which made firing her a risky bet. So the company put her on a six-month "performance improvement program" to document her deficiencies — and to find out if she could mend her ways. She couldn't, and, Cassilly notes, her client "had to suffer through her poor performance during the whole period."

Early this year, Cassilly got a call from the client. They had just discovered that the woman, an office administrator, had stolen thousands of dollars from the company, and they promptly dismissed her. "It was almost a case where the company was delighted to find out they were the victim of theft," Cassilly says, as opposed to having to defend far more subjective performance evaluations.

Even in the face of theft, Revolution Partners, a small investment banking advisory firm in Boston, balked before showing one of its employees the door. The woman had used her company credit card for a personal shopping spree and plane ticket, but Revolution retained an employment attorney, got the woman to sign a form waiving her right to sue for wrongful dismissal, and after she was fired took no legal action to recover the amounts improperly charged.[23] "We're a little firm, and the last thing I need is to spend a lot of time on a lawsuit, whether it's warranted or not," says Peter Falvey, one of Revolution's co-founders.

Falvey isn't alone. A number of defense attorneys and HR managers said companies they work for prefer to buy themselves peace of mind over facing the prospect of being sued. "They don't want the publicity or the expense," says Robert J. Nobile, an attorney at Seyfarth Shaw in New York. "Some of them say, Hey, we'll swallow our pride and pay 10 grand now rather than 100 grand later.'" That's an approach that makes IAC's Taylor shudder. "If that becomes your norm, then you train the plaintiffs' bar and your departing employees that they should expect something on the way out, no matter how poorly they perform[24]," he says.

Many observers put much of the blame for fear of firing on HR. "The problem is much more with HR managers being nervous Nellies than it is a problem in actual legal exposure[25]," says consultant Grote. The bigger risk is retaining poor performers, not terminating them, he says, provided the firing is done properly.

Indeed, at most companies HR is essentially a support function that gets called in only when a personnel problem has reached the crisis stage. [26] At that point, the best they may be able to do is suggest the kind of risk-avoidance measures that drive managers crazy — such as requiring that an employee's deficiencies actually be documented in writing for an extended period before he or she is fired. This can be avoided, says Amy Rasner, a former HR manager in the fashion industry, if human resources personnel are teamed with line managers, working with them on an ongoing basis to develop and communicate specific, measurable performance objectives to employees.

In interview after interview, attorneys and HR execs say the biggest problem they confront in terminations is the failure of managers to have these kinds of conversations. In a 2005 Hewitt Associates[27] (HEW) survey of 129 major US corporations, 72% said managers' ability to carry out performance management discussions and decisions effectively was the part of their personnel evaluation process most in need of improvement. [28]

The reasons for this, of course, are varied. Some managers simply see the whole review process as a bureaucratic waste of time. It's also not easy to do. Many supervisors have been promoted into their jobs because they excelled in operations, not because they are skilled as managers. What's more, they've often spent a lot of time working alongside the very people they now oversee, so giving candid feedback to friends and former peers may be awkward. Managers in this position are "the biggest chickens on earth[29]," says Fred Kiel, an executive-development consultant at KRW International Inc. [30] in Minneapolis.

Ironically, when it came to handling personnel issues involving Mody, GE managers appear to have done most things right, offering regular and candid performance appraisals and involving HR and legal personnel at an early stage when matters began to sour. In trial exhibits and testimony, Mody's GE supervisors described him as a talented but prickly worker. Performance reviews and other documents faulted both his people and leadership skills.

But in the trial against GE, Mody's attorney, Scott R. Lucas of Stamford[31], Conn., laid out the details of what he labeled a campaign of retaliation against his client. Following a July, 2002, memo in which Mody accused the company of discrimination, Lucas told jurors, Mody's boss began complaining that he was absent and tardy too often. In a court filing, Lucas called this "a contrived performance issue," and says Mody was also "falsely criticized for lack of output."

What's more, just six weeks after having given Mody a "very favorable review," his boss gave Mody a "very poor and critical evaluation," according to the filing. Mody was excluded from various conferences and removed from "meaningful contribution" to projects. At one point, Mody's boss allegedly told him: "There are things I can ask you to do that if I asked you to do them, you would just quit." The last straw for Mody came when he returned from medical leave and was asked to do an assignment that he alleged was low-level and intentionally demeaning.

On July 18, jurors awarded Mody about $1.1 million in back pay and compensatory damages and — in one of several aspects of the case being challenged by GE — a tidy $10 million in punitive damages. Even for a company as big as GE, an $11.1 million verdict is plenty of cause to justify a fear of firing. But Mark S. Dichter, head of the employment practice at Morgan Lewis & Bockius[32] in Philadelphia, thinks that's the wrong lesson to draw from the Mody case and other similar lawsuits. "I can design HR policies that can virtually eliminate your risk of facing employment claims, but you'll have a pretty lousy workforce," says Dichter. "At the end of the day[33], you have to run your business."

(*BusinessWeek*, April 23, 2007)

New Words and Expressions

litigation	n.	诉讼, 起诉
skittish	a.	易受惊吓的, 易惊慌的
spar	v.	争论, 辩论
disparagingly	ad.	以贬抑的口吻, 以轻视的态度
dialysis	n.	血液透析
run-in	n.	争吵, 争论
retaliation	n.	报复, 报仇
sack	v.	解雇
whistleblower	n.	告密者, 揭发者
reverse	v.	颠倒, 倒转
potent	a.	有力的, 有效的
meritless	a.	缺乏法律依据的
covet	a.	垂涎, 觊觎
severance	n.	解雇费, 分割
screwup	n.	把事情弄糟搞砸的人
crook	n.	骗子
litigious	a.	可导致诉讼的
conglomerate	n.	集团企业, 联合大企业
divergent	a.	分歧的, 背道而驰的
slob	n.	懒汉, 粗俗汉, 笨蛋
solitaire	n.	单人纸牌戏, 单人跳棋
underling	n.	部下, 下僚, 下属
infraction	n.	违反, 侵害
perpetuate	v.	使永久存在, 使继续
vet	v.	审查, 修正
blindside	v.	突然袭击
plaintiff	n.	[律] 起诉人, 原告

mistreatment	n.	虐待
demote	v.	使降级，使降职
misconduct	n.	不正当的行为，处理不当
cloak	v.	掩饰，借口
propensity	n.	习性，倾向，嗜好
traumatic	a.	受创伤的
undue	a.	不适当的
dueling	n.	决斗，较量
contortional	a.	扭歪的，弯曲的
perverse	a.	反常的，违反常情的
balk	v.	犹豫不决，畏缩不前
shudder	v.	战栗，发抖
prickly	a.	多刺的，易生气的人
tardy	a.	行动缓慢的，磨蹭的
demeaning	a.	贬低身份的
lousy	a.	很糟的，无用的

problem workers	问题雇员
medical leave	病假
spar over	争论，辩论
promotion prospect	晋升前景
court documents	法庭文件，法庭档案
flat out	竭尽全力，用全速
in retaliation for	打击，报复
defense attorney	辩护律师
line managers	各级负责人，各级主管
take root in	生根，扎根于
find fault with …	找茬，挑毛病
mass layoffs	大规模裁员
intangible slights	无形的侮辱，轻视
come forward	自告奋勇，挺身而出
post-traumatic stress disorder	创伤后应激障碍
beat back	击退
office administrator	办公室管理人员
be teamed with …	与……合作
back pay	欠薪

Notes

1. According to court documents, Mody's bosses claimed he spoke disparagingly of his co-workers, refused an assignment as being beneath him, and was abruptly taking days off and coming to work late. 根据法院文件，穆迪的上级声称他轻视同事，拒绝接受他认为是有损其身份的工作任务，还经常旷工迟到。

   句中的"beneath"意为"不值得，有失身份"，"abruptly"意为"突然地，支离破碎地"。

2. The run-ins resumed with his managers, whom he had accused flat out of discriminating against him because of his race and age. 他和经理继续争辩着，并指责经理因为他的种族和年龄而歧视他。

   句中的"whom"引导非限制性定语从句，"flat out"意为"竭尽全力，极力地"。

3. It doesn't take an advanced degree in human resources to recognize that the situation was a ticking time bomb. 在人力资源领域，人们不难发现这种情况就像一枚定时炸弹。

   句中的"ticking time bomb"意为"定时炸弹"，"ticking"指钟表指针滴滴答答的声音。

4. If this can happen to GE, a company famed for its rigorous performance reviews, with an HR operation that is studied worldwide, it can happen anywhere. 通用公司一向以严格的业绩管理而闻名，它的人力资源管理模式在世界各地被研究学习，如果连通用都发生了这种事情，那么其他任何公司也很有可能发生。

   句中的"a company"是同位语。

5. Over the past 40 years federal, state, and local lawmakers have steadily expanded the categories of workers who enjoy special legal protection — a sprawling group that now includes women, minorities, gays, whistleblowers, the disabled, people over 40, employees who have filed workers' compensation claims, and workers who have been called away for jury duty or military service, among others. 40多年以来，联邦、州和地方议员一直致力于扩大受法律特别保护的雇员的范围，现在这些群体包括妇女、少数民族、同性恋、检举人、残疾人、40岁以上的公民、提起赔偿诉求的雇员及参加陪审团或服兵役的人员，等等。

   句中的"that now includes"引导定语从句。

6. reverse-discrimination 逆差别待遇或反向歧视

   这是指由于改善歧视黑人或妇女等政策过度而使白人或男人蒙受不利。

7. Terrified of lawsuits, they let unproductive employees linger, lay off coveted workers while retaining less valuable ones, and pay severance to screwups and even crooks in exchange for promises that they won't sue. 因为害怕诉讼，他们让效率不高、保留价值不大的雇员留下，而解雇那些迫切需要的雇员，向滋事闹事者甚至向骗子支付解雇费，以换取他们不再诉讼的承诺。

   句中的"terrified"是过去分词作状语。

8. IAC/Inter ActiveCorp   美国电子商务集团（全球最大的在线旅游服务商）
9. Addison   英国爱达讯科技公司

    其全称为"Addison Limited Technology"，是专业综合布线生产商，主要提供非屏蔽双绞线、屏蔽双绞线等各种铜缆，同时还提供光缆布线系统，是较早期的电缆 OEM 制造商。

10. That's because most fail to give the kind of regular and candid evaluations that will allow a company to prove poor performance if a fired employee hauls them into court.   那是因为当被解雇员工将这些公司送上法庭的时候，它们中的大部分无法提供可以证明员工表现不佳所需的定期而又客观的鉴定评价。

    句中的"because"引导表语从句。

11. Perry Ellis International   美国派瑞·艾力斯国际公司

    它是美国首屈一指的服装公司，拥有一系列占主导地位的男、女装品牌。其每年的零售总额高达十亿美元。

12. Kenneth Cole Productions Inc.   凯尼斯·柯尔制造公司（世界著名鞋履设计制造商）

13. The notion that American workers are employed "at will"— meaning, as one lawyer put it, you can be fired if your manager doesn't like the color of your socks — took root in the laissez-faire atmosphere of the late 19th century, and as an official matter is still the law of the land in every state ...   美国人自由被雇佣的理念源于 19 世纪晚期的自由政策，正如一名律师所说的那样，自由雇佣是指哪怕经理不喜欢你短袜的颜色也可以解雇你。从官方角度来看，目前这种理念仍然存在于各州的地方法律中……

    句中的"the law of the land"指地方法律。

14. Donald Trump   唐纳德·特鲁普

    美国传媒热衷追逐的人物，曾是美国《商业周刊》封面人物，也曾出现在全美最畅销的八卦杂志《国家询问报》的头条新闻。《间谍》杂志宣称"特鲁普是一个浅薄庸俗的暴发户"，而美国著名讽刺连环漫画《杜恩斯比利》的主编也把特鲁普作为头号攻击对象。

15. Collective-bargaining agreements outlined the specific kinds of infractions that could lead to termination, and set up procedures for discipline and review that a company must follow before a worker can be fired.   集体谈判协议列出了具体的可以导致雇佣关系终止的违约情况，并制定了在解雇员工之前公司所应遵循的行政和复审程序。

    句中的 infractions 指违反协约或协议规定。

16. Equal Employment Opportunity Commission   公平就业机会委员会

    1965 年在历史性的《1964 年民权法》第 7 条的基础上，美国通过了公平就业机会法案。根据这一法案，联邦政府成立了公平就业机会委员会（EEOC）。这个机构的职责就是保障民权法得到充分执行，鼓励工人了解自己的合法权益，并争取和保护自己的权益。

17. Edwards Angell Palmer & Dodge   爱德华－安琪－帕尔默 & 道奇律师事务所

    该律师事务所为全球 100 强律师事务所之一。

18. Last year the US Supreme Court increased the legal risk to business by ruling that improper retaliation can involve acts far short of firing or demoting someone.   去年，美国最高法院判决不正当的报复行为即使远没有达到解雇或降职的程度，也会违反有关法案，这增加了公司的法律风险。

句中的"far short of firing or demoting someone"作定语，修饰前面的"improper retaliation"（不正当的报复行为）。

19. Fearing their jobs may be in jeopardy, they may quickly contact HR with an allegation of discrimination or call a corporate hotline to report misconduct, thereby cloaking themselves in the protection of anti-retaliation law. 由于担心会被解雇，他们可能会迅速和人力资源部门联系，声称受到歧视，或是打公司的热线电话来反应处理不当的问题，因为这样他们就可以披上反报复法的保护外衣了。

20. Orrick Herrington & Sutcliffe 美国奥睿律师事务所（世界著名律师事务所）

21. Kettering Adventist Healthcare Network 凯特灵基督保健网络
    它位于美国代顿，包括2家中心医院，3家一般医院和1所医学院。

22. the US Court of Appeals for the Sixth Circuit 联邦上诉法院第六巡回审判庭
    该法院的管辖范围包括密歇根州、俄亥俄州、阿肯色州和田纳西州。

23. The woman had used her company credit card for a personal shopping spree and plane ticket, but Revolution retained an employment attorney, got the woman to sign a form waiving her right to sue for wrongful dismissal, and after she was fired took no legal action to recover the amounts improperly charged. 这名妇女用公司信用卡购买机票并疯狂购物，但Revolution公司聘请了一名就业律师，让该妇女签署了一份文件，要求她放弃以不正当的解职为由起诉公司的权利，在解雇她之后，公司也没有采取任何法律行动去追回被滥用的金额。
    句中的"improperly charged"是过去分词作定语，修饰前面的"amounts"（金额）。

24. If that becomes your norm, then you train the plaintiffs' bar and your departing employees that they should expect something on the way out, no matter how poorly they perform. 如果这成为了你的行为准则，那么就会使你的原告律师和离职员工认为不管他们的表现是如何糟糕，在离开公司时都应该期待些什么。
    句中的"bar"指律师业，"on the way out"意为"离开公司"。

25. The problem is much more with HR managers being nervous Nellies than it is a problem in actual legal exposure. 问题不在于实际的法律诉讼，而更多地在于人力资源经理们过于胆小怕事。
    句中的"nervous Nellies"是美国习语，指胆小怕事的人，"Nelly"是女孩常用名。

26. Indeed, at most companies HR is essentially a support function that gets called in only when a personnel problem has reached the crisis stage. 事实上，在大多数公司里，人力资源部门只有在人员问题出现了危机时，才会被要求参与进来帮助公司渡过难关。
    句中的"that"引导定语从句，"support function"意为"支撑函数，支撑功能"。

27. Hewitt Associates 翰威特咨询公司
    翰威特咨询公司是全球最大的综合性人力资源外包管理和人力资源管理咨询公司。

28. In a 2005 Hewitt Associates (HEW) survey of 129 major US corporations, 72% said managers' ability to carry out performance management discussions and decisions effectively was the part of their personnel evaluation process most in need of improvement. 在2005年翰威特咨询公司对美国129家主要公司的调查中，72%的人认为在员工评估过程中最需要提高的是经理

们组织业绩管理讨论和有效决策的能力。

句中的"most in need of improvement"是介宾短语作定语。

29. the biggest chickens on earth　这里指最聪明和能力最强的人。
30. KRW International Inc.　美国著名咨询公司
    该公司主要为公司高管提供各种管理咨询服务，以提高他们的领导能力。
31. Stamford　史丹福咨询公司（世界著名咨询公司）
32. Morgan Lewis & Bockius　摩根路易斯律师事务所（世界50强律师事务所）

　阅读小知识（1）

用批判的眼光来阅读

　　从表面上来看，英美等国报刊有着相对的自由。报刊均非公办，不代表政府，因此常常标榜"客观"、"公正"，然而它们是有政治倾向的。第二次世界大战后，西方一些政客、报人曾以"铁幕国家"（iron curtain country）称呼苏联和东欧社会主义国家，意指这些国家为阻止本国人民同西方进行交流，特别是为政治和意识形态的交流，设置了障碍。后又以"竹幕"（bamboo curtain）污蔑中国。西方一些经贸报刊在报道中国经济的同时往往也对中国的人权横加指责，同时对他们本国的一些问题也想当然地归咎于中国的快速经济发展和货币政策及国民消费。我们应提高警惕，学会用批判的眼光去阅读，平时不断加强学习，多了解国家政策和国情，在阅读中不能人云亦云，做西方报人的传声筒。

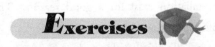

I Decide whether the following statements are true (T) or false (F).

1. Mody's bosses decided to lay off Mody, because they thought that Mody's behavior was improper and his health situation was deteriorating. (　　)
2. The court ruled that GE's termination of Mody was improper and awarded him a large sum of money as damages, the award that was made to his being fired in retaliation for complaining about discrimination. (　　)
3. It seems to the author that such an award is fair and justified, because it is a good case that employees can follow in protecting their rights across the world. (　　)
4. According to the text, the local lawmakers have expanded steadily the categories of workers who enjoy special legal protection, which can improve the work efficiency and working condition. (　　)
5. To fire an employee, HR department needs to conduct years of performance evaluations of him

or her; therefore HR department faces the toughest challenge in the company. (   )

6. The statement that his employment was "at will", means that in today's US workplace, employers can more easily fire a worker. (   )

7. The fear of firing is so prevalent in the US, because, according to the author, workers can wield a potent weapon not only by a good discrimination claim, but also through resorting to the protection of anti-retaliation law. (   )

8. After 1991, when Congress allowed punitive damages and jury trials in job discrimination cases, litigation in the area exploded, but many more cases were not settled in court, but quietly well beforehand. (   )

9. Many employers would have to engage in abnormal and at times perverse litigation avoidance for the sake of costs and distraction of lawsuits in their daily business operation. (   )

10. The text shows that the author is sympathetic to the Mody case and critical of the employers in the US corporations. (   )

II Choose one answer that best suits the following statements.

1. It is often the supervisors themselves who bear much of the blame when HR says someone cannot be fired, because _____.
   A. the supervisors mostly cannot give the kind of regular and candid evaluations that will allow a company to prove poor performance if a fired employee takes a legal action against the company
   B. the supervisors excelled in operations, but not in management matters
   C. the supervisors were not the group with good awareness
   D. the supervisors felt it awkward to cooperate with their workers

2. The prohibitions against retaliation exist for a good reason. That is, they can well protect the rights of workers, but some attorneys are suspicious that _____.
   A. workers' rights cannot be effectively protected
   B. workers may abuse the prohibition
   C. workers can improve their work efficiency
   D. workers would try to engage in litigation avoidance

3. Companies were very cautious about firing employees, but despite that, they still faced the risk of losing a lawsuit when they were accused by their employees, because, it seems to the author, _____.
   A. HR departments were only support function, and could not offer the valid details on poor performance of the employees fired
   B. supervisors were not in the position of offering the candid and objective evaluation of their employees' performance
   C. the anti-retaliation law might be capitalized on by workers to their favor
   D. workers have improved awareness of work ethics

4. But it is often the supervisors themselves who bear much of the blame when HR says someone

cannot be shown the door.

The underlined part of this sentence means that _____.

A. someone cannot be led astray

B. someone is not allowed to be promoted

C. someone cannot be fired

D. someone has no potential of becoming an efficient employee

5. What's more, they have often spent a lot of time working alongside the very people they now oversee, so giving candid feedback to friends and former peers may be awkward. Managers in this position are "the biggest chickens on earth."

The underlined part means that _____.

A. managers in this position are the most challenged group

B. managers in this position are the group who has the least experience in conducting effective evaluation of those underperforming workers

C. managers in this position are very sophisticated in handling the complaints

D. managers in this position are most incapable of improving the labor-employer relations

III Translate the following passages into Chinese.

1. The fear of firing is particularly acute in the HR and legal departments. They don't directly suffer when an underperformer lingers in the corporate hierarchy, but they may endure unpleasant indirect consequences if that person files a lawsuit. Says Dick Grote, an Addison (Tex.) talent management consultant: "They don't get their bonuses based on the number of lawsuits they win. They get their bonuses based on the number of lawsuits they don't get involved in."

   This set of divergent incentives puts line managers in a tough position. When they finally decide to get rid of the underperforming slob who plays PC solitaire all day in her cubicle, it can be surprisingly tough to do. And that, in turn, affects productive workers. "Few things demotivate an organization faster than tolerating and retaining low performers," says Grant Freeland, a regional leader in Boston Consulting Group's organization practice.

2. The cost and distraction of lawsuits lead many employers to engage in contortional, and at times perverse, litigation avoidance. Defense attorney Cassilly offers the story of one of her clients, a hospital in the Southeast forced to reduce its ranks because of budget cuts. The head of one department elected to let go a female employee in favor of keeping a more junior male, whom he had spent a great deal of effort to recruit and whom he felt was more valuable. But the hospital overrode that choice and laid off the man out of concern that it would be more exposed in a lawsuit by the woman.

IV Write a summary of this text.

Asia's Skills Shortage

(Author Unknown)

Despite its booming economies and huge numbers of people, Asia is suffering a big shortage of skills. And it is about to get worse

It seems odd. In the world's most populous region the biggest problem facing employers is a shortage of people. Asia has more than half the planet's inhabitants and is home to many of the world's fastest-growing economies. But some businesses are being forced to reconsider just how quickly they will be able to grow, because they cannot find enough people with the skills they need.

In a recent survey, 600 chief executives of multinational companies with businesses across Asia said a shortage of qualified staff ranked as their biggest concern in China (See Chart 1) and South-East Asia. It was their second-biggest headache in Japan (after cultural differences) and the fourth-biggest in India (after problems with infrastructure, bureaucracy and wage inflation). Across almost every industry and sector it was the same.

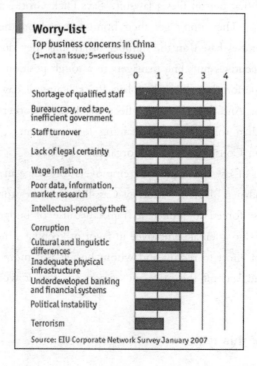

Chart 1

Old Asia-hands may find it easy to understand why there is such concern. The region's rapid economic growth has fished out the pool of available talent, they would say. But there is also a failure of education. Recent growth in many parts of Asia has been so great that it has rapidly transformed the type of skills needed by businesses. Schools and universities have been unable to keep up.

Taking Wing

This is especially true for professional staff. Airlines are one example. With increasing deregulation, many new carriers are setting up and airlines are offering more services to meet demand. But there is a dreadful shortage of pilots. According to Alteon Training[1], the commercial-pilot training arm of Boeing, India has fewer than 3,000 pilots today but will need more than 12,000 by 2025. China will need to find an average of 2,200 new pilots a year just to keep up with the growth in air travel, which means it will need more than 40,000 pilots by 2025. In the meantime, with big international airlines training only a few hundred pilots a year, Asian airlines have taken to poaching them, often from each other. Philippine Airlines[2], for instance, lost 75 pilots to overseas airlines during the past three years. China has been trying to lure pilots from Brazil, among other places.

Similar problems are realizing the legal profession, which is suffering from a grave shortage of lawyers and judges. This can cause a long backlog of cases and other complications in what are sometimes rudimentary legal systems.[3] It can damage the way business is done, for instance in dealing with intellectual property or settling contract disputes. According to the All-China Lawyers Association[4], the country has only 122,000 lawyers. That is 70,000 fewer than California where the population is only 37m (against China's 1.3 billion). Many business people might argue that California is overlawyered, but there are parts of China without any lawyers at all.

A report presented at the Chinese Party Congress in March by the Jiu San Society[5], a group of progressive Chinese intellectuals, stressed the shortage of doctors. There are only 4,000 general practitioners in China. But if the government is to achieve its ambition of establishing community hospitals for the country's 500m urban residents, it will need 160,000 doctors to staff them. There is a huge shortage of nursing staff as well.

The scarcity of accountants is already having a regional impact. In order to list their shares in Hong Kong or Shanghai, many Chinese companies are busy preparing internationally acceptable accounts and statutory reports.[6] With the country's own bean-counters trained in Communist-era systems — which never paid heed to capitalist ideas like profits or assets — accountants are being lured to the mainland from Hong Kong and the rest of the region. A senior manager at one of the big audit firms recently arrived in Hong Kong after a long stint in Russia, took one look at his firm's ambitious growth plans and asked: "How are we going to do this without enough staff?"

Technical skills, particularly in information technology, are lacking in many parts of the region, even India. One of the main concerns is that there are not enough skilled graduates to fill all the jobs being created in a vibrant sector.[7] Nasscom[8], which represents India's software companies, has estimated that there could be a shortfall of 500,000 IT professionals by 2010. This means companies recruiting at job fairs in India have to make lucrative offers to capture the most promising students. Even a junior software-engineer can expect to take home $45,000 a year.

There is also a severe shortage of good managers. A study by the McKinsey Global Institute predicts that 75,000 business leaders will be needed in China in the next ten years. It estimates the current stock at just 3,000 to 5,000. And that assessment could prove optimistic. The study, which covered a broad spectrum of businesses and surveyed more than 80 human-resources managers, found that less than "10% of Chinese job candidates, on average, were suitable for work in a foreign company." In engineering, for example, graduates were criticized for being too immersed in theory and not enough in practice.[9] It concluded that the available pool of engineering talent in China was no larger than that in Britain, which now has a mostly service economy.

China is even suffering from something of a brain drain. In recent years the Chinese have been able to travel abroad more freely to study and acquire skills. But many do not return. A recent report by the Chinese Academy of Social Sciences[10] found that between 1978 and 2006, just over 1m Chinese went to study overseas and some 70% of them did not go back. The brightest are often tempted to stay abroad by local employers, because the competition for jobs has become global.

The skills shortage comes in two forms: higher staff turnover and rising wage costs. Pay rates for senior staff in many parts of Asia already exceed those for similar staff in much of Europe. The going rate for a human-resources director working for a medium-to-large multinational in Shanghai is now $250,000 a year, and that is for "someone who has probably never even left China[11]," says Vanessa Moriel, the managing partner of Human Capital Partners[12], a Shanghai-based consulting firm. The chief executive of an international business based in India can expect to earn $400,000-500,000, with many earning well over $750,000, according to Korn/Ferry[13], a consultancy. For a chief finance officer the average pay is now $194,000 in China, $159,000 in Thailand, $157,000 in Malaysia and $73,000 in India. Wages for lower-level staff are also rising quickly, increasing by 14% in Indonesia last year, 11% in India and 8% in China — well above the rates of inflation in each country.

Another Year, Another Job

A high staff-turnover rate helps to force up wage costs, and turnover-rates can exceed 30% a year in some places in Asia. Fiducia[14], a Hong Kong-based consultancy, reckons that the additional hiring and training costs of operating in Asia add a further 15% to the basic costs of employing someone. Factories in southern China now plan for a 4% loss of staff just in the week immediately after Chinese New Year, because people seem to like to start the new year with a new job. In middle management, the average retention period of an employee in Shanghai is just 1.8 years, with human-resources managers among the most difficult to keep. Some job applicants are known as "jumpers" because of their tendency to switch jobs every two years.

Struggling with high staff-turnover is harder still when many firms are also trying to expand. Last year Flextronics[15], a big electronics manufacturer, wanted to increase staff numbers in Shenzhen from 27,000 to 43,000. But to get a net increase of 16,000 people, it had to hire more than 20,000 because over the same period it had 4,000 employees leave.

As well as excessive wage inflation there is also "title inflation" and "responsibility inflation". Relatively inexperienced local managers are sometimes given ever-grander titles — much to the chagrin of their counterparts from Europe and America, who can find themselves sitting beside much less able and more junior colleagues described as "Senior Executive Vice President" or "Regional Chairman".[16] But these honors are handed out for a reason: many employers in Asia have found that awarding new titles to employees every 18 months or so can be a good way to keep them.

Giving greater responsibility to staff is more troublesome. Yet many inexperienced managers in China are being given powerful regional roles or are promoted to positions where they lack sufficient knowledge or ability. Even though they may not seem ready for the job, it is often seen as the only way to keep them on the payroll.

A Problem for Years to Come

As if all this were not bad enough, the Asian talent shortage is set to get worse. The predicted inflow of investment, together with the growth of local companies and the rising expectations of foreign investors — especially as other markets are slowing — means that the pressure to find and keep staff is mounting.[17]

Demography will also play a big role, especially as labor forces in both China and Japan shrink over the next two decades. This means, for instance, that the already difficult job of finding creative software-engineers will become ever harder in northern Asia, which in turn will increase demand for staff in India and other markets where demographic problems do not exist.

But that only points to an even bigger threat which may take a generation to fix: education. In much of South-East Asia most people are educated only to the age of 12. More than half of the women in India are illiterate. Nearly two-thirds of the children in government primary schools in India cannot read a simple story. Half cannot solve simple numerical problems.

China's educational difficulties are different — and often linked to the country's history. Universities were closed during the Cultural Revolution and few well-educated people entered the workforce for over a decade. This has resulted in a lost generation of business people between the ages of 50 and 60, exactly the age group from where many of China's corporate leaders should be drawn today.[18]

Those who were children (and typically without siblings because of China's one-child policy) after the Cultural Revolution have other things to deal with. Their parents had often been sent for re-education in the fields and many were brought up far away from home by strangers. Perhaps in response to this harshness, they have brought up their own children rather indulgently. What is known as the "little emperor syndrome" is a particular weakness in boys. Many older Chinese believe this younger generation, doted on by grandparents and parents, lacks a work ethic. It has even become a bit of a slur to say of someone that "they were born in the 1980s".

Girls born after the Cultural Revolution are much less likely to have been spoilt, which means some employers see them as good hires. Liam Casey, the boss of PCH China Solutions[19], a contract-manufacturer in southern China, says he once noticed in a shopping mall that there were typically groups of seven people or groups of three. The groups of seven consisted of two sets of grandparents, parents and a boy, those of three comprised parents and a daughter. He says he realized then that girls were valued less by society and that if he hired them and showed them loyalty, they would be more loyal in return. [20] This is one reason, he says, that his business has much lower rates of staff turnover than his rivals' businesses do.

But even hiring women is getting harder. In Zhuhai another foreign manufacturer which hires staff from all over China says it prefers to recruit women too. The managers believe that women are generally harder-working and tend to stay longer. But schools and universities have cottoned on to this now and set quotas on the number of women that firms can recruit. [21] The company says that for every group of women it selects, it now has to hire a share of men too.

Team Building

In the face of so many problems, what can employers do? Building a skilled workforce is as much about a company's general attitude as its tactics, says Michael Bekins, the managing director of Korn/Ferry in Hong Kong. The first part of that mindset is realizing that retention is more important than recruitment, he says. He thinks all managers in Asia should be explicitly measured on their ability to keep a team together.

Some ways of doing that are more obvious than others. Paying higher wages to employees, say most managers and recruitment specialists, is certainly not enough. Pay should be seen as only part of any package. Delaying bonus payments with a reward at the end of say, three years, can work well, but increases costs. Offering career planning, training, "personal-development road maps", mentoring and the rest of the modern HR kitbag seems to go down well (See Chart 2), though managing expectations is critical. One company in South-East Asia has a "welcome the boomerangers" policy, making it easy for anyone who has left to come back. The big accounting firms have programs to keep in touch with people who leave.

Some employers argue that you should focus on the family not just the employee. Offering support for children's education and helping the families of staff resettle can build loyalty. With expatriates, this is crucial. According to one consultant, 85% of expatriates in China leave because their families do not like living there. Life can be especially hard in smaller cities, where there are few other foreigners, international schools or decent restaurants and little to do in your time off. Many spouses complain of feeling like prisoners in their gated communities while their partners are away, heady with the thrill of running the firm's fastest-growing division.

There are less obvious ways to keep people too. A prestigious brand can be valuable in more ways than one; Asians seem attracted to the idea of working for well-known firms. Having a fashionable office can be a big help. And providing courses in stress management or etiquette can be attractive. So is giving staff club memberships. Even providing staff with the latest PDAs and mobile phones can work wonders (See Chart 2). And, if a company has a canteen, it should make sure it hires a good chef.

One of the more creative options for employers is to offer flexible working hours and sabbaticals. Although these are unusual in Asia, they can help staff who has young children or elderly parents to care for. But there are some dangers. It is common, especially in China, for employees to

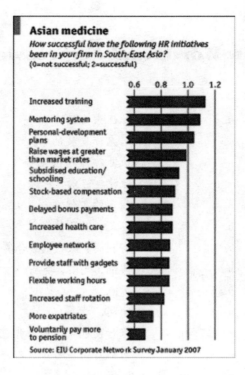

Chart 2

run private businesses on the side. Giving them more time for outside activities may not be in a company's best interests. It could also be counterproductive in some parts of Asia, where workers want a job in order to make as much money as fast as they can.

Hiring Asians who have been educated overseas and bringing them back does not always work. They often expect to be paid a lot. Some demand expatriate packages with paid flights back to America or Europe. They may also be out of touch with local developments. But the biggest difficulty is that their colleagues frequently resent them. This is especially so in China, where one of the politer names for returning people is *hai gui* or sea turtles. A similar attitude sometimes turns up in India too. Companies find that the turtles tend to fit in best in the finance industry or in privately owned businesses.

With such a mismatch between supply and demand in Asia's labor markets, companies will have to become better at hiring good staff and keeping them. But as some companies will always be better at this than others, the job-hopping and poaching are set to continue for many years, until education and training catch up. The consequences of that are stark. "It will limit the growth. It has to," says Korn/Ferry's Mr. Bekins. It means that without talented recruiting policies, some firms may end up scaling back their bold Asian growth-plans.

(*Economist*, August 18, 2007)

New Words and Expressions

backlog	n.	积压未办的事
rudimentary	a.	未充分发展的
practioner	n.	执业律师或医生等
heed	n.	注意，留意
stint	n.	指定的工作
shortfall	n.	不足，不足量
lucrative	a.	有利的，赚钱的，合算的，待遇好的
chagrin	n.	懊恼，气愤，委屈
slur	n.	污点
mentoring	n.	顾问，指导
kitbag	n.	旅行皮包，行囊，背包
boomeranger	n.	回锅员工，回归员工
sabbatical	n.	休假
counterproductive	a.	产生相反效果的，使达不到预期目标的
poaching	n.	猎头
stark	a.	严厉的，荒凉的

be home to ...	是……的家乡，家园
wage inflation	工资增长
red tape	繁琐的手续，官僚作风
staff turnover	员工流动
old Asia-hands	对亚洲了解比较多的老手
Chinese Party Congress	中国党代会
statutory report	法定报告
pay heed to	注意，留意
audit firm	审计所
brain drain	人才流失
pay rate	付费标准，工资率
chief finance officer	首席财务总监
retention period	停留期，在某一单位的工作时间
numerical problems	算术题，计算题
the Cultural Revolution	文化大革命

Unit 6 Human Resources

work ethic	职业道德
cotton on	理解
team building	团队建设
recruitment specialist	招聘专家
stress management	压力管理，压力调节
club membership	会员身份
on the side	作为兼职，另外
be out of touch with ...	对……不熟悉的
job-hopping	跳槽
scale back	按比例缩减，相应缩减

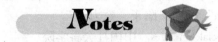

1. Alteon Training　翱腾航训公司
   波音公司全资子公司，拥有遍布全球的航空训练中心网络，并针对波音 787 梦想飞机客户，推出了一种颇具创意的获取训练资源的全新模式，长期为航空公司提供有效的战略性解决方案。

2. Philippine Airlines　菲律宾航空公司
   菲律宾航空公司是亚洲第一家航空公司，拥有 60 年的历史，菲律宾航空公司的机队由宽体机及窄体机组成，包括波音 747-400 型、空客 A340-300 型、空客 A300-300 型、空客 A320、波音 734-400 型和波音 737-300 型等。

3. This can cause a long backlog of cases and other complications in what are sometimes rudimentary legal systems.　在一些不太健全的司法体系里，这会造成案件积压，并带来其他一些复杂问题。
   句中的"in"引导介宾短语作状语。

4. All-China Lawyers Association　中华全国律师协会
   该协会成立于 1986 年 7 月，社会团体法人，是全国性的律师行业自律性组织，依法对律师实行行业管理。中华全国律师协会的最高权力机构为全国律师代表大会。

5. Jiu San Society　九三学社
   九三学社是以科学技术界高、中级知识分子为主的具有政治联盟特点的政党，是接受中国共产党领导、同中国共产党亲密合作、致力于建设中国特色社会主义事业的参政党，其前身为抗日战争后期，一批进步学者发扬五四运动的反帝爱国精神，以民主科学为宗旨，在重庆发起成立的"民主科学座谈会"，后为纪念 1945 年 9 月 3 日抗日战争和世界反法西斯战争的伟大胜利，改建为"九三学社"。

6. In order to list their shares in Hong Kong or Shanghai, many Chinese companies are busy preparing internationally acceptable accounts and statutory reports.　为在香港或上海上市，很多中国公司正忙着准备各种国际上接受的会计报表和法定报告。

句中的"list"意为"上市"。

7. One of the main concerns is that there are not enough skilled graduates to fill all the jobs being created in a vibrant sector. 一个主要问题是在一个富于变化的行业,没有足够的、训练有素的毕业生去满足新增的工作岗位。

   句中的"being created in a vibrant sector"作定语修饰前面的"jobs"(工作岗位)。

8. Nasscom 印度软件和服务公司协会

   全称为 National Association of Software and Service Companies,成立于 1986 年,是一个非盈利性组织,是印度 IT 及其相关服务行业的尖端组织。Nasscom 的成员公司广泛地从事于软件开发业、软件服务业、互联网相关产业、电子经济及 IT 相关服务业等电子经济领域。Nasscom 还提供各种印度 IT 方面相关信息的查询服务。

9. In engineering, for example, graduates were criticized for being too immersed in theory and not enough in practice. 譬如在工程领域,毕业生被批评为太注重理论,而缺乏实践。

   句中的"be immersed in"意为"陷于,致力于"。

10. Chinese Academy of Social Sciences 中国社会科学院

    中国社会科学院于 1977 年 5 月建立,是中国哲学社会科学研究的最高学术机构和综合研究中心。中国社会科学院学科齐全,人才集中,资料丰富,进行创造性地理论探索和政策研究,肩负着从整体上提高中国人文社会科学水平的使命。

11. The going rate for a human-resources director working for a medium-to-large multinational in Shanghai is now ＄250,000 a year, and that is for someone who has probably never even left China. 目前在上海大中型跨国公司中就职的人力资源总监的收入是 25 万美元,而这还只是给那些可能从来没有出过国的人的报酬。

    句中的"and"此处有递进的语气。

12. Human Capital Partners HCP 咨询公司

    HCP 咨询公司是欧洲顾问集团成员之一。欧洲顾问集团成立于 1968 年,由英国、法国、意大利和德国四方合作者共同创办成立。现在这个国际集团在 9 个不同的国家拥有 20 个办事处,是全球顶尖顾问公司之一。

13. Korn/Ferry 光辉国际

    光辉国际是著名的猎头公司,全球最大的高级管理人才顾问公司,成立于 1969 年,总部设在美国洛杉矶。光辉国际为财富 500 强企业中的近半数公司提供过服务,其中超过半数是 CEO、CFO、COO、董事会成员或其他高等级的职位。光辉国际曾经为奥运会举荐一位奥运会 CEO,1984 年的洛杉矶奥运会主席尤伯罗思成为第一位来自民间的奥运会管理者,这次奥运营利 2.5 亿美元,使奥运会首次变为赚钱的生意。光辉国际分别于 1995 年和 1997 年开设北京及上海办事处。

14. Fiducia 德鑫管理咨询公司

    该公司成立于 1982 年,总部位于香港,公司主要为跨国公司提供外包和咨询服务。

15. Flextronics 伟创力公司

    伟创力公司是业界领先的端到端电子元件生产服务供应商,向通讯、网络、计算机、医药及消费品市场的众多 OEM 客户提供设计、工程及制造服务,被公认为是在全球电子元件生产服务领域最大、盈利状况最好的企业。

16. Relatively inexperienced local managers are sometimes given ever-grander titles — much to the chagrin of their counterparts from Europe and America, who can find themselves sitting beside much less able and more junior colleagues described as "Senior Executive Vice President" or "Regional Chairman".　有时，当地一些经理经验相对不足，但头衔却很高，欧美经理们经常发现自己和一些能力较弱、职位较低但却被冠以"高级行政主管"或"地区主席"的同事坐在一起，这让他们有些懊恼。

    句中的"who"引导非限制性定语从句。

17. The predicted inflow of investment, together with the growth of local companies and the rising expectations of foreign investors — especially as other markets are slowing — means that the pressure to find and keep staff is mounting.　投资流入预期，当地公司增长，国外投资者期望加大，尤其是在其他市场放缓的情况下，这都意味着发现和留住员工的压力在加大。

    句中的谓语是"mean"，主语是破折号前面的部分。

18. This has resulted in a lost generation of business people between the ages of 50 and 60, exactly the age group from where many of China's corporate leaders should be drawn today.

    这导致从商人员在 50 岁和 60 岁之间出现断层，而中国很多公司恰恰就是在这一群体中选拔领导的。

    句中的"the age group"是同位语。

19. PCH China Solutions　普诚华信息科技咨询公司

    深圳一家外资公司，主要承接外包业务，给想要销售产品的外国公司与能为他们生产这些产品的中国供应商牵线搭桥。

20. He says he realized then that girls were valued less by society and that if he hired them and showed them loyalty, they would be more loyal in return.　他说当时他意识到女孩在社会上不太受重视，如果雇佣她们，并教她们学会忠诚，她们将会以更加忠诚作为回报。

    句中两个"that"引导两个从句，并列作"realized"的宾语。

21. But schools and universities have cottoned on to this now and set quotas on the number of women that firms can recruit.　但是学校和大学已经意识到这些，并对公司招聘的女性数量设置了配额。

    句中的"cotton on"意为"理解"。

阅读小知识（2）

日本部分著名企业介绍

1. 丰田汽车公司（Toyota）

该公司是世界十大汽车工业公司之一，日本最大的汽车公司。它创立于 1933 年，现在已发展成为以汽车生产为主，业务涉及机械、电子、金融等行业的庞大工业集团。

丰田汽车公司有很强的技术开发能力，而且十分注重研究顾客对汽车的需求，因而在它发展的各个不同历史阶段创出不同的名牌产品，而且以快速的产品换型击败欧美竞争对手。早期的丰田牌、皇冠、光冠、花冠汽车名噪一时，近来的克雷西达、雷克萨斯豪华汽车也极负盛名。丰田汽车公司总部在日本东京。

丰田汽车公司与韩国的现代汽车公司结成合作伙伴关系。

2. 本田汽车公司（Honda）

本田汽车公司是1948年以生产自行车助力发动机起步的，它一直以"梦想"作为原动力，以"商品"的形式不断为个人和社会提供更广泛的移动文化。

现在，本田汽车公司已经发展成为从小型通用发动机、踏板摩托车到跑车等各个领域都拥有独创技术，并不断研发、生产新产品的企业。从创业之初，本田汽车公司一直本着"让世界各地顾客满意"的理念不断开拓自己的事业。以"如何让当地顾客满意"为宗旨，本田汽车公司不仅建立了为提供适合当地的商品及服务的广阔销售服务网络，还建立了在当地生产和研发新产品的一整套体制。

目前除日本之外，本田汽车公司在全世界29个国家拥有120个以上的生产基地，通过摩托车、汽车和通用产品，每年惠顾的客户多达1 700万以上。

在全球环境问题日益突出的当今，本田汽车公司在产品研发、生产和销售等各项企业活动中努力把解决大气污染、降低CO_2排放量、有效利用资源和能源等作为课题，为达到产品排放清洁化、降低燃料消耗、实现生产线的"绿色工厂化"等采取了一系列措施，为减少对地球环境的影响做出了积极贡献。

3. 日立公司（Hitachi）

日立公司（Hitachi）是全球最大的综合跨国集团之一，总部位于日本东京，在世界各地拥有控股子公司956家，员工约33万人。

日立公司在广泛的事业领域中为社会提供着系统、产品及服务，其中包括信息通信系统、电子设备、电力/产业系统、数字媒体/家用电器、高性能材料、物流及服务、金融服务等领域。

4. 日产汽车公司（Nissan）

日产汽车公司是日本大型汽车制造公司。其前身是1933年成立的汽车制造公司，1934年取现名。其总部在东京，是日本第二大汽车生产商。

该公司除生产各型汽车外，还涉足机床、工程机械、造船和航天技术等领域，是一个庞大的跨国集团公司。日产汽车公司的汽车产品分实用型汽车（即货车、小型客货车和四轮驱动车）、豪华型轿车和普通型轿车。实用型汽车的品牌有巴宁、途乐、皮卡和佳碧等；豪华型轿车的品牌有公爵、蓝鸟、千里马、无限、光荣、桂冠和总统等；普通型轿车的品牌有阳光、自由别墅、地平线和兰利等。几十年来，日产汽车公司的技术与产品受到全世界消费者的喜爱。

5. 松下电器公司（Panasonic）

松下电器公司为日本最大的综合性电子技术设备制造厂家。该公司的前身是创业者松下幸之助和夫人及内弟井植岁男3人于1918年创立的松下电器器具制作所，1929年改称松下电器制作所，1935年12月改成股份公司并用现名。

松下电器公司注意到电子技术对人类发展所起的作用，坚持不懈地开发新技术、新产品，先后同荷兰飞利浦电器公司、美国西方电器公司和美国无线电公司进行技术合作，20世纪60年代发展成为日本家用电器的最大生产厂家，70年代其家用电器的生产居世界首位。该公司经营范围广，产品主要包括电视机、录像机、冰箱、洗衣机、微波炉等家用电器，以及办公自动化设备、工厂生产自动化设备及各种集成电路、电子元器件等几乎所有种类的电子产品。除国内拥有60多家子公司外，国外也有近60家子公司。松下电器公司的总部设在大阪。

6. 索尼公司（Sony）

索尼公司是世界上民用和专业视听产品、游戏产品、通信产品和信息技术等领域的先导者之一。它在音乐、影视、计算机娱乐及在线业务方面的成就也使其成为全球领先的个人宽带娱乐公司。公司在截止到2007年3月31日结束的2006财政年度中的合并销售额达703亿美元。在公司发展的60多年时间里，作为一家具有高度责任感的全球化企业，索尼一直致力于以优秀的产品和服务，帮助人们实现享受更高品质娱乐生活的梦想。目前，索尼公司在全球120多个国家和地区建立了分公司、子公司和工厂；集团70%的销售来自于日本以外的其他市场；数以亿计的索尼用户遍布世界各地。

以"全球本土化"的运营策略为目标，索尼公司于1996年10月在北京设立了统一管理和协调在华业务活动的全资子公司——索尼（中国）有限公司。

7. 东芝公司（Toshiba）

东芝公司原名东京芝浦电气株式会社，1939年由株式会社芝浦制作所和东京电气株式会社两家日本公司合并而成。

20世纪80年代以来，东芝公司从一个以家用电器、重型电机为主体的企业转变为包括通信、电子在内的综合电子电器企业。进入90年代，东芝公司在数字技术、移动通信技术和网络技术等领域取得了飞速发展，东芝公司已成功地从家电行业的巨人转变为IT行业的先锋。

1995年，东芝（中国）有限公司成立，强化了东芝公司对在华企业的综合管理职能和战略制定职能。迄今为止，东芝公司在中国设立合资、独资公司达60家，投资总额逾80亿元人民币，员工总数约17 000人。中国已经毋庸置疑地成为东芝全球事业的重要支柱。

8. 日本电气股份有限公司（NEC Corporation）

日本电气股份有限公司（NEC Corporation）简称日本电气或日电或NEC，是一家跨国信息技术公司，总部位于日本东京港区（Minato-Ku）。NEC为商业企业、通信服务及政府提供信息技术（IT）和网络产品。它的经营范围主要分成三个部分：IT解决方案、网络解决方案和电子设备。IT解决方案主要是向商业企业、政府和个人用户提供软件、硬件和相关服务。网络解决方案主要是设计和提供宽带系统、移动和无线通信网络系统、移动电话、广播和其他系统。NEC 的电子设备包括半导体、显示器及其他的电子器件。NEC 还生产面向国际市场的 Versa 系列笔记本电脑和面向日本国内市场的 Lavie 系列笔记本电脑。NEC 还是地球模拟器（Earth Simulator）的发明者，这是当今世界上最快的超级计算机。NEC 是住友集团（Sumitomo Group）的成员。在过去的 5 年中，NEC 的美国专利申请量一直都位前四名，平均每年获得批准的专利为 1 764 项。

在使用目前的名字之前，即 1983 年之前，公司被称为日本电气有限公司（Nippon Electric Company Ltd.），现在在日本国内仍然使用这个名字。

9．富士通（Fujitsu）

日本富士通株式会社（Fujitsu）创立于 1935 年 6 月，总资产为 340 亿美元，销售额为 445 亿美元，员工总数为 151 000 人。富士通的事业涉及通信、计算机、半导体、软件服务和研究开发、空调等领域。富士通在日本、美国、欧洲、中国等世界上许多国家设立了研发中心、生产基地和销售及售后服务网络。富士通是全球第三大 IT 及服务公司，全球前五大服务器和 PC 机生产商，是日本大型的空调企业集团之一。

富士通于 20 世纪 70 年代进入中国，在通信、计算机、软件开发、半导体及高新技术的研究开发等领域与中国进行合作并取得了丰硕的成果。三十年来，富士通在中国的总投资金额超过 19 亿人民币，共设立 37 家公司。除了商业性的投资经营活动，富士通还积极投身于中日两国的社会、文化交流事业，并在环境保护领域做出贡献。

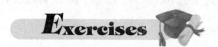

I Discuss and answer the following questions.

1. Why has the shortage of the talent become a headache in Asia?
2. Do you agree to such a statement of "China is even suffering from something of a brain drain?" in this text? Why?
3. What forms does the skill shortage come in?
4. What causes a high turn-over rate among employees in Asia, particularly in China?
5. What impact does the high turn-over rate make on the talent market?
6. What recipes can you propose to improve loyalty of employees?

II Decide whether the following statements are true (T) or false (F).

1. In Asia, a shortage of qualified staff has become the biggest headache in many multinational corporations. （   ）
2. The biggest reason for such a shortage is the declining of population in this region. （   ）
3. Because of the scarcity of accountants in China, many accountants or those from Hong Kong are lured to the mainland. （   ）

4. It seems to the author that a shortage of good managers in China is caused by far fewer qualified university graduates in recent years. (   )
5. In Shanghai, technical engineers are among the group the hardest to keep, the reason being that Shanghai's fast growing manufacturing industry needs large numbers of skilled labor and engineers. (   )
6. In order to keep the middle management, many companies based in Asia offer grander titles and responsibilities to relatively inexperienced local managers. (   )
7. The problem of talent shortage cannot be resolved in a short period of time, and it will get worse, because of the local markets that are slowing in the near future. (   )
8. To address the problem of skills shortage involves many measures, and no single solution is often taken as efficient by many HR personnel. (   )
9. Many expatriates' families cannot immediately be accustomed to the new settlement in Asia, therefore offering a flexible working schedule cannot be an ideal solution. (   )
10. In Asia, some firms are gripped by job-hopping and poaching, the impact of which is that their growth will be somewhat hampered in the future. (   )

III Group discussion.

1. What are the factors contributing to the skills shortage in Asia? Can you summarize them?
2. What are effective ways to build up the loyalty of employees to their companies?
3. Can Asia solve the problem of the talent shortage in the near future? Why?
4. How can we develop the sense of team work nowadays in China's companies?

Case Study
Why does China's Labor Law raise concerns in the US?

Fake DVDs and the undervalued renminbi have been the main points of discussion in the US about the rise of the Chinese economy. But another issue is gathering steam in the US — a new law that seeks to boost the employment rights of Chinese workers and give trade unions more influence.

While the bill was discussed behind closed doors by legislators in Beijing last week and the latest version is still a secret, the law is the subject of an increasingly bitter war of words in the US between business groups and trade unions unhappy about outsourcing jobs to Asia.

Last week the United Steelworkers, one of the biggest industrial unions, came out in favour of the law and accused US business groups of trying to block reforms. Leo Gerard, the USW president, criticized what he called the American Chamber of Commerce's "immoral campaign to undermine Chinese workers rights".

In a sign of the increasingly complex relationship between two countries with closely linked economies but vastly different political systems, Chinese supporters of the bill have even toured the US to rally opinion. Liu Cheng, a law professor at Shanghai Normal University, visited members of Congress and unions last month. "I told them that the business groups just want to maintain their sweatshops to protect their low-price strategy," he said on his return.

Business groups fiercely deny strong-arming China into weakening its legislation. The Shanghai office of Amcham insisted it "has never lobbied against, and is not lobbying against, the draft labor contract law".

Aside from the furore in the US, the bill is a delicate issue in China. The government has pledged to reduce income inequality and supporters say 200,000 Chinese sent in opinions on the first draft of the labour bill, a sign of intense public interest. Yet policymakers do not want to deter investment by companies in sectors such as textiles, some of whom are already shifting production to Vietnam and Bangladesh because of rising labour costs.

The new labour law is designed primarily to prevent abuse of migrant workers by establishing stronger employment contracts and giving trade unions more say. Supporters say it will reduce the number of people employed as vulnerable temporary staff but companies argue it will make it too hard to dismiss workers.

When the first draft was released last year it prompted opposition from foreign business groups, who argued it was a return to the communist "iron rice bowl" of guaranteed jobs and benefits and could discourage foreign investment.

Since then western business groups have moderated their public criticism and a second draft released in December watered down some provisions. "Along with lots of other businesses, we put forward our position and the government listened," says the head of a western business group.

But multinational companies operating in China remain worried. A survey of 436 companies conducted this year by law firm Baker & McKenzie and consultants Hewitt Associates found more than half thought the bill would have a negative or very negative impact.

While some of the precise terms of the new law are still fiercely contested, there are two broader areas of debate. Amcham and the European Chamber of Commerce say labour abuse in China is due to poor implementation of existing rules rather than an absence of laws. "The biggest criticism that I have personally is that they are trying to use a law to solve a political issue," says Andreas Lauffs, a partner at Baker & McKenzie.

Supporters accept this is a problem but say an improved law would be easier to implement. "The point of the new law is to increase the cost of violating," says Professor Liu.

The other issue concerns the official Chinese trade union federation, the All-China Federation of Trade Unions. Industry executives say they are reluctant to see it win more power because it is, in effect, an offshoot of the Communist party.

However, with the Chinese economy becoming more important the ACFTU has gained some credibility, especially since its successful campaign to open trade union branches in Wal-Mart stores in China.

(Adapted from *The Financial Times Limited*, May 2, 2007)

Supplementary Reading

Japan's Lost Generation

Ian Rowley and Kenji Hall

Japan Inc. is back, but millions of young workers have been left behind by just about any measure. Japan is back. The economy is growing at 2% a year, company profits are soaring, and land prices are rising. Unemployment, meanwhile, is down to 4% as Japan Inc. has started hiring again, with many college grads receiving multiple job offers. Suddenly, the future looks bright for a new generation of Japanese.

Try telling that to Sadaaki Nehashi. The 31-year-old contract worker at delivery company Yamato Transport makes just $1,100 a month sorting packages — about a third of the average income for full-time employees in Japan. That's a step up from when he landed the job six years ago, though not enough for Nehashi to afford a place of his own, so he lives at his parents' modest home in central Tokyo. "I've had to lower my expectations a bit," says Nehashi, who graduated from university with a degree in marine biology in 2000. "But if I had waited around for a full-time job, I might have been waiting forever."

If a rising tide lifts all boats, then why are millions of Japanese like Nehashi treading water? There's an entire generation of people in their late 20s and early 30s who came of age during Japan's so-called lost decade, a stretch of economic stagnation that started to ease in 2003. Through that period, with Japanese companies in retrenchment mode, young people faced what came to be known as a "hiring ice age." Many settled for odd jobs or part-time work to make ends meet but hoped eventually to find their way into regular employment with the stars of corporate Japan. Instead, they're being passed over in favor of new graduates — a serious problem in a country that still values lifetime employment and frowns on miscarried job-hopping.

This group is called the "lost" or "suffering" generation. Some 3.3 million Japanese aged 25 to 34 work as temps or contract employees — up from 1.5 million 10 years ago, according to the Ministry of Internal Affairs. These young people have earned various less-than-desirable classifications in hierarchy-conscious Japan. They might be *keiyakushain*, or contract workers, typically lower-paid than full-time staff, with fewer benefits and minimal job security. Or they're *hakenshain* (people employed by temp agencies); freeters (those who flit from one menial job to the next); or, at the bottom, NEETS (an acronym coined in Britain that stands for not employed, in education, or in training). The plight of such folks was the subject of a recent TV drama called Haken no Hinkaku, or *Dignity of the Agency Worker*, the saga of a twenty something temp who must put up with the snobbery of full-time colleagues despite her long list of qualifications.

Skills Shortage

With Japan's economy on the mend, you'd expect the ranks of the underemployed to shrink fast. But the number of agency and contract workers continues to swell. To spur employment during the lean years, Tokyo made it easier for companies to add temporary employees. Now, even with fat times back, big employers are reluctant to take those people on permanently.

In their defense, Japanese companies say people from the lost generation aren't equipped to move into the middle rungs of the corporate world. "No matter how much companies want to hire from among this pool, many in their early 30s just don't have the needed skills," says Toshihiro Nagahama, senior economist at Dai-Ichi Life Research Institute. Employers also fear that *freeters* who have drifted from one job to another will be less loyal than ambitious grads hoping to work their way up through the ranks.

These millions of young people face a life that's vastly different from that of their parents. For Japan's postwar baby boomers, jobs provided certainty, spurring them to partner and procreate. Faced with insecurity, many of Japan's twenty-and-thirty somethings are doing neither. The number of marriages fell to 714,000 in 2005 from 1 million-plus in the 1970s. That could exacerbate a drop in Japan's birthrate, already among the lowest in the developed world. "You don't get maternity pay, and you have no job to return to — that makes it hard," says Masako Ikeda, a 30-year-old who works at a video game company in Tokyo but is employed by a job agency.

The suffering generation also suffers from more mental illness. Workers in their 30s accounted for 61% of all cases of depression, stress, and work-related mental disabilities last year, up from 42% in 2002, according to a study by the Japan Productivity Center for Socio-Economic Development. "Because of the anxiety stemming from job insecurity, it is quite natural that these people have problems," says Susumu Oda, the psychiatrist in charge of the survey.

The fate of the likes of Nehashi and Ikeda worries Japan's economists. If members of the lost generation don't land higher-paying, salaried jobs, they won't have much pocket change to spend or funds to sock away for their old age. Credit Suisse Group (CS) estimates these people could saddle Japan's taxpayers with \$67 billion a year in retirement and health-care costs if their number remains at current levels for the next three decades.

Tokyo is waking up to the problem. Last year it set targets for paring the ranks of the underemployed, and it is offering companies \$2,500 for each new hire of a freeter aged 25 to 34. And in September, the Health, Labor & Welfare Ministry unveiled projects to help *NEETS* join the workforce. It plans to double the number of *NEET* outreach centers, staffed by psychologists and job counselors, to 50 this year and to increase training schools to 40 from the current 25. "The government is finally realizing that it has a crisis on its hands," says Yosaku Sato, director of the

Bunka Gakushu Cooperative Network, a nonprofit based on the outskirts of Tokyo that receives $200,000 a year in public funds to run training and placement services targeted at young people.

Some companies are pitching in, too. Toyota Motor Corp. (TM), which has tripled the number of workers it employs on short-term contracts to 10,000 since 2001, put 943 into permanent positions last year and plans to convert 1,200 more by next March. Phone company Nippon Telegraph & Telephone Corp. (NTT) and Fast Retailing Co., owner of the Uniqlo clothing chain, have announced similar plans.

Rankled Ranks

Meanwhile, some disgruntled Japanese contract workers are pressing for changing the old-fashioned way. Electronics giant Canon Inc. (CAJ) is in the spotlight after Hideyuki Ohno, a 32-year-old temporary worker at the company's Utsunomiya factory, near Tokyo, organized 17 other temps into a union. His beef: After seven years on the job, he's still employed by an agency, not Canon. Ohno, who earns $2,200 a month polishing glass lenses for steppers, the complex machines used to make semiconductors, says he hasn't had a raise in five years. "I heard my salary was nearly half of a regular staffer of the same age, but I tried not to care about it too much," says the father of two. Then Ohno read in a newspaper that Canon may have violated employment law for not offering him a permanent position after his many years with the company. That spurred him to file a complaint with the Labor Standards Office.

Despite growing profits, Canon still relies heavily on outside help. In 2006, it increased its ranks of contract employees by 19%, to 37,000; permanent staff rose 4%, to 50,753. Canon declined to comment on Ohno's case but says it treats temporary workers fairly and follows all labor laws.

Ohno says the dispute has opened a rift between temps and full-timers at the plant where he works. After he launched his lawsuit, tape was put on the floor to demarcate the line between permanent employees and temps. "We used to all work together," says Ohno. "But now they don't even say, Good morning."

(*BusinessWeek*, May 28, 2007)

Answer and discuss the following questions:

1. What does the title of this passage imply?
2. Why are companies in Japan reluctant to hire this group of employees, known as "Lost Generation"?
3. What implications will they have for Japan's labor market?
4. How will Japanese government plan to solve this problem?

Unit 7

Corporate Culture
企业文化

A McKinsey[1] of Pop Culture?

Steve Stoute is making hot sellers out of cold brands by turning execs on to "the tanning of America."[2]

Tom Lowry

Several months into his new job as vice-president of US marketing and advertising for General Motors (GM), Mike Jackson came to the conclusion that the automaker was just not cool enough. Young, urban trendsetters on the East and West Coasts were not paying attention to GM's cars. The message being sent to consumers, Jackson says, was all wrong. "We worried far too much about the sheet metal, color, etc.," he explains. "What we really needed to worry about was connecting emotionally with our consumers." So Jackson picked up the phone last spring and called Steve Stoute.

More executives overseeing brands that have gone stale are turning to the 36-year-old consultant and former music executive for help. Stoute's agency, Translation Consultation & Brand Imaging, offers to imbue brands with a combination of hip-hop ethos[3] and practicality to help reposition products, from Chevy Impalas to Crest Whitestrips to Reese's peanut butter cups. The end result is for brands to resonate with a younger, more trendy audience. Other successful entrepreneurs have emerged from the hip-hop scene, such as Russell Simmons and Sean "P. Diddy" Combs, to help put urban fashion and lifestyle into the mainstream. But Stoute is more closely aligned with a new guard of innovation consultants providing strategies that go beyond tricked-out sneakers and jeans. His message: Companies have not embraced the changes in the culture to be able to talk to a new generation of consumers. "So many executives," says Stoute, "are lost in the confines of their own building." Besides GM, Stoute has successfully taken his mantra to clients that include McDonald's (MCD), Procter & Gamble (PG), Hershey[5] (HSY), Microsoft (MSFT), and Estée Lauder[6] (EL).

Now Stoute seems to be gaining respect on Madison Avenue. Interpublic Group of Companies Inc.[7] (IPG), the $6.2 billion-a-year global advertising conglomerate, is in talks with Stoute to buy a majority stake in Translation, say sources close to those talks. If the deal is closed, IPG would get schooled on Stoute's approach to brands and access to celebrities, while Translation would gain entrée to IPG's large client base and deeper pockets.[8]

As an African American with strong relationships to hip-hop artists (music icon Jay-Z is a good friend and business partner), Stoute knows how easy it is to pigeonhole Translation as a black ad agency. He immodestly characterizes his firm as "a McKinsey of pop culture." By that he means that Translation is called upon by companies facing strategic challenges. "These are companies who know they have to take advantage of global trends, but at the same time are afraid of jeopardizing core businesses," says Stoute. "We show them how to walk that thin line. It often comes down to showing them the language and tonality needed to reach consumers."

But Stoute also says he's helping executives understand a phenomenon that he refers to as the "tanning of America." It's a generation of black, Latino, and white consumers who have the same "mental complexion," he says, based on "shared experiences and values." Rap and hip-hop, starting in the late 1980s when white suburban kids began snapping up music by mostly inner-city artists, provided the first glimpse into this shift.[9] "Rap was a litmus test for where the culture was headed," he says.

To connect McDonald's to this world, Stoute helped create its "I'm lovin' it" ad campaign featuring pop star Justin Timberlake[10]. That was relatively easy. To top executives, it was all about coming up with a new ad. Stoute has encouraged them to go much further and told them they could be blowing a big opportunity for reaching young adults. They have a million-plus young people working for them who come to the job every day ashamed of what they were wearing. "The uniforms are ugly," says Stoute. "If the workers were actually proud of what they were wearing, it could be a huge opportunity to promote the brand. Those kids wouldn't want to change after work and stuff it in a knapsack."

Stoute suggested McDonald's hire top designers to redo the uniforms under urban-centric brands such as Sean John, Rocawear, FUBU, American Apparel, and Tommy Hilfiger[11]. The chain is considering the move. "We know the cutting edge comes from the African American and Hispanic communities," says Bill Lamar, McDonald's senior vice-president of marketing, "but then crosses all people."

Stoute knows those communities well. Raised in Queens, NY, he was barely out of his teens when he became a road manager for rap act Kid 'n Play.[12] He would go on to become a manager for rapper Nas and a young female hip-hop soul singer named Mary J. Blige, now one of the music industry's biggest successes, who won three Grammy Awards this year. From there, Stoute was recruited by Sony Music (SNE) and later Interscope Records of the Universal Music Group[13] (V). But he was becoming fascinated with the broader playing field of brands. He left music to join veteran ad man Peter Arnell as a partner in his business, the Arnell Group[14]. At Arnell in 2003, Stoute worked with Reebok[15], at the time a stagnant brand that needed to revamp its image. He brokered Reebok's ad campaign with Jay-Z, whose S. Carter Collection by Rbk (Jay-Z's real name is Shawn Carter) made Reebok a big hit on city streets. "Steve was very good at getting our whole organization to buy in on this new direction," says former Reebok CEO Paul Fireman, who worked closely with Stoute to revive the brand. There was resistance from the organization. "Sometimes the fear factor rose quickly," says Fireman. "But he made a very strong case for why we needed to be more cosmopolitan." The breakthrough for Stoute was convincing Reebok's executives that you couldn't position the sneakers on performance capabilities.[16] "Nike (NKE) had that locked up," says Stoute. "Instead, they needed to align the brand to the sound and rhythm of sports, with fashion."

"RETAIL THEATER"

Following the sale of the Arnell Group to ad giant Omnicom[17] (OMC), Stoute in 2004 launched Translation with a 10% investment from his old employer, Interscope Records. Now housed in the penthouse of a 12-story Midtown Manhattan building, Translation employs nearly 50 people. Stoute has his own method for keeping in touch with contemporary culture. He frequently invites his cohorts to join him for what he calls "Retail Theater." He loves going to department stores and malls to watch people. "I like to see how they touch fabric, or view a display," he says. "Or listen to what they say to their husbands. For me, it is more fun than going to the movies."

Stoute works most closely with two top deputies. Charles Wright, Translation's chief strategy officer, spent seven years in marketing and product management at major record labels including Motown and Virgin[18]. Stoute's other deputy is Vice-President for Strategy John McBride, an industrial designer by training who last worked as a research scientist and project director in Eastman Kodak's[19] (EK) innovation hub.

Once a client hires them, Stoute, Wright, and McBride often brainstorm ideas early on with sketches, music, and video clips. When Hewlett-Packard Co.[20] came calling three years ago, the challenge was to create HP brand awareness in the home entertainment area. Compared with slick products from Apple (AAPL) and Sony, says McBride, HP wasn't regarded as a real player, making it hard for the PC maker to claim "we're cool, too." So Translation started by signing Gwen Stefani to sing her hit *Hollaback Girl*[21] to help promote digital cameras. Most recently, during HP's "The Computer Is Personal Again" campaign, Stoute once again called on Jay-Z, who helped launch ads in which the rapper is heard but his face is never seen. That helped give HP celebrity appeal, says McBride.

Still, not all of Stoute's ideas fly. Some companies view them as just too far out. When he tried to help Coors (TAP) overhaul its brand, he suggested less emphasis on the brand's "rugged" image or its brewing processes and more effort to create a new high-end aura. Says Stoute: "We were attempting to make Coors an arbiter in the renaissance of sophisticated beer drinking." The pitch makes it.

But Stoute's most important test will be changing perceptions about GM. The assignment is to help the carmaker increase awareness for its models among a growing and influential buyer group, 18- to 34-year-olds who live in clustered metro areas on the coasts and along the perimeter of the southern US.[22] The task is to get them to think about GM the way they were already thinking about Toyota (TM) and other Japanese models. The mandate, says Stoute, was "to think of ways to spark contagious consumer behavior."

So far, Translation has helped GM to redeploy Tiger Woods[23] from the Buick brand to what Stoute believes is a more convincing role, as a spokesman for all of GM. "Tiger and GM share similar values of integrity and, most importantly, diversity," he says. Stoute also connected GM with Jay-Z on Jay-Z Blue, a branded, lavender-tinted, electric blue that will be available on the GMC Yukon[24]. Translation is also creating a campaign for the reissue of the Camaro, the iconic 1970s muscle car. Stoute is talking with the advertising agencies responsible for all GM models about marketing alternatives, such as social media, that go beyond traditional TV and print outlets.

It's still too early to tell if GM is reaching new consumers. Unsurprisingly, Stoute believes the results so far are positive. Look no further, he says, than the January debut of Jay-Z Blue. From Detroit to Beijing, the news was featured on the front pages of 26 national and international Sunday papers.

On the night of the premiere of Jay-Z Blue, Stoute was in Detroit backstage in a green room. He had flown in from New York with Jay-Z to introduce the color and help kick off a GM-sponsored fashion show of cars and celebrities, the first of its kind for the automaker. As Stoute sipped a Budweiser (BUD) in a large, heated tent erected for the event not far from GM's headquarters, he mingled with supermodel Petra Nemcova, actor Christian Slater, and Oscar winner Jennifer Hudson. Not far from the spread of catered food were surfing star Laird Hamilton and model and actress Carmen Electra. GM's marketing chief Jackson gushed that the glamorous scene had just the kind of glitzy excitement that he had hoped would envelop GM when he hired Stoute.

FEELING CHEVY

Since that big night, Stoute has focused most intently on the stodgy Chevrolet brand. The challenge was to make Chevys more appealing to those with "a metro mindset, that 34-year-old independent-thinking person," says Ed Peper, general manager of Chevrolet. "One of the first things Steve asked us was: Do you know that there have been 700 songs written about Chevy? Why aren't you leveraging that?'" It became abundantly clear to Peper that Chevy hadn't done enough to marry its brand with music. So Stoute suggested bringing in Grammy-winning hip-hopper TI to help sell the Impala. An ad campaign featuring TI's song *Top Back* first aired on MTV (VIA) and Black Entertainment Television in early February. Chevy, in turn, sponsored TI's latest music video. TI appears in another spot that GM is calling "Ain't We Got Love," which launched during the Super Bowl. The spot also features Mary J. Blige, Dale Earnhardt Jr., and a group of regular folks fawning over their cars. "It's damn near an emotion driving a Chevy," says Stoute. "We want people to feel that."

(*BusinessWeek*, March 26, 2007)

New Words and Expressions

trendsetter	n.	（思想、服装式样等方面的）创新者
stale	a.	不新鲜的，陈旧的
imbue	v.	灌输，注入，浸染
ethos	n.	社会思潮，风气
sneaker	n.	胶底运动鞋
confine	n.	界限，边界
pigeonhole	v.	分类，归档
tonality	n.	音调，色调
Latino	n.	拉丁美洲人
rap	n.	说唱
litmus	n.	石蕊
knapsack	n.	（帆布或皮制）背包
redo	v.	再做，重做
penthouse	n.	（高楼大厦顶部的）阁楼
cohort	n.	支持者，同谋者，同党
slick	a.	光滑的，熟练的，华而不实的
overhaul	v.	彻底检查，大修
rugged	a.	粗糙的，粗犷而朴实的
brewing	n.	酿造
aura	n.	气氛，气味，光环
arbiter	n.	权威人士
renaissance	n.	复兴，复活，新生
perimeter	n.	周长，周界
mandate	n.	命令，训令，要求
spark	v.	发动，鼓舞，使有朝气
contagious	a.	易传染的，有感染力的
lavender-tinted	a.	淡紫色的
reissue	n.	重新发行
iconic	a.	图标的
premiere	n.	初次演出
backstage	ad.	在后台，秘密地
sip	v.	吸吮
supermodel	n.	超级名模

gush	v.	涌出
glamorous	a.	富有魅力的，迷人的
chevy	a.	追逐
stodgy	a.	暗淡的，平凡的，庸俗的
air	v.	宣扬，显示
fawn	v.	奉承，讨好，说好话
sheet metal		金属片，金属薄板
tricked-out		豪华的，有各种各样装置的
get schooled on		接受……训练，教导，学习
cutting edge		最前沿的位置，最先进的
soul singer		美国黑人灵歌歌手
buy in		大批引进，大宗买进
lock up		锁上
muscle car		跑车（美国人的叫法），肌肉车
social media		社会媒体
fawn over		讨好，非理性地喜爱

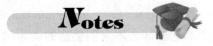

1. McKinsey 麦肯锡
   此处引申为影响、宣传和拿来主义，这里用"A McKinsey of Pop Culture"作题目，是突出流行文化在商业经营中的影响。

2. Steve Stoute is making hot sellers out of cold brands by turning execs on to "the tanning of America." 通过让执政官们接受"美国肤色"的概念，史蒂夫·斯托特正在使许多不为人关注的品牌变得火暴。
   句中的"the tanning of America"指美国各群体所共同拥有的心理肤色，指代各群体共同接受的流行文化。

3. hip-hop ethos 嘻哈主义
   按照字面解释，"hip"意为"臀部"，"hop"是"跳跃"的意思，实际上它是一种生活文化的统称。它起源于20世纪70年代美国纽约一些穷困黑人和南美洲人所住的布鲁克林区，因为物质生活匮乏，他们很穷，每天无所事事，所以大都在街上闲逛，有的人打篮球，有的人就在街上放着音乐随着音乐尽情地表演，有的人则通过喷画、涂鸦、即兴演唱发泄情绪，便出现了"hip-hop"。它融合了黑人的语言、音乐、舞蹈、生活方式等，包括很有押韵节奏表演的饶舌说唱、跳霹雳舞、街头涂鸦及很酷的卷发装扮等。

4. from Chevy Impalas to Crest Whitestrips to Reese's peanut butter cups 从雪佛莱羚羊到佳洁

士深层洁白牙贴，再到好时公司的花生酱口味的雪糕
Chevy 指雪佛莱汽车，Crest Whitestrips 属于宝洁公司推出的产品。

5. Hershey 好时公司（美国第一大糖果生产商）

6. Estée Lauder 雅诗兰黛

雅诗兰黛是化妆品领域的知名公司，该公司宣传的对美丽的信念是"世界上没有丑女人，只有懒女人"。

7. Interpublic Group of Companies Inc. 美国国际公众企业集团公司

该公司是全球商业传播的领导者，与奥尼康姆、WPP、阳狮集团和电通为全球五大广告业巨头，是美国第二大、世界第四大广告与传播集团。其业务范围包括广告、直效行销、市场研究、公关、健康咨询、会议与活动、媒体专业服务等。其旗下拥有三个全球运作的广告公司——麦肯环球广告（McCann-Erikson）、灵狮广告（Lowe&Partners）、博达大桥广告（FCB）和优势麦肯、Initiative 媒介及公关公司万博宣伟（Weber Shandwick）等。

8. If the deal is closed, IPG would get schooled on Stoute's approach to brands and access to celebrities, while Translation would gain entrée to IPG's large client base and deeper pockets.
一旦这桩交易成功，国际公众企业集团公司就可以将斯托特独特的品牌营销方法收入囊中，并且还可以借此接近与其关系密切的一些嘻哈界名人，而斯托特也可以接触到国际公众企业集团公司极为庞大的客户群，同时获得更雄厚的资金支持。
句中的"celebrities"指嘻哈界的名人，"deeper pockets"指雄厚的资金支持。

9. Rap and hip-hop, starting in the late 1980s when white suburban kids began snapping up music by mostly inner-city artists, provided the first glimpse into this shift. 20 世纪 80 年代，当城郊的白人孩子们开始沉迷于那些城区艺术家们创造的音乐时，说唱和嘻哈音乐诞生了，它让人们开始了解到这种心理肤色的变化和趋同。
句中的"shift"指心理肤色的变化和趋同。

10. Justin Timberlake 贾斯汀·廷伯莱克

说唱乐界的天王级人物，他于 1995 年和另外 4 个男孩组成了偶像组合"超级男孩"，他们签约后的首张唱片 *No Strings Attached* 成为美国流行音乐排行榜历史上首张在第一周内销量超过 200 万张的唱片，其中还诞生了单曲排行榜的冠军作品 *It's Gonna Be Me*。后来乐队解散，贾斯汀转型，其著名歌曲有《爱你无罪》和《泪流成河》。

11. Sean John, Rocawear, FUBU, American Apparel, and Tommy Hilfiger

均为著名休闲品牌，其中 Sean John 是肖恩·康姆斯创立的一个做工精良但定位不高的品牌，Rocawear 是美国数一数二的嘻哈品牌，FUBU 是美国最具代表性的年轻都市休闲品牌，American Apparel 是著名时尚 T 恤品牌，Tommy Hilfiger 是著名休闲品牌，中文译名汤美·希菲格。

12. Raised in Queens, NY, he was barely out of his teens when he became a road manager for rap act Kid 'n Play. 在纽约著名的黑人区长大的斯托特刚刚十几岁的时候就已经成为了说唱乐组合 Kid 'n Play 乐队的领队。
句中的"Queens, NY"是美国著名的黑人区。

13. the Universal Music Group 环球唱片公司

20 世纪全球最大的唱片、音像制品制作出版发行集团，其前身是 Polygram（宝丽金）

唱片公司，1972 年由德国 Polydor International 与荷兰 Phonogram 联合组建。1961 年，Polygram 通过 Philips 将美国 Mercury（水星）唱片公司收归旗下。1980 年，又将名扬全球的英国 Decca 唱片公司收归旗下。后来 Polygram 又先后收购了美国 A&M 公司、Motion 公司及英国 Island 公司。1997 年以后，随着一线歌手的逐渐离开与淡出，宝丽金唱片的声势也大为削弱，最终于 1998 年被环球媒体及通讯公司收购并组成环球唱片公司。

14. Arnell Group　阿内尔集团
    美国纽约广告传播集团，隶属世界上最大的广告和市场营销企业宏盟集团（Omnicom Group）。

15. Reebok　锐步（世界著名运动鞋品牌）

16. The breakthrough for Stoute was convincing Reebok's executives that you couldn't position the sneakers on performance capabilities.　斯托特的突破使锐步的高管们相信不能够从表演的角度去定位运动鞋。
    句中的 "performance capabilities" 指表演能力，而不是实际中的运动感觉。

17. Omnicom　宏盟集团
    宏盟集团是世界最大的广告和市场营销企业，是一家战略控股公司。在运营上，宏盟集团包括四大部分：由 3 家全球性广告公司，即 DDB、BBDO 及 TBWA 所组成的网络；由全球 175 家营销服务公司组成的网络；众多美国一流的本土广告公司组成的网络；由两家世界著名的媒体策划和购买服务商，即 OMD 和 PHD 组成的传媒集团。宏盟集团旗下的广告公司长期以来被公认为全球最富创意的公司。

18. Motown and Virgin　摩城和维京（著名唱片品牌）

19. Eastman Kodak　伊斯曼－柯达公司
    世界上最大的摄影器材及相关产品生产公司，总部设在纽约，在美国本土及世界各地设立 50 多个分公司和近 30 个联营公司，主要产品有照相机、电影摄影机、复印机、缩微机、照相胶片、电影胶片、医用 X 光胶片、航空摄影胶片、印相纸、洗印化学品、合成纤维、塑料、染料、食品添加剂、胶粘剂、增塑剂等 30 000 多种。

20. Hewlett-Packard Co.　惠普公司
    世界最大的计算机公司之一，同时是全球领先的计算、成像解决方案与服务的供应商，致力于通过简单的信息终端产品、功能完备的电子化服务和永续运行的互联网基础架构来使科技与其所带来的利益达及个人和企业。

21. *Hollaback Girl*　《哈啦女孩》
    由美国著名的 Ska-Punk 风格的 No Doubt 乐队女主唱格温史蒂芬尼演唱。

22. The assignment is to help the carmaker increase awareness for its models among a growing and influential buyer group, 18- to 34-year-olds who live in clustered metro areas on the coasts and along the perimeter of the southern US.　斯托特必须提高该品牌在影响力巨大且数量仍在不断增长的都市年轻消费群体中的知名度。这一消费群体的年龄介于 18 岁至 34 岁之间，生活在美国东西海岸的大城市及南部滨海各州。
    句中的 "18- to 34-year-olds" 是前面 "buyer group" 的同位语。

23. Tiger Woods　泰格·伍兹（世界高尔夫界传奇人物）

24. GMC Yukon　通用育空河

GMC 是通用集团旗下的商用车部门，有 Envoy（使节）、Canyon（峡谷）、Sierra（西拉）、Yukon（育空河）、Safari（旅行）等一系列车型。

阅读小知识（1）

企业文化

1. 企业文化理论的提出

20 世纪 80 年代初，美国哈佛大学教育研究院的教授泰伦斯·迪尔和麦肯锡咨询公司顾问艾伦·肯尼迪在长期的企业管理研究中积累了丰富的资料。他们在 6 个月的时间里，集中对 80 家企业进行了详尽的调查，写成了《企业文化——企业生存的习俗和礼仪》一书。该书在 1981 年 7 月出版后，就成为最畅销的管理学著作。它用丰富的例证指出：杰出而成功的企业都有强有力的企业文化，即为全体员工共同遵守，但往往是自然约定俗成的而非书面的行为规范，并有各种各样用来宣传、强化这些价值观念的仪式和习俗。正是企业文化——这一非技术、非经济的因素，导致了这些决策的产生、企业中的人事任免，小至员工们的行为举止、衣着爱好、生活习惯。在两个其他条件都相差无几的企业中，由于其文化的强弱，对企业发展所产生的后果就完全不同。

2. 企业文化的要素

迪尔和肯尼迪把企业文化整个理论系统地概述为 5 个要素，即企业环境、价值观、英雄人物、文化仪式和文化网络。企业环境是指企业的性质、企业的经营方向、企业的外部环境、企业的社会形象、企业与外界的联系等方面。它往往决定企业的行为。价值观是指企业内成员对某个事件或某种行为好与坏、善与恶、正确与错误、是否值得仿效的一致认识。价值观是企业文化的核心，统一的价值观使企业内成员在判断自己行为时具有统一的标准，并以此来选择自己的行为。英雄人物是指企业文化的核心人物或企业文化的人格化，其作用在于作为一种活的样板，给企业中其他员工提供可供仿效的榜样，对企业文化的形成和强化起着极为重要的作用。文化仪式是指企业内的各种表彰、奖励活动、聚会及文娱活动等，它可以把企业中发生的某些事情戏剧化和形象化，以生动地宣传和体现本企业的价值观，使人们通过这些生动活泼的活动来领会企业文化的内涵，使企业文化"寓教于乐"。文化网络是指非正式的信息传递渠道，主要是传播文化信息。它是由某种非正式的组织和人群，以及某一特定场合所组成，它所传递出的信息往往能反映出职工的愿望和心态。

3. 企业文化的内容

根据企业文化的定义，其内容是十分广泛的，但其中最主要的应包括以下几点。

1) 经营哲学

经营哲学也称企业哲学,是一个企业特有的从事生产经营和管理活动的方法论原则。它是指导企业行为的基础。一个企业在激烈的市场竞争环境中面临着各种矛盾和多种选择,所以要求企业有一个科学的方法论来指导,有一套逻辑思维的程序来决定自己的行为,这就是经营哲学。

2) 价值观念

所谓价值观念,是人们基于某种功利性或道义性的追求而对人们(个人、组织)本身的存在、行为和行为结果进行评价的基本观点。可以说,人生就是为了价值的追求,价值观念决定着人生追求行为。价值观不是人们在一时一事上的体现,而是在长期实践活动中形成的关于价值的观念体系。企业的价值观是指企业职工对企业存在的意义、经营目的、经营宗旨的价值评价和为之追求的整体化、个异化的群体意识,是企业全体职工共同的价值准则。只有在共同的价值准则基础上才能产生企业正确的价值目标。有了正确的价值目标,才会有奋力追求价值目标的行为,企业才有希望。

3) 企业精神

企业精神是指企业基于自身特定的性质、任务、宗旨、时代要求和发展方向,并经过精心培养而形成的企业成员群体的精神风貌。企业精神要通过企业全体职工有意识的实践活动体现出来。因此,它又是企业职工观念意识和进取心理的外化。

企业精神是企业文化的核心,在整个企业文化中起着支配的地位。企业精神以价值观念为基础,以价值目标为动力,对企业经营哲学、管理制度、道德风尚、团体意识和企业形象起着决定性的作用。可以说,企业精神是企业的灵魂。企业精神通常用一些既富于哲理,又简洁明快的语言予以表达,便于职工铭记在心,时刻用于激励自己;同时也便于对外宣传,容易在人们脑海里形成印象,从而在社会上形成个性鲜明的企业形象。例如王府井百货大楼的"一团火"精神,就是用大楼人的光和热去照亮、温暖每一颗心,其实质就是奉献服务;北京西单商场的"求实、奋进"精神,体现了以求实为核心的价值观念和真诚守信、开拓奋进的经营作风。

4) 企业道德

企业道德是指调整本企业与其他企业之间、企业与顾客之间、企业内部职工之间关系的行为规范的总和。它是从伦理关系的角度,以善与恶、公与私、荣与辱、诚实与虚伪等道德范畴为标准来评价和规范企业。企业道德与法律规范和制度规范不同,不具有强制性和约束力,但具有积极的示范效应和强烈的感染力,当被人们认可和接受后具有自我约束的力量,因此它具有更广泛的适应性,是约束企业和职工行为的重要手段。

5) 团体意识

团体即组织,团体意识是指组织成员的集体观念。团体意识是企业内部凝聚力形成的重要心理因素。企业团体意识的形成使企业的每个职工把自己的工作和行为都看成是实现企业目标的一个组成部分,使他们对自己作为企业的成员而感到自豪,对企业的成就产生荣誉感,从而把企业看成是自己利益的共同体和归属。因此,他们就会为实现企业的目标而努力奋斗,自觉地克服与实现企业目标不一致的行为。

6) 企业形象

企业形象是企业通过外部特征和经营实力表现出来的,被消费者和公众所认同的企业总体印象。由外部特征表现出来的企业的形象称表层形象,如招牌、门面、徽标、广告、商标、服饰、营业环境等,这些都给人以直观的感觉,容易形成印象;通过经营实力表现出来的形象称深层形象,它是企业内部要素的集中体现,如人员素质、生产经营能力、管理水平、资本实力、产品质量等。表层形象是以深层形象为基础,没有深层形象这个基础,表层形象就是虚假的,也不能长久地保持。

7) 企业制度

企业制度是在生产经营实践活动中所形成的,对人的行为带有强制性,并能保障一定权利的各种规定。从企业文化的层次结构看,企业制度属中间层次,它是精神文化的表现形式,是物质文化实现的保证。企业制度作为职工行为规范的模式,使个人的活动得以合理进行,内外人际关系得以协调,员工的共同利益受到保护,从而使企业有序地组织起来为实现企业目标而努力。

4. 企业文化的三个层面

1) 精神文化层

企业精神文化的构成包括:企业核心价值观、企业精神、企业哲学、企业伦理、企业道德等。

2) 制度文化层

制度文化包括企业的各种规章制度及这些规章制度所遵循的理念,包括人力资源理念、营销理念、生产理念等。

3) 物质文化层

企业物质文化的构成包括厂容、企业标识、厂歌、文化传播网络。

企业的精神层为企业的物质层和制度层提供思想基础,是企业文化的核心,而制度层约束和规范精神层和物质层的建设;企业的物质层为制度层和精神层提供物质基础,是企业文化的外在表现和载体。总之,三者互相作用,共同形成企业文化的全部内容。

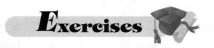

I Decide whether the following statements are true (T) or false (F).

1. According to Jackson, many executives only paid attention to the fashion of autos, but they should really worry about consumers' emotions. (　　)
2. More executives of brands need to follow the trend of young generation. (　　)
3. As Interpublic Group of Companies Inc (IGP) was in talks with Stoute to buy a majority of stakes in Translation, both of them could mutually gain benefits. (　　)
4. Stoute is helping executives understand the rap and hip-hop so that they can have better inspirations for brand designing. (　　)
5. In the US, the uniforms of employees at the chain of McDonald's are not fashionable, which should have been changed to promote the brand. (　　)

6. Stoute first worked as manager for some singers and record companies, where he was fiercely engaged in advertisement to make biggest successes. (   )
7. Stoute came through the resistance of Reebok to convince the organization's executives that they should reposition their brand. (   )
8. Stoute worked with two top deputies and often brainstormed ideas after he discussed with customers at department stores and malls. (   )
9. Translation Consultation & Brand Imaging successfully helped HP Co. to create brand awareness in the home entertainment area by working closely with some rap and hip-hop singers. (   )
10. Stoute adopted two different approaches to the promotion of auto images of GE and Chevy. (   )

II Choose one answer that best suits the following statements.

1. It seems to Stoute that lots of companies _____.
   A. had no idea of good marketing strategies
   B. were not well prepared for the changes in the culture so as to best suit the needs of a younger and more trendy audience
   C. did not think of hip-hop music as a viable means to promote the images of their products
   D. ignored the importance of brand awareness
2. The "tanning of America" which was referred to as by Stoute means _____.
   A. the mainstream of American black minority
   B. rap and hip-hop fans
   C. a litmus test for where the culture was headed
   D. a younger generation sharing the same value and experience
3. Stoute was successful in his business and the reason was that _____.
   A. he was becoming fascinated with the broader playing field of brands
   B. he could invite many singing stars to join his publicity
   C. he could assemble the available resources he had to help companies to position their products to satisfy the needs of trend-conscious customers or other certain group of customers
   D. he was sensitive to rap and hip-hop music and digital products
4. Stoute's agency, Translation Consultation & Brand Image, offers to imbue brands with a combination of hip-hop <u>ethos</u> and practicality to help reposition products from Chevy Impalas to Crest Whitestrips to Reese's peanut butter cups.
   The underlined part in the above sentence means _____.
   A. music beats   B. tone   C. attribute   D. music language
5. The spot also features Mary J. Blige, Dale Earnhardt Jr. , and a group of regular folk, <u>fawning over</u> their cars.
   The underlined part in the above sentence means _____.
   A. frowning upon   B. focusing on
   C. loving   D. paying heed to

Ⅲ **Translate the following passage into Chinese.**

Once a client hires them, Stoute, Wright, and McBride often brainstorm ideas early on with sketches, music, and video clips. When Hewlett-Packard Co. came calling three years ago, the challenge was to create HP brand awareness in the home entertainment area. Compared with slick products from Apple (AAPL) and Sony, says McBride, HP wasn't regarded as a real player, making it hard for the PC maker to claim "we're cool, too." So Translation started by signing Gwen Stefani to sing her hit *Hollaback Girl* to help promote digital cameras. Most recently, during HP's "The Computer Is Personal Again" campaign, Stoute once again called on Jay-Z, who helped launch ads in which the rapper is heard but his face is never seen. That helped give HP celebrity appeal, says McBride.

Ⅳ **Write a summary of this text.**

Managing Diversity in Corporations

Susan Caminit

Among the most challenging — and potentially rewarding — aspects of corporate life is the country's increasingly diverse workforce. Whether defined generationally, radically, or culturally, there's no question that the make-up of the American workforce is a virtual mirror of the global marketplace in which most companies find themselves competing.[1]

Harnessing the power of such diversity is in the best interest of employers, workers, and society at large, research shows. For corporations, the blending of disparate ideas, cultures, and values from a wide range of stakeholders is a key driver of innovation. For the communities in which these companies do business, diversity helps foster a better way of life by offering opportunities for small minority-and women-owned businesses to thrive.

Not to be overlooked, of course, is the tremendous economic clout wielded by a diverse consumer base. For instance, by 2010 the buying power of African-American and Hispanic consumers — just two of many slices of the demographic pie — is likely to exceed the GDP of Canada, the ninth-largest economy in the world, according to the Selig Center for Economic Growth at the University of Georgia. When you add in the buying power of Asians and Native Americans, the total comes to more than $2.7 trillion. Few companies can ignore those numbers.

Yet despite this overwhelming presence in American commerce, African-Americans and other people of color are still under-represented in senior levels of management and on the boards of public companies, research shows. For instance, this year, just seven African-Americans are CEOs of

Fortune 500 companies, up from six last year. African-Americans hold just 8.1% of all board seats at America's top 500 corporations, according to the Executive Leadership Council[2], a networking organization of senior African-American business executives. "Corporations are increasingly embracing the wisdom that diversity in the workplace works," says Dennis Hayes, acting CEO of the NAACP. "Some companies are very aggressive in this area, but many others are moving slower than we would like to see."

Grooming Future Leaders

The ways in which companies choose to address and foster diversity in the workforce are varied. Some have established the position of chief diversity officer. In fact, according to research by Cornell University, which has established a diversity certification program, there are 25 large companies with diversity chiefs who report to the CEO or someone else in the C-suite[3].

Some companies, such as UPS[4], the package delivery and supply chain management firm, take a different approach. At UPS, there is no diversity officer, but rather a diversity council headed by CEO Mike Eskew. "The belief is that the issue of diversity could not be — and is not — below the top person in the company", explains Aileen Hernandez, one of the two outside members of the company's 20-person diversity council. "And when the CEO is sitting in on every morning, listening and asking questions, you know people are taking this seriously," she says. "Mike ends every morning with, 'We're doing good work, but we can do better.'"

Aside from measuring issues such as the number of minorities moving into management positions, or the turnover rate of women and minorities, UPS includes outreach as part of its diversity efforts. Since 1989, the company has participated in the Black Executive Exchange Program[5] (BEEP), a national initiatives that provides African-American students at about 84 historically black colleges and universities with perspectives about the world of business.

Janice Johnson, who manages BEEP for UPS, explains that between 75 and 100 employees — or visiting professors as they are known in the program — spend about two days a year at different schools. They speak to students about their experiences as black executives in a traditionally white business world and provide students with positive role models.[6] "A lot of students don't know what it takes to make it in the business world, or think that we made it just like that," Johnson says. "We're there to tell them not to use race as an excuse. Start preparing early, do the work — and we tell them to be the best persons for the job."

Managing the Melting Pot

Extending diversity initiatives to the company's supplier base is essential for its success, explains Frits Valsaint, manager of supplier diversity at UPS. Indeed, UPS is among a growing universe of corporations that realize that their supplier base needs to be as diverse as their customer base if they are to succeed in the years ahead. The numbers support that belief. According to the National Minority Supplier Development Council[7], some of America's biggest companies purchased more than $100 billion worth of goods and services from minority-owned firms in 2006. Last year UPS spent $700 million with diverse suppliers, $150 million of which was with about 1,200 minority-owned firms.

Doing business in over 200 countries means that UPS needs creative and cost-effective solutions for its customers. "Our diverse supplier base brings innovation and cost savings and helps us compete," says Valsaint. "Because they're often smaller companies, they're used to being creative with solutions."

For its part, UPS works with its diverse supplier base to help position them for changes in the global landscape. For instance, Valsaint explains that UPS encourages its minority suppliers to move away from commodity-type businesses that are often crushed on price by overseas competitors. Case in point: the minority-owned business that makes uniforms for UPS[8]. In order for this company to survive — and thrive — Valsaint says he encouraged it to begin sourcing non-apparel items overseas for UPS. "If we can help these companies see that they need to move towards services, we can help them succeed," he says. "The US is exporting more services than product overseas these days."

Target, the giant retailer with more than 1,500 stores across the US, also believes that diversity has to start at the top. CEO Bob Ulrich says he understands that diversity both within the company and through its supplier base is the only way to meet the needs of its diverse customer base.

"Diversity is something we integrate into all aspects of our business," writes Ulrich on the company's website. "Our ability to offer an exceptional shopping experience depends on team members who understand the diverse communities we serve." Adds Joe Mudd, senior manager for minority and women business development: "Few of us have 'diversity' in our titles. It's just part of the fabric of the corporation." Indeed, 41% of Target's total employee base — and 24% of officials and managers — are classified as diverse.

To fortify the company's belief in a diverse workforce, Target offers all employees a series of training classes on appreciating differences, communication styles, managing inclusion, and the multicultural workplace.[9] The company also supports a variety of Diversity Business Councils within the organization that address and support particular minority groups, including those for African-Americans, Asians, Hispanics, and gay, lesbian, bisexual, and transgender employees.

With new stores seeming to sprout up in communities every week, Target is in a unique position to make an immediate impact on the cities and towns where it does business, Mudd says. For instance, when Target is building a new store, it works with local small and minority-owned contractors and building-supply companies.

"Using local companies helps us in a number of ways, including helping to strengthen the businesses that will be our customers in that location," Mudd says.

What lies ahead for companies grappling with diversity, considering the rapid shift in demographics in the US and around the world[10]? Hopefully, continued effort to better manage the melting pot, mentor a more diverse group of leaders-in-waiting, and offer more opportunity to minority suppliers. None of this is easy. All of these are complex managerial tasks that need to be constantly refined, updated, and expanded. But with global competition becoming an ever-greater challenge for US firms, it is surely the organizations with the most foresight and commitment to this philosophy that will succeed.

(*Fortune*, August 23, 2007)

New Words and Expressions

harness	v.	利用，控制
disparate	a.	异类的，不同的
stakeholder	n.	利益相关人，股东
wield	v.	支配，掌握
under-represented	a.	代表较少的，缺少代表的
groom	v.	培训，培植
outreach	n.	伸出，延展，范围
crush	v.	挤压，镇压
fortify	v.	增强（体力，结构等），使坚强
lesbian	n.	同性恋女子
transgender	n.	跨性别者
grapple	v.	抓紧，抓牢
foresight	n.	远见，深谋远虑
sprout up		出现，往外钻
building-supply companies		建筑公司
grapple with		抓紧，抓牢

Notes

1. Whether defined generationally, radically, or culturally, there's no question that the make-up of the American workforce is a virtual mirror of the global marketplace in which most companies find themselves competing. 不论是从世代、根源、还是从文化角度划分，毫无疑问，美国劳动力的构成就是很多公司相互竞争的全球市场的一面镜子。
句中的"whether"引导让步条件状语从句。

2. Executive Leadership Council 执行官领导委员会
该委员会为美国非营利组织，主要由非裔美国人中的高级企业主管组成。

3. C-suite 高级主管
因为 CEO、CIO、CTO 等每个主管都是以 C 开头，所以称为 C-suite。

4. UPS 联合包裹服务公司
世界上历史最悠久、规模最庞大、实力最雄厚的快递公司。UPS 拥有强大的自主性机群、先进的快件分拣系统和信息软件体系及多种服务品种，可以提供完善的国际到付服务。

5. Black Executive Exchange Program　黑人执行官交换项目

   这是一个自发性的非盈利项目，用于资助非裔美国人中的执行官去大学作客座教授，其目的是交流学习经历、培养新的领导人和激励人们通过出色的表现取得更大的成就。

6. They speak to students about their experiences as black executives in a traditionally white business world and provide students with positive role models.　他们与学生交流在传统上属于白人的商业领域中担任黑人主管的经历，并为学生树立积极的榜样。

   句中的"role model"意为"榜样"。

7. National Minority Supplier Development Council　美国全国少数民族供应商发展理事会

   其宗旨是为美国企业和少数民族公司之间建立联系，以便给少数民族公司更多的商业机会。

8. ... UPS encourages its minority suppliers to move away from commodity-type businesses that are often crushed on price by overseas competitors. Case in point: the minority-owned business that makes uniforms for UPS.　……联邦包裹服务公司鼓励少数民族供应商从商品领域撤出，这些领域由于国外公司的竞争而使价格压得很低。譬如联邦包裹服务公司的制服就是由一家少数民族公司制作的。

   句中的"case in point"意为"一个恰当的例子，有关的案例"。

9. To fortify the company's belief in a diverse workforce, Target offers all employees a series of training classes on appreciating differences, communication styles, managing inclusion, and the multicultural workplace.　为加强公司员工多元化的信念，塔吉特公司给员工提供了一系列培训课程，包括差异分析、沟通风格、包容管理和员工文化多元化，等等。

   句中的Target是美国第二大零售商集团。

10. What lies ahead for companies grappling with diversity, considering the rapid shift in demographics in the US and around the world?　考虑到美国甚至全球的人口变化，对那些信奉多元化的公司来说，等待他们的是什么呢？

    句中的"lie ahead"意为"面临，面对"；"considering"是介词，意为"鉴于，考虑到"。

阅读小知识（2）

绿色营销

英国威尔斯大学肯毕提（Kenpeattie）教授在其所著的《绿色营销——化危机为商机的经营趋势》一书中指出："绿色营销是一种能辨识、预期及符合消费的社会需求，并且可带来利润及永续经营的管理过程。"绿色营销观念认为，企业在营销活动中要顺应时代可持续发展战略的要求，注重地球生态环境保护，促进经济与生态环境协调发展，以实现企业利益、消费者利益、社会利益及生态环境利益的协调统一。所谓绿色营销，是指企业在生产经营过程中，将企业自身利益、消费者利益和环境保护利益三者统一起来，并以此为中心，对产品和服务进行构思、设计、销售和制造。具体来说，绿色营销是指企业以环境保护为经营指导思想，以绿色文化为价值观念，以消费者的绿色消费为中心和出发点的营销观念、营销方式和营销策略。它要求企业在经营中贯彻自身利益、消费者利益和环境利益相结合的原则。

目前，西方发达国家对于绿色产品的需求非常广泛，而发展中国家由于资金、消费导向和消费质量等原因，还无法真正实现对所有消费需求的绿化。以我国为例，目前只能对部分食品、家电产品、通信产品等进行部分绿化；而发达国家已经通过各种途径和手段，包括立法等，来推行和实现全部产品的绿色消费，从而培养了极为广泛的市场需求基础，为绿色营销活动的开展打下了坚实的根基。以绿色食品为例，英国、德国绿色食品的需求完全不能自给，英国每年要进口该食品消费总量的80%，德国则高达98%。这表明，绿色产品的市场潜力非常巨大，市场需求非常广泛。

绿色营销只是适应21世纪的消费需求而产生的一种新型营销理念，也就是说，绿色营销还不可能脱离原有的营销理论基础。因此，绿色营销模式的制定和方案的选择及相关资源的整合还无法也不能脱离原有的营销理论基础，可以说绿色营销是在人们追求健康（health）、安全（safe）、环保（environment）的意识形态下所发展起来的新的营销方式和方法。

经济发达国家的绿色营销发展过程已经基本上形成了以"绿色需求—绿色研发—绿色生产—绿色产品—绿色价格—绿色市场开发—绿色消费"为主线的消费链条。

绿色营销观要求企业家要有全局、长远的发展意识。企业在制定企业发展规划和进行生产、营销的决策和管理时，必须时刻注意绿色意识的渗透，从"末端治理"这种被动的、高代价的对付环境问题的途径转向积极的、主动的、精细的环境治理。在可持续发展目标下，调整自身行为，从单纯追求短期最优化目标转向追求长期持续最优化目标，将可持续性目标作为企业的基本目标。

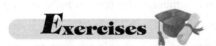

Exercises

I Discuss and answer the following questions.

1. What can employers benefit from harnessing the power of diverse workforce?
2. Do you agree that within corporations, the blending of disparate ideas, cultures, and values from a wide range of stakeholders is a key driver of innovation? If yes, in what way?
3. Why is it important to extend diversity initiatives to the company's supplier base?
4. What are effective approaches for enhancing employees' appreciation of cultural diversity?
5. Why is solution to the diversity issue the one that calls for a continued and long-term endeavor by corporate employees?

II Decide whether the following statements are true (T) or false (F).

1. The increasingly diverse workforce in the US is the showcase of the global marketplace of fierce competition. (   )
2. The purchasing power of diverse consumers in the US cannot afford to be ignored because of its

great economic influence. (   )

3. In many big corporations listed on the stock markets in the US, senior level of management and boards of directors are fully staffed by many African-Americans and other people of color. (   )

4. Business executives are increasingly aware of the importance of diversity in the workplace. (   )

5. The companies in US adopted different approaches to address and foster diversity in the workforce. (   )

6. Extending diversity initiatives to the company's subsidiaries or affiliates can help the company achieve better performance. (   )

7. Some executives held that diversity should be integrated into all aspects of business. (   )

8. To foster diversity within corporation needs time to enhance employees' appreciation of cultural differences and communication styles and etc. (   )

9. The communities where ethnic minorities are concentrated should be the most important areas that corporations need to care for. (   )

10. As the global competition is intensifying, corporations should constantly refine or update their managerial style in dealing with cultural diversity, and also need develop foresight and commitment to this issue. (   )

Ⅲ Group discussion.

1. What is cultural shock? Can you explain the meaning of this term?
2. What should we pay more attention to the diversity in the workplace nowadays against the backdrop of increasing globalization?
3. What can we do to address the issue of cultural diversity and its resulted cultural differences or even cultural clashes in the work environment of multinationals based in China?

Case Study

Is Guanxi a lubricant?

Guanxi. It's the first word any businessperson learns upon arriving in China. Loosely translated, *guanxi* means "connections" and, as any China veteran will tell you, it is the key to everything: securing a business license, landing a distribution deal, even finding that coveted colonial villa in Shanghai. Fortunes have been made and lost based on whether the seeker has good or bad *guanxi*, and in most cases a positive outcome has meant knowing the right government official, a relationship nurtured over epic banquets and gallons of XO brandy.

Now, like so many things in China, the old notion of *guanxi* is starting to make room for the new. Businesspeople — local and foreign — are tapping into emerging networks that revolve around shared work experiences or taking business classes together. Networking that once happened in private rooms at chichi restaurants now goes on in plain view — at wine-tastings for the nouveau riche, say, or at Davos-style confabs such as the annual China Entrepreneurs Forum held annually at China's Yabuli ski resort. By tapping into these informal groups, Western companies can theoretically improve their understanding of the marketplace, hire the best talent, and find potential business partners.

Guanxi goes back thousands of years and is based on traditional values of loyalty, accountability, and obligation — the notion that if somebody does you a favor, you will be expected to repay it one day. One of Asia's most successful businessmen, Hong Kong billionaire Li Ka-shing, has parlayed his *guanxi* particularly astutely over the years, in the process winning valuable licenses and permission to build huge real estate developments. Playing the *guanxi* game is still imperative, and especially for foreign investors. Knowing that Party boss (or his children) remains not just a competitive advantage but an admission ticket.

As China increasingly meshes its economy with the rest of the world, its ascendant professional and entrepreneurial classes are beginning to see the value of networking among themselves. "More and more Chinese who studied or worked overseas understand how to build these networks," says Yang Yuanqing, chairman of Lenovo Group (LNVGY), the big Chinese computer manufacturer.

Many of China's networkers meet through an American or European MBA program. Gary Wang attended Insead, the famous French business school outside Paris. Today he runs a YouTube (GOOG) wanna be called Tudou that was built largely on connections made at B-school. His partner, Dutchman Marc van der Chijs, was married to one of Wang's classmates. A fellow alum who worked at Ogilvy & Mather Worldwide (WPP) helped out with public relations. And another Insead grad, Helen Wong, a partner at Granite Global Ventures, helped Wang raise $8.5 million after a friend heard him speak at the China Europe International Business School (CEIBS) in Shanghai. "Without knowing all these people through Insead," says Wang, "Tudou probably never would have happened."

Executive MBA programs, all the rage now in China, have become *Guanxi* Central. Targeted at senior executives and high-powered entrepreneurs, the programs are attracting some of China's most successful businesspeople. "It's important to have friends in different industries and meet people from different cities," says Zhou Junjun, who runs the Chinese operations of a South Korean systems integrator and did an Executive MBA at the Cheung Kong Graduate School of Business in Beijing.

The school recently began offering an ultra-exclusive CEO program that accepts 40 people. It has attracted a veritable who's who of Chinese business, including Jack Ma, founder of the online exchange Alibaba.com, which raised $1 billion in an IPO earlier this month. Ma and his 39 classmates have created an alumni association.

It's a serious club: Members who miss one of the mandatory annual meetings must pay a $10,000 fine (which is donated to charity). The alums also gather almost weekly for meals or rounds of golf (one member has his own 36-hole course), where they share ideas and business gossip. "*Guanxi* is an evolving thing," says Chang Sun, managing director of private equity firm Warburg Pincus Asia and a charter member. "It used to mean access; once you had it you could open doors. Now it's relationships that can inform and educate you."

Multinational companies, of course, provide rich opportunities for networking, too — and some are trying to goose the *guanxi*. Ogilvy Public Relations Worldwide holds an annual party for former employees, many of whom now work for O&M clients, including Lenovo, Johnson & Johnson, and solar-panel maker Suntek. McKinsey has plenty of alumni who have moved into senior posts at major companies and startups. "Obviously, they became a valuable network for us," says Andrew Grant, who runs the firm's China practice in Shanghai.

Procter & Gamble (PG) China "graduates" have their own Web site, where they post everything from new job prospects to potential tennis partners. Jerry Liu, who joined P&G along with 80 other college recruits in 1997, recalls an intense bonding experience. "When you join the company, it's like entering another college," says Liu, who subsequently did an MBA at the University of Michigan and used his P&G connections to land a job at Coca-Cola (KO) in Shanghai.

If one thing has remained the same for foreigners in China, it is this: Cracking the *guanxi* code still takes hard work and perseverance. Schmoozing at an alumni barbecue or wine tasting goes only so far when trying to build relationships of any lasting value. After the first 30 minutes at these functions, say people who have attended, foreigners and locals almost invariably break off into separate groups. What's more, Chinese businesspeople are more experienced and globally savvy than they were just a few years ago. They're looking for business connections who can help them expand outside China or get their company listed on a foreign exchange. "People want something more professional and strategic from their relationships," says Li Yifei, Viacom's chief representative in China. "They want to know how good your *guanxi* is back home."

(Adapted from *BusinessWeek*, November 19, 2007, by Frederk Balfour)

Supplementary Reading

Beyond the Green Corporation

By Pete Engardio

Under conventional notions of how to run a conglomerate like Unilever, CEO Patrick Cescau should wake up each morning with a laser-like focus: how to sell more soap and shampoo than Procter & Gamble Co. But ask Cescau about the $52 billion Dutch-British giant's biggest strategic challenges for the 21st century, and the conversation roams from water-deprived villages in Africa to the planet's warming climate.

The world is Unilever's laboratory. In Brazil, the company operates a free community laundry in a SóPaulo slum, provides financing to help tomato growers convert to eco-friendly "drip" irrigation, and recycles 17 tons of waste annually at a toothpaste factory. Unilever funds a floating hospital that offers free medical care in Bangladesh, a nation with just 20 doctors for every 10,000 people. In Ghana, it teaches palm oil producers to reuse plant waste while providing potable water to deprived communities. In India, Unilever staff help thousands of women in remote villages start micro-enterprises. And responding to green activists, the company discloses how much carbon dioxide and hazardous waste its factories spew out around the world.

As Cescau sees it, helping such nations wrestle with poverty, water scarcity, and the effects of climate change is vital to staying competitive in coming decades. Some 40 percent of the company's sales and most of its growth now take place in developing nations. Unilever food products account for roughly 10 percent of the world's crops of tea and 30 percent of all spinach. It is also one of the world's biggest buyers of fish. As environmental regulations grow tighter around the world, Unilever must invest in green technologies or its leadership in packaged foods, soaps, and other goods could be imperiled. "You can't ignore the impact your company has on the community and environment," Cescau says. CEOs used to frame thoughts like these in the context of moral responsibility, he adds. But now, "it's also about growth and innovation. In the future, it will be the only way to do business."

A remarkable number of CEOs have begun to commit themselves to the same kind of sustainability goals Cescau has pinpointed, even in profit-obsessed America. For years, the term "sustainability" has carried a lot of baggage. Put simply, it's about meeting humanity's needs without harming future generations. It was a favorite cause among economic development experts, human rights activists, and conservationists. But to many US business leaders, sustainability just meant higher costs and smacked of earnest UN corporate-responsibility conferences and the utopian idealism of Western Europe. Now, sustainability is "right at the top of the agendas" of more US CEOs, especially young ones, says McKinsey Global Institute Chairman Lenny Mendonca.

You can tell something is up just wading through the voluminous sustainability reports most big corporations post on their Web sites. These lay out efforts to cut toxic emissions, create eco-friendly products, help the poor, and cooperate with nonprofit groups. As recently as five years ago, such reports — if they appeared at all — were usually transparent efforts to polish the corporate image. Now there's a more sophisticated understanding that environmental and social practices can yield strategic advantages in an interconnected world of shifting customer loyalties and regulatory regimes.

Embracing sustainability can help avert costly setbacks from environmental disasters, political protests, and human rights or workplace abuses — the kinds of debacles suffered by Royal Dutch Shell PLC in Nigeria and Unocal in Burma. "Nobody has an idea when such events can hit a balance sheet, so companies must stay ahead of the curve," says Matthew J. Kiernan, CEO of Innovest Strategic Value Advisors. Innovest is an international research and advisory firm whose clients include large institutional investors. It supplied the data for this *BusinessWeek* Special Report and prepared a list of the world's 100 most sustainable corporations, to be presented at the Jan. 24–28 World Economic Forum in Davos, Switzerland.

The roster of advocates includes Jeffrey Immelt, CEO of General Electric Co., who is betting billions to position GE as a leading innovator in everything from wind power to hybrid engines. Wal-Mart Stores Inc., long assailed for its labor and global sourcing practices, has made a series of high-profile promises to slash energy use overall, from its stores to its vast trucking fleets, and purchase more electricity derived from renewable sources. GlaxoSmithKline discovered that, by investing to develop drugs for poor nations, it can work more effectively with those governments to make sure its patents are protected. Dow Chemical Co. is increasing R&D in products such as roof tiles that deliver solar power to buildings and water treatment technologies for regions short of clean water. "There is 100 percent overlap between our business drivers and social and environmental interests," says Dow CEO Andrew N. Liveris.

Striking that balance is not easy. Many noble efforts fail because they are poorly executed or never made sense to begin with. "If there's no connection to a company's business, it doesn't have much leverage to make an impact," says Harvard University business guru Michael Porter. Sustainability can be a hard proposition for investors, too. Decades of experience show that it's risky to pick stocks based mainly on a company's long-term environmental or social-responsibility targets.

Nevertheless, new sets of metrics, which Innovest and others designed to measure sustainability efforts, have helped convince CEOs and boards that they pay off. Few Wall Street analysts, for example, have tried to assess how much damage Wal-Mart's reputation for poor labor and environmental practices did to the stock price. But New York's Communications Consulting Worldwide (CCW), which studies issues such as reputation, puts it in stark dollars and cents. CCW calculates that if Wal-Mart had a reputation like that of rival Target Corp., its stock would be worth 8.4 percent more, adding $16 billion in market capitalization.

Serious money is lining up behind the sustainability agenda. Assets of mutual funds that are designed to invest in companies meeting social responsibility criteria have swelled from $12 billion in 1995 to $178 billion in 2005, estimates trade association Social Investment Forum. Boston's State Street Global Advisors alone handles $77 billion in such funds. And institutions with $4 trillion in assets, including charitable trusts and government pension funds in Europe and states such as California, pledge to weigh sustainability factors in investment decisions.

Why the sudden urgency? The growing clout of watchdog groups making savvy use of the Internet is one factor. New environmental regulations also play a powerful role. Electronics manufacturers slow to wean their factories and products off toxic materials, for example, could be at a serious disadvantage as Europe adopts additional, stringent restrictions. American energy and utility companies that don't cut fossil fuel reliance could lose if Washington joins the rest of the industrialized world in ordering curbs on greenhouse gas emissions. Such developments help explain why Exxon Mobil Corp., long opposed to linking government policies with global warming theories, is now taking part in meetings to figure out what the US should do to cut emissions.

Investors who think about these issues obviously have long time horizons. But they encounter knotty problems when trying to peer beyond the next quarter's results to a future years down the road. Corporations disclose the value of physical assets and investments in equipment and property. But US regulators don't require them to quantify environmental, social, or labor practices. Accountants call such squishy factors "intangibles." These items aren't found on a corporate balance sheet, yet can be powerful indicators of future performance.

If a company is at the leading edge of understanding and preparing for megatrends taking shape in key markets, this could constitute a valuable intangible asset. By being the first fast-food chain to stop using unhealthy trans fats, Wendy's International Inc. may have a competitive edge now that New York City has banned the additives in restaurants. McDonald's Corp., which failed to do so, could have a future problem.

Rising investor demand for information on sustainability has spurred a flood of new research. Goldman Sachs, Deutsche Bank Securities, UBS, Citigroup, Morgan Stanley, and other brokerages have formed dedicated teams assessing how companies are affected by everything from climate change and social pressures in emerging markets to governance records. "The difference in interest between three years ago and now is extraordinary," says former Goldman Sachs Asset Management CEO David Blood, who heads the Enhanced Analytics Initiative, a research effort on intangibles by 22 brokerages. He also leads Generation Investment Management, co-founded in 2004 with former Vice-President Al Gore, which uses sustainability as an investment criterion.

Perhaps the most ambitious effort is by Innovest, founded in 1995 by Kiernan, a former KPMG senior partner. Besides conventional financial performance metrics, Innovest studies 120 different factors, such as energy use, health and safety records, litigation, employee practices, regulatory history, and management systems for dealing with supplier problems. It uses these measures to assign grades ranging from AAA to CCC, much like a bond rating, to 2,200 listed companies. Companies on the Global 100 list on *BusinessWeek's* Web site include Nokia Corp. and Ericsson, which excel at tailoring products for developing nations, and banks such as HSBC Holdings and ABN-Amro that study the environmental impact of projects they help finance.

Some of Innovest's conclusions are counterintuitive. Hewlett-Packard and Dell both rate AAA, for example; market darling Apple gets a middling BBB on the grounds of weaker oversight of offshore factories and lack of a "clear environmental business strategy." An Apple spokesman contests that it is a laggard, citing the company's leadership in energy-efficient products and in cutting toxic substances. Then there's Sony Corp. vs. Nintendo. Wall Street loves the latter for a host of reasons, not least that its Wii video game system, the first to let users simulate actions such as swinging a sword or tennis racket, was a Christmas blockbuster. Sony, meanwhile, has a famously dysfunctional home electronics arm, and was embarrassed by exploding laptop batteries and long delays in bringing out its PlayStation 3 game console. Nintendo's stock has more than tripled in three years; Sony's has languished.

Viewed through the lens of sustainability, however, Sony looks like the better bet. It is an industry leader in developing energy-efficient appliances. It also learned from a 2001 fiasco, when illegal cadmium was found in PlayStation cables bought from outside suppliers. That cost Sony $85 million, says Hidemi Tomita, Sony's corporate responsibility general manager. Now, Sony has a whole corporate infrastructure for controlling its vast supplier network, helping it avert or quickly fix problems. Nintendo, a smaller Kyoto-based company focused on games, shows less evidence of the global management systems needed to cope with sudden regulatory shifts or supplier problems, says Innovest. A Nintendo spokesman says it meets all environmental rules and is "always reviewing and considering" the merits of new global sustainability guidelines.

Here's another Rorschach test. Which is the best investment: Exxon Mobil, BP, or PetroChina? Exxon, one of the best-performing energy biggies of the past five years, seems like the obvious stock pick. PetroChina Co. is riskier but also alluring. It's a prime supplier of fuel to booming China, has seen revenues and profits rocket, and has been a hot stock for two years. Analyst Shahreza Yusof of Aberdeen Asset Management PLC rates the company a buy. Because of its access to China's market and new reserves, he writes, one day it will be as big as today's major oil giants — "if not bigger."

By contrast, BP seems to disprove the sustainability thesis altogether. CEO John Browne has preached environmentalism for a decade, and BP consistently ranked atop most sustainability indexes. Yet in the past two years it has been hit with a refinery explosion that killed 15 in Texas, a fine for safety violations at a refinery in Ohio, a major oil pipeline leak in Alaska, and a US Justice Dept. probe into suspected manipulation of oil prices. Browne has recently announced his retirement. BP's shares have slid 10 percent since late April. Exxon's are up around 12 percent.

Innovest still rates BP a solid AA, while labeling Exxon a riskier BB. And PetroChina? Innovest gives it a CCC. Here's why: BP wins points for plowing $8 billion into alternative energies to diversify away from oil and engages community and environmental groups. Exxon has done less to curb greenhouse gas emissions and promote renewables and has big projects in trouble spots like Chad. "I would still say Exxon is a bigger long-term risk," says Innovest's Kiernan. PetroChina is easier to justify. Begin with its safety record: A gas well explosion killed 243 people in 2003; another fatal explosion in 2005 spewed toxic benzene into a river, leaving millions temporarily without water. PetroChina has been slow to invest in alternative energy, Innovest says, and its parent company has big bets in the Sudan.

Do Innovest's metrics make a reliable guide for picking stocks? Dozens of studies have looked for direct relationships between a company's social and environmental practices and its financial performance. So far the results are mixed, and Kiernan admits Innovest can't prove a causal link. That's little help to portfolio managers who must post good numbers by year's end. "The crux of the problem is that we are looking at things from the long term, but we're still under short-term review from our clients," says William H. Page, who oversees socially responsible investing for State Street Global Advisors.

Yet Kiernan and many other experts maintain sustainability factors are good proxies of management quality. "They show that companies tend to be more strategic, nimble, and better equipped to compete in the complex, high-velocity global environment," Kiernan explains. That also is the logic behind Goldman Sachs's intangibles research. In its thick annual assessments of global energy and mining companies, for example, it ranks companies on the basis of sustainability factors, financial returns, and access to new resource reserves. Top-ranking companies, such as British Gas, Shell, and Brazil's Petrobras, are leaders in all three categories. For the past two years, the stocks of elite companies on its list bested their industry peers by more than 5 percent — while laggards underperformed, Goldman says.

Still, BP's woeful performance highlights a serious caveat to the corporate responsibility crusade. Companies that talk the most about sustainability aren't always the best at executing. Ford Motor Co. is another case in point. Former CEO William C. Ford Jr. has championed green causes for years. He famously spent \$2 billion overhauling the sprawling River Rouge (Mich.) complex, putting on a 10-acre grass roof to capture rainwater. Ford also donated \$25 million to Conservation International for an environmental center.

But Ford was flat-footed in the area most important to its business: It kept churning out gas-guzzling SUVs and pickups. "Having a green factory was not Ford's core issue. It was fuel economy," says Andrew S. Winston, director of a Yale University corporate environmental strategy project and co-author of the book *Green to Gold*.

The corporate responsibility field is littered with lofty intentions that don't pay off. As a result, many CEOs are unsure what to do exactly. In a recent McKinsey & Co. study of 1,144 top global executives, 79 percent predicted at least some responsibility for dealing with future social and political issues would fall on corporations. Three of four said such issues should be addressed by the CEO. But only 3 percent said they do a good job dealing with social pressures. "This is uncomfortable territory because most CEOs have not been trained to sense or react to the broader landscape," says McKinsey's Mendonca. "For the first time, they are expected to be statesmen as much as they are functional business leaders." Adding to the complexity, says Harvard's Porter, each company must custom-design initiatives that fit its own objectives.

Dow Chemical is looking at the big picture. It sees a market in the need for low-cost housing and is developing technologies such as eco-friendly Styrofoam used for walls. CEO Liveris also cites global water scarcity as a field in which Dow can "marry planetary issues with market opportunity." The UN figures 1.2 billion people lack access to clean water. Dow says financial solutions could help 300 million of them. That could translate into up to \$3 billion in sales for Dow, which has a portfolio of cutting-edge systems for filtering minute contaminants from water. To reach the poor, Dow is working with foundations and the UN to raise funds for projects.

Philips Electronics also is building strategies around global megatrends. By 2050, the UN predicts, 85 percent of people will live in developing nations. But shortages of health care are acute. Among Philips' many projects are medical vans that reach remote villages, allowing urban doctors to diagnose and treat patients via satellite. Philips has also developed low-cost water-purification technology and a smokeless wood-burning stove that could reduce the 1.6 million deaths annually worldwide from pulmonary diseases linked to cooking smoke. "For us, sustainability is a business imperative," says Philips Chief Procurement Officer Barbara Kux, who chairs a sustainability board that includes managers from all business units.

Such laudable efforts, even if successful, may not help managers make their numbers next quarter. But amid turbulent global challenges, they could help investors sort long-term survivors from the dinosaurs.

(*BusinessWeek*, Jan. 19, 2007)

Answer and discuss the following questions:

1. Why does Unilever pay so much attention to environment and community?
2. Do you think that Green notion is vital to the future growth and innovation of businesses? Why?
3. Even many profit-obsessed American companies also commit themselves to the sustainability goals through eco-friendly and socially responsible practices. Why do they change their business practices?
4. In what way does those eco-friendly and socially responsible practices of corporations add to their assets and reputation? Can you cite an example from the passage to illustrate this point?
5. What proposals can you present to executives of our Chinese companies after you have read this passage?

Unit 8

Entrepreneur

企 业 家

Carlos Slim, the Richest Man in the World

The son of a Mexico City shopkeeper has built a staggering $59 billion fortune. Fortune's Stephanie Mehta tells the inside story of how he made it to the top.

Stephanie N. Mehta

I remember there was a time when the value of his enterprises was very low, recalls Patrick, the youngest son of Carlos Slim Helú. It was the early 1980s, and Mexico was in the depths of a massive financial crisis. Periodically the elder Slim would round up his three teenage sons for an economics lesson. Sitting them down in the living room of the family home, Slim would produce a single handwritten list. One line would show, for instance, how a Mexican insurance company was selling for far less than a similar American insurer. Another would show that compared with European candy or cigarette makers, Mexican manufacturers were drastically undervalued. "It was a very, very long time ago," says Patrick, "but I absolutely remember him teaching us at an early age."

For Slim, a onetime math instructor, this was no mere academic exercise. Yes, he wanted to instill in his sons the same lesson his father — a Lebanese immigrant who started acquiring real estate in Mexico City during the Revolution of 1910 — taught him: Though Mexico will have its ups and downs, don't ever count the country out.¹ But Slim wasn't just teaching, he was buying. He spent $55 million on an insurance company. He took a stake in retailer Sanborns². He invested in a hotel chain.

Now those early investments are paying off big time.³ His three heirs — Carlos Jr., 40; Marco Antonio, 39; and Patrick, 38, run day-to-day operations at various Slim businesses and are increasingly making strategic decisions, while their father, who had heart surgery in 1997, pulls back. And Slim's investments in downtrodden Mexico? They laid the foundations of a sprawling, $150 billion business empire whose growth in recent months has turned Carlos Slim Helú into the world's richest man.

By our calculations, the 67-year-old Slim has amassed a $59 billion fortune, based on the value of his public holdings at the end of July. This number puts him just ahead of perennial No. 1, Microsoft founder Bill Gates, whose net worth is estimated to be at least $58 billion. But Gates is selling off his single greatest source of wealth, Microsoft stock, to fund his foundation, while Slim's fortune is growing at a stunning clip.[4] His net worth jumped $12 billion this year alone. His family's holdings represent more than 5% of Mexico's 2006 gross domestic product, and Slim-controlled companies make up one-third of the $422 billion Mexican Bolsa[5], or stock exchange.

Portly and often puffing a cigar, Slim could pass for a latter-day Latin American J. P. Morgan. But with his dominant stakes in everything from phones to finance, his business profile more closely resembles that of John D. Rockefeller, who likewise thrived in a loosely regulated environment.[6] (For the record, though, even in current dollars Rockefeller's wealth pales in comparison to Slim's: At his death in 1937, Rockefeller was worth $20.3 billion, representing one fifty-second of 1937 US GDP.) The average Mexican encounters a Slim-owned business when she visits an ATM, drives a car, stops for coffee, and especially when she picks up the phone — Slim's Teléphonos de México controls 92% of the country's phone lines, and his América Móvil wireless service has a 70% market share. George W. Grayson, a professor of government at the College of William & Mary[7], coined the term "Slimlandia" to describe how entrenched the Slim family's companies are in the daily life of Mexicans.

It's not a reverential term. Many Mexicans hoped privatization, which began in the early 1990s, would create competition and drive prices down drastically. That hasn't happened. "Slim is one of a dozen fat cats in Mexico who impede that country's growth because they run monopolies or oligopolies," says Grayson. "The Mexican economy is highly inefficient, and it is losing its competitive standing vis-a-vis other countries because of people like Slim."

Fortune Global 500: América Móvil[8]

"The accusations are not well-founded," Carlos Jr. fires back during an interview. He then pulls out an analyst's report showing how the average price of long-distance phone service in Mexico compares with that in other countries. Mexico is third cheapest, according to the report, behind the US and Finland. (A recent study by the World Bank paints a different picture, showing that Mexico's rates for monthly service and residential phone hookups are among the highest in the developing world.)

Wooing the public isn't exactly a favorite activity for the Slims. "I think sometimes when you are successful in business," says Slim in heavily accented English, "you have others trying to turn public opinion against you because they are trying to compete with you." Slim, however, is beginning to court public opinion, pledging earlier this year to increase the size of his charitable foundations. Meanwhile, his sons are doing what the Slims do best: making more money.

Unit 8　Entrepreneur

　　Anyone expecting to find monuments to the Slim financial empire in Mexico City — a gleaming TelMex tower jutting out of the skyline or an América Móvil stadium — would leave disappointed. In fact, América Móvil Latin America's largest provider of wireless services, is housed in a converted tire factory. The juxtaposition of austerity and wealth can be quite odd, as evidenced by a recent visit to the headquarters of Inbursa, Slim's financial business.[9] Just beyond the lobby is a makeshift art gallery that features a rotating selection of paintings on loan from the Museo Soumaya, a Slim-financed fine-arts museum named after his wife, who died in 1999. The room is a bit shabby. It is poorly lit and smells faintly of cigarettes; several large crates are propped against one of the walls. "We had several El Grecos[10] here," Arturo Elias Ayub, Slim's son-in-law and spokesman, says matter-of-factly. There's also a folding table in the center of the room. "Mr. Slim sometimes likes to eat his lunch here," Elias adds.

　　The famous Slim thrift — he used to show up for business meetings wearing a cheap calculator watch — extends across the entire company. Years ago he wrote "official principles" for Grupo Carso, his industrial conglomerate, which is distributed annually to all employees. One tenet translates into English as follows: "Maintain austerity in prosperous times (in times when the cow is fat with milk); it accelerates corporate development and avoids the need for drastic change in times of crisis.[11]" So, for example, TelMex's net debt equals Ebitda[12], or earnings before interest, taxes, depreciation, and amortization, a statistic that's unheard-of in its industry, where debt is typically three times cash flow. América Móvil actually has less debt than Ebitda. "They're rabid about costs," says New York-based Citi investment research analyst Patrick Grenham. "They borrow as little as possible and very carefully."

　　Slim inherited his head for numbers — and his knack for bottom-fishing — from his father, Julian, who fled to Mexico in 1902 to avoid the Ottoman Empire's military draft. Julian Slim started a general store and bought commercial real estate in downtown Mexico City during the 1910 Revolution. He required his young son to record his childhood purchases in notebooks; Slim, a bit of a pack rat, keeps some of the ledgers on a shelf in his office.

　　Though he taught math to make money in college, Slim graduated with a degree in engineering from the National Autonomous University of Mexico in the early 1960s. He then started a stock brokerage in Mexico City and began to acquire industrial companies he deemed bargains. He would reinvest the cash from those businesses or use it to acquire additional properties, and he named his holding company Grupo Carso ("Carso" is an amalgam of his first name and Soumaya's).

　　Then came the crash of the Mexican economy in 1982. The country defaulted on foreign-debt payments, investors fled Mexico, and companies traded for centavos on the peso. Slim was able to scoop up assets on the cheap. All the while, he was schooling his heirs on his investments, occasionally even seeking their counsel to test their business savvy, such as the time he asked 12-year-old Patrick if he should acquire cigarette maker Cigatam[13] (he did). "You make it fun," Slim says. "It is one thing to listen to a father lecture. It is better to learn from experience."

　　The Mexican economy eventually recovered, and by the late 1980s Slim was one of the country's most successful businessmen. When the government put the state-owned telephone

233

company, Teléphonos de México, up for sale, Slim jumped. He partnered with SBC (now AT&T, Fortune 500) and France Télécom[14] to buy 20% of the company in late 1990 for about $2 billion — a fair price, based on other phone companies' market values at the time. What rankled would-be competitors of TelMex (including US long-distance companies such as MCI) were the terms of the privatization: Slim and company got what amounted to a seven-year guarantee of monopoly status at a time when phone companies around the world had the money — and will — to expand into new markets. [15]

Further clouding the deal was the fact that Slim was a huge contributor to Carlos Salinas de Gortari's PRI party[16]. In his book about Mexican politics Bordering on Chaos, author Andrés Oppenheimer describes a 1993 dinner party in which Salinas's people solicited 30 Mexican businessmen for contributions. According to Oppenheimer's account, Slim was willing to give but told the group he "wished the funds had been collected privately, rather than at a dinner, because publicity over the banquet could 'turn into a political scandal.'" Oppenheimer writes that the businessmen present pledged to contribute an average of $25 million apiece. A Slim rep declined to comment.

"He made his billions because of an extremely close and advantageous relationship with the Salinas government," says professor Grayson of William & Mary. More recently Slim has been pragmatically investing in multiple parties, a common practice among Mexico's oligarchs.

Slim's cozy relationships weren't limited to powerful government officials. In the 1990s many of Mexico's trade associations were struggling financially because membership in the groups, once compulsory, had become voluntary, and some businesses stopped paying dues. Slim began supporting many of the associations. A trade group leader confessed to a US researcher that he was glad for the financial help, but it certainly kept him from complaining too loudly about phone rates in Mexico.

Middle- and working-class Mexicans are less reticent, says Marco Múoz, assistant director at the Teresa Lozano Long Institute of Latin American Studies at the University of Texas. They, too, feel Slim hasn't been a good steward of TelMex: Many Mexicans hoped the privatization would produce new operators and lower rates; instead, the company has a virtual monopoly more than 15 years after the government got out of the phone business.

That is due in part to Slim's masterful neutralization of his opponents. AT&T and MCI told local and US regulators that TelMex consistently stymied their efforts to expand in Mexico by setting exorbitant rates to connect calls to TelMex's network. [17] Meanwhile, consolidation in the US — which reduced the landscape to just two big carriers — worked to Slim's advantage. AT&T, of course, is now owned by SBC, Slim's original partner in TelMex. And Verizon[18] (Charts, Fortune 500) just agreed to sell a bunch of wireless and wireline assets in Latin America to Slim. (CEO Ivan Seidenberg got to know the Mexican businessman a few years ago when he was trying to buy MCI and had to cut a deal with Slim, who turned out to be one of the largest owners of the bankrupt company's distressed debt.)

Even as Slim was keeping competitors out of Mexico, he was looking to expand beyond his home country. AT&T CEO Randall Stephenson, who worked in Mexico from 1992 to 1996 overseeing SBC's investments, vividly remembers talking strategy with Slim in 1995. "It's always a late night with Carlos," says Stephenson, who recalls him laying out his plans to go into the rest of Latin America and bet big on wireless. Slim began acquiring wireless assets in the region, and he also took advantage of the dot-com crash in 2000 to scoop up phone assets that had gone belly-up, including AT&T Latin America, which provided him with a backbone for moving traffic throughout the region. [19]

During a recent visit with Slim, Stephenson says he "pulls out this piece of paper, and he keeps on unfolding and unfolding." It was a handwritten table of all the major communications companies in the world. (Slim doesn't use computers.) In one column he had listed all the companies he owns or controls. Elsewhere he listed the other players, along with their revenue and operating and net incomes. "I took the sheet and made a comment about one of the companies, and he starts going through all the financial metrics for the company," Stephenson says, grinning. "He's got all that information in his head."

Another executive at a US Telco remembers being summoned to a pitch meeting in Mexico City a few years back, when Slim was looking to invest in busted phone companies. Slim grilled the group for a couple of hours, asking a seemingly endless number of questions concerning minute details about the business, such as margin information for each of the company's segments. Only after Slim left the room did the stunned executive realize that in addition to doing due diligence, Slim had gleaned valuable information about the competition. (An obsessive baseball buff — especially when it comes to the Yankees — Slim also has a moneyball memory for sports stats. In 1998 he even penned an article in a local magazine extolling the performances of historical baseball figures, both famous and obscure.)

Though Carlos Sr. gets most of the credit for building the Slim empire, the various companies for years have been managed by a network of relatives and confidants. While he was undergoing heart surgery in 1997, all eyes were suddenly on his sons. "When I was sick a few years ago, they were very young," says Slim. Still, "they were in charge, and nobody knew I was gone."

I have been whisked into a sparsely furnished conference room at Inbursa's Mexico City offices, waiting to meet the eldest son of the world's richest man. Security guards pace outside the door. Suddenly Carlos Slim Domit (Domit was his mother's maiden name) walks into the room unannounced, sleeves of his dress shirt rolled up, and apologizes for running late. Though Carlos Sr. has announced no formal succession plans, his eldest son and namesake may end up being the de facto public face of the Slim family (he now runs Grupo Carso, the most complex of Slim's three holding companies). It is a role that suits him: Friends and business associates say all the sons are social, but Carlos Jr. is the most charismatic of the three. A bachelor who enjoys car racing (observing, not driving), he seems to genuinely like interacting with the public. Unlike the children of many international moguls, he and his brothers didn't go to European boarding schools or pursue advanced degrees at B-schools abroad. They studied business as undergraduates in Mexico, and they learned on the job.

For Carlos Jr., that meant working at his father's banking operations in his teens, during breaks from school. He went on to join Sanborns (an old-style emporium known for its lunchtime cafeteria crowd), making frequent early-morning trips to La Merced market in an unsavory part of Mexico City to help purchase produce. Eventually Carlos Jr. took over the chain, and under his watch Sanborns became Mexico's No. 1 bookseller and music retailer. Since 1998 he's been running Grupo Carso.

If Carlos is the customer service guy, Marco Antonio is the moneyman. An intense fellow who has inherited his father's mind for math, the middle son has been in his current job, chairman of Inbursa, since 1992, when he was just 24. The stock has performed respectably but hasn't outpaced the broader market. The laid-back youngest son, Patrick, works with brother-in-law Daniel Hajj at América Móvil (Charts). That stock, traded on the New York Stock Exchange and the Bolsa, has tripled since Patrick became chairman in 2004 and has emerged as the greatest source of the Slim family's wealth.

The Slims have also had their share of clunkers, such as the Carlos Jr.-led 1999 purchase of a 15% stake in CompUSA, which has been a disaster. It was all part of a plan to build an Internet business in both the US and Mexico that included dial-up Internet operator Prodigy and a Spanish-language portal.[20] For once, the Slims' timing was terrible. They unwound their US prodigy investment as consumers flocked to broadband, but held onto CompUSA too long. The company was squeezed by direct sellers like Dell (Charts, Fortune 500) as well as by electronics retailers like Circuit City[21]. Earlier this year CompUSA announced plans to shutter half its 250 stores and the Slims have said they would consider selling the business. "If we have to make mistakes, we make small mistakes," Slim says. "We prefer no mistakes, of course, but small mistakes are the best mistakes."

A few days after my first set of interviews, the entire Slim family, including grandchildren, was set to take a vacation together on the beaches of western Mexico near the Sea of Cortez. I asked how many people were going, and Slim's son-in-law Arturo Elias, who was sitting in on the session with Carlos Jr., started to count the family members in his head. "The only bachelor is Carlos," Elias said, smiling. "And my father," Carlos added. "So we count them as a couple," Elias joked.

By all accounts the family seems to enjoy spending time together. The elder Slim and his sons and sons-in-law meet for dinner every Monday night in la casa familiar, the family house. "My mother and father were very close to us," Carlos Jr. told me. "They taught us to try to be happy with your life and also to be conscious of the responsibility we have as a prosperous clan."

The issue of responsibility is one that is already dominating the thinking of family members and outsiders alike, given Slim's new designation as the richest man in the world. He has a "historical opportunity to become the Rockefeller of Latin America," says Jose Antonio Rios, a former Global Crossing and Teléonica executive who now runs a US real estate holding company. "A wealthy, powerful family like the Slims could be a tremendously positive factor in the next 25 years of development in Latin America."

What form will that take exactly? The Slims' three main foundations have roughly $4 billion today, and they've pledged at least another $6 billion over the next several years. Among the causes: institutes for health and education, each seeded with $500 million to start. Slim has been a big backer of Nicholas Negroponte's One Laptop Per Child initiative[22], and Bill Clinton recently convinced Slim to donate at least $100 million to his foundation's efforts to reduce poverty in Latin America. He also has invested heavily in refurbishing Mexico City's Centro histórico, or downtown. That said, the family tends to embrace economic development rather than donations as a way of eradicating poverty. "I think the best way to help people is not to give them money but to give them a job," says Marco Antonio. "We support education, health, and employment — that's what people need for a better life." Carlos Sr. caught a lot of flak from the Mexican press and US commentators earlier this year when he was quoted as saying that he had no intention of "going around like Santa Claus" distributing his wealth.[23]

Indeed, Slim seems to have a slightly different view of how he might give back. A few years ago he won an award from the World Education and Development Fund for his work on infrastructure in the developing world. His entire family accompanied him to the dinner in New York City. In his acceptance speech, Slim explained his life's work: "Many people want to leave a better world for their children," he told the crowd. "I'm trying to leave better children for my world."

(*Fortune*, August 20, 2007)

New Words and Expressions

staggering	a.	令人惊愕的
undervalue	v.	价值低估
onetime	a.	过去的，从前的
instill	v.	慢慢地灌输
downtrodden	a.	被践踏的，被踩蹋的，被压制的
sprawling	a.	四处蔓生的，四处蔓延的
amass	v.	收集，积聚（尤指财富）
perennial	a.	终年的，长期的
stunning	a.	足以使人晕倒的，极好的
pale	v.	变苍白，失色
entrenched	a.	确立的，不容易改的（风俗习惯）
reverential	a.	可敬的
oligopoly	n.	求过于供的市场情况
well-founded	a.	有根据的，言之有据的
hookup	n.	连接，转播，接线

woo	v.	招致,惹出(祸事等),招惹
court	v.	向……献殷勤,设法获得支持
gleaming	a.	若隐若现
juxtaposition	n.	毗邻,并置,并列
austerity	n.	朴素,节俭,苦行
makeshift	a.	权宜之计的,凑合的
tenet	n.	原则
rabid	a.	疯狂的,狂暴的,激烈的
knack	n.	诀窍
amalgam	n.	混合物
default	v.	疏忽职责,拖欠
centavo	n.	分(菲律宾和拉丁美洲的货币单位)
peso	n.	比索(货币单位)
rankle	v.	(怨恨、失望等)使心痛,激怒
rep	n.	推销员,跑街
pragmatically	ad.	实际地,实用主义地,专断地
oligarch	n.	寡头政治成员
reticent	a.	沉默寡言的,有保留的,含蓄的
steward	n.	管家,管事
stymie	v.	从中作梗,完全妨碍
exorbitant	a.	过度的,过高的,昂贵的
telco	n.	电话中枢办公室
grill	v.	拷问,严厉盘问
glean	v.	搜集(情报或事实),发现,找到
obsessive	a.	强迫性的,分神的,成见(性)的
buff	n.	爱好者,迷
moneyball	n.	为钱打球
extol	v.	赞美,颂扬
confidant	n.	心腹朋友,知己
whisk	v.	飞跑,疾过,飞奔
namesake	n.	同名的人,同名物
de facto	a.	事实上的,实际的
charismatic	a.	神赐能力的,超凡魅力的
mogul	n.	显要人物,有权势的人
B-school	n.	商学院
emporium	n.	商场,商业中心,大百货商店
unsavory	a.	难吃的,令人讨厌的
outpace	v.	发展快过,胜过,超过

clunker	n.	由于太旧而不太好用的东西
prodigy	n.	惊人的事物，神童，奇观
portal	a.	手提的
unwind	v.	展开，放松
shutter	v.	关闭，装以遮门
refurbish	v.	再刷新，整修
eradicate	v.	根除
flak	n.	谴责，反对
round up		围捕，使集拢
count out		点数，拳击中判输
hotel chain		旅馆连锁
big time		第一流，最高级，欢乐时刻
pull back		撤退
matter of factly		实事求是地，事实上
folding table		折叠桌
bottom fishing		抄底
pack rat		什么东西都不肯扔的人
scoop up		铲起
go belly-up		完蛋，垮台
public face		公众形象，公众面孔
laid back		个性随和的，松散的
dial up		通过电话线拨号上网
sit in on		出席
acceptance speech		提名演讲，得奖发言

Notes

1. Yes, he wanted to instill in his sons the same lesson his father — a Lebanese immigrant who started acquiring real estate in Mexico City during the Revolution of 1910 — taught him: Though Mexico will have its ups and downs, don't ever count the country out. 他的确是想把父亲教授给他的东西再传授给儿子们，他的父亲是名黎巴嫩移民，在 1910 年大革命时期开始收购房地产，他父亲告诉他：虽然墨西哥会有起伏变动，但这个国家是有希望的。句中的"ups and downs"指"起伏变动，涨跌"；"don't ever count the country out"是双重否定，"count out"原意是"判定失败"，这里和前面的"not"一起表示墨西哥的前景是有希望的。

2. Sanborns 桑伯恩斯零售公司

墨西哥最大最具规模的连锁餐厅，首家店成立于 1903 年。

3. Now those early investments are paying off big time.　现在那些早期投资获得了巨大的回报。
   句中的"pay off"意为"回报，赢利"；"big time"意为"第一流，最高级"。

4. But Gates is selling off his single greatest source of wealth, Microsoft stock, to fund his foundation, while Slim's fortune is growing at a stunning clip.　为了给基金会融资，盖茨正出售他唯一的财富来源——微软股票，而同时斯利姆的财富却以惊人的速度增长。
   句中的"clip"在此处意为"快速"。

5. Mexican Bolsa　墨西哥证券交易所

6. But with his dominant stakes in everything from phones to finance, his business profile more closely resembles that of John D. Rockefeller, who likewise thrived in a loosely regulated environment.　但他在电话和金融等各个领域的大量投资，使他的商业形象更类似于约翰·洛克菲勒，洛克菲勒同样也是在一个政府管制较为宽松的环境下发家的。
   句中的"who"引导非限制性定语从句。

7. College of William & Mary　威廉玛丽学院
   美国第二所高等学府，在哈佛之后（1636 年）、耶鲁之前（1701 年），为纪念 1688 年英国光荣革命后共同主政的威廉三世与玛丽二世而称威廉玛丽学院。校友中有三位美国总统：杰弗逊（1762 年毕业）、门罗、泰勒和四位联邦高等法院大法官（其中有著名的马歇尔）。《独立宣言》的起草人杰弗逊尤其令威廉玛丽学院引以为豪。威廉玛丽学院一直注重本科教学，被评为公立大学中最注重教学的学校

8. América Móvil　墨西哥美洲电信公司
   该公司 2000 年成立于墨西哥市，是拉美领先的运营商，同时也是全球最大的无线运营商之一。

9. The juxtaposition of austerity and wealth can be quite odd, as evidenced by a recent visit to the headquarters of Inbursa, Slim's financial business.　节俭和财富同时并存非常不可思议，最近去斯利姆的英博沙金融集团总部一行却证明了这一点。
   句中的"as"引导非限制性定语从句，"as"指代前面整个分句。

10. El Greco　埃尔·格雷柯
    意大利矫饰主义画家，是一名狂热的宗教画家。

11. Maintain austerity in prosperous times (in times when the cow is fat with milk); it accelerates corporate development and avoids the need for drastic change in times of crisis.
    在繁荣时期保持节俭可以使公司加速发展，并在危机时期避免产生剧烈的变动。

12. Ebitda　未计利息、税项、折旧和摊销前的利润
    全称为"earnings before interest, tax, depreciation and amortization"，常用来计算公司经营业绩。

13. Cigatam　雪茄堂（墨西哥万宝路香烟的制造商）

14. France Télécom　法国电信
    它是法国主要的电信公司，在全球拥有 22 万多名员工，近 9 000 万位顾客（包含法国的海外省份），拥有许多事业群，例如万那杜（Wanadoo, 法国第一大，亦为全欧洲第二大的网络服务供应商）、Orange SA（法国第一大手机服务公司）及负责数位通信网路商

业服务的易宽特公司（Equant），2006 年停止使用易宽特及万那杜这两个品牌，并将两者整合至 Orange。

15. What rankled would-be competitors of TelMex (including US long-distance companies such as MCI) were the terms of the privatization: Slim and company got what amounted to a seven-year guarantee of monopoly status at a time when phone companies around the world had the money — and will — to expand into new markets.　令墨西哥电信的竞争对手（包括 MCI 在内的美国长途电话公司）恼怒的是私有化的条件：斯利姆和公司获得了长达 7 年的垄断地位，而就在这一时期全球的电信公司手握大量资金急切地开拓新型市场。
句中的"MCI"指美国微波通信公司，2005 年被 Verizon 公司收购。

16. Carlos Salinas de Gortari's PRI party　埃内斯托·塞迪略·庞塞·德莱昂的革命制度党（埃内斯托·塞迪略·庞塞·德莱昂于 1994 年 12 月至 2000 年 11 月担任墨西哥总统）

17. AT&T and MCI told local and US regulators that TelMex consistently stymied their efforts to expand in Mexico by setting exorbitant rates to connect calls to TelMex's network.　美国电话电报公司和微波通信公司告诉当地和美国的管理者：墨西哥电信一直通过收取高额的网络连接费来阻止他们在墨西哥扩展业务。
句中的"stymie one's efforts to"意为"阻止或妨碍某人做某事"。

18. Verizon　美国韦里逊通信公司
该公司是弗莱森电信公司兼并了 MCI 后新成立的公司，弗莱森电信公司成立于 1983 年，主要提供电信服务，拥有 4 个部门分管国内与国外电信服务。弗莱森电信公司是由贝尔大西洋公司（Bell Atlantic）与美国通用电话电气公司（GTE）于 2000 年 5 月合并而成（兼并金额 600 亿美元），是美国第一大地方电话公司和第二大电信服务商，拥有 1.12 亿固定电话接入线和 2 800 万移动用户。该公司也是世界上最大的话簿出版和在线话簿检索公司。

19. Slim began acquiring wireless assets in the region, and he also took advantage of the dot-com crash in 2000 to scoop up phone assets that had gone belly-up, including AT&T Latin America, which provided him with a backbone for moving traffic throughout the region.　斯利姆开始在该地区收购无线资产，同时也抓住了 2000 年网络热潮的机会，低价收购了一些经营不善的电信资产，包括美国电话电报公司拉美部，这笔交易使斯利姆以后在该地区的扩展畅通无阻。
句中的"moving traffic"意为"畅通无阻"。

20. It was all part of a plan to build an Internet business in both the US and Mexico that included dial-up Internet operator Prodigy and a Spanish-language portal.　它是在美国和墨西哥开展因特网业务计划的一部分，包括拨号上网运营商普罗迪奇公司和一家西班牙语的端口。
句中的普罗迪奇公司是 1984 年由 IBM 与 Sears 公司合创的一家网络服务公司，并于 1988 年正式独立经营，2001 年被 SBC 公司收购。

21. Circuit City　电路城（美国专业消费类电子产品零售企业）

22. Nicholas Negroponte's One Laptop Per Child initiative　尼可拉斯·尼葛洛庞帝的"人人电脑"计划
该计划由麻省理工大学教授尼可拉斯·尼葛洛庞帝发起，目的是弥补发达国家和发展中国家之间的数字鸿沟。

23. Carlos Sr. caught a lot of flak from the Mexican press and US commentators earlier this year when he was quoted as saying that he had no intention of "going around like Santa Claus" distributing his wealth. 老卡罗斯说他没有任何打算"像圣诞老人那样四处"散发钱财，今年年初，当这些话被转载引用之后，他遭到了墨西哥媒体和美国评论人士的广泛批评。

阅读小知识（1）

1. 企业家精神

在关于企业的理论探讨中，大家认同企业的经营管理在很大程度上就是对资源进行合理有效的配置。一般情况下，经济学认为资源包括资本、土地、劳动力和企业家，而企业家并非像前三者那样简单，它还包括企业家素质、企业家才能、企业家精神等多种要素。在现代企业的发展中，企业家精神日益受到重视，甚至被称为是一种最稀缺的资源。

企业家精神中最重要的要素是：开创精神、冒险精神、拼搏精神和牺牲精神。因为有开创精神，企业家才会领导大家开拓新的市场、拓展新的业务领域、迈向新的发展层面；因为有冒险精神，企业家才敢在大家犹豫不决的时候拍板决定，挑战新的困难、迎接新的机遇；因为有拼搏精神，企业家才愿和大家一起不屈不挠、废寝忘食地进行调查研究，讨论、分析并寻找企业发展的新机遇；因为有牺牲精神，企业家才能在得当管理、有效领导的基础之上给人才以铺垫，为企业的未来思索良方。

然而，问题似乎也接踵而来。同样是优秀的企业家，包括职业经理人，在自我精神意愿良好的情况下，许多人却无法启动企业良性运转，无法带动员工积极工作。这样的矛盾并不鲜见，其中的原因除了对行业的认同和熟悉程度、企业的机制和产权、市场的变化和扭曲之外，一个更重要的原因是没有发掘和培养"员工精神"。

2. 员工精神

员工精神是企业发展必不可少的条件，员工精神的培养就是要员工明白为什么要孜孜不倦、兢兢业业地去工作。对于员工精神的整合，应该重视的是以下几个方面。

一是勤奋。其实企业本身就是一部勤奋的历史。无论是创业的领导者还是追随者，在创业史中都扮演的是勤奋努力、不屈不挠的角色。在相对稳定的企业发展中，更是要用勤奋的精神激励自己和同仁。因为拥有勤奋精神，在工作中才会时刻努力、任劳任怨、用心思、想办法不断地提高工作水平，从工作中获得享受，并把勤奋视做自己的品质。

二是忠诚。作为企业内的一员，忠诚是一种品质，更是一种精神。这种精神会让企业的员工视企业为自己的企业，视工作为自己的本分，不会因为工作的困难而放弃企业，不会因为暂时的障碍而背离企业。

三是互助。这是一种朴素的精神，也是一个民族的传统美德。但是有些企业的员工由于物质利益的原因而渐渐地放弃互助的精神。企业领导者要有意识地去培养大家的互助精神，让团结的气氛、共进的场面成为企业的平常景象。

四是追求。没有追求就没有思想，没有思想就没有思路，没有思路就没有效率。所以，在实际的工作中要不断地传输不可放弃追求的信念，把追求作为一种精神，一直延续下去。

3. 组织精神

组织精神是企业家精神和员工精神的融合体，是企业的创新精神、学习精神、拼搏精神、勤奋精神、服务精神、追求精神的融合体。对于企业的组织精神，不能简单地理解为"组织文化"，文化是惯常性的东西，主要在于理解和培养做事的风格和方法，而精神却在于做事的原动力和做事时表现出来的始终如一的思想和行为状态。

从整体的角度看来，组织的精神也需要不断地去培养和锻造。在市场经营的过程中，可以着手去做一些惯例性的工作。

第一是关于共同战略目标的树立和强化。企业家、员工、企业都是战略组织中的一员，必须在统一的目标指引之下，才能有共同的认识和向心力。目标的合理性和挑战性有助于这三者的相互配合，战略目标必须依赖于实际的市场状况，又不能拘泥于现存的市场数据分析，而是把一个合理、准确、清晰而又激动人心的目标呈现在众人面前。

第二是所有的成员主动不断地追求先进的科学技术和工作方法。对新技术、新方法的追求和使用代表着未来的工作效率，证明着所有成员的时代性特征，更是体现了组织科学化的理念和工具化的运营模式。

第三主要是鼓励。在现代管理中，人们通常强调的是激励而不是鼓励。事实上鼓励的作用比激励尤甚，原因在于鼓励的自发性而不是被迫性。激励是以目标、期望、满足等因素来刺激人们的工作激情，而鼓励则以温情、人性、关怀等方式来感动人们。同时，精神的塑造离不开外在的形象。外在的形象主要体现在环境、服装、制度等，而内在的形象则体现于人们的言语态度、行为模式、对危机的处理方法等因素上。这些同样需要由外而内的渐次培养和塑造。

I Decide whether the following statements are true (T) or false (F).

1. Carlos Slim Helú, influenced by his father, also tries to teach his sons how to make money. (   )
2. Slim is the richest man just next to Bill Gates, but he will go ahead of Gates in assets, because Slim's fortunes are growing at a stunning clip. (   )
3. Slim family's companies have great influence on the daily life of Mexicans, and are comparable to John D. Rockefeller of American history in their wealth. (   )
4. Slim's financial business makes him a wealthy person who lives a thrifty life, but is generous in donation. (   )

5. The Mexican economy is highly efficient, which is greatly contributed to by Slim' family, and state's poverty is accordingly alleviated, because of Slim's charitable foundations. (   )
6. When Mexican economy encountered a crash in 1982, Slim was losing big fortunes, therefore he instructed his sons how to make investment and learn to be business-savvy. (   )
7. Slim has a virtual monopoly on the phone market, which can be mainly accounted for by his close association with local government. (   )
8. It seems to Slim that business experience is more valuable than book knowledge acquired at MBA schools. (   )
9. Slim was not concerned about charitable work before, therefore Slim family was expected or convinced by foreign leaders to donate more money to the fund. (   )
10. Slim thinks that the best solution to poverty is to create more jobs for society. (   )

II Choose one answer that best suits the following statements.

1. Compared with John D. Rockefeller in the US, Slim family's companies _____.
   A. have made more investment in buying state-owned companies
   B. have more clout over the daily life of the nation
   C. can grow at a staggering rate
   D. have become less diversified in real estate industry

2. Slim's privatization features that _____.
   A. it turns Mexican nation into a highly efficient economy
   B. it amasses huge wealth and delivers the wealth evenly among the people
   C. it strengthens its monopoly over some industries, driving the price up steadily
   D. it has increased the size of the charitable foundation of the family

3. The fact that Slim is successful in business is mainly due to _____.
   A. his business-savvy mind, quickness in catching business opportunities and good relations with government
   B. his thrifty style in running business
   C. his monopoly status and good image of company
   D. his experience inherited from his father

4. AT&T and MCI told local and US regulators that TelMex consistently stymied their efforts to expand in Mexico by setting exorbitant rates to connect calls to TelMex's network.
   The underlined word in the above sentence means _____.
   A. strengthened   B. put an end to   C. thwarted   D. doubled

5. What rankled would-be competitors of TelMex (including US long-distance companies such as MCI) were the terms of the privatization: Slim and company got what amounted to a seven-year guarantee of monopoly states at a time...
   The underlined word in the above sentence means _____.
   A. wrecked   B. raked   C. annoyed   D. quelled

III Translate the following passages into Chinese.

1. Slim inherited his head for numbers — and his knack for bottom-fishing — from his father, Julian, who fled to Mexico in 1902 to avoid the Ottoman Empire's military draft. Julian Slim started a general store and bought commercial real estate in downtown Mexico City during the 1910 Revolution. He required his young son to record his childhood purchases in notebooks; Slim, a bit of a pack rat, keeps some of the ledgers on a shelf in his office.

2. Indeed, Slim seems to have a slightly different view of how he might give back. A few years ago he won an award from the World Education and Development Fund for his work on infrastructure in the developing world. His entire family accompanied him to the dinner in New York City. In his acceptance speech, Slim explained his life's work: "Many people want to leave a better world for their children," he told the crowd. "I'm trying to leave better children for my world."

IV Write a summary of this text.

Shanghai Rising

China struggles to build a livable city inside a world-class business capital.

(Author Unknown)

Benjamin Wood swings his bulky frame over the saddle, straps on his helmet, and settles onto a vintage motorcycle with sidecar. The American architect kicks the engine into life with a single thrust and pulls into the rush-hour traffic coursing through Shanghai's trendy Xintiandi district. He soon steers down a narrow street and enters another world. While Xintiandi is all luxury shops and outdoor cafés, in surrounding neighborhoods the sidewalks are full of people playing mah-jongg in their pajamas, washing dishes at outdoor taps, or popping dumplings into bubbling oil.[1] Life goes on much as it has for the past half-century.

As the bike gathers speed, Wood's white silk jacket flaps in the wind. Passing between some of the fast-disappearing courtyard houses of Shanghai, he waves at locals making dinner. "They know me pretty well in this neighborhood, because I like to ride through here a lot," he says, raising his voice to be heard over the growling motor. "What they don't know," he adds with a hint of regret, "is that I'm also the guy who is going to make this way of life disappear."

Although few might recognize Wood, virtually anyone who has spent more than a day or two in Shanghai will know Xintiandi. The rebuilt neighborhood is Wood's first and best-known work in China, a collage of cobblestone streets, narrow alleyways, and graceful tiled roofs.[2] Xintiandi, which translates as "New Heaven and Earth," has become one of Shanghai's top tourist destinations. Foreigners love it because it evokes the colonial era and is one of the few neighborhoods to escape the wrecker's ball, while locals are drawn to the bistros, bars, and boutiques that lend it a Western cachet.

Wood's work at Xintiandi has become a symbol of the changing aspirations China has for Shanghai. In 1992, Deng Xiaoping declared that Shanghai would be "the head of the dragon" pulling the country into the future, and the Chinese have poured tens of billions of dollars into rebuilding the city after a half-century of neglect. The pace has slackened after a scandal over municipal pension money spent on questionable real estate deals, but the city is still booming.[3]

Problem is, Shanghai has long preferred megaprojects that blindly ape the kind of high-rise developments that scream "modernity" but have little to do with traditional Chinese culture. Until Ben Wood, that is. Xintiandi represents Wood's signature style: Instead of calling in the bulldozers, he imagines a rundown neighborhood as something refreshed. He refurbishes old buildings, saves the facades of others while gutting their interiors, and designs new structures that blend in.

That graceful melding of old and new fits Shanghai's ambitions as it steams toward its third decade of hypergrowth. Like Renaissance Florence, London in the 1800s[4], or New York early in the 20th century, Shanghai aims to muscle its way into a top spot in the global economic order — a role it played back in the 1920s. Today, Shanghai is the mainland's most populous city, with 18 million residents. It's home to the Asia headquarters of more than 150 global corporations, including General Motors (GM), IBM, and Alcatel-Lucent[5] (ALU). And multinationals are boosting their commitment. GM today employs some 1,800 white-collar workers in the city, 60% more than in 2004, while Citibank now has 2,000 employees there, up from 80 in 1999. "Shanghai has very visible ambitions to be a major financial center in the region and perhaps beyond," says Richard Stanley, CEO of Citigroup China.

Expatriates love Shanghai's nightlife, while skilled young Chinese and migrant laborers have rushed to cash in on the city's surging economy. Shanghai is growing at 12% — even faster than the 10.7% expansion that China as a whole saw in 2006 — and the city's gross domestic product was $136 billion last year. That's less than half of London's, but Shanghai's growth is three times as fast the British capital's. And Shanghai has attracted some $120 billion in foreign direct investment since 1992, including commitments of $14.6 billion last year, or 23% of China's total FDI for 2006. "You are witnessing the greatest transformation of a piece of earth in history. It's mind-boggling," says Greg Yager, vice-president of Baltimore design firm RTKL Associates[6], which has done planning work in the city.

The opportunities in Shanghai have attracted scores of foreign architects, who have helped craft one of the world's most extraordinary skylines. In the financial district of Pudong, which until two decades ago was little more than rice paddies and small factories, the 88-story Jin Mao Tower (designed by Chicago's Skidmore, Owings & Merrill[7]) is home to GM, Credit Lyonnais[8], and

IBM. Next door, the 101-story Shanghai World Financial Center (from New York's Kohn Pederson Fox Associates[9]) — originally planned as the world's tallest building, but now eclipsed by Taiwan's Taipei 101 — is about three-quarters completed. Across the Huangpu River, the 66-story Plaza 66 (by Atlanta-based John Portman & Associates[10]) houses General Electric, BP, and KPMG[11]. And the once-dilapidated Bund, the erstwhile Wall Street of Asia on the riverfront, has been re-energized with packed nightclubs, tony boutiques, and trendy restaurants.[12] "Shanghai is a dynamic, exciting, increasingly multicultural city," says Robert Pallash, president for Asia at auto-parts maker Visteon Corp.[13] (VC), which moved its regional headquarters to Shanghai from Japan in 2003. One reason the city won out over Bangkok, Hong Kong, and Singapore: It's an easier sell for expats. "It's very important to attract people from the global organization," Pallash says.

Attracting locals is equally important. The legions of migrants flocking to Shanghai are filling Visteon's factories, as well as those of Intel (INTC), Philips, Honeywell[14], and scores of other multinationals. And the city's universities are churning out thousands of engineering grads every year, which provides a steady supply of researchers for labs run by corporations from around the world. At its facility in Zizhu Science Park[15], 18 miles southwest of the center, Intel Corp. now employs 1,000 people, up from about 40 in 2000. A decade ago, "it was difficult to find a high-quality office building," and qualified workers were scarce, says Wang Wen-hann, general manager of the lab. Today, "all these factors have matured," he says.

Overstretched Infrastructure

In neighborhood after neighborhood, though, eight-lane expressways and steel-and-glass behemoths crowd out gracious townhouses and tenements dating to the early 20th century.[16] The city has doubled its housing stock over the past two decades, but most of those new homes are in soulless skyscrapers. And many of Pudong's towers stand alongside the 100-yard-wide Century Avenue, a thoroughfare that's nearly impossible to cross and lacks so much as a kiosk selling newspapers, let alone a sidewalk café.[17] The district represents "a failure to create a livable urban environment," says Tom Doctoroff, the chief executive for Greater China at ad agency JWT Co.[18]

That's a problem for a place with mega-ambitions. If companies find that Shanghai has become too pricey or too congested for the kinds of employees they want to attract, it may quickly fall from the global hot list. Top-quality office space today costs more than in Midtown Manhattan, and expatriates typically pay $5,000 to $10,000 or even more in monthly rent. The air can be unbreathable, and the highways are clogged much of the day. "You have a city whose infrastructure is totally stretched," says Steve Mullinjer, managing partner at executive search firm Heidrick & Struggles[19] in Shanghai (HSII). "It's like a wild horse ... with no way to rein it in."

Controlling that runaway horse is Job One in Shanghai, and how Shanghai grapples with that issue is important for all of China. Hundreds of millions of migrants are likely to move to the mainland's cities in coming decades, and much of the rest of the country looks to the city for cues. So if Shanghai bulldozes its history to build highways, you can bet that many other cities will follow suit.[20] Since 2000 the number of cars on the mainland has tripled, and Shanghai and Beijing are already ringed with single-family homes and new communities accessible only by car. With 1.3

billion people, the mainland can ill afford the kind of suburban culture that many seem to want. "The government is now more aware of quality-of-life issues," says Daniel Vasella, chairman of pharmaceutical giant Novartis[21] and head of the International Business Leaders Advisory Council for the Mayor of Shanghai[22]. "They realize that if you can't deliver a good standard of living, people won't want to live there."

Perhaps that's why the Chinese have taken so readily to Ben Wood. The 59-year-old architect, whose white beard and ruddy complexion make him seem more like a good old boy from his native Georgia than a hotshot designer, was drawn to Shanghai's street life and the crowded tenements known as shikumen. These two-story buildings, a mélange of Chinese and Western styles with carved stone details, had remained largely untouched since the Communists took over in 1949. But when Wood arrived in Shanghai in 1998 to design Xintiandi, they were rapidly being razed.

At the Xintiandi site, Wood suggested saving the structures and creating a walking district that would preserve the sense of community of old Shanghai. That was a revelation to the city fathers, who until then had struggled to find an alternate way of expressing Shanghai's newfound confidence and affluence. Having proved it can replicate the West in districts such as Pudong, the city was looking for a second wave of development that wouldn't just import styles wholesale, but could give shape to its aspirations as a world-class metropolis.[23] Wood "understands the relationship between new and old buildings," says Wu Jiang, deputy director of the Shanghai Urban Planning Bureau.

If Wood has been good for Shanghai, Shanghai has been equally good to Wood. He kept a relatively low profile in the US, but in China he's a true star. Xintiandi's success has spawned countless imitators on the mainland, and Wood has received more than a dozen major commissions. Today he runs a studio of 30 draftsmen and designers, and inquiries from prospective clients roll in almost daily.[24] He is working on a mountain resort, a development similar to Xintiandi in the western city of Chongqing, and another in Hangzhou, a lakeside city 120 miles southwest of Shanghai. Wood "is totally different from other foreigners practicing in China," says Ma Qingyun, a Shanghai architect and now dean of the School of Architecture at the University of Southern California. "He is quite into the human side."

To keep Shanghai's growth from tearing apart its urban fabric, the city is building nine new communities on the periphery that are expected to house a total of a million or more newcomers by 2020. These projects, called "One City, Nine Towns," were planned as self-sufficient satellite cities where residents can live, work, and shop, without having to travel into central Shanghai. Each was also designed thematically to resemble the cities of other countries or cultures — a notion some dismiss as frivolous. In Fencheng, for instance, a Spanish group is creating streetscapes inspired by Barcelona's Ramblas promenade. Albert Speer, son of Hitler's favorite architect, is the brains behind Anting, a community modeled after small cities in Germany and home to the Shanghai Formula One circuit[25] as well as Volkswagen's[26] (VLKAY) joint-venture auto factory. And Thames Town looks like an English village with cobblestone streets, half-timbered Tudor buildings, red telephone boxes, and a statue of Sir Winston Churchill. "It's farcical," Wood says. "Why pretend you are living in some fantasy land?"

Wood's contribution to the nine town's effort is less garish. In Qingpu, on the southwestern edge of Shanghai, he is working on an 830-unit residential complex that draws its inspiration from the area's ancient canals, bridges, and walkways. His aim, he says, is to create buildings on a human scale that relate to their environs. "The biggest problem in China is that the Forbidden City is burned into every brain," says Wood. "It's symmetrical, monumental, and out of scale."

China's modern-day mandarins can be equally intrusive. In 2004, Rockefeller Group International, the New York-based property development arm of Mitsubishi, hired Wood to plan a 30-acre site the developers call Rock Bund. The project will incorporate a 1928 art deco theater and more than two dozen colonial-era buildings. Rockefeller seemed to have everything going for it, including the support of Shanghai municipality government.

Despite the headaches, Wood isn't one to shrink from a challenge. A latecomer to architecture, he didn't start practicing until he was 36. By that time he had flown fighter jets with the US Air Force and founded a mountaineering school and a French restaurant in Colorado. At 31, he enrolled in a graduate architecture program at the Massachusetts Institute of Technology. He soon started his own firm with Ecuadoran Carlos Zapata and broke into the big leagues in 1998 with a commission to rebuild Soldier Field, the Chicago Bears' stadium[27].

When Wood was in the middle of the Soldier Field project, he got a call from Hong Kong. Would he pick up a business-class ticket waiting for him at the airport and come ASAP? Two days later, Wood was being whisked by limo to the offices of Vincent Lo, chairman of property group Shui-On[28]. The meeting lasted five minutes. "He told me, I want you on the next plane to Shanghai and back here tomorrow morning," Wood recalls.

After a few hours wandering the dilapidated neighborhoods that would become Xintiandi, Wood returned to Hong Kong to make his pitch. He cited Boston's Faneuil Hall Marketplace[29] and mountain villages in Italy as potential models. As luck would have it, Lo was a fan of the Boston development and had spent time in Tuscany[30]. "After half an hour, I said, This is the man I want to work with," says Lo, who gave Wood the job over three competing architects. Within six months, some 1,600 families had been relocated to new developments far from their old homes — not always happily, despite having indoor plumbing and their own kitchens for the first time. "We did things like take off their roofs to speed up the process," Wood says.

The irony of Xintiandi's success is that surrounding blocks have been bulldozed for luxury developments, spelling the end of the local charm that attracted Wood in the first place.[31] Lo now wants to turn adjacent property into a theater district that will rival Broadway[32] or London's West End[33]. Although a few handsome brick buildings will be saved, the expanded site will also include four theaters, a 68-story office tower and high-end apartments. The outdoor dining, meanwhile, won't be at dumpling stands, but at upscale restaurants. "The real tragedy is not the disappearance of the old buildings, but of life on the streets," Wood says.

As Shanghai's transformation continues apace, Wood is likely to be there to watch it unfold and lend a hand where he can. In 2003, he moved full-time to Shanghai, one of the few foreign architects to make such a commitment. On any given evening, you're likely to find him holding court in the DR Bar, a Xintiandi watering hole he designed and owns, or treating guests to grilled salmon and steaks in his two-story penthouse, followed by a soak in the outdoor hot tub with views of the city's ever-changing skyline.[34] Will he ever go back to the US? Don't bet on it. Shanghai's growth still offers plenty of opportunities, especially for an architect who understands that it takes more than tall buildings to make a truly global capital. "If Shanghai is unable to provide the quality of life of a world city like Paris or London, it will never become a major financial center," Wood says. "But the wild west atmosphere is being replaced by more sophisticated development strategies. And this will ultimately be to Shanghai's advantage."

(*BusinessWeek*, February 19, 2007)

New Words and Expressions

strap	v.	用带缚住，用带捆扎
vintage	a.	最佳的，过时的
sidecar	n.	（附于摩托车旁的）边车，跨斗
pop	v.	抛出
dumpling	n.	（有馅的）包子，汤团
bubble	v.	起泡，沸腾
flap	v.	鼓翼而飞，飘动
collage	n.	大杂烩
cobblestone	n.	圆石，鹅卵石
alleyway	n.	小巷，窄街
wrecker	n.	肇事者
bistro	n.	小酒馆，小咖啡店
cachet	n.	公务印章，标记
aspiration	n.	热望，渴望
slacken	v.	松弛，放慢，减弱
megaproject	n.	巨无霸工程
ape	v.	模仿
rundown	n.	裁减，纲要
facade	n.	正面，外观
melding	n.	混合，合并
expatriate	n.	移居国外的人
mind-boggling	a.	令人难以想象的，难以置信的
boggle	v.	畏缩不前，犹豫
skyline	n.	地平线，以天空为背景映出轮廓

paddy	n.	稻，谷
dilapidated	a.	毁坏的，要塌似的，荒废的
erstwhile	a.	以前的，往昔的
riverfront	n.	（城镇的）河边地区，河边陆地
tony	a.	高贵的，时髦的
expat	n.	移居国外的人
grad	n.	毕业生，校友
behemoth	n.	巨兽，庞然大物
tenement	n.	经济公寓住宅，房屋
thoroughfare	n.	通路，大道
kiosk	n.	亭子
congested	a.	拥挤的
ruddy	a.	红的，红润的
hotshot	a.	杰出的，极好的
mélange	n.	混融，混合
raze	v.	夷为平地
spawn	v.	产生，引起
periphery	n.	外围
thematically	ad.	主题上，有主题地
frivolous	a.	轻浮妄动的，无意义的
streetscape	n.	街景画
promenade	n.	散步场所
Tudor	a.	都铎式建筑式样的
farcical	a.	引人发笑的，闹剧的，滑稽的
garish	a.	炫耀的，过分装饰的
intrusive	a.	打扰的，插入的
limo	n.	豪华轿车
plumbing	n.	水管装置，管道工程
upscale	a.	高消费阶层的，质优价高的
apace	ad.	快速地，急速地
blind in		调和，掺入
tony boutique		时尚店
win out		战胜
churn out		艰苦地做出
crowd out		挤出，推开，驱逐
single-family home		普通独立住宅
roll in		蜂拥而来

out of scale	不合规定比例
art deco	艺术装饰
make one's pitch	定居
dumpling stand	卖包子的摊位
hold court	接受大批的崇拜者

Notes

1. While Xintiandi is all luxury shops and outdoor cafés, in surrounding neighborhoods the sidewalks are full of people playing mah-jongg in their pajamas, washing dishes at outdoor taps, or popping dumplings into bubbling oil. 虽然新天地都是豪华商店和室外咖啡馆,但周围街道两旁聚集了很多人,有的穿着睡衣在打麻将,有的在室外的水池里洗餐具,而有的则在做煎包。
   句中的"popping dumplings into bubbling oil"直译是把包子或馅饼扔到滚烫的油里面,这里是指做煎包或油饼。

2. The rebuilt neighborhood is Wood's first and best-known work in China, a collage of cobblestone streets, narrow alleyways, and graceful tiled roofs. 这块重建的区域是伍德在中国的第一件也是最知名的作品。错落有致的鹅卵石街道,窄窄的小巷,还有雅致的瓦制屋顶。

3. The pace has slackened after a scandal over municipal pension money spent on questionable real estate deals, but the city is still booming. 在市社保基金被用于有问题的房地产交易丑闻之后,上海的发展速度减缓了,但仍然很繁荣。

4. Renaissance Florence, London in the 1800s 意大利文艺复兴时期的佛罗伦萨和19世纪的伦敦(它们都是当时世界著名的经济中心)

5. Alcatel-Lucent 阿尔卡特-朗讯
   它是阿尔卡特和朗讯合并后的新公司,总部位于法国巴黎,同时于朗讯总部所在地美国新泽西州设立美国运营总部,以年销售额计算,该公司为全球第一大电信设备巨头。

6. RTKL Associates RTKL联合公司
   它是世界上最大的建筑设计公司之一,1946年创办,提供建筑、都市规划、结构工程、空调水电设备工程、室内设计、园景绿化设计、标志路牌系统设计等各种多元化整体专业服务。2007年被国际咨询与工程公司ARCADIS收购。

7. Skidmore, Owings & Merrill
   它是美国最大的建筑工程师事务所之一,1936年由Louis Skidmore、John O. Merrill和Nathaniel Owings在芝加哥创办,现为世界第三大设计公司。

8. Credit Lyonnais 里昂信贷银行
   它是法国的一家大商业银行,1863年成立,法国政府拥有其66.15%的股份,总行现已迁至巴黎。它的一级资本为106.97亿美元,在法国银行排名中列第2位,在世界大银行排名中列第12位。

9. Kohn Pederson Fox Associates　科恩-佩德森-福克斯建筑事务所

   国际知名的建筑师事务所，在美国纽约和英国伦敦都设有工作室，在中国上海的业务范围也日益拓展，该事务所致力于为公共机构和个人提供设计服务，业务范围涵盖建筑设计、规划设计、城市设计、产品设计和设计制图等领域。

10. John Portman & Associates　约翰波特曼建筑设计事务所

    它成立于1953年，国际上公认的具有建筑设计与工程施工双重资质的企业，办公地点分别位于美国佐治亚州的亚特兰大及中国的上海，针对建筑设计、总体规划、建筑策划、结构工程、项目管理等方面提供全面的专业设计服务。

11. KPMG　毕马威国际

    总部位于荷兰阿姆斯特丹，与普华永道、安达信、安永、德勤等并称为国际五大会计公司。

12. And the once-dilapidated Bund, the erstwhile Wall Street of Asia on the riverfront, has been re-energized with packed nightclubs, tony boutiques, and trendy restaurants.　黄浦江畔，曾经荒废的外滩，当年亚洲的华尔街，也恢复了昔日的活力，到处是灯红酒绿的夜总会、高级时装专卖店和时髦餐厅。

    句中的"riverfront"指黄浦江畔。

13. Visteon Corp.　伟世通公司

    它是全球知名的汽车零部件集成供应商，总部位于美国密歇根州，伟世通公司在汽车电子领域提供的主要产品包括音响、信息娱乐、驾驶信息、动力总成控制和照明。目前，伟世通公司在全球汽车电子供应商中处于领军地位，为配合发展迅速的中国业务，伟世通公司亚太总部迁至上海，并成立了亚太区采购中心及中国研发中心。

14. Honeywell　美国霍尼韦尔国际公司

    该公司成立于1999年，由原世界两大著名公司——美国联信公司及霍尼韦尔公司合并而成。原美国联信公司的核心业务为航空航天、汽车和工程材料。原霍尼韦尔公司的核心业务为住宅及楼宇控制技术和工业控制及自动化产品。在全球，其业务涉及航空产品及服务、住宅及楼宇控制和工业控制技术、自动化产品、特种化学、纤维、塑料、电子、先进材料、交通和动力系统及产品等领域。

15. Zizhu Science Park　上海紫竹科学园区

    高科技产业密集区，是目前中国唯一的"政府搭台，企业唱戏，高校提供资源"并完全以市场化模式运作的园区。在整个开发主体中，政府、高校和民营企业各占一半的股份，既保持了政府在政策运作、项目审批中的权威优势，又融合了民营企业高效、快速、灵活的市场运作优势。

16. In neighborhood after neighborhood, though, eight-lane expressways and steel-and-glass behemoths crowd out gracious townhouses and tenements dating to the early 20th century.　但是，在每个街区里，8车道的快速路和巨大的钢铁玻璃建筑物代替了20世纪初的雅致的连排别墅和公寓楼。

    句中的"crowd out"原意是"驱逐，赶走"，这里意为"代替，取而代之"。

17. And many of Pudong's towers stand alongside the 100-yard-wide Century Avenue, a thoroughfare that's nearly impossible to cross and lacks so much as a kiosk selling newspapers, let alone a sidewalk café.　浦东的许多高楼矗立在宽达100码的世纪大道旁，这是一条几

乎不可穿越的大道，路边甚至没有一个报亭，更不用说咖啡馆了。
句中的"let alone"意为"更不用说，何况"。

18. JWT Co.　智威汤逊公司
该公司始创于1864年，是全球第一家广告公司，现隶属于WPP集团。

19. Heidrick & Struggles　海德思哲国际咨询公司
该公司是全球最大的提供企业领袖搜寻和企业领导咨询服务的专业公司，提供从首席执行官（CEO）、董事会成员到公司高级管理人才的搜索咨询服务。

20. So if Shanghai bulldozes its history to build highways, you can bet that many other cities will follow suit.　所以如果上海强行修建大量高速公路，可以打赌很多中国城市将紧随其后。
句中的"bulldoze"意为"胁迫，强行"，"you can bet"意为"你可以下注，可以打赌"。

21. Novartis　瑞士诺华公司
它是全球制药和消费者保健行业居领先位置的跨国公司，总部设在瑞士巴塞尔。

22. International Business Leaders Advisory Council for the Mayor of Shanghai　上海市市长国际企业家咨询会议
该会议的宗旨是向市长提供有助于提高上海经济发展水平、加速上海经济改革和发展的信息与建议，会议每年的主题与上海不同阶段的发展重心密切相关。

23. Having proved it can replicate the West in districts such as Pudong, the city was looking for a second wave of development that wouldn't just import styles wholesale, but could give shape to its aspirations as a world-class metropolis.　发现可以在浦东这样的区域复制西方风格之后，上海正热切期望着第二波发展浪潮的到来。这一次，上海不只是全面引进西方风格，还要展现其要成为世界大都市的梦想。
句中的"that"引导定语从句，修饰"development"；"give shape to"意为"形成，表达，展现"；"aspiration"意为"对美好事物的渴望或梦想"。

24. Today he runs a studio of 30 draftsmen and designers, and inquiries from prospective clients roll in almost daily.　目前，伍德经营着一个由30名绘图和设计人员组成的工作室，每天都会有很多客户前来咨询。
句中的"inquiries"做第二个分句的主语，谓语是"roll in"；此处"roll in"意为"蜂拥而来"。

25. Shanghai Formula One circuit　上海一级方程式赛车场
它是世界一级方程式赛车锦标赛（F1）上海站举办地。一级方程式大奖赛是目前世界上速度最快的、费用最昂贵、技术最高的比赛，它是赛车运动中等级最高的一种。每年观看F1的观众人数与奥运会和世界杯的观众人数相比毫不逊色。所谓"方程式"赛车，是指按照国际汽车运动联合会（FISA）规定标准制造的赛车。这些标准对"方程式"赛车的车长、车宽、车重、发动机的功率、排量、是否用增压器及轮胎的尺寸等技术参数都做了严格的规定。

26. Volkswagen　大众汽车公司
它是德国汽车制造公司，在中国和一汽与上汽合作，分别被称为一汽大众和上海大众。

27. Soldier Field, the Chicago Bears' stadium　芝加哥熊队战士体育场（橄榄球芝加哥熊队的比赛主场地）

Unit 8 Entrepreneur

28. Shui-On 香港瑞安集团（主营房地产、建筑和建筑材料业务）
29. Faneuil Hall Marketplace 波士顿芬威市场
    该市场均由 19 世纪的建筑改装而成，具有独特的味道，有 100 多家个性商店。
30. Tuscany 托斯卡尼（意大利文艺复兴发祥地）
31. The irony of Xintiandi's success is that surrounding blocks have been bulldozed for luxury developments, spelling the end of the local charm that attracted Wood in the first place. 具有讽刺意味的是，新天地的成功就是推倒周围的建筑，建设豪华社区，而这也意味着上海最初吸引伍德的魅力要消失了。
    句中的第一个"that"引导表语从句，第二个"that"引导定语从句修饰前面的"charm"；"spelling"是现在分词作状语；"spell the end of"意思是"意味着……终结"。
32. Broadway 百老汇
    1900 年前后，许多戏院就在百老汇大道两旁和附近的街上建立。20 世纪 20 年代是百老汇戏剧区域最旺盛时期，剧场林立，达到七八十家。位于百老汇大道与第 42 街交叉口的时代广场成了全市的娱乐中心，也是市民集会欢乐的场所。后来百老汇的戏剧区域渐渐缩小、渐渐北移，到现在还剩下近 40 家戏院。纽约是美国戏剧文化之都，其他城市的戏剧称为地方戏。纽约有着世界级的影响力，任何一出戏只要在百老汇的某一剧场获得了成功，就会名扬全美国和英语世界，甚至整个西方世界，于是该剧就会在各地被邀请演出。因此，百老汇在极大程度上就成了美国戏剧的代名词。
33. London's West End 伦敦西区
    伦敦西区是与纽约百老汇齐名的世界戏剧中心，每天都有几十部最新最流行的音乐剧在这里上演。
34. On any given evening, you're likely to find him holding court in the DR Bar, a Xintiandi watering hole he designed and owns, or treating guests to grilled salmon and steaks in his two-story penthouse, followed by a soak in the outdoor hot tub with views of the city's ever-changing skyline. 每个晚上，你都会发现他在新天地 DR Bar 酒吧里处理事务，这是他自己设计和拥有的一个水池，或者在他的两层阁楼里用烤大马哈鱼或牛排招待客人，然后在户外的浴缸里泡个澡，欣赏大上海玄妙变幻的夜空。
    句中的"hold court"原意是"国王上朝，接受朝拜"，这里指"处理事务"；"holding court"和"treating"是选择性并列平行结构；"ever changing"意为"变幻不定，一直变化"。

阅读小知识（2）

企业创新

熊彼特（J. Schumpeter，1883—1950）的经典著作《经济发展理论》的正式出版，标志着创新理论的正式确立。在熊彼特创新理论中，企业是创新主体，而创新者就是企业家，因此熊彼特的"创新"概念接近于"企业创新"概念。然而，它是一个经济概念，并不是人们在一般定义上理解的"创造新东西"或"守旧"的反义词，并强调其目的是获得潜在利润或经济效益。

创新是一个多元性的概念，具有内在的动态性。到底什么是创新？经济学家认为，创新是企业家首次以商业目的向经济中引入的能给社会或消费者带来价值追加的新事物。这个观点得到广泛认可，具有普遍意义。但是，它过于抽象，不具备可操作性，只能用作衡量"什么是创新"的准则，而企业需要的是从管理的角度分析和说明创新。

为此，我们首先要解决创新的价值衡量问题。不少人只强调创新的技术领先性，而忽视创新的商业性和应用性，因此他们的"创新"注定要失败。创新的价值在于创造价值和独特性。所以，衡量创新价值的尺度应该是看它创造了多少消费者价值和社会价值，创造了多少可以转化为商业优势的独特性，而不是看投入了多少研发费用、技术有多先进、有没有知识产权和专利。这样看待创新，必然有利于企业形成正确的创新机制。

从本质上讲，创新是一个多元性的概念，首先表现为创新来源的多样化。许多人认为，研发是创新的唯一来源。但在现实中，创新绝不仅仅来自研发，而是源自很多方面——意外发现、人类对清洁能源的需要、可持续发展、市场、用户、设计、经济结构、管制变化……甚至某个失败的项目都可能产生创新机遇。例如，青霉素就是弗莱明的意外发现。作为创新之源，这些渠道的重要性不低于研发。

创新多元性的第二个方面是其内涵非常丰富。创新远远不止是技术创新和产品创新，还包括业务流程创新、商业模式创新、管理创新、制度创新、服务创新及创造全新的市场以满足尚未开发的顾客需要，甚至是新的营销和分销方法等。星巴克、eBay、维基百科都是极其出色的商业模式创新。品牌管理、事业部制则是价值卓越的管理创新。这些都表明，创新经济决不仅限于高技术部门。

创新在程度上的巨大差别是创新多元性的第三个重要方面。既有微处理器这种革命性创新，也有外观设计变化这类渐进性创新，还有结构式创新、跳跃式创新及随身听（索尼）这种创造空缺市场的创新等。深受社会关注的行业标准一般都是由结构式创新所形成的主导设计转化而来的，施乐914复印机、IBM-PC及福特早年推出的T型车都是这样。

互联网和全球化大大扩展了创新构思的来源和协作范围，创新的多元性还意味着正确寻找和选择创新构思及有效组织实施创新，并在适当的时间限度内把创新带向市场，也就是企业创新方式的创新。2006年，IBM召集数十万精英在互联网上展开创新风暴，出资10亿美元以求最佳创新理念。宝洁则提出，到2010年必须有一半的创新来自外部。

参与者的多样化也是创新多元性的一种体现。创新不是某个部门或少数几个人的任务，而是遍布整个企业的思维方式。现代的创新甚至不能局限于一个企业的内部，而是呈现出网络化协作的特征，研发和设计部门、合作企业、用户、供应商、大学、政府，甚至竞争对手，都可能参与其中。

现代创新还有一个显著特征：仅靠单纯的技术创新一般说来无法取得商业成功。一方面，创新包含的知识产权和技术越来越多，单个技术创新不能保证整个创新成功；另一方面，企业要想从某个技术创新中取得实际的商业利益，常常需要其他多种创新的配合。苹果电脑推出iPod产品时用了7种创新，其中包括音乐下载平台iTunes这一商业模式创新。

创新的动态性和变化性特点表明，任何关于创新概念的解释都不能算是最终的定义。20世纪90年代，创新的主要议题是技术、质量控制和降低成本。

其实，创新并非什么高深莫测的神话，而是人类最普遍的行为。有句话非常形象地描述了创新的真谛：创新无处不在，无人不能。

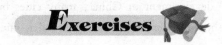

I Discuss and answer the following questions.

1. Why has Benjamin Wood's work at Xintiandi in Shanghai become a symbol of the changing aspirations China has for Shanghai?
2. What does Shanghai, the rapidly changing city, lack in its infrastructure building?
3. What makes the city of Shanghai, a city of dreams for Wood?
4. What are challenges posed to Wood's career in Shanghai?

II Decide whether the following statements are true (T) or false (F).

1. Shanghai is a city which has long preferred the high skyline and modern style of buildings, while ignoring traditional Chinese culture. (   )
2. The melding of old and new in Shanghai has become a must in its endeavor to become a top spot in the global economic order. (   )
3. Shanghai is a dynamic, exciting city where it has greater allure to people from the global organization than locals. (   )
4. It seems to Wood that many newly built architectures fit the mega-ambitions of this city, but they lack souls. (   )
5. According to the author, Shanghai is not only the trend-setter of the style or fashion, but also the model for other cities to follow in the layout of infrastructure. (   )
6. If the city's infrastructure is stretched, it will cause many problems which will impede the growth of the city. (   )
7. In architecture designing, Wood tries to preserve the color of tradition, while looking for new aspirations as a world-class metropolis. (   )
8. Wood's designing efforts in nine towns focus on the self-sufficient, and environement-friendly layout with a mélange of traditional Chinese style and Western culture tinges. (   )
9. Wood comes to Shanghai for his new career, just because he thinks Shanghai can spawn golden opportunities for him. (   )
10. Wood believes that a truly global city should have a high quality of life not only for business people but also for local residents. (   )

III Group discussion.

1. What do you think are the sensible ways to preserve the traditional styles of those cities whose landscapes are being transformed now in mainland China?
2. Now many cities in China are packed and crowded and skylines are already irregular. What can you suggest will be done to underscore their unique styles, both traditional and modern?
3. In the previous decades' development in China, many cities bulldozed their histories to build highways, high-rises or shopping centers, and such trend is intensifying now, what recipes can you present for such a practice?

Case Study

What can you learn from his work?

When Bob Iger became Disney's CEO in 2005, he quickly established himself as the anti-Michael Eisner. He made peace with his feisty predecessor's adversaries. He acted swiftly to make ABC hits like Desperate Housewives available online. And he oversaw the release of Disney's High School Musical movies, which have contributed to operating income growth of 20 percent during Iger's tenure.

Disney's (Fortune 500) stock price, too, is up 36 percent since he took over, but the king of the Magic Kingdom has his challenges. The Hollywood writers' strike threatens to erode ABC's ratings resurgence, and the slowing economy could hurt theme park attendance. How does Iger, 55, hope to tackle those issues — and still get home for dinner with his wife and two sons, as he regularly does when in L.A.? He shared his efficiency tips over a cup of coffee with *Fortune's* Devin Leonard.

1. Get up before dawn. I get up at 4:30 in the morning, seven days a week, no matter where I am in the world. It's a time of day when I can be very productive without too much interruption. I ride a bike and use aerobic equipment twice a week, and work out with a trainer, lifting weights. It's a good time to think. I believe that exercise relieves stress and contributes to an improvement in stamina, which in a job like this you absolutely need.

2. Be punctual. Meetings need to start on time. I'm zealous about that because my day needs to be managed like clockwork. If people are late for meetings, the meetings tend to go late, which throws off my agenda thereafter. I frequently start the meeting even if all the people expected to be in attendance aren't there. I don't need to say to people, "Be on time." They know.

3. Lose your driver. I drive myself to and from work. I love the privacy. It's one less person to talk with. I'm not antisocial. While I'm going home, I talk on the phone. Plus I love listening to music. Classic rock is always at the top of the list, from the Stones to the Beatles and Bob Dylan. I have a fondness for jazz, particularly for jazz singers, Billie Holiday and Ella Fitzgerald all the way through the Sinatra era.

4. Write notes. It's rare that I will spend time with our talent. But I try to let them know if I've appreciated something they've done, like when Katherine Heigl from Grey's Anatomy — whom I've never met — won an Emmy. That's when I'll take my fountain pen and use my trusty Disney stationery, and write a nice, simple note. I think that goes a long way with people.

5. Put history to work. When I was 12, a friend of my dad's carved a beautiful Winston Churchill figurine out of wood for me. It's been with me since. Churchill had a real appreciation for the balance between heritage and innovation. There's something to be said for that at Disney. We had a meeting recently with Disney's animation chief, John Lasseter about Mickey Mouse, and we wanted to do research for it. I downloaded old Walt Disney shorts onto my iPhone, and in the white space of my life I watched the classic Mickey films so we could think about what Mickey's personality and his voice should be like in today's world.

There's huge value to our heritage. But it needs to be carefully balanced with innovation — and not just what is new today, but what will be new in the future.

(Adapted from *Fortune*, December 10, 2007, by Devin Leonard)

Supplementary Reading

Confessions of a CEO

Being "ruthlessly aggressive" took Dominic Orr to the top of the corporate world. And it nearly ruined his life, reports Fortune's Stephanie Mehta.

Stephanie N. Mehta

On a spring morning in 1998, Dominic Orr woke up as he did every day, in the dark. While his children slept, he showered, checked his phone and e-mail messages, and drove from his Saratoga, Calif., home to a breakfast meeting nearby. When he emerged an hour or so later, he stopped cold.

In the early-morning light, he saw his dark-green Infiniti J30 covered with deep dents. The taillights were smashed, and the body was riddled with chips and scratches. Orr could hardly believe his eyes. When had this happened? Who could possibly have done it? His stress level was already higher than it had ever been. As the CEO of Alteon WebSystems, a Silicon Valley data-networking company that was poised to go public, he spent months on the road meeting with business partners and wooing clients. The few hours he had at home were spent answering e-mails, phoning potential hires, or reviewing marketing plans. Eighteen- and 20-hour days had often been the norm when he worked at Hewlett-Packard (Fortune 500), but now his responsibilities were far greater. He couldn't afford to screw anything up.

His home life had become equally stressful; lately the only thing his family did together was argue. The night before, Orr had made a rare appearance for family dinner but was irritated to find his 15-year-old son, Alvin, chatting on the phone, no doubt racking up another $200 long-distance bill. Orr shouted at his son for keeping him, his wife, Teresa, and their 11-year-old daughter, Adria, waiting to eat, and threatened to take away Alvin's computer.

Now, standing in front of his wrecked car, on the phone with Teresa, it dawned on him that the damage hadn't occurred while he was at breakfast, it had happened the night before, and he had been so wrapped up in work that he simply hadn't noticed till the sun came out. Later that day Alvin confessed to having attacked the car in a fit of rage. "I tried to destroy something that mattered to him," Alvin recalled recently.

For two decades talk in the American workplace has centered on "balance." Institutes and think tanks study it. Forward-thinking bosses are supposed to encourage it. Policies like telecommuting and flextime and sabbaticals are designed to foster it.

Even so, "the fact of the matter is that in today's job market there are only two tracks — the fast track and the slow track," says Robert Reich, former Labor Secretary and the author of a new book called *Supercapitalism*. "The only track that leads to better jobs is the fast track. That means working all hours, it means giving up time with family, and it means very large sacrifices."

Orr made those sacrifices willingly. But climbing the corporate ladder hadn't just stretched his time, it had changed his temperament. He prided himself on being "ruthlessly aggressive" at work. How could he come home and just turn that off? Now, he realized, the grotesque result of those choices was parked in front of him.

Several months after his son's outburst, Orr found himself in a therapist's office in Menlo Park, Calif. There was no doubt in Orr's mind that his obsession with his job had alienated him from his family. "I was astounded to find out how he felt," Orr would later say, describing his relationship with Alvin. "I discovered I had no relationship with my son."

And he was starting to realize that his lack of a personal life made him an unappealing boss — and, to his dismay, perhaps a poor leader. Then the therapist, John Cayton, asked him a simple question: "What is your goal?" There were a million possible answers: Get his son back. Cope with the stress of working constantly. Feel less regret. Be a better executive. In an unexpected moment of clarity, Orr blurted out, "I want to die a complete man."

He didn't exactly know what that meant at the time. But in that moment Orr opened the door to a nine-year struggle during which his marriage would end, he would take a company public and then sell it, plunge into depression, drop out of the workforce, and take another company public, all while searching for a way to be a good boss and a good person.

Nine years after that counseling session Orr, 56, arranged to meet me, saying he wanted to talk about his "journey." I had heard of him — I knew he was the CEO of a publicly held wireless-equipment company called Aruba Networks — but we had never spoken. "I've repeated patterns in my life," he said cryptically as we settled into a small conference room for the first in a series of long conversations. He stopped, and then looked up. "Let me tell you my story."

If there was one quality Dominic Orr always possessed in abundance, it was endurance. Selina Lo, who worked with Orr at HP and Alteon, says she used to marvel at his ability to work straight through international flights; he would turn to his expense reports if he ran out of other projects in midair. (A fellow passenger who was trying to sleep once scolded Orr for his intensity in shuffling receipts.) While running Alteon, he regularly would get off planes on a Saturday or Sunday and drive straight to the office for meetings.

Some executives might have considered the birth of a child a reason to slow down, but not Orr: The day after second child Adria was born in Hong Kong, Orr, then an executive at HP, was on a plane back to California to meet with the CEO. ["Adria's mom still talk(s) bitterly about it," he recalls in an e-mail.] The following year, Orr traveled to a sales conference the day after his mother's death, holding up her funeral for three days.

It sounds extreme, but in many ways Orr was repeating the patterns of his own father. Raised on the island of Macau, Orr, who has four older sisters and one younger brother, rarely saw his father. His family was prominent and wealthy: Orr's great-grandfather owned gambling houses, the relatively modest precursors to the mega-casinos that now blanket Macau. Orr's father had a number of business interests, including an antique shop, an import-export business, and a film-financing operation. He spent most of his time in Hong Kong, where the film and import-export businesses were based. When he would return to Macau — roughly once a month, for a weekend — the household would buzz as maids cleaned and cooks prepared extra food. Orr thought it all perfectly normal. "I didn't see anything wrong with getting married, having kids, and focusing on my career," he says. "That's the value system I grew up with."

Years later Orr's father was diagnosed with cancer. The family's income stream dried up as the businesses were downsized, and Orr's parents and younger brother decamped to an apartment in Hong Kong, where the older man could get medical treatment. The family's change of fortune stuck with Orr. "I guess I always, subconsciously and consciously, wanted to recreate the environment I grew up in," he says.

In 1969, at age 18, Orr left for the US to pursue a degree in physics from the City College of New York. He soon started corresponding with Teresa Wong, the 18-year-old sister of an acquaintance. "When he started writing me, I thought, 'What is this boy trying to do?' remembers Teresa. "My sister told me to write back, as a chance to practice my English. The missives evolved into a long-distance courtship, and the two married ten years after Orr wrote his first letter. He completed a Ph. D. in neurobiology at Caltech, and Alvin was born three years later in Pasadena.

Teresa, now a full-time philanthropist, says she only fully realized the extent of Orr's obsessive tendencies once they were married. "I was puzzled by Dom's behavior," she says during a telephone call from Beijing. "He could be so charming and affectionate, but he also had an explosive temper."

Orr took a job in marketing at HP and soon became a rising star in the organization, winning promotions that required the family to move first to Hong Kong, then 2.5 years later to Singapore. Even while based abroad, Orr traveled for work constantly. Lo, then working at HP, says that after he transferred to Asia, she would see him in the halls of the California offices every three weeks or so. "It was like he never left."

The long absences, however, were taking a toll on the Orr family. When Adria was 2 years old, Teresa says, she forgot what her father looked like. And the emotional separation between Orr and his family soon turned into a physical one. In 1991, Orr got a promotion to work with HP in Japan, and rather than move to yet another foreign city, Teresa decided to take the children back to California the following year.

The Tokyo assignment was a tough one. Orr had to downsize HP's Asian workforce through retirements and reassignments. Employees lost face with their families, and Orr says the wife of one displaced worker called him, begging him to rehire her spouse. For the first time in his skyrocketing career, Orr, who always thought of himself as a compassionate manager, began to wonder whether being a business success was compatible with being a good human being.

"What right do I have" to mess with people's lives? he asked his boss and mentor, Wim Roelandts, now CEO of chipmaker Xilinx. Roelandts lectured him about the greater good. "Look at the jobs you're saving," Roelandts, told him.

Orr hated the experience and longed to work for a company that was growing, not shrinking. In 1994 he accepted a job as vice president of product management with Synoptics, a midsized maker of data-networking equipment. He informed his family he'd be rejoining them in California via a one-page fax, a puzzle he'd made up that yielded the answer: "It is Synoptics."

By 1996, two years into his tenure at Synoptics (which had merged with Wellfleet Communications and changed its name to Bay Networks), Orr was offered the CEO job at Alteon. Here was a chance to build a company and shape its culture from the ground up. Despite his hard-driving ways, Orr had no trouble assembling a team to jump to Alteon.

"It is like a drug," says Lo of working for Orr. She was trying to take a sabbatical when he lured her aboard. "He gives you all the support you need, but he stretches you beyond what you thought you were capable of." Shirish Sathaye, Alteon's head of engineering, remembers asking Orr to help him with recruitment. "If someone turned me down, I would tell him, 'I understand, I just want you to meet with my CEO.' He never failed to win someone over."

The one place Orr didn't seem capable of winning someone over was at home. By 1998 he and Alvin were fighting about grades, school, phone bills, and just about everything else. Adria says she hid out in her room a lot. Orr and Teresa battled too, about Orr's long hours and lack of relationship with his children. Teresa says she also learned that Orr was in love with someone else — Orr acknowledges that but won't elaborate.

Then came that night in 1998 when Alvin reached his breaking point. He was on the phone with a girl he'd met online. Orr had bought him the technology to make Internet calls on his computer, but Alvin had never installed the gear. Their argument escalated when Alvin refused to join the family for dinner; it turned out he and the girl were calling it quits. Later that night Alvin took a fireplace poker to his dad's car. When the handle broke off, he picked up his skateboard, striking it, wheels down, into each panel of the car.

"I was going for maximum cost of repair by damaging separate parts of the car," he says.

A few months later, Teresa moved out of the house. She also made a heartbreaking decision: She knew that if she took the kids — which she desperately wanted to do — they would grow up without a father. The only way to ensure that they saw their dad, she decided, was for the two children to stay with him in the house.

So Teresa installed herself in a townhouse nearby and every day would come back to the house in the afternoon to see her kids and prepare meals before heading back to her flat in the evenings. "I cried driving home every night," she remembers. The couple divorced in March 1999.

Meanwhile, the principal of Alvin's school suggested that the father and son get professional help, and referred them to John Cayton, a counselor with the Mental Research Institute of Palo Alto, a family-therapy clinic that does a brisk business in absentee-parent cases. Orr, who says he had always considered therapy a "sissy thing," found himself reluctantly meeting regularly with Alvin and Cayton, a psychotherapist.

Cayton thinks he eventually won Orr over by speaking his language, suggesting, for example, that instead of acting like Alvin's manager, Orr might try being his consultant.

Cayton helped Alvin, in turn, deal with his anger, and over a period of months the father and son were able to start having civil, if strained, conversations. Orr says he was so impressed that he decided to work with Cayton one-on-one in an effort to restore some balance to his life. It was an extremely difficult time to embark on such a quest. Orr was hoping to take Alteon public; employees were working like crazy to develop and market products, and Orr had never been under more pressure. He had tried to foster a positive, creative vibe at Alteon and had adopted the phrase "brutal intellectual honesty" as a rallying cry for the corporate culture. (He borrowed the phrase from Tench Coxe, a venture investor in Alteon.) Orr says he had hoped people would be brutally honest with themselves: He didn't want people championing their own inferior ideas, for example.

Unfortunately, far too many people at the company were being brutal to others. Orr once delivered an expletive-filled speech to a group of employees, not even realizing he was using coarse language until marketing executive David Callisch brought it to his attention. It occurred to Orr that if Cayton could temper personal interactions, perhaps the therapist could help him improve the culture at Alteon.

So in the winter of 1999, Orr invited Cayton to the office. "He introduced me as his spiritual coach, and I just wanted to crawl under the table," sighs Cayton, who goes by the nickname Karuna — a Buddhist term meaning "compassion." Recalls Lo: "I really did not trust having a shrink in the company."

Cayton's approach — he has lived in Nepal and melds Eastern and Western schools of thought — also rubbed her the wrong way. "I felt this guy had no professional business background — he went to Tibet and was a semi-monk or something."

Cayton wasn't able to change the Alteon culture — Orr says the executives were too accustomed to the fast-paced style of a startup. And Alteon was about to undergo a much more dramatic change: In 2000, Canadian telecom giant Nortel Networks bought the company for nearly $8 billion.

It should have been Orr's crowning achievement as a CEO. Instead, he was savaged. Investors railed against him for selling cheap. He got a barrage of angry e-mails from employees and stockholders. Callisch, the marketing executive, remembers tucking into a bowl of ice cream and watching David Letterman on TV when the phone rang: Orr was on the line, apologizing profusely for not getting a better price for Alteon. "He was on the verge of tears — he was that distraught," recalls Callisch. (In retrospect, Orr got a very good price for Alteon shareholders. Had he held out, the subsequent telecom collapse surely would have knocked billions off the company's valuation.) It only got worse. Nortel required Orr to stay as a senior executive just as the tech bubble was deflating. Orr once again found himself downsizing. "I was in a crisis," he remembers. "I wasn't sleeping or eating. It was like my father died — it was that level of depression." Once again he was questioning whether he could be both a good executive and a good person. Orr's crisis proved to be another turning point.

"Part of the problem with working with executives is that when they are at the peak of their success, they are too high to focus on real change," says Cayton, who now has his own practice specializing in executive coaching. "Change usually doesn't happen until they're in a conflicted, difficult state of mind."

In his conversations with Cayton in the summer of 2001, Orr happened upon the term hikari — Japanese for "light." The word resonated on a deep level. Light is what had been missing from his life — and the word conveyed the urgency of Orr's mission. He began to think of hikari as "speed to enlightenment." But could he achieve hikari and thrive in the corporate world? "I made the resolution I would never work again if I could not find the answer to be yes," he says. On Oct. 31, 2001, he left Nortel and devoted himself almost full-time to finding hikari.

Orr now had time on his hands, and so did Alvin. A smart young man but a lackluster student, Alvin started taking classes at a local community college while still in high school and opted to get a high school equivalency degree. A friend of Orr's suggested he try to motivate Alvin with a long trip, and in early 2002 the two set off for Tokyo to study Japanese. They'd go to class, do homework, gossip about their classmates, and shop for their apartment. "It was definitely one of the happiest and most memorable times of my life," Orr says. The getaway proved to be good for Alvin too. Teresa remembers visiting her son in Japan and seeing a changed young man, one who kept his room tidy and studied diligently. "I saw the boy I wanted to bring up," she says.

When Orr got back from Japan, he found himself resisting offers to return to work. (His Alteon stock was worth hundreds of millions when the company was sold, and he didn't need the money.) Particularly persistent was a startup called Aruba Networks, founded and funded by a few of his Alteon pals. Orr agreed to invest in the company and to serve as an advisor. But he declined to run the business. Hikari beckoned. He set about reconnecting with Adria. Throughout her middle-school years, he'd never seen her run track. Now she was in high school at a boarding school in Pebble Beach, Calif., a two-hour drive away, and suddenly he started showing up to watch her run. He learned to cook so that he could share meals with his kids and, in an attempt to develop a hobby, started doing his own landscaping. By the end of 2002, he finally felt ready to go back to work. He, Adria, and Alvin seemed to be getting along well. At age 52, "I was too young not to participate in business again," he said. Vivace Networks, a company in which he'd invested his own money — and his siblings' — was struggling and in need of an interim CEO. Feeling guilty about putting family funds into the company, he agreed to step in. He also figured it was time to test his newfound sense of balance in the real world.

Instead of being Orr's triumphant return, the experience was a personal disaster. Orr says the other financiers thought he was going to fix all the company's problems. In a January 2003 e-mail to the Aruba founders (who were still trying to woo him), he described his state of mind: "Even though I felt we had made great progress on the business side at Vivace, I declared to my counsellor [sic] that I had failed — I had put in 14-hour days, I felt that I was losing my calm; I started to ignore/delay my personal responsibilities."

He helped the founders sell Vivace to another telecom-equipment maker in 2003, but he knew he wasn't ready to take on another CEO job. Not yet.

Orr retreated again, building a new house — he took pains to use the same floor plan as the family's original home so as not to upset Adria — and participating in a philanthropy workshop sponsored by the Hewlett Foundation. For Orr, who had never been particularly civic-minded, the experience was formative. Until then he'd thought of "dying a complete man" only in terms of his own life. Now he realized there was another component. In March 2005, just a month after moving into his remodeled home, Orr went to West Africa and began working with Inveneo, a group that helps provide Internet connections in remote and poor areas.

Early last year, Aruba Networks came calling again. The company was getting ready for its IPO, and the board wanted a CEO with a track record taking companies public. One name kept coming up: Dominic Orr. It had been three years since the Vivace debacle, and Orr thought he might be ready. A talk with Adria, by then a freshman at Brown, helped convince him he was. "If it is what you love, then you should go back," Adria recalls telling him. "You're good at it, and you have changed."

"I'd like to hijack the meeting to address some competitive issues," Orr says. He is literally sitting on the edge of his seat in a conference room at Aruba's Sunnyvale, Calif., headquarters. He may have mellowed, but he's no pushover. Aruba, which sells wireless networking gear to corporations, competes with the likes of Cisco (Fortune 500) and Motorola (Fortune 500) in a brutally competitive field. (A sign on his office wall reads THE WEAK ARE KILLED, THE WOUNDED ARE EATEN.) Yet there are visible signs he's trying to temper the culture of "brutal honesty." Early on, he brought in a consultant — not a spiritual coach — to help shape Aruba's corporate culture through training and workshops. During the monthly management meeting I observed in July, the discussion was interrupted by a mariachi band, part of a monthly program to celebrate employees' birthdays. Though it felt a bit like a scene out of The Office, it's part of Orr's bid to create a fun workplace. "Where's the margarita machine?" one worker asks.

"I think he is free to be a good CEO without feeling a sense of desperation around the challenge," says Geoffrey Moore, the Silicon Valley-based consultant and author. Moore has known Orr for more than a dozen years and considers him a top-tier leader. "Before, his identity was so deeply at stake. Now it is like, 'I know how to do this.'"

For Orr, the balancing act doesn't necessarily mean working fewer hours (he typically gets about four hours of sleep a night), but working different hours. "If he's in Boston for business, he'll drive down to Providence to take Adria for dinner," says Aaron Bean, Aruba's head of human resources, who also worked for Orr at Alteon. "The old Dom would have immediately hopped on an airplane to Chicago for a sales call."

Melding compassion and capitalism has been difficult as well. "This is definitely a work in progress," he writes in an e-mail. Orr tries to heed the advice of Xilinx's Roelandts, who reminded him that tough decisions benefit the overall enterprise. Cayton coaches him that "harsh actions do not equate to being wrong, and soft actions do not equate to being right."

Day to day, Orr simply tries to be an empathetic leader, taking workers' and peers' feelings into consideration before he acts. Still, his family's feelings are now paramount. "I have been increasingly taking Alvin and Adria's opinions ... in my decisions on matters big or small," he says. Dominic and Teresa speak periodically, mostly about the kids and their charity work. And Dominic's relationship with Alvin is getting better — slowly.

One of my last meetings with Orr is over dinner at a Singaporean restaurant in the Bay Area. Cayton is there, and so is Alvin, now 25. We've been discussing the family dynamic circa 1992, and Orr is talking about all the transcontinental moves. He begins, "When we moved back to Palo Alto ..." Alvin interrupts: "First of all, we didn't move from Singapore to Palo Alto. Mom and I moved. You moved from Singapore to Japan."

Orr stares at his plate and nods. "That's right," he says quietly. Alvin turns to me and continues, "I understand why he loved work. It's where he found his escape. But then he shouldn't have gotten married and had kids." A look of pain crosses Orr's normally placid face.

But then, just as suddenly, there are moments that remind Orr why he did. Leaving the restaurant, Alvin casually slings his arm around his dad's shoulder. Alvin plans to head out for a drink later that night with Callisch, now a marketing executive at Ruckus Wireless and Alvin's current boss.

He wants his dad to join them. "You should come," Alvin says, with genuine feeling. Orr smiles and says he'll think about it. In that moment of closeness with his son, he sees a glimmer of light.

(*Fortune*, November 2, 2007)

Answer and discuss the following questions:

1. Can you offer a brief account of the stressful home life of Orr in the past?

2. What made Orr change his attitude towards work and family life?
3. What did he do to improve his corporate culture and relations with his family members?
4. How do you think could Orr become both a good executive and a good father or husband?
5. What do you think is the real meaning of the term "hikari" which came from Japanese culture?
6. Do you think Orr has turned into a successful executive and father at the same time towards the end of this story? Why?

Unit 9

Trade Organizations and Conferences on Cooperation

贸易机构与合作会议

Text A

2007 Leaders' Declaration

**FIFTEENTH APEC ECONOMIC LEADERS' MEETING
"STRENGTHENING OUR COMMUNITY, BUILDING
A SUSTAINABLE FUTURE"**[1]

Sydney, Australia, 9 September, 2007

  We, the Leaders of the Asia-Pacific Economic Cooperation[2] (APEC) forum, gathered in Sydney, Australia on 8-9 September 2007. Recalling that APEC was established in Australia in 1989, we reflected with great satisfaction on the strong economic performance of the region since that time. We agreed that our collective commitment to regional economic integration, to free and open markets and to the security of our people has contributed substantially to the strength of our economies and the significant improvement in the welfare and prosperity of our people.[3]

  Promoting open, efficient, transparent and flexible economies is vital to continuing economic growth and the building of a strong and sustainable future for our Asia-Pacific community. This provides the best protection against economic volatility and disruption caused by natural disasters and other threats to sustainable growth.[4] Each of us has agreed to play our part to support long-term prosperity. We will demonstrate strong leadership in pursuit of this objective in order to further improve the lives of our people. We have instructed Ministers to give new momentum to work in APEC in support of structural economic reform in member economies.

  We are confident that robust economic growth will continue and that we can make further progress in our goal to reduce poverty and increase living standards. We will remain alert and responsive to developments and circumstances that might impact directly the attainment of our goal.

Climate Change, Energy Security and Clean Development

We addressed the challenges of climate change, energy security and clean development. Our resolve on this issue is outlined in a separate statement issued at this meeting.

Primacy of the Multilateral Trading System

The Doha Round of World Trade Organization (WTO)[5] negotiations are at a critical juncture. Open markets generate prosperity and development. Expansion of trading opportunities contributes to economic growth and higher living standards. APEC economies account for almost fifty per cent of world trade, and we are, therefore, all major stakeholders in a strong, expanding rules-based multilateral trade system.[6]

Reflecting both the critical juncture faced by the WTO Doha Round, and our continued resolve to achieve a successful conclusion in these negotiations so important to each of our economies, we have issued a separate statement setting out the urgent need for progress and pledging our commitment to work with renewed energy to deliver an ambitious and balanced result.[7]

Regional Economic Integration

APEC economies' commitment to open markets and economic cooperation has generated substantial regional integration. We have all benefited. Economic growth in the region has outstripped the rest of the world and the number of people living in poverty in the region has halved since 1989.

We welcomed and endorsed a report from our Ministers on ways to promote further economic integration in the Asia-Pacific region. We have agreed to accelerate efforts towards this objective by:

- further reducing barriers to trade and investment including through free trade agreements and regional trading arrangements;
- improving economic efficiency and the regional business environment, including capital markets; and
- facilitating integration in sectors such as transportation, telecommunications, mining and energy.

We have asked Ministers and officials to carry forward this work and report back to us in 2008 with a summary of steps taken to promote regional economic integration.

Free Trade Agreements and Regional Trading Arrangements

A successful conclusion to the Doha Round remains our primary trade priority. Regional and bilateral free trade arrangements also play a valuable role in accelerating trade and investment liberalization and in bringing our economies closer together.

We took note of the views of the APEC Business Advisory Council[8] on the importance of enhancing the convergence of trade agreements in the region.

Through a range of practical and incremental steps, we will examine the options and prospects for a Free Trade Area of the Asia-Pacific[9] (FTAAP).

Improving economic efficiency and the business environment, including a new emphasis on structural reform

We have taken note of the views of our business leaders on the impact of global production networks and the integration of regional markets on business risks, costs and competitiveness. Regional economic integration requires not only enhanced trade and investment liberalization and facilitation but also greater attention to "behind-the-border" issues that impact on trade and commerce.[10] We pledge to provide individual and collective leadership to improve the business environment by addressing these issues. In that regard, we:

- agreed on the need to further improve the efficiency of our domestic markets, raise productivity, enhance the resilience of our economies and sustain strong rates of growth through structural reform. We welcomed efforts to intensify work on our Leaders' Agenda to Implement Structural Reform[11] (LAISR) and have asked Ministers to build on this work.
- acknowledged the importance of strengthening domestic institutions that support structural reform and agreed to convene a meeting at the ministerial level in 2008 to address structural reform priorities in the region.
- welcomed the new APEC Trade Facilitation Action Plan[12] which will reduce trade transaction costs by a further five per cent by 2010.
- agreed to continue to strengthen protection and enforcement of intellectual property rights (IPR) in the region. We recognized that a strong knowledge-based economy requires a comprehensive and balanced IPR system, as well as an environment that encourages creativity and innovation and provides the tools for successful management and utilization of IPR.[13] We also agreed to continued efforts by APEC economies to combat the sale of counterfeit and pirated goods at markets involved in this activity.
- emphasized the critical importance of investment to economic growth and development and agreed that the region should take steps to improve the investment climate. This will require liberalization of investment regimes, enhancing the promotion and protection of investment and domestic reforms to strengthen financial institutions and markets. We agreed to undertake a study of bilateral investment agreements and core investment-related elements of existing FTAs with a view to developing principles for investment agreements.[14]
- acknowledged the importance of deep and liquid capital markets, including private capital markets, to support productive investment and manage risks in economies and to enhance economic development and regional integration. We asked our Finance Ministers to explore options for broadening the institutional base and range of instruments available in regional financial markets, recognizing the important role played by financial intermediaries.
- reaffirmed our commitment to combat corruption and promote good governance in order to build prosperity and a predictable business environment. The APEC statement on "Fighting Corruption through Improved International Legal Co-operation" reinforces our strong

commitment to strengthening cooperation on extradition, prosecution, mutual legal assistance and the recovery of proceeds of corruption.[15] We endorsed the complementary Anti-Corruption Principles for the Public and Private Sectors with their codes of conduct and urged full implementation of these practical measures to combat corruption.[16]

Enhancing Human Security

We are repeatedly reminded of our region's vulnerability to natural disasters and the devastating human and economic costs arising from threats to human security. We recognized that we all face new risks and challenges to people and economies — including from the potential spread across borders of terrorism, pandemics, illicit drugs and contaminated products, and the consequences of natural disasters. We affirmed that human security is essential to economic growth and prosperity.

We resolved to enhance our cooperation on challenges to human security and in so doing to remain closely attuned to the needs of business. We reaffirmed our commitment to dismantle terrorist groups, eliminate the danger posed by the proliferation of weapons of mass destruction and to protect our economic and financial systems from abuse by terrorist groups. We welcomed the ongoing development of APEC's trade recovery programme to facilitate trade recovery after a terrorist attack and encouraged economies to undertake pilot projects. We endorsed APEC's voluntary Food Defence Principles[17] to help protect the food supply against deliberate contamination. We instructed Ministers to work towards more consistent security measures that reduce transaction costs, and to enhance cooperation with the private sector.

We agreed on the need to further strengthen APEC's efforts to build community resilience and preparedness for emergencies and natural disasters. We welcomed APEC's work to address and prevent threats to the customs, maritime, aviation, and mass transit sectors as well as to enhance pandemic preparedness and our ability to fight infectious diseases, including HIV/AIDS. To that end, we endorsed the APEC guidelines to ensure that economies continue to function in times of pandemic and guidelines to help create a supportive environment in the workplace for workers living with HIV/AIDS. We agreed to support the sharing of influenza specimens in a timely manner and to promote transparent, fair and equitable access to vaccines and other benefits that derive from them.

We agreed on the need to develop a more robust approach to strengthening food and consumer product safety standards and practices in the region, using scientific risk-based approaches and without creating unnecessary impediments to trade. Additional capacity building in this area is a priority. We directed Ministers to undertake further work in this important area and report on progress.

We recognized the ongoing economic risks associated with high and volatile energy prices and affirmed that rising energy demand in the Asia-Pacific can best be met by expanded trade and investment to boost supply and greater efficiency in use. We agreed that energy security is best met through efficient energy markets, characterized by free and open trade, secure and transparent frameworks for investment, clear price signals, market transparency, effective governance and competition.[18]

Strengthening APEC

We are committed to ongoing efforts to strengthen APEC and to make it more efficient and responsive. We welcomed the decision by Ministers to increase substantially member contributions, the establishment of a new APEC Policy Support Unit[19] and on the appointment of an Executive Director for a fixed term.

We particularly recognized the benefits that have flowed from sharing experiences among our diverse economies and the provision of economic and technical assistance to assist in the implementation of APEC commitments. We expressed appreciation to those member economies providing voluntary contributions to fund a new Policy Support Unit and the increasing number of economies making contributions to APEC's capacity building programmes.

We discussed the issue of APEC membership and agreed it was important to manage the possible entry of new members in a manner that ensures that the momentum APEC has developed towards regional integration and open economies is enhanced.[20] We agreed to revisit the issue of membership in 2010.

We welcomed the offer of the United States of America and the Russian Federation to host APEC in 2011 and 2012 respectively.

We endorsed in full the Joint Statement of Ministers at the 19th APEC Ministerial Meeting.

We welcomed the invitation from the President of Peru to meet again in Lima in 2008.

New Words and Expressions

volatility	n.	反复无常
disruption	n.	瓦解，中断
attainment	n.	达到
primacy	n.	首位，首要
juncture	n.	时刻，关头
stakeholder	n.	利益攸关的共同参与者
outstrip	v.	超过，胜过
convergence	n.	集中，收敛
incremental	a.	逐渐增长的，递增的
behind-the-border	a.	边境背后的
resilience	n.	反弹，恢复力
counterfeit	a.	伪造的，假冒的
intermediary	n.	中间人，媒介
extradition	n.	引渡
prosecution	n.	诉讼，检举，起诉
pandemics	n.	全国（全世界）性的流行病，大疫
illicit	a.	违法的

Unit 9 Trade Organizations and Conferences on Cooperation

proliferation	n.	扩散
equitable	a.	公平的，公正的，合理的
governance	n.	统治，管理，统辖

regional economic integration	区域经济一体化
give momentum to ...	给……提供动力
reduce poverty	扶贫
energy security	能源安全
clean development	清洁发展
free trade agreement	自由贸易协定
take note of	记录下来
in that regard	在那一点上
counterfeit and pirated goods	假冒伪劣产品
deep and liquid capital markets	成熟透明的资本市场
code of conduct	行动守则，管理法典
illicit drugs	毒品，非法毒品
remain closely attuned to ...	和……保持紧密一致（协调）
pilot projects	试点项目
mass transit sectors	公共交通部门
to that end	为此目的
risk-based approaches	以风险评估管理为基础的措施
price signals	价格信号
effective governance	有效监管
joint statement	联合声明

Notes

1. "Strengthening Our Community, Building a Sustainable Future" "加强大家庭建设，共创可持续未来"
   这是2007年亚太经合组织商业峰会的主题，主要讨论亚太地区经济、贸易、能源、环境、教育等领域面临的突出问题和解决办法，亚太经合组织商业峰会是亚太经合组织年会期间的一个重要论坛。

2. Asia-Pacific Economic Cooperation 亚洲太平洋经济合作组织
   简称亚太经合组织，英文简称APEC，是亚洲太平洋地区级别最高，影响最大的区域性经济组织。APEC的宗旨和目标是相互依存，共同利益，坚持开放的多边贸易体制和减少区域贸易堡垒。其会标是呈绿、蓝、白三色的地球状，其含义是：在地球上用太平洋这一半代表APEC经济体，绿色和蓝色表示亚太人民期待着繁荣、健康和福利的生活，白色代表着和平和稳定，边缘阴影部分代表着亚太地区发展和增长富有活力的前景，中间是白色的 APEC 4 个英文字母。领导人非正式会议是亚太经合组织最高级别的会议。会议就有关经济问题发表见解，交换看法，会议形成的领导人宣言是指导亚太经合组织各项工作的重要纲领性文件。部长级会议是亚太经合组织决策机制中的一个重要组成部分。会议的主要任务是为领导人非正式会议做准备、贯彻执行领导人非正式会议通过的各项指示、讨论区域内的重要经济问题和决定亚太经合组织的合作方向与内容。高官会议是亚太经合组织的协调机构，通常由当年举办领导人非正式会议的东道主主办，每年举行 3 至 4 次会议，主要负责执行领导人和部长级会议的决定，审议各工作组和秘书处的活动，筹备部长级会议、领导人非正式会议及其后续行动等事宜。秘书处于 1992 年 9 月在新加坡设立，为 APEC 各层次的活动提供支持与服务。秘书处最高职务为执行主任，任期一年，由每年亚太经合组织会议东道主指派。副执行主任由下届 APEC 会议东道主指派，一年之后成为执行主任。工商咨询理事会是亚太经合组织的常设机构，主要任务是对亚太经合组织贸易投资自由化、经济技术合作及创造有利的工商环境提出设想和建议，并向领导人和部长级会议提交咨询报告。理事会的主要任务是鼓励工商界人士参与亚太经合组织合作进程。

3. We agreed that our collective commitment to regional economic integration, to free and open markets and to the security of our people has contributed substantially to the strength of our economies and the significant improvement in the welfare and prosperity of our people. 我们一致认为对区域经济一体化、自由开放市场和民众安全的集体承诺大幅提高了本地区的经济力量和民众的福利生活水平。

句中的"that"引导的从句作"agree"的宾语。

4. This provides the best protection against economic volatility and disruption caused by natural disasters and other threats to sustainable growth. 这可以有效地预防自然灾害和其他威胁可持续增长事件所带来的经济动荡和混乱。

5. World Trade Organization（WTO） 世界贸易组织

WTO 成立于 1995 年 1 月 1 日，其前身是关税和贸易总协定（GATT），其总部在瑞士日内瓦。WTO 是世界上最大的多边贸易组织，成员的贸易量占世界贸易的 95% 以上。WTO 与世界银行、国际货币基金组织被并称为当今世界经济体制的"三大支柱"。WTO 的基本职能包括制订和规范国际多边贸易规则，组织多边贸易谈判和解决成员之间的贸易争端。WTO 的宗旨是：提高生活水平，保证充分就业，大幅度和稳定地增加实际收入和有效需求，扩大货物和服务的生产与贸易，按照可持续发展的目的，最有效地运用世界资源，保护环境，并以不同经济发展水平下各自需要的方式，采取各种相应的措施；积极努力，确保发展中国家，尤其是最不发达国家在国际贸易增长中获得与其经济发展需要相称的份额。WTO 的具体目标是：建立一个完整的、更具活力和永久性的多边贸易体制，以巩固原来的关贸总协定为贸易自由化所做的努力和乌拉圭回合多边贸易谈判的所有成果。为实现这些目标，各成员应通过互惠互利的安排，切实降低关税和其他贸易壁垒，在国际贸易中消除歧视性待遇。WTO 的地位是：WTO 是具有法人地位的国际组织。WTO 的最高决策权力机构是部长大会，至少每两年召开一次会议，可对多边贸易协议的所有事务做出决定。部长大会下设总理事会和秘书处，负责 WTO 的日常会议和工

Unit 9 Trade Organizations and Conferences on Cooperation

作。总理事会设有货物贸易、服务贸易、知识产权三个理事会和贸易与发展、国际收支、行政预算三个委员会。秘书处设总干事一人。

6. APEC economies account for almost fifty per cent of world trade, and we are, therefore, all major stakeholders in a strong, expanding rules-based multilateral trade system. 亚太经合组织的经济几乎占世界贸易的一半，因此我们都是一个强大的、不断发展和规范的多边贸易体系的利益相关者。

   句中的"rules-based"意为"以规则为基础的，规范的"。

7. Reflecting both the critical juncture faced by the WTO Doha Round, and our continued resolve to achieve a successful conclusion in these negotiations so important to each of our economies, we have issued a separate statement setting out the urgent need for progress and pledging our commitment to work with renewed energy to deliver an ambitious and balanced result. 世贸组织多哈回合谈判正处于关键时刻，我们决心要在这些对每个经济体来说具有重要意义的谈判中取得圆满成功。鉴于以上考虑，我们已单独发表了一个声明，表明了对取得谈判进展的迫切需要，承诺会继续努力以取得一个完美平衡的结果。

   句中的"reflecting"是现在分词作状语。

8. APEC Business Advisory Council 亚太工商咨询理事会

   亚太经合组织的常设机构，主要任务是对亚太经合组织贸易投资自由化、经济技术合作及创造有利的工商环境提出设想和建议，并向领导人和部长级会议提交咨询报告。理事会的主要任务是鼓励工商界人士参与亚太经合组织合作进程。

9. Free Trade Area of the Asia-Pacific 亚太自由贸易区

   1993年提出，2006—2007年启动，创建"亚太自由贸易区"可能对全球产生巨大的正面影响。占世界经济规模一半的这些成员，只要实现任何接近于自由贸易的目标，都会比多哈回合谈判哪怕最雄心勃勃的成果带来更大的益处，因为多哈回合谈判最多只是试图适当减少市场准入障碍。其影响的分布将会与多边协议不同：APEC成员将会获益，而许多非APEC成员却要受贸易转移之苦。

10. Regional economic integration requires not only enhanced trade and investment liberalization and facilitation but also greater attention to 'behind-the-border' issues that impact on trade and commerce. 区域经济一体化不仅要求贸易投资进一步自由化和便利化，还要求更多地关注对商业贸易有影响的"边境背后"的问题。

    句中的"behind-the-border issues"意为"边境背后"的问题，指除关税和其他边境措施之外，具有影响国际贸易性质的国内政策和国内法律所引出的众多与贸易有关的问题。

11. Leaders' Agenda to Implement Structural Reform 关于实施结构改革的领导人议程

    其目的是重申APEC成员要履行进行结构改革的承诺，结构改革的目的是使成员们的经济体制能更好地适应市场经济的运作，以充分发挥亚太地区经济增长的潜能。

12. APEC Trade Facilitation Action Plan 贸易加强行动计划

    该计划每两年一期，旨在降低贸易成本，促进APEC成员之间的贸易交往。

13. We recognized that a strong knowledge-based economy requires a comprehensive and balanced IPR system, as well as an environment that encourages creativity and innovation and provides the tools for successful management and utilization of IPR. 我们认识到：强大的知识经济，

必须有完善和平衡的知识产权体系和鼓励创新和革新的环境，同时提供能够成功管理和使用知识产权的工具。

句中的"recognized"后是宾语从句，"requires"和"provides"并列作宾语从句的谓语。

14. We agreed to undertake a study of bilateral investment agreements and core investment-related elements of existing FTAs with a view to developing principles for investment agreements. 我们同意着手研究双边投资协议及现存自由贸易协议中与投资相关的核心部分，以完善投资协议准则。

    句中的"with a view to"意为"着眼于，以……为目的"。

15. The APEC statement on "Fighting Corruption through Improved International Legal Co-operation" reinforces our strong commitment to strengthening cooperation on extradition, prosecution, mutual legal assistance and the recovery of proceeds of corruption. 亚太经合组织"通过促进国际法律合作打击贪腐"的声明，强调了我们的承诺，这些承诺包括加强在引渡、诉讼、司法互助及追回贪污所得等方面的合作。

16. We endorsed the complementary Anti-Corruption Principles for the Public and Private Sectors with their codes of conduct and urged full implementation of these practical measures to combat corruption. 我们同时也批准了一项补充性的"公私部门反贪原则"及相应的行为准则，并呼吁充分落实这些反贪措施。

    句中的"endorsed"和"urged"并列作句子的谓语。

17. APEC's voluntary Food Defence Principles 亚太经合组织自愿性食品防卫原则

    该原则包括预防、防范、应对、恢复及有效沟通，这些原则对于国际上防范恐怖主义从食物供给源头进行污染有着重要的作用。

18. We agreed that energy security is best met through efficient energy markets, characterized by free and open trade, secure and transparent frameworks for investment, clear price signals, market transparency, effective governance and competition. 我们一致认为有效的能源市场能够最有效地促进能源安全，有效的能源市场特征包括贸易自由开放、投资环境安全透明、价格信号清晰、市场透明、有效的政府管理及竞争机制等。

    句中的"characterized"是过去分词作定语修饰前面的"efficient energy markets"（有效的能源市场）。

19. APEC Policy Support Unit APEC 政策支持小组

    该小组在 APEC 秘书处内设立，可以提升秘书处在政策研究和活动评估方面的能力。

20. We discussed the issue of APEC membership and agreed it was important to manage the possible entry of new members in a manner that ensures that the momentum APEC has developed towards regional integration and open economies is enhanced. 我们讨论了亚太经合组织成员国的议题，一致认为在处理可能的新成员加入提案时，应确保 APEC 的影响力，该影响力一直使 APEC 朝着区域一体化和经济开放的方向发展。

    句中"APEC has developed towards regional integration and open economies"作定语修饰前面的"momentum"（动力、势头、影响力）。

Unit 9 Trade Organizations and Conferences on Cooperation

 阅读小知识（1）

1. 经济一体化（Economic Integration）

经济一体化是指两个或两个以上的国家在现有生产力发展水平和国际分工的基础上，由政府间通过协商缔结条约，建立多国的经济联盟。在这个多国经济联盟的区域内，商品、资本和劳务能够自由流动，不存在任何贸易壁垒，并拥有一个统一的机构来监督条约的执行和实施共同的政策及措施。

广义的经济一体化即世界经济一体化，指世界各国经济之间彼此相互开放，形成相互联系、相互依赖的有机体。

狭义的经济一体化，即地区经济一体化，指区域内两个或两个以上国家或地区，在一个由政府授权组成的并具有超国家性的共同机构下，通过制定统一的对内对外经济政策、财政与金融政策等，消除国别之间阻碍经济贸易发展的障碍，实现区域内互利互惠、协调发展和资源优化配置，最终形成一个政治经济高度协调统一的有机体的过程。

1）经济一体化的形式

根据各参加国的具体情况和条件及它们的目标要求，经济一体化的形式有自由贸易区、关税同盟、共同市场和经济联盟4种形式。

（1）自由贸易区。自由贸易区是指由签订自由贸易协定的国家组成的贸易区。成员国之间免征关税和取消其他贸易限制。

（2）关税同盟。关税同盟是指两个或两个以上国家为了取消彼此之间的关税或各种贸易壁垒，建立共同的对外关税而缔结的同盟。关税同盟内部商品自由流通和自由竞争。关税同盟在一体化程度上比自由贸易区更进了一步。

（3）共同市场。共同市场是指在关税同盟基础上实现生产要素的自由流动，在同盟内建立关税、贸易和市场一体化，其最终目标是要实现完全的经济联盟。

（4）经济联盟。经济联盟是经济一体化的最终发展目标和最高级的形式。它要求其成员国在实现关税、贸易和市场一体化的基础上，建立一个超国家的管理机构，在国际经济决策中采取同一立场，行使统一的货币制度和组建统一的银行机构，进而在经济、财政、货币、关税、贸易和市场等方面实现全面的经济一体化。

2）经济一体化的特征

经济一体化的特征包括：相互给予的贸易优惠、成员国之间的自由贸易、共同的对外关税、生产要素的自由流动、经济政策的协调、统一的经济政策。

2. 欧洲联盟

欧洲联盟简称欧盟（European Union，EU），是由欧洲共同体（European Communities）发展而来的，是一个集政治实体和经济实体于一身、在世界上具有重要影响的区域一体化组织。1991年12月，欧洲共同体马斯特里赫特首脑会议通过《欧洲联盟条约》，通称《马斯特里赫特条约》（简称《马约》）。1993年11月1日，《马约》正式生效，欧盟正式诞生，总部设在比利时首都布鲁塞尔。

1）成立过程

欧洲统一思潮存在已久，在第二次世界大战后进入高潮。1946年9月，英国首相丘吉尔曾提议建立"欧洲合众国"。1950年5月9日，法国外长罗伯特·舒曼提出欧洲煤钢共同体计划（即舒曼计划），旨在约束德国。1951年4月18日，法、意、联邦德国、荷、比、卢6国签订了为期50年的《关于建立欧洲煤钢共同体的条约》。1955年6月1日，参加欧洲煤钢共同体的6国外长在意大利墨西拿举行会议，建议将煤钢共同体的原则推广到其他经济领域，并建立共同市场。1957年3月25日，6国外长在罗马签订了建立欧洲经济共同体与欧洲原子能共同体的两个条约，即《罗马条约》，于1958年1月1日生效。1965年4月8日，6国签订了《布鲁塞尔条约》，决定将欧洲煤钢共同体、欧洲原子能共同体和欧洲经济共同体统一起来，统称欧洲共同体（简称欧共体）。该条约于1967年7月1日生效。欧共体总部设在比利时布鲁塞尔。1991年12月11日，欧共体马斯特里赫特首脑会议通过了建立"欧洲经济货币联盟"和"欧洲政治联盟"的《欧洲联盟条约》。1992年2月1日，各国外长正式签署《马约》。经欧共体各成员国批准，《马约》于1993年11月1日正式生效，欧共体开始向欧洲联盟过渡。1993年11月1日《马约》正式生效，欧共体更名为欧盟。这标志着欧共体从经济实体向经济政治实体过渡。1995年，奥地利、瑞典和芬兰加入，使欧盟成员国扩大到15个。欧盟成立后，经济快速发展，1995年至2000年间经济增速达3%，人均国内生产总值由1997年的1.9万美元上升到1999年的2.06万美元。欧盟的经济总量从1993年的约6.7万亿美元增长到2002年的近10万亿美元。

2002年11月18日，欧盟115国外长会议决定邀请塞浦路斯、匈牙利、捷克、爱沙尼亚、拉脱维亚、立陶宛、马耳他、波兰、斯洛伐克和斯洛文尼亚10个中东欧国家入盟。2003年4月16日，在希腊首都雅典举行的欧盟首脑会议上，上述10国正式签署入盟协议。2004年5月1日，这10个国家正式成为欧盟的成员国。这是欧盟历史上的第五次扩大，也是规模最大的一次扩大。2007年1月，罗马尼亚和保加利亚两国加入欧盟。欧盟经历了6次扩大，成为一个涵盖27个国家、总人口超过4.8亿的当今世界上经济实力最强、一体化程度最高的国家联合体。2003年7月，欧盟制宪筹备委员会全体会议就欧盟的盟旗、盟歌、铭言与庆典日等问题达成了一致。根据宪法草案：欧盟的盟旗为蓝底和12颗黄星图案，盟歌为贝多芬第九交响曲中的《欢乐颂》，铭言为"多元一体"，"欧洲日"为5月9日。

2）欧元

欧盟的统一货币为欧元（euro），1999年1月1日正式启用。除英国、希腊、瑞典和丹麦外的11个国家于1998年首批成为欧元国。2000年6月，欧盟在葡萄牙北部城市费拉举行的首脑会议批准希腊加入欧元区。2002年1月1日零时，欧元正式流通。2006年7月11日，欧盟财政部长理事会正式批准斯洛文尼亚在2007年1月1日加入欧元区，这将是欧元区的首次扩大。同时，该国将成为新加入欧盟的10个中东欧国家中第一个加入欧元区的国家。2008年1月1日，马耳他和塞浦路斯加入欧元区，使欧元区国家增至15个。

3）欧盟的主要组织机构

（1）欧洲理事会（European Council），即首脑会议，由成员国国家元首或政府首脑及欧盟委员会主席组成，负责讨论欧洲联盟的内部建设、重要的对外关系及重大的国际问题。欧洲理事会每年至少举行两次会议。欧洲理事会主席由各成员国轮流担任，任期半年，顺序基本按本国文字书写的国名字母排列。欧洲理事会是欧盟的最高权力机构，在决策过程中采取协商一致通过的原则。欧洲理事会下设总秘书处。

（2）欧盟理事会，即部长理事会，主席由各成员国轮流担任，任期半年。

（3）欧盟委员会（Commission of European Union），是欧洲联盟的常设机构和执行机构，负责实施欧洲联盟条约和欧盟理事会做出的决定，向理事会和欧洲议会提出报告和立法动议，处理联盟的日常事务，代表欧盟对外联系和进行贸易等方面的谈判等。在欧盟实施共同外交和安全政策范围内，欧盟委员会只有建议权和参与权。欧盟委员会总部设在比利时首都布鲁塞尔。

（4）欧洲议会（European Parliament），是欧洲联盟的执行监督和咨询机构，在某些领域有立法职能，并有部分预算决定权，并可以三分之二多数弹劾欧盟委员会，迫其集体辞职。议会大厦设在法国斯特拉斯堡，议会秘书处设在卢森堡。自1979年起，欧洲议会议员由成员国直接普选产生，任期5年。

此外，欧盟机构还包括设在卢森堡的欧洲法院和欧洲审计院。

（5）欧洲法院是欧盟的仲裁机构，负责审理和裁决在执行欧盟条约和有关规定中发生的各种争执。现有15名法官和9名检察官，由成员国政府共同任命。

（6）欧洲审计院负责欧盟的审计和财政管理。欧洲审计院于1977年成立，由12人组成。

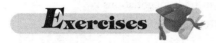

I Decide whether the following statements are true（T）or false（F）.

1. The leaders of the APEC showed reserved satisfaction with the economic growth in this region, because they thought that the goal established by them had not been attained as agreed. （　　）

2. The economic growth in the Asia Pacific region has caught up with the rest of the world, and the number of people living in poverty has reduced by half since 1989. （　　）

3. The acceleration of trade and investment liberalization and improvement in economic ties of APEC members depends on the efforts in promotion of regional and bilateral free trade. （　　）

4. It seems to the leaders that domestic institutions of APEC member nations that support structural reform are vital to the regional economic growth. （　　）

5. Protection and enforcement of intellectual property rights and the combat against corruption can help clear the business environment of adverse factors that affect the investment and economic growth, because these two issues have already become the most serious problems in this region. （　　）

6. Among all new risks and challenges facing the nation, terrorism has become the most formidable threat to human security. （　　）

7. According to the leaders of the APEC, it is necessary to develop a more effective mechanism to enhance food and consumer product safety standards and practices in this region. （　　）

8. Effective and transparent energy markets should be established to ensure energy security. (   )
9. The APEC member nations, although different in their political systems, can share the experiences of their economic development and are cooperative enough in the implementation of APEC commitments. (   )
10. The APEC, a permanent institution, which was established in Australia in 1989, has contributed a great deal to the economic integration and improvement in the welfare and prosperity of this region. (   )

II Choose one answer that best suits the following statements.

1. It remains the primary trade priority for APEC to reach a successful conclusion in the Doha Round negotiation, because _____.
    A. this region needs to have a good mechanism of negotiation to address the problem
    B. this region is not responsive to the trade disputes
    C. this region has become a major influential economic player in strong, expanding rules-based multilateral trade system
    D. this region can need an approach to achieve its structural reforms

2. Regional economic integration requires APEC nations to _____.
    A. liberalize and facilitate investment only
    B. remove the obstacles in trade negotiations
    C. protect and enforce IRP and fight against corruption and terrorism
    D. both liberalize the trade and investment and address the domestic issues of those nation members

3. In countering new risks and challenges, the APEC leaders called for member nations to make further efforts to _____.
    A. dismantle terrorist groups and improve trade recovery programme
    B. conduct cooperation on challenges to human security and build or develop more effective mechanism to meet emergencies and natural disasters as well as set up rigorous standards for food and consumer product safety
    C. make them more efficient and responsive to new business climate
    D. produce more measures that help reduce transaction risks and undertake pilot projects

4. We agreed on the need to further strengthen APEC's efforts to build community <u>resilience</u> and preparedness for emergencies and natural disasters.
    The above underlined word means _____.
    A. readily recovering capacity from setbacks   B. flexibility
    C. resistance   D. resuscitation

5. Regional economic integration requires not only enhanced trade and <u>investment</u> liberalization and facilitation but also great attention to "<u>behind-the-border</u>" issues that impact trade and commerce.
    The above underlined word means _____.
    A. back-door-deal   B. domestic   C. international   D. behind-the-scene

Unit 9 Trade Organizations and Conferences on Cooperation

III Translate the following passages into Chinese.

1. Promoting open, efficient, transparent and flexible economies is vital to continuing economic growth and the building of a strong and sustainable future for our Asia-Pacific community. This provides the best protection against economic volatility and disruption caused by natural disasters and other threats to sustainable growth. Each of us has agreed to play our part to support long-term prosperity. We will demonstrate strong leadership in pursuit of this objective in order to further improve the lives of our people. We have instructed Ministers to give new momentum to work in APEC in support of structural economic reform in member economies.

2. We resolved to enhance our cooperation on challenges to human security and in so doing to remain closely attuned to the needs of business. We reaffirmed our commitment to dismantle terrorist groups, eliminate the danger posed by the proliferation of weapons of mass destruction and to protect our economic and financial systems from abuse by terrorist groups. We welcomed the ongoing development of APEC's trade recovery programme to facilitate trade recovery after a terrorist attack and encouraged economies to undertake pilot projects. We endorsed APEC's voluntary Food Defence Principles to help protect the food supply against deliberate contamination. We instructed Ministers to work towards more consistent security measures that reduce transaction costs, and to enhance cooperation with the private sector.

IV Write a summary of this text.

East Asia Exposes Limits of Regional Trade Deals

Alan Beattie

The trade diplomacy of east Asia has become so blindingly complex that even the metaphors are getting muddled. The subtitle of one academic paper on free trade agreements (FTAs) suggests using "spaghetti bowls as building blocs[1]". Another describes "a patchwork of bilateral hub-and-spoke FTAs in a noodle bowl[2]."

These curious attempts to express the new world of Asian trade reflect the confusion surrounding rapidly proliferating regional trade deals and bilateral agreements. Attempts to illustrate this new trade architecture graphically are just as clumsy as the verbal analogies, variously resembling modern art, an electrical circuit board or, yes, a noodle bowl.

This complexity is accentuated by the suspension of the so-called Doha round of global trade talks, since July, with its slim chances of swift resuscitation reduced further by the Democrats' clean sweep of Congress last week.³ With multilateral negotiations at a standstill, attention has shifted to bilateral and regional trade agreements.

Though such deals claim to lower import tariffs and other barriers to trade, orthodox trade economists such as Jagdish Bhagwati, the Columbia academic who coined the spaghetti metaphor (adapted to noodles for use in Asia), say they often do more to complicate trade than ease it. Certainly, he says, they do not deserve the name of free-trade agreements.

But his is a minority view. One particularly tangled bowl of noodles will assemble in Vietnam this week: the oddly-named Asia-Pacific Economic Co-operation (APEC). Rumors are swirling that the US might revive an old idea of turning the 21-member APEC into a regional trade agreement (RTA) to secure a collective lowering of trade protection in the region. But like its rivals, the Association of South-East Asian Nations[4] (ASEAN) and the newer "east Asia summit", APEC continues to resemble a motley collection of governments in search of a common project.

The intrinsic problem with all these forums is that the region contains such a variety of economies and political systems. This means that in the short to medium term, any pact to cut tariff or regulatory protection tends to sink to the lowest common denominator.

No association like ASEAN, which contains both rich, globalized Singapore and the desperately poor and repressive Burma, is likely to serve as the basis for a serious trade deal. No agreement including South Korea and Japan can include radical agricultural liberalization for fear of alarming their heavily protected rice farmers. Korean insistence on excluding rice in talks over a Korea-ASEAN FTA, for example, prompted Thailand — one of the most efficient rice producers — to refuse to participate in the agreement.

No agreement that excludes the US makes much sense. Despite the rapid growth in intra-east Asian trade in the past few years, many countries retain strong trading links to the US. Such links are a strong deterrent to the creation of an Asian-only "customs union" — a regional trading area that imposes the same tariff on imports from any non-member — because some countries within it will want to lock in low tariffs with their biggest customer.⁵ Precisely this problem has occurred within the Latin American "Mercosur[6]" customs union, which Uruguay has threatened to quit because it wants a deeper bilateral deal with the US.

While no east Asian trading area would mean much without the US, neither would it without China, whose trade with south-east Asia has been growing rapidly and whose FTA with ASEAN is one of the few that may prove to have some substance. But the protectionist Sinophobia flourishing in Washington, likely to be given even freer rein given the new Democratic dominance on Capitol Hill, precludes any substantive regional trade pact including both China and the US.⁷

It seems very likely that actual trade will carry on growing regardless of bureaucratic wrangling. Rarely has there been such a contrast between the dynamism of a regional economy and faltering official attempts to build a free trade area therein.⁸ Years of rapid growth have turned much of east Asia into one big assembly line, with Japan, Korea or Chinese Taiwan specializing in design and high-skill engineering while labor-intensive assembly takes place in Thailand or China. The average ratio of exports plus imports to gross domestic product is more than 130 per cent in south-east Asia,

Unit 9 Trade Organizations and Conferences on Cooperation

far higher than in Latin America, Africa or Europe.

This dynamism, however, has little to do with formal trade pacts. "Surprising as it may seem, all this regional trade creation happened outside the aegis of regional trade agreements," says Richard Baldwin, professor of international economics at the Graduate Institute of International Economics in Geneva. He cites a study by Jetro, a Japanese government-backed organization that promotes trade and investment, finding that less than 10 per cent of the capacity of a trade pact signed by ASEAN in 1991 was actually used. The "information technology agreement", an open global association whose member countries commit to eliminating tariffs on IT products, has outflanked it in that sector.[9] Unilateral liberalization, most recently practised by China, has done more to open up markets in east Asia than have bilateral or plurilateral agreements.

But this has not stopped the trade diplomacy caravan proceeding, if only in circles.[10] APEC, whose members include the US, Chile, Canada and Mexico, was launched in 1994 with the aim of achieving "free and open trade and investment in the Asia-Pacific" by 2010 for industrialized countries. It has since done little to achieve that end except, in its early years, acting as a discussion forum for governments who were unilaterally cutting tariffs.

The rival Association of South East Asian Nations (ASEAN), which holds its annual meeting next month in the Philippines, was founded in 1967 and emerged as a political bloc of five anti-communist countries in a region that was often a theatre of cold war combat. That purpose redundant after 1989, it signed a trade deal in 1991 and its membership has expanded to 10. It has since agreed separate bilateral trade deals with China and Korea, and there is intermittent talk of adding Japan into a supersized "ASEAN plus three".

The newest knot in the regional cat's-cradle is the "east Asia summit", comprising the "ASEAN plus three" 13 and India, Australia and New Zealand, with some other countries, including Russia, as observers. They will gather again this year just after December's ASEAN meeting, the definition of east Asia stretched to breaking point by a proposal from Malaysia that Pakistan be admitted.[11]

Few businesses are planning business strategies based on faith that a regional trading pact will take off. Michael Gadbaw, head of government relations for General Electric, says that any form of trade liberalization is beneficial — "We should use every avenue we can" — though multilateralism is the best. But as for APEC, ASEAN or the east Asia grouping, he says, "hopes are high but expectations are more realistic".

The US government's preferred vehicle for integration is, unsurprisingly, the one it helped set up: APEC. A senior US trade official says: "The entity that, notwithstanding all of its weaknesses, has done the most and has the most legs is APEC ... what the various ASEAN and 'ASEAN plus' deals have achieved is pretty thin gruel.[12]"

But by US officials' own admissions, it will take a lot of work to turn APEC even into a useful policy forum like the Organization for Economic Co-operation and Development[13], the Paris-based club of rich country governments. "The APEC architecture is very unwieldy and there is no secretariat, which places a lot of strain on the host country," the senior US trade official says. "Even building the kind of rudimentary architecture that other groups like the OECD have would be enormously helpful in turning this organization into the kind of thing that can achieve the lofty goals it was set up for.[14]"

In the absence of effective regional co-operation, bilateral deals have rushed in to fill the hole. There are now dozens in east Asia with more to come. Peter Mandelson, European Union trade commissioner, has departed from traditional EU practice and launched a full-throated campaign of bilateral deal-seeking.

Some bilaterals, notably the ones signed by the US with Singapore and Australia, have real bite, with extensive rules protecting intellectual property rights and opening up agricultural markets. Most, particularly those signed between two developing countries, are more to do with foreign policy posturing than increasing trade. Razeen Sally, a London School of Economics academic, says: "The predictable results of foreign policy-driven FTA negotiations light on economic strategy are bitty, quick-fix sectoral deals.[15]"

The US trade official concurs: "Bilateral FTAs being pursued by China and Japan, and Korea to some extent, risk falling to the lowest common denominator. As someone once quipped: they are neither F nor T nor A.[16]"

Is there any way to knit these partial deals into a regional tapestry of free trade? Such an outcome would require heavily simplifying the vastly complex "rules of origin" — the regulations determining the minimum level of an export product's value that has to be added in-country to benefit from a nation's special market access. Without rules of origin, trade pacts are close to meaningless. Chinese-made goods could be touched down on the quay in Penang, relabeled "Made in Malaysia" and then be re-exported to any country with which Malaysia had a trade deal.

But with the fragmented supply chains of east Asia, aggregating multiple rules of origin for different products from different countries under different trade deals is immensely complex. Prof Sally says that the interaction of bilateral and regional rules of origin will get so complicated that exporters will find it easier and cheaper to pay the standard tariff available to all WTO members than to try to get the lowest tariff possible. "Little trade will be created," he says. "But there will be more work for customs officials."

(*Financial Times*, November 13, 2006)

New Words and Expressions

blindingly	ad.	盲目地，摸索地
metaphor	n.	隐喻，暗喻
spaghetti	n.	意大利面条

Unit 9 Trade Organizations and Conferences on Cooperation

patchwork	n.	拼缝物，拼缀物，拼凑物
hub-and-spoke		中心辐射型，星型
accentuate	v.	强调，加重
resuscitation	n.	复生，复兴
standstill	n.	停止，停顿
tangled	a.	缠结的，紊乱的
swirl	v.	旋转，传播
motley	a.	混杂的，好坏杂合的
intrinsic	a.	固有的，内在的，本质的
pact	n.	合同，公约，协定
denominator	n.	分母，共同特性
sinophobia	n.	恐华（对中国事物的怀疑或恐惧）
preclude	v.	排除
substantive	a.	独立存在的，真实的，有实质的
wrangling	n.	辩驳，争吵
dynamism	n.	活力，推动力
faltering	a.	犹豫的，支吾的
aegis	n.	保护，庇护，支持
outflank	v.	包抄，以计胜过，阻挠，挫败
plurilateral	a.	多边的
caravan	n.	旅行队，商队
intermittent	a.	间歇的，断断续续的
gruel	n.	稀粥，燕麦粥
unwieldy	a.	笨拙的，不实用的，难使用的
rudimentary	a.	根本的，未发展的
full-throated	a.	喧嚣的，放开喉咙的
deal-seeking	n.	寻求达成协议
quick-fix	a.	权宜的，应急的
concur	v.	同意，赞成
quip	v.	讥讽，嘲弄
tapestry	n.	织锦，挂毯
east-Asia summit		东亚峰会
lock in		禁闭，锁定，锁入
breaking point		断裂点
light on		停留在

Notes

1. spaghetti bowls as building blocs   以盛意大利面条的碗为基础

   这里是比喻，指自由贸易协定就像碗里的面条，一根根地绞在一起，剪不断，理还乱，混乱不堪。

2. a patchwork of bilateral hub-and-spoke FTAs in a noodle bowl   面碗里拼凑着一堆星形的双边自由贸易协定

   这里也是比喻，指各经济体都与多个其他经济体分别签订双边自由贸易协定，然后混杂在一起。此处的 noodle bowl 指区域经济组织。

3. This complexity is accentuated by the suspension of the so-called Doha round of global trade talks, since July, with its slim chances of swift resuscitation reduced further by the Democrats' clean sweep of Congress last week.   7月份，多哈回合全球贸易谈判的中止加剧了这种复杂态势，而快速恢复多哈回合谈判的可能性本来就很小，又因为上周民主党在国会的彻底胜利而使这种可能性进一步降低了。

   句中的"resuscitation"原意是"复兴"，此处指恢复谈判。

4. Association of South-East Asian Nations   东南亚国家联盟（东盟）

   其前身是由马来西亚、菲律宾和泰国3国于1961年7月31日在曼谷成立的东南亚联盟。1967年8月7日至8日，印度尼西亚、新加坡、泰国、菲律宾四国外长和马来西亚副总理在泰国首都曼谷举行会议，发表了《东南亚国家联盟成立宣言》，即《曼谷宣言》，正式宣告东南亚国家联盟成立。现在东盟已成为东南亚地区以经济合作为基础的政治、经济、安全一体化合作组织，并建立起一系列合作机制。东盟除印度尼西亚、马来西亚、菲律宾、新加坡和泰国5个创始成员国外，20世纪80年代后，文莱（1984年）、越南（1995年）、老挝（1997年）、缅甸（1997年）和柬埔寨（1999年）5国先后加入该组织，使东盟由最初成立时的5个成员国发展到10个成员国。观察员国为巴布亚新几内亚。东盟的10个对话伙伴国是：澳大利亚、加拿大、中国、欧盟、印度、日本、新西兰、俄罗斯、韩国和美国。东盟的宗旨是：以平等和协作精神，共同努力促进本地区的经济增长、社会进步和文化发展；遵循正义、国家关系准则和《联合国宪章》，促进本地区的和平与稳定；同国际和地区组织进行紧密和互利的合作。东盟的主要机构有首脑会议、外长会议、常务委员会、经济部长会议、其他部长会议、秘书处、专门委员会及民间和半官方机构。首脑会议是东盟最高决策机构，外长会议是制定东盟基本政策的机构，常务委员会主要讨论东盟外交政策，并落实具体合作项目。1994年7月成立了东盟地区论坛，1999年9月成立了东亚－拉美合作论坛，10+3和10+1合作机制也应运而生，2002年1月又启动东盟自由贸易区。

5. Such links are a strong deterrent to the creation of an Asian-only "customs union" — a regional trading area that imposes the same tariff on imports from any non-member — because some countries within it will want to lock in low tariffs with their biggest customer.   这些联系对建

立单一的亚洲"关税同盟"是个极大的障碍，关税同盟区要求对任何非成员国征收同样的进口关税，但是有些成员国却想给予自己最大的贸易伙伴锁定较低的关税。

句中的"biggest customer"在此处指那些非成员国贸易伙伴。

6. Mercosur 南方共同市场

简称南共市，是南美地区最大的经济一体化组织，也是世界上第一个完全由发展中国家组成的共同市场。1991年，阿根廷、巴西、乌拉圭和巴拉圭4国总统在巴拉圭首都亚松森签署《亚松森条约》，宣布建立南方共同市场。1995年1月1日，南共市正式启动，关税联盟开始生效。此后，南共市先后接纳智利、玻利维亚、秘鲁、厄瓜多尔和哥伦比亚等国为其联系国。该组织的宗旨是：通过有效利用资源、保护环境、协调宏观经济政策、加强经济互补，促进成员国科技进步，最终实现经济政治一体化。南共市的最高决策机构为理事会。首脑会议每年至少举行一次，必要时可召开多次。南共市的执行机构为共同市场小组，负责实施条约和理事会做出的决议，其行政秘书处设在乌拉圭首都蒙得维的亚。2006年7月，南共市正式吸收委内瑞拉为第五个成员国。

7. But the protectionist sinophobia flourishing in Washington, likely to be given even freer rein given the new Democratic dominance on Capitol Hill, precludes any substantive regional trade pact including both China and the US.   但是华盛顿贸易保护主义者的恐华情绪有所抬头，如果民主党在国会里占据统治地位，恐华情绪可能会进一步蔓延，这就排除了中美签订任何实质性区域贸易协定的可能性。

句中的"Capitol Hill"指代美国国会。

8. Rarely has there been such a contrast between the dynamism of a regional economy and faltering official attempts to build a free trade area therein.   很少会有这样的对比局面，一方面区域经济充满活力，而另一方面官方建设自由贸易区的努力却收效不大。

句中的"rarely"是具有否定含义的词，放在句首，句子要倒装。

9. The "information technology agreement", an open global association whose member countries commit to eliminating tariffs on IT products, has outflanked it in that sector.   《信息技术协定》是一个开放的全球性协会，其成员国承诺取消IT产品的关税，该协定在信息技术领域已经超越了东盟的某些协议。

句中的"an open global association"是同位语，"it"指东盟的有关协议。

10. But this has not stopped the trade diplomacy caravan proceeding, if only in circles.   但这并没有阻止贸易外交活动的进行，只要在这个圈里，这还会继续下去。

句中的"if only"意为"只要"，这里指只要还是当前这样的情况，该活动还会继续进行下去。

11. They will gather again this year just after December's ASEAN meeting, the definition of east Asia stretched to breaking point by a proposal from Malaysia that Pakistan be admitted.   在刚刚结束的11月份东盟会议之后，他们将再次开会，东亚的定义也因马来西亚提议巴基斯坦加入东盟而延伸到了极限。

12. The entity that, notwithstanding all of its weaknesses, has done the most and has the most legs is APEC ... what the various ASEAN and "ASEAN plus" deals have achieved is pretty thin gruel.   尽管有很多缺点，但APEC却是做得最多的，也是最有成效的……而东盟和

"东盟+"各项协议的效果却是微乎其微。

句中的"have legs"原意为"走得快，出名快"，这里指"有效，有效果"。

13. Organisation for Economic Co-operation and Development 经济合作与发展组织

简称经合组织，前身是1948年4月成立的欧洲经济合作组织。1960年12月14日，加拿大、美国及欧洲经济合作组织的成员国等20个国家签署公约，决定成立经济合作与发展组织。1961年9月30日，该组织在法国巴黎正式宣告成立。其宗旨和原则是：促进成员国经济和社会的发展，推动世界经济增长，帮助各成员国制定和协调有关政策，以提高各成员国的生活水平，保持财政的相对稳定，鼓励和协调成员国为援助发展中国家做出努力，帮助发展中国家改善经济状况，促进非成员国的经济发展。经合组织是一个政府间的国际经济组织，总部设在法国巴黎。经合组织最初有20个创始成员国：奥地利、比利时、加拿大、丹麦、西班牙、美国、法国、希腊、爱尔兰、冰岛、意大利、卢森堡、挪威、荷兰、葡萄牙、联邦德国、英国、瑞典、瑞士、土耳其。20世纪六七十年代，日本（1964）、芬兰（1969）、澳大利亚（1971）、新西兰（1973）先后加入；进入90年代，墨西哥（1994）、捷克（1995）、匈牙利（1996）、波兰（1996）和韩国（1996）相继加入。目前，经合组织成员总数为30个。经合组织下设200多个专业委员会和工作组。秘书处是经合组织的常设机构，负责该组织的日常工作。

14. Even building the kind of rudimentary architecture that other groups like the OECD have would be enormously helpful in turning this organisation into the kind of thing that can achieve the lofty goals it was set up for. 即使是像OECD等其他组织那样，只建立基本的机构设置，对实现它所制定的宏伟目标的帮助也是巨大的。

句中"rudimentary architecture"在此处指组织的基本机构设置。

15. The predictable results of foreign policy-driven FTA negotiations light on economic strategy are bitty, quick-fix sectoral deals. 可以预见，那些外交政策推动经济战略的谈判结果仅仅是一些片面和权宜的行业部门协议。

句中的"light on"意为"停留在，着眼于"，"quick fix"意为"权宜的，应急的"。

16. As someone once quipped: they are neither F nor T nor A. 正如有人曾经戏谑地那样：他们既不是F，也不是T，更不是A。

这里用"既不是F，也不是T，更不是A"表示没有共同点，比较混乱。

阅读小知识（2）

1. 北美自由贸易区（Freedom Trade Region of North America）

北美自由贸易区是包括加拿大、墨西哥和加勒比海诸国在内的北美共同市场。1980年，美国总统里根就提出建立北美自由贸易区的设想。80年代中期以后，美国在国际经济中的优势地位逐渐丧失，而日本的实力在急剧增强，欧洲统一大市场在迅速发展。

美国和加拿大为了加强北美地区的竞争能力和各自经济发展的需要，从1986年开始谈

Unit 9 Trade Organizations and Conferences on Cooperation

判签订"自由贸易协定",作为建立北美自由贸易区的第一步。经过漫长的谈判历程,1988年1月2日,美、加两国正式签订美加自由贸易协定,建立美加自由贸易区,1989年1月1日正式生效。按照这个协定,两国将在10年内分三次取消一切关税,大幅度降低非关税壁垒。美国还同墨西哥签署了《自由贸易协议大纲》,并就两国贸易自由化的细节问题进行谈判。此外,美国还以加勒比海诸国不采取损害美国利益的措施为条件单方面对它们提供地区性特惠待遇,这在美国历史上还是第一次。1993年8月13日,美国、加拿大和墨西哥同时宣布,三国已就北美自由贸易协议的劳务和环境附加条约达成协议,从而为三国通向北美自由贸易道路扫清了障碍。北美自由贸易区建立后,有利于形成一个包括贸易、投资、金融和劳动力流动的一体化共同市场,从而把北美地区的经济合作推向一个新的发展阶段。

1994年1月1日,由美国、加拿大、墨西哥3国共同签署的北美自由贸易协定正式生效,北美自由贸易区宣告诞生。

北美自由贸易区是世界上第一个由发达国家和发展中国家联合组成的贸易集团,成员国之间经济上既有较大互补性和相互依存性,又有明显的不对称性。北美自由贸易区的建立对北美、拉美,以致对冷战结束后新的世界经济格局的形成,都将产生重大而深远的影响。

2. 中国东盟自由贸易区(CAFTA)

中国东盟自由贸易区指在中国与东盟10国之间构建的自由贸易区,即"10+1"。

2000年9月,在新加坡举行的第四次东盟与中国(10+1)领导人会议上,中国提出建立中国-东盟自由贸易区的建议,得到东盟有关国家的赞同。2001年11月,在文莱举行的东盟首脑会议期间,中国和10个东盟成员国宣布了将在未来十年内建成自由贸易区的目标。2002年11月4日,第六次东盟与中国领导人会议在柬埔寨首都金边举行。中国和东盟10国领导人签署了《中国与东盟全面经济合作框架协议》,宣布2010年建成中国-东盟自由贸易区,从而启动了中国-东盟自由贸易区的进程。进程分两个阶段:一是用10年的时间完成所有关税和非关税的削减,消除双方之间存在的关税及非关税壁垒;二是建立一个综合框架,包含市场一体化的一系列措施,如投资促进、贸易便利化及和谐的贸易和投资规则与标准。

建立中国-东盟自由贸易区,是中国和东盟合作历程中历史性的一步。它充分反映了双方领导人加强睦邻友好关系的良好愿望,也体现了中国和东盟之间不断加强的经济联系,是中国与东盟关系发展中新的里程碑。中国-东盟自由贸易区的建成将会创造一个拥有18亿消费者、近2万亿美元国内生产总值、1.2万亿美元贸易总量的经济区。按人口算,这将是世界上最大的自由贸易区;从经济规模上看,这将是仅次于欧盟和北美自由贸易区的全球第三大自由贸易区,由中国和东盟10国共创的世界第三大自由贸易区,是发展中国家组成的最大的自由贸易区。

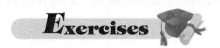

1 Discuss and answer the following questions.

1. What is the US policy towards economic integration in East Asia?

2. Why is it so difficult to implement the policy on free trade agreements in the this region?
3. What are the best solutions to the challenges facing East Asia?
4. What outlook can you forecast for such a blueprint in free trade agreements in this region?

II Decide whether the following statements are true (T) or false (F).

1. The trade diplomacy of east Asia is so complicated that even analogies cannot describe it sufficiently well. (　　)
2. Due to different economic and political systems of this region, it is difficult to sign pacts to cut tariffs or regulate protection. (　　)
3. It seems that South Korea and Japan will not agree to radical agriculture liberalization, because they are big rice producers and exporters. (　　)
4. According to the author, the east Asia trading area cannot successfully establish an Asia-only "Customs Union" without participation of the US and China. (　　)
5. The fact that not many formal trade pacts were signed by ASEAN had somewhat affected the dynamic growth of this regional economy. (　　)
6. ASEAN, founded in 1967 as a political bloc in the region, has now become an effective entity in promoting trade cooperation and bilateral trade deals as its membership was constantly expanding. (　　)
7. APEC was preferred by the US government to promote the economic integration in this region, because it has proved to be an effective approach to help achieve regional cooperation. (　　)
8. It seems to some US trade officials that bilateral FTAs being pursued by China, Japan and Korea will possibly turn out to be resultless and the least efficient. (　　)
9. The biggest challenge for bilateral FTAs is the complex rules of origins, because these rules are hard to compromise. (　　)
10. It can be concluded that the WTO rules will be adopted as a replacement by ASEAN member nations in the near future to address the issues of tariffs. (　　)

III Group discussion.

1. What do you think are the factors that contribute to the difficulty in free trade agreement signing in East Asia?
2. Do you think that China will play a vital role in establishing free trade zone of ASEAN? Why?
3. Can APEC serve as a device to help set up a low tariff zone in this region? Why?
4. What do you think are effective solutions to the varied rules of origin in this region?

Unit 9 Trade Organizations and Conferences on Cooperation

Case Study
Is the European Union an economic giant with surprisingly little clout?

A QUARTER of the way into a devastating new book about the European Union, one of the authors, Simon Everett, offers a comforting prediction about the EU's long-term global heft. With an economy that he says produces an annual $12 trillion (8.8 trillion) in added value and more than 450 million rich consumers, Europe will remain at the top table of world trade negotiations "for decades to come", he writes. But then comes a sharp prod. "The question, then, is to what purpose?"

It is a question that is too rarely asked. What is EU power for, notably in the economic sphere, where it is a genuine force: as marketplace, financial centre and (with America) dominant source of the standards and norms that govern the world? Is the mission to "master" globalization, to quote a former trade commissioner, Pascal Lamy? Or is it to "shape" globalization so that "Europeans prosper" in a "new and better global order", to quote the European Commission's president, José Manuel Barroso?

A collection of essays being published next week by a Brussels think-tank, Bruegel, constructs a careful case that the EU is a "fragmented power" in which institutions, member governments and citizens do not agree on how to exploit or defend Europe's economic strengths. This, even though history has bequeathed to Europeans a privileged status in international economic governance. Half the G8 group of rich countries come from the EU, as do nearly a quarter of the executive board members of the International Monetary Fund.

In the words of the book's editor, André Sapir, Europe's "over-representation" is "exactly mirrored" by the under-representation of emerging economies. At the same time, Europe's fragmented position causes it "to punch below its weight", writes Mr. Sapir (already known in Brussels for the furore over his 2004 report, written for the European Commission, on the EU's failure to focus on growth and rational spending).

Eurocrats seem unsure whether to be cocky or anxious about Europe's position in the world. They never tire of noting that the euro is the second global currency and that the EU is the world's biggest market, largest exporter, biggest aid donor and largest foreign investor. At the same time, national governments and citizens plead for Europe to unite more and speak with a single voice on scary new challenges such as energy security, controlling migration or adjusting to China's rise. Mr. Sapir and his fellow authors are also keen on unity, arguing that aggregating powers at the European level might put special interests in their place. The book calls for a new "high representative" for external economic policy, to match the real-life high representative for foreign and security policy.

Appeals for the Europeans to centralise their way out of trouble are problematic, of course. They play badly in Eurosceptical countries such as Britain. They can also seem circular:

Europe needs more unity, because Europe is not united. Try asking Peter Mandelson, the trade commissioner, who (on paper) has sole authority to speak for all 27 EU members on trade. That has not stopped him being hobbled by a French-led coalition determined to limit concessions offered on farm subsidies in the Doha round of world trade talks (which are stalled partly as a result).

There is also the tiny problem that, on economic matters, the EU does not agree what unity might be for. The new book catalogues endless philosophical gulfs. Are world trading rules an end in themselves, as some argue, answering public calls for globalization to do less harm? Or are they tools for improving market access and the elimination of trade barriers, which will defuse hostility to globalization by bringing jobs, growth and lower prices? And what about aid? The EU may be, cumulatively, the world's largest donor, but the Nordics hate links between aid and commercial interests whereas others blatantly use aid as an arm of trade policy, to channel money to former colonies or to scatter small sums around the globe to boost their profiles. The chunk of European aid disbursed directly by Brussels is little better, the book finds, citing the conclusion of a Swedish study that "neither recipient needs nor recipient merits" play a big role in aid allocation.

A common energy policy is similarly much talked about, but European governments do not agree whether greater competition or more national champions are the right way to maketheir energy markets more robust. Even assuming that the EU thrashed out a common position on energy, what would it bring to the negotiating table? The EU is a mature market, already committed to trimming its use of carbon-laden fossil fuels, notes the book. Next to China and India, its importance is shrinking.

Smaller Europe, Bigger World

And that is the final problem: even if the EU could unite, a Europe that has a static or even shrinking population has far less weight in the world than it once did. This leads Mr Sapir and his co-authors to an intriguing argument in favour of more centralisation. If relative decline is inevitable, Europeans might as well consolidate what clout they have left, and get some credit for being generous to rising powers. Take the question of pooling EU seats at the IMF, to free up chairs for emerging economies. If Europeans do not budge up, bodies like the IMF may simply lose credibility. In a phrase nicely calculated to get the attention of well-lunched Eurocrats, the book suggests: "If Europe refuses to share its place at the table, it may find itself increasingly short of dining partners in consequence."

Mr Sapir does not deny that there are different national interests within the EU. "The question to be asked is if we are even efficiently pursuing our national interests with the current system," he says. Over-represented and underpowered, Europe "will have to move at some stage." Adjusting gracefully to its declining importance in a new global order might give European power a purpose for years to come.

(Adapted from *Economist*, Sep. 6, 2007)

Supplementary Reading

Ten Years after Marrakesh: the WTO and Developing Countries
Supachai Panitchpakdi

Honorable Minister Mechahouri, Ladies and Gentlemen:

It is indeed a great honor to join you here today to mark the ten year anniversary of the Marrakesh Agreement establishing the World Trade Organization. In the words of His Majesty King Hassan II at the closing ceremony, the establishment of the WTO represented "a gigantic leap forward towards broader and more intensive international co-operation". I am also very pleased, personally, to be back in the beautiful city where, ten years ago, I was representing my own country, Thailand.

Just a couple of days ago we commemorated another anniversary — the 60th anniversary of the D-Day landings. And this reminded me of Morocco's very early association with discussions about the shape of the post war international order. Morocco's hosting of the Casablanca Conference of 1943 marked the beginning of a series of Allied conferences to prepare the end of the Second World War and a strong and enduring peace. It is widely recognized that economic tensions, including spiraling trade retaliation, hastened the march to war. The founders of the post-war economic order had the foresight to recognize that economic co-operation must be central to achieve a lasting peace. This is perhaps most clearly encapsulated in the words of President Roosevelt to the Bretton Woods conference in 1944. He reflected that "Commerce is the life blood of a free society." He also urged that "we must see to it that the arteries which carry that blood stream are not clogged again, as they have been in the past, by artificial barriers created through senseless economic rivalries". From this imperative, were built the three pillars of the post-war international economic order: the International Monetary Fund; the International Bank for Reconstruction and Development (the World Bank) and the multilateral trading system embodied in the GATT.

The GATT was essentially an ad hoc arrangement — created because of the failure to implement the Havana Charter which would have given birth to the International Trade Organization. It was only forty-seven years later that the GATT evolved here in Marrakesh into a fully fledged international organization — the World Trade Organization.

My predecessor, Peter Sutherland, described the Marrakesh Agreement as a "priceless cargo" and the "greatest trade agreement in history". He was right. After 7 years of tortuous negotiations, over 100 Ministers signed the Final Act containing 28 agreements and appended to by some 26,000 pages of national tariff and services schedules. In so doing they created a stronger, clearer and extended framework for the conduct of international trade, underpinned by a more effective and reliable dispute settlement mechanism. Progress was also made in opening markets, building upon the work of previous GATT rounds.

Now, ten years down the line, it is perhaps timely to reflect back on the hopes expressed at Marrakesh that the WTO would usher in a new era of global economic co-operation. Are we on the way to realizing those expectations? Yes, I do believe we are on the right track, particularly because the multilateral trading system embodied in the WTO is about more than just trade liberalization. It is about Members' commitment to the rules they have created governing the conduct of trade with each other.

Let me support my optimism by touching more specifically upon, what I think, have been the five key developments in the multilateral trading system over the last ten years. Firstly, the role played by the multilateral trading system during the Asian Financial Crisis. Secondly, the WTO's record in settling trade disputes. Thirdly, accessions to the WTO. Fourthly, an increased focus of the WTO on technical assistance and capacity building for developing countries. And finally the launch of the Doha Development Agenda.

As concerns the first point, I was Thailand's Deputy Prime Minister and Minister of Commerce when the Asian Financial Crisis broke out in the 1990s. It was nerve racking to see the dramatic drop in exchange rates which threatened to drain Asia of foreign exchange. It was a rough ride. But looking back on these events I am struck most by how that crisis was contained and reversed within a relatively short period of time. The majority of the five countries most affected by the Asian Financial Crisis had regained their pre-crisis income levels within a couple of years. Of course, there were a lot of factors at play in determining this recovery. But certainly one of them was the discreet role played by the multilateral trading system. In the face of an increase in exports from Asia, Members honored their WTO commitments, kept their markets open and resisted calls for protectionism at home.

The five Asian countries had a combined trade deficit of forty billion dollars at the outbreak of the crisis in 1996 and managed to record a trade surplus of more than eighty billion dollars two years later. These countries' exports to Western Europe and North America increased in the crisis years of 1997 and 1998 by 22 and 16 per cent at a time when global merchandise trade stagnated in value terms.

Not only this, but Members pressed ahead with the Financial Services negotiations that were ongoing in the WTO at that time — and brought them to a successful conclusion. Asian countries were able to export their way to recovery and the crisis was prevented from spreading more broadly. It is particularly significant that the Financial Services negotiations were concluded outside a broader round of trade negotiations.

Without a strong multilateral trading system, the consequences of the Asian Financial Crisis could have been unimaginably worse. Today, the developing Asian region is one of the brightest spots on the global economic map.

The second development I want to talk about is dispute settlement. One of the key achievements of the Uruguay Round was to strengthen the multilateral trading system's framework for settling disputes. The panel process was made more automatic and binding and a body of appeal

Unit 9 Trade Organizations and Conferences on Cooperation

was created. The new dispute settlement system has commonly been referred to as the jewel in the crown of the multilateral trading system.

Over the last ten years, more dispute settlement cases have been taken to the WTO than were brought to the GATT in nearly fifty years of its existence. To date, 311 complaints have been filed in the WTO, leading to the composition of 100 panels and nearly 70 Appellate Body proceedings. In the last five years nearly sixty per cent of all cases initiated in the WTO have been brought by developing countries. The increase in dispute settlement activity may, of course, be a reflection of the fact that the WTO system of agreements, and therefore Members' rights and obligations, are far more extensive than was the case under the GATT. But it also clearly reflects Members' confidence in the system. Such confidence is based no doubt in part on the willingness of Members to implement Panel and Appellate Body rulings and recommendations. In this regard losing parties have already fully implemented Panel and Appellate Body reports in 90 per cent of the cases and are working in good faith to implement those reports in the remaining cases.

My third point relates to accession to the WTO. A good measure of the success of any institution is certainly its ability to attract new Members. Again the WTO's record has been decisive. Over the last ten years, the WTO has welcomed 19 new Members to its table, bringing the total WTO membership up to 147 at the moment. These have included major players like China — now the world's fourth largest trader. Recent accessions have also included some of the world's smallest and most vulnerable countries like Nepal. A further 25 countries are in the process of negotiating accession. Today, WTO Membership covers 92 per cent of the world's population and 95 per cent of world trade.

Another measure of the success of the trading system is its ability to adapt and respond to the needs of its Members. Today, the vast majority of WTO Members are developing countries and their ability to actively participate in the system has become a much higher priority than ever before — particularly with the launch of new trade negotiations under the Doha Development Agenda. There is, on the one hand, a much more widespread acceptance of the central role trade can play in fostering economic growth — a prerequisite for development. On the other hand, there is an appreciation that new commitments undertaken by WTO Members will be bound by the rule of law and underpinned by a strong dispute settlement mechanism. Hence, developing countries have a bigger stake in setting the agenda, formulating proposals that reflect their priorities and interests and also understanding the implications of the positions of others.

Many developing countries expressed strong concerns about their capacity to participate in the negotiations, and more generally to exercise their WTO rights and obligations, because of limited human resources. The WTO has responded to this need, by significantly ramping up the number and range of technical assistance activities, and cooperating more closely with other international agencies. There is also emphasis being placed on capacity building.

Since the launch of the Doha Development Agenda, Moroccan officials have participated in some 37 technical assistance activities, of varying lengths of time. One new initiative which has been highly successful is the regional three-month trade policy courses: two of them in Africa (one in

Kenya and one in Morocco). The aim of these courses is not only to provide intensive training in all aspects of the WTO for African officials, but also to develop local capacity for training and analysis by involving regional teachers and academics. Morocco hosted the first of these courses for francophone African countries in Casablanca two years ago, and will host it for the second time in Rabat later this year.

Finally, proof of the strength of multilateral co-operation in trade was signaled by the launch of the Doha Development Agenda two and a half years ago in Qatar. This was not, as you will know, an easy endeavour. An attempt to launch negotiations in Seattle two years previous had ended in failure, creating widespread mistrust and resentment among WTO Members which took some time to overcome.

On reflection, it seems the Seattle experience impressed upon Members the need for the WTO to be inclusive if it is to be sustainable. It was a hard lesson learned, and what emerged from the Doha Ministerial meeting was a broad and ambitious work programme built upon difficult compromises and characterized by an unprecedented focus on the needs and priorities of developing countries. In parallel we have seen a much more intense focus by WTO Members on procedural transparency.

The development dimension of the Doha Development Agenda cuts across the whole length and breadth of the whole work programme. Market access for developing country exports is, of course, a central component. We know that if developing countries are to grow their way out of poverty, more must be done to remove barriers facing their exports of goods and services. All three areas of market access — agriculture, manufactures and services are on the table in the negotiations. While developed country tariffs are on average low, developed countries still maintain tariff peaks and escalation in product areas of interest to many developing countries, including labor-intensive manufactures and agriculture. Indeed, since agricultural products and textiles and clothing account for more than 70 per cent of poor countries' exports, the potential benefits from liberalization could be quite large indeed.

Developing countries, however, should also not shy away from the opportunity the round presents to strategically open up their own economies, including to other developing countries' exports. The evidence is clear that those developing countries which have derived the greatest benefits from the multilateral trading system, and most successfully integrated their economies into the global economy, are those which have pursued sound economic policies, including maintaining liberal trade and investment regimes.

There are also elements of the Work Programme which have a specific "development" focus — among them: negotiations to make special and differential treatment more precisely effective and operational; implementation issues and work programmes on: small economies; least-developed countries; trade, debt and finance and trade and transfer of technology.

Developing countries have also identified other areas of the negotiations as being of key interest. One example is strengthening disciplines on anti-dumping to ensure it is not used as a covert form of protectionism — not only by developed countries, but also by other developing countries too.

Strengthened disciplines on anti-dumping are all the more important because of the rapidly approaching phase for final removal of quotas on textiles and clothing products under the ATC.

The Doha Development Agenda now stands at a critical juncture. Because of missed deadlines and the setback at Cancun, we have lost a lot of precious time. But, Members have now strongly recommitted themselves to make progress on some key issues by the end of July. These issues include developing what we call "frameworks for modalities" on agriculture and non-agricultural market access and agreeing on the treatment of cotton within the negotiations and a solution to the so-called Singapore issues. In addition, there is a growing consensus that Members would also like to see some advances in the area of special and differential treatment. These issues were among the most difficult to resolve at Cancún and are regarded as crucial to unlocking progress across the board. This is one unique opportunity to get the DDA back on track. If we miss this deadline, it is likely the rest of 2004 will be unproductive as far as making progress in the DDA is concerned, and probably much of 2005 as well.

It is clear to me that most WTO Members are aware of the urgency of the situation and we have seen some real flexibilities being shown, which is very encouraging. The European Union, for example, has indicated its willingness to consider the elimination of export subsidies which is a major step forward. The EU has also very substantially modified its position on the Singapore issues. I recently attended a meeting of Ministers from Least Developed Countries in Senegal — they too showed a willingness to be accommodating. We need to see at the same time, more indications of flexibility from the highest political levels as well as a dynamic process in Geneva which can focus on working out the finer details.

Ten years ago, His Majesty King Mohammed, standing in this very building, spoke to the historical significance of the Marrakesh meeting in establishing the legal and institutional pillar of international trade in the twenty-first century. We should be immensely proud of the achievements of the last decade. The trading system has shown its resilience in the face of financial turbulence and it has contained and resolved over 300 trade disputes between its Members, providing for greater stability and predictability in global commercial exchanges. The WTO is moving towards becoming a truly universal organization — welcoming new countries, some of whose membership would have been unthinkable not so long ago. The multilateral trading system has proved that it is responsive to the needs of its Membership by realigning its priorities to provide more support to its poorer members. It has also shown that it is a dynamic organization — through the commitment undertaken by Members at Doha to further reform and strengthen the WTO — a commitment which was undertaken, against a background of considerable economic and political uncertainty. The challenge ahead is to make good on the political investment made at Doha, so that trade can play its role in generating economic growth and raising incomes and living standards around the world.

Before closing, may I thank Minister Mechahouri and the Government of Morocco again for holding this conference and for your warm and generous hospitality? Morocco has a very special place in the history of the multilateral trading system.

Thank you.

Answer and discuss the following questions:

1. Why was the Marrakesh Agreement described as a "Priceless cargo" and the "greatest trade agreement in history"?
2. Has the WTO ushered in a new era of global economic cooperation ten years after Marrakesh? Why?
3. According to the author, how did the five countries get recovery from the Asian Financial Crisis? And what underlies their success?
4. Can you describe the multilateral trading system's framework for dispute settlement in the WTO?
5. Do developing countries have more capacity to participate in the negotiation or exercise their WTO right or obligation? Why?
6. Why does the author think that it is more important for the developing countries to strengthen disciplines on antidumping in the WTO?
7. Why does the Doha Development Agenda now stand at a critical juncture?
8. Can you summarize the achievements made by the WTO over the past decade?

参 考 文 献

[1] 萨缪尔森. 经济学. 19 版. 北京：商务印书馆，2013.
[2] 陈祥国，刘涛，钟立君，等. 国际商务英语报刊选读. 北京：中国商务出版社，2006.
[3] 科特勒. 营销管理. 14 版. 北京：中国青年出版社，2008.
[4] 狄瑞鹏. 商务英语工商管理知识精要. 北京：清华大学出版社，2003.
[5] 兰磊. 英美报刊核心商务术语释义. 北京：中国对外经济贸易出版社，2003.
[6] 马建国. 英文报刊导读. 北京：外语教学与研究出版社，2012.
[7] 帕利瑟. 牛津商务词典. 上海：上海外语教育出版社，2003.
[8] 魏杰. 企业文化塑造. 北京：中国发展出版社，2009.
[9] 周学艺. 美英报刊文章阅读. 北京：北京大学出版社，2007.
[10] 张键. 报刊英语研究. 上海：上海外语教育出版社，2011.